Encyclopedia of
AMERICAN AUTOMOBILES

Contributors:

Glenn Baechler   Keith Marvin
Hugh Durnford   Court Myers
Bill Emery   G. Marshall Naul
David Filsell   T. R. Nicholson
G. N. Georgano   Michael Sedgwick
Roland Jerry   Michael Worthington-Williams

E. P. Dutton and Company Inc., New York

Encyclopedia of AMERICAN AUTOMOBILES

Edited by G. N. Georgano

This book was designed and produced by
Rainbird Reference Books Ltd,
Marble Arch House, 44 Edgware Road, London, W2,
for E. P. Dutton & Co Inc,
201 Park Avenue South, New York, N.Y. 10003
and first published in the U.S.A. in 1971

House Editor: Peter Coxhead
Designer: Michael Mendelsohn

The material in this book, emended and fully revised, has been
extracted from *The Complete Encyclopedia of Motorcars*, first
published by E. P. Dutton & Co Inc in 1968

Library of Congress Catalog Card Number 79-147885
SBN 0-525-097929

The text was photoset by BAS Printers Ltd, Wallop, Hampshire
The book was printed by Westerham Press Ltd, Westerham, Kent
and bound by Dorstel Press Ltd, Harlow, Essex

Printed in Great Britain

ACKNOWLEDGMENTS

For valuable help in many different ways, I would particularly like to thank G. Marshall Naul and also the Public Relations Department of automobile manufacturers who so readily gave me advance data on their 1971 models, and the following individuals:

Alvin J. Arnheim
Doug Bell
Albert R. Bochroch
John A. Conde
Dennis C. Field
Randall Gould
Colin Hilton
H. C. Hopkins
E. E. Husting
David K. James
Stan James
Lars Kile Jr
W. S. Jaro
Beverly Rae Kimes
Frank Kurtis
Dr. Alfred S. Lewerenz
W. J. Lewis

Thomas Maylone
Warren K. Miller
Bruce Baldwin Mohs
David L. Morse
Harry Pulfer
Peter A. Readyhough
E. T. Reynolds
Arthur Rippey
Martin Schacht
Thomas L. Sherred
Charles Stowell
E. R. Tarnowsky
Brian K. Thomas
Robert Tuthill
Roger van Bolt
William Watson
Joe H. Whitney

All photographs have been credited in their captions, but I would like to make special acknowledgment to the following, who have lent generously from their private collections:

David Filsell
Maurice Harrison
Jacques Kupélian
Dr Alfred S. Lewerenz

Lucien Loreille
Keith Marvin
Kenneth Stauffer
Michael Worthington-Williams

I would also like to thank the following museums, journals, and libraries for their generous help in searching out and lending many rare photographs:

Antique Automobile: William S. Jackson, Editor

Autocar, London: Maurice A. Smith, DFC, Editor; Bill Banks; Mrs K. Maynard; Miss Hazel Dumayne

Automobile Manufacturers' Association, Detroit: Peter B. Teeley

Automotive History Collection, Detroit Public Library: James J. Bradley

Autosport, London: Miss Peggie O'Mahony; Michael Hollingshead

Gilltrap's Museum, Coolangatta, New South Wales: Mrs K. Gilltrap

Harrah's Automobile Collection, Reno: E. R. Tarnowsky

Henry Ford Museum, Dearborn, Mich.: Leslie R. Henry

Indianapolis Motor Speedway Museum: Karl Kizer

Long Island Automotive Museum, Glen Cove, L.I.: Henry Austin Clark Jr

Montagu Motor Museum, Beaulieu, Hants: Lord Montagu of Beaulieu; Michael Ware; Derek Maidment

Motor, London: Mrs E. Welch

Musée de l' Automobile, Le Mans: Comte Bernard de Lassée

The Raben Collection, Nysted: Baron J. O. Raben-Levetzau

The Veteran Car Club of Great Britain, London: Dennis C. Field, Librarian; Brian Dinsley, Librarian; Mrs Joan Das, Secretary

G. N. GEORGANO

CONTRIBUTORS

Glenn Baechler   Keith Marvin

Hugh Durnford   Court Myers

Bill Emery   G. Marshall Naul

David Filsell   T. R. Nicholson

G. N. Georgano   Michael Sedgwick

Roland Jerry   Michael Worthington-Williams

CONTENTS

Acknowledgments   5
Contributors   6
Color Plates   8
Introduction   9
Abbreviations   11
The Encyclopedia   13
Glossary   215
Index   219

COLOR PLATES

1 **1902 RAMBLER** 8hp runabout. Owned by Baron J. A. Raben-Levetzau. Photo: Bernard.

2 **1904 CADILLAC** 8½hp limousine. Owned by Mrs M. E. Bowden. Photo: Derrick E. Witty.

3 **1909 LOZIER** Model H Briarcliff four-seater toy tonneau. Owned by Dr Russell B. Hunsberger. Photo: William S. Jackson.

4 **1913 MERCER** Type 35 Raceabout. Owned by Dr Samuel Scher. Photo: Copyright Henry Austin Clark Jr, Glen Cove, New York.

5 **1914 STUTZ** Bearcat roadster. Photo: Automobile Quarterly.

6 **1914 LOCOMOBILE** 48hp roadster. Owned by Baron J. A. Raben-Levetzau. Photo: Raben.

7 **1922 PIERCE ARROW** 38hp roadster. Owned by Baron J. A. Raben-Levetzau. Photo: J. Bache.

8 **1920 DETROIT ELECTRIC** coupé. Owned by Baron J. A. Raben-Levetzau. Photo: Bernard.

9 **1922 WILLS SAINTE CLAIRE** V-8 roadster. Photo: Copyright Wm A. C. Pettit III.

10 **1926 KISSEL** speedster. Owned by J. K. Lilly III. Photo: Spooner Studio, Falmouth, Mass.

11 **1909 FORD** Model T 20hp touring car. Owned by Baron J. A. Raben-Levetzau. Photo: Bernard.

12 **1927 PACKARD** 39.2hp sedan. Owned by Baron J. A. Raben-Levetzau. Photo: Raben.

13 **1929 DUESENBERG** Model J town car. Coachwork by Barker. Owned by James E. Dougherty. Photo: John R. Price.

14 **1935 AUBURN** Type 851 speedster. Loaned by Vintage Tyre Supplies Ltd to The Montagu Motor Museum.

15 **1937 CORD** Model 812 convertible coupé. Owned by Kenneth Brewer. Photo: Copyright Henry Austin Clark Jr, Glen Cove, New York.

16 **1941 LINCOLN** Continental convertible. Owned by Gerald Meek. Photo: Copyright Henry Austin Clark Jr, Glen Cove, New York.

17 **1948 TUCKER** sedan. Photo: Copyright Wm A. C. Pettit III.

18 **1960 CHEVROLET** Corvair sedan. Photo: General Motors Corporation.

19 **1967 SHELBY** Cobra 4 27 CS hardtop coupé. This is one of the thirty-six Competition Street Cobras built. Owned by Michael B. Clark. Photo: William S. Jackson.

20 **1968 AUBURN** 866 Replica Speedster. Owned by Glen Pray. Photo: William S. Jackson.

21 **1971 AMERICAN MOTORS** Gremlin sub-compact sedan. Photo: American Motors Corporation.

1 1902 RAMBLER

2 1904 CADILLAC

3 1909 LOZIER
4 1913 MERCER

5 1914 STUTZ

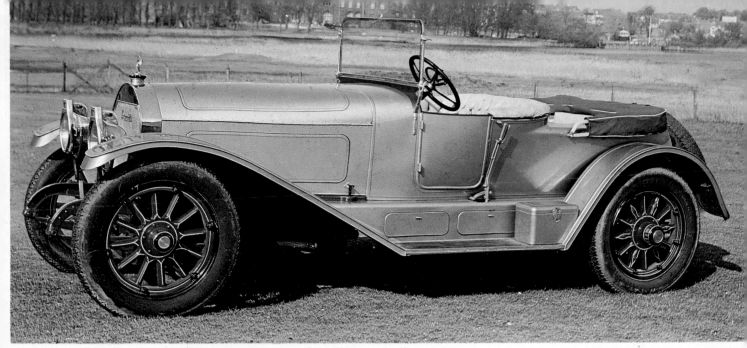

6 1914 LOCOMOBILE
7 1922 PIERCE ARROW

8 1920 DETROIT ELECTRIC

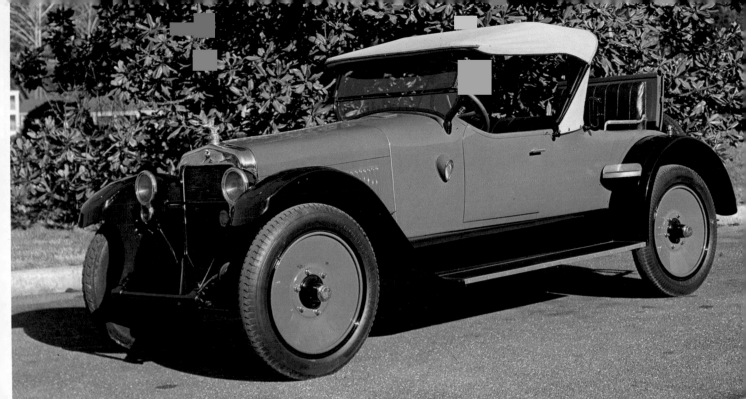

9 1922 WILLS SAINTE CLAIRE
10 1926 KISSEL

11 1909 FORD

12 1927 PACKARD

13 1929 DUESENBERG
14 1935 AUBURN

15 1937 CORD
16 1941 LINCOLN

17 1948 TUCKER
18 1960 CHEVROLET

19 1967 SHELBY COBRA

SUNRISE PHARMACY

INTRODUCTION

In this book we aim to give balanced biographies of over 1,640 makes of car which have been built for sale in the United States and Canada over the past eighty years. All commercially-built passenger cars are included, but the following points should be noted:

1 In order to exclude the hundreds of home-built specials, we insist that there must be reasonable evidence of intention to manufacture cars for sale to the public. We are well aware that this is not a water-tight limitation, for to establish 'intention to manufacture' one would have to read the minds of car builders long dead. In the early days of the industry, hundreds of amateur mechanics thought they could do as well as Henry Ford, and took a small stand at their local auto show on which to exhibit their hastily-assembled prototype. If no interested customers appeared, this was often the end of the make, and sometimes the builder never even formed a company. The formation of a company, the announcement of a price, the issue of a catalog, are all fairly safe indications of intention to manufacture, and yet there have been stock promotion schemes which did all these things and yet had no aim beyond that of selling bogus shares, and never made a car. These are not included, although there are borderline cases which rate an entry, where at least one car was built. Cars built by an organization for their own use, and not for sale, are not included. Also excluded are the pioneer cars by such inventors as Roper and Nadig, for, interesting though they were, they were in no sense even would-be production cars.

2 As this is an encyclopedia of automobiles and not of commercial vehicles, only those cars which were built for private use as passenger-carrying vehicles are included. Estate cars and station wagons are mentioned where relevant, but mobile homes built on truck chassis, although normally used by private individuals, are not included.

3 Motorcycles are obviously excluded, but the fully-bodied two-wheeled Moore is listed.

4 We have excluded Dune Buggies and All-Terrain vehicles. There are over fifty makes of these machines, mostly similar in design, and it is felt that they are not passenger transportation vehicles in the way that other automobiles covered in the book are.

5 Only those vehicles which are supplied complete or as complete kits are included. This eliminates makers of fiberglass bodies for Volkswagen and other chassis, even though these are sometimes listed as makes of automobile.

Adherence to these principles will explain the absence from the encyclopedia of a number of makes which have appeared in other lists. Having established which makes were to be included, the next problem was to determine the treatment each make should receive. It is obviously impossible to list every model made by each firm, and no attempt has been made to do so. However we have indicated the broad line of development, mentioning any technical features which were distinctive for the period. In pioneer days, when wheel or tiller steering was used, each system is mentioned, but after 1900 it may be assumed that steering was by wheel unless stated otherwise. On makes with a long history we have indicated the introduction of such features as shaft drive, electric starting and lighting, front wheel brakes, and so on. The expression 'a thoroughly conventional car' may seem annoyingly vague to some readers, but it cannot be denied that by about 1910 car design had settled down to a pattern embracing a front-mounted, in-line, water-cooled engine, driving via a three- or four-speed sliding pinion transmission and propeller shaft to bevel-geared rear axle. Any deviations from this pattern, such as V-engine layout, air-cooling, planetary transmission or belt drive, are mentioned. Wherever possible we have given the horsepower rating (see Glossary) or cubic capacity, and number of cylinders. Sporting activities are mentioned where they are relevant, and whenever cars were built for Grand Prix or other racing.

The dating of cars, especially in the captions to illustrations, may cause confusion because of the discrepancy between the model year and the calendar year. Normally the date given is the year in which the car was made (this follows the practice of the Dating Committee of the Veteran Car Club of Great Britain). However an exception has to be made for those cars announced as (for example) 1971 models, even though they were made during the last quarter of 1970. This is especially important with American cars, where the next season's models are almost always announced in September or October. The Mercury was introduced in November 1938 (hence a starting date of 1938 in our entry) but even the first cars made were always thought of as 1939 models, and are thus described in the caption. The only known example of a two year discrepancy is that of the Palmer-Singer company, which announced late in 1913 its 1915 models, in a frantic attempt to capture the public's attention.

The makes are listed in alphabetical order, but the following points should be noted:

1 Makes having Christian names as part of their make-up are classified under the Christian name, e.g., Guy Vaughan, not Vaughan, Guy.

2 Makes beginning with Mc are listed between Maytag and Mecca, not at the beginning of the letter 'M'.

3 Makes beginning with De are classified under the letter 'D'. Thus De Leon is found in D, not L.

4   Makes beginning with Le or La are classified under the letter 'L'. Thus La Salle is found in L, not S.

5   Makes using initial letters joined by '&', such as S. & M. Simplex, or S. & S., are classified as if they were spelled 'Sand . . .'

We are well aware that the quality of some photographs leaves much to be desired, but where nothing better was obtainable, we felt that readers would rather see an indifferent photograph than none at all.

Any corrections or additions which readers may think desirable for future editions will be very welcome. They should be sent to the Editor, c/o Rainbird Reference Books Ltd, Marble Arch House, 44 Edgware Road, London W2, England.

ABBREVIATIONS

aiv   automatic inlet valve(s)

bhp   brake horsepower

CDN   Canadian (make)

ci   cubic inch(es)

dohc   double overhead camshaft(s)

ft   foot (feet)

fwb   four wheel brakes

fwd   front wheel drive

GP   Grand Prix

GT   Gran Turismo

hp   horsepower

hr   hour(s)

ht   high tension

ifs   independent front suspension

in   inch(es)

ioe   inlet over exhaust

irs   independent rear suspension

lb   pound(s)

lt   low tension

lwb   long wheelbase

moiv   mechanically operated inlet valve(s)

mpg   miles per gallon

mph   miles per hour

ohc   overhead camshaft(s)

ohv   overhead valve(s)

oiv   overhead inlet valve(s)

psi   pounds per square inch

rpm   revolutions per minute

sec   second(s)

sv   side valve(s)

swb   short wheelbase

ABBOTT and ABBOTT-DETROIT 1909–1918
1 Abbott Motor Car Co, Detroit, Mich. 1909–1915
2 Consolidated Car Co, Detroit, Mich. 1916
3 The Abbott Corp, Cleveland, Ohio 1916–1918
The Abbott-Detroit was a conventional car using 4- and 6-cylinder Continental and 8-cylinder Herschell-Spillman engines. By 1916 production was running at 15–20 units per day, and it was to improve on this figure that the company moved to a larger factory at Cleveland. However, they over-reached themselves, and in April 1918 they were declared bankrupt. The Cleveland-built cars were generally known simply as Abbott, although in some lists the name Abbott-Detroit persisted.

1911 ABBOTT-DETROIT 30hp touring car. *The Veteran Car Club of Great Britain*
1910 ACME (i) 50hp touring car. *Automotive History Collection, Detroit Public Library*

A.B.C. 1906–1910
1 Autobuggy Manufacturing Co, St Louis, Mo. 1906–1908
2 A.B.C. Motor Vehicle Manufacturing Co, St Louis, Mo. 1908–1910
Originally known as the Autobuggy, this car was a typical high-wheel motor buggy whose excellent ground clearance made it popular in rural America. Powered by a 10/12hp 2-cylinder engine, it used a system of friction transmission by cone and two bevel wheels, one for forward movement, one for reverse. This gave a maximum speed of 30mph in either direction. Later models included more conventional roadsters with 2- or 4-cylinder air- or water-cooled engines. The company name was derived from the initials of the designer, A. B. Cole.

ABLE EIGHT *see* VERNON

ACADIA 1904
Ernest R. Kelly, Wilmington, Del.
This was a very small two-passenger runabout with the engine under the seat. It was steered by wheel, had a single chain-drive and wire wheels.

ACADIAN (CDN) 1962 to date
General Motors Corp of Canada, Oshawa, Ont.
Acadian and Beaumont are the brand names of General Motors cars sold in Canada. The original Acadian was based on the Chevy II and known as the Acadian Canso. In 1963 a larger model became available with the Chevelle body, known as the Acadian Beaumont. From 1966 to 1969 it was sold simply as the Beaumont, and for 1970 was replaced in Pontiac showrooms by the Pontiac Tempest and the Le Mans. (Although based on Chevrolet designs, Acadians were marketed by Pontiac in Canada.) Since 1968 the Acadian has been imported from Michigan as a reduction in tariffs has reduced the necessity to make cars in Canada.

ACE (i) 1920–1922
Apex Motor Corp, Ypsilanti, Mich.
An assembled car which used at various periods, a Gray-Bell 4-cylinder and Herschell-Spillman and Continental 6-cylinder engines. The Ace differed from other cars of its time because of the 'traditional' squared lines of its coachwork. The make was absorbed into the American Motor Truck Co of Newark, Ohio.

ACE (ii) *see* FRONTENAC (*iii*)

ACME (i) 1903–1910
Acme Motor Car Co, Reading, Pa.
Acme was an outgrowth of the Reber Manufacturing Co which made the Reber car. The Acme was available in at least nine different models during its existence. Early models had 2- or 4-cylinder engines. Later cars were much larger, with 6-cylinder engines and ball-bearing transmission; they cost $3–5,000. The car was sold with an optimistic 'perpetual guarantee'.

ACME (ii) 1908–1909
Acme Motor Buggy Manufacturing Co, Minneapolis, Minn.
This car was a short-lived high-wheel motor buggy.

ACME (iii) (CDN) 1910–1911

Acme Motor Carriage and Machinery Co Ltd, Hamilton, Ont.

This firm was organized to manufacture touring cars, taxicabs and commercial vehicles with bodies built in Hamilton and mechanical parts imported from the United States.

ACME (iv) *see* XENIA

ADAMS 1911

Adams Bros Co, Findlay, Ohio

The Adams Model C had a 4-cylinder engine of 25/30hp. This was a five-passenger touring model, but the main interest of this manufacturer was in commercial vehicles.

ADAMS-FARWELL 1904–1913

The Adams Co, Dubuque, Iowa

After six years of experiments, the Adams-Farwell with a 20hp 3-cylinder radial rotary engine was put on the market in 1904, followed by a 40/45hp 5-cylinder model in 1906. The cylinders and crankcase revolved in a horizontal plane about a fixed shaft, power being transmitted by bevel gears to a 4-speed transmission (3-speed after 1908), and thence by single chain to the rear axle. The engine was mounted under the rear seat ahead of the axle. The rotating mass of the engine acted as a flywheel and gave excellent cooling.

The 1904 models included a convertible brougham in which the driver's seat in front could be closed up, and control devices transferred inside for driving from the rear seat. The 40hp model had a short hood, and the general appearance of a conventional car. After 1908 the forward control model was dropped, but no new models appeared and only small changes were made to the existing range for the rest of the make's life. Prices reached $3,500 for the 40hp touring car by 1912.

ADELPHIA 1920

Winfield Barnes Co, Philadelphia, Pa.

This medium-sized auto had a wheelbase of 114in and right-hand drive. It was built for export only. The 4-cylinder engine was by Herschell-Spillman. This make probably never got beyond the prototype stage.

ADRIA 1921–1922

Adria Motor Car Corp, Batavia, N.Y.

The Adria appeared briefly on the automotive lists, offered as an assembled car with a 4-cylinder Supreme motor.

ADVANCE 1909–1911

Advance Motor Vehicle Co, Miamisburg, Ohio

This company took over the business of Hatfield Motor Car Co of Miamisburg, which had made the Hatfield (i). The Advance was a typical motor buggy with large diameter wheels and solid rubber tires.

A.E.C. (ANGER) 1913–1914

Anger Engineering Co, Milwaukee, Wis.

The two models of the A.E.C. used 6-cylinder engines. One was a T-head of 42ci, and the other, of 366ci was an L-head. The larger automobile with a 4-speed transmission cost $2,500. The smaller $2,000 model had a 3-speed transmission.

AEROCAR (i) 1906–1908

The Aerocar Co, Detroit, Mich.

The Aerocar was an ambitious venture, available in five different models, both air-cooled and water-cooled. The Model F, a touring car offered in 1907 and 1908, was on a 115in wheelbase, powered by a 4-cylinder engine with 5in bore and stroke.

AERO CAR (ii) 1921

Sheldon F. Reese Co, Huron, S.Dak.

This was the name applied to a tiny propeller-driven two-passenger

roadster which was to sell for $160. This vehicle had a tread of 30in with wheelbase of 60in and with a 6hp, 2-cylinder engine, weighed about 150lb. Production was unlikely although a prototype was built.

AEROCAR (iii) 1948 to date

Aerocar Inc, Longview, Wash.

The brainchild of retired Navy Commander Molt B. Taylor, the Aerocar is a four-passenger sedan which can be fitted with wings and take to the air, the 4-cylinder 143hp Lycoming engine driving a rear-mounted propeller. Commander Taylor has built seven prototypes since 1948 and claims that he could sell Aerocars at $10,000 each if enough buyers came along.

AERO-TYPE *see* PAGÉ

AIRPHIBIAN 1950–1956

Continental Inc, Danbury, Conn.

This was an airplane-cum-automobile combination, powered by a

1906 ADAMS-FARWELL 40/45hp touring car. *Harrah's Automobile Collection*

1925 AJAX (iii) sedan, with C. W. Nash. *American Motors Corporation*

165bhp engine which gave an air speed of 120mph and a road speed of 55mph. The four small wheels were independently sprung. Unlike most such vehicles, the Airphibian passed the prototype stage, was fully licensed by the Federal Aviation Agency, and offered for sale.

AIRWAY 1949–1950
T. P. Hall Engineering Co, San Diego, Calif.

The Airway was one of the many post-war minicars which failed to get into large-scale production. It carried two passengers and weighed 775lb. Its air-cooled engine gave 45mpg. It was to sell for $500.

AJAX (i) 1901–1903
Ajax Motor Vehicle Co, New York, N.Y.

The Ajax was a typical light electric runabout with an open two-passenger body, spindly bicycle-type wheels and optional fenders.

AJAX (ii) 1914–1915
Ajax Motors Co, Seattle, Wash.

This Ajax company offered a car in three wheelbase lengths with a 6-cylinder engine available in sleeve-valve or conventional poppet valve form, 'changeable from one to the other at comparatively little expense'.

AJAX (iii) 1925–1926
Ajax Motors Co, Racine, Wis.

The Ajax Company was a subsidiary of Nash and the 6-cylinder cars they built were Nash in everything except name. Manufacturing operations were in the Mitchell factory acquired by Nash interests in 1924. The car was not a success and was continued as the Nash Light Six in 1926.

ALAND 1916–1917
Aland Motor Car Co, Detroit, Mich.

This car had a very advanced 4-cylinder engine of 155ci. It used four overhead valves per cylinder, with a single camshaft. Aluminum alloy pistons were standard. The chassis was fitted with very early internal expanding brakes on all four wheels. The wheelbase was 122in and the two-passenger and five-passenger models cost $1,500 with wire wheels.

ALBANY 1907–1908
Albany Automobile Co, Albany, Ind.

The Albany models, surrey and runabout, were rather crude vehicles, with false hoods and solid rubber tires. The single or 2-cylinder air-cooled engines were of 6/7hp and 18/20hp respectively.

ALCO 1905–1913
1 American Locomotive Automobile Co, Providence, R.I. 1905–1908
2 American Locomotive Co, Providence, R.I. 1908–1913

The Alco was a high quality car built by a subsidiary of a well-known locomotive manufacturing firm. The cars were built under Berliet license and up to 1908 were known as American Berliet. It was claimed that parts were interchangeable so that there would be no delays in repair work for Alco owners who might be touring in France. The first models were chain-driven 4-cylinder machines, of 24 and 40hp, but shaft drive was introduced in 1907, while 1909 saw a 16hp 4-cylinder model mainly for taxicab work, and a 60hp 6-cylinder car. The latter was the most famous Alco model, and was made with expensive open and closed bodywork priced at $6,000 to $7,250. In 1909 and 1910 Alco cars won the Vanderbilt Cup.

ALDO 1910–1911
Albaugh-Dover Co, Chicago, Ill.

The Aldo was a motor buggy for two passengers. Its engine was an air-cooled, opposed 2-cylinder type. It had planetary transmission with double chain drive and tiller steering.

ALLEN (i) 1913–1914
Allen Iron & Steel Co, Philadelphia, Pa

The first models of the Allen used a 2-cylinder air-cooled engine. In 1914, these two-passenger cars had a 4-cylinder water-cooled engine, friction transmission and shaft drive. With a 108in wheelbase and a 44in track, these cost $450.

ALLEN (ii) 1914–1922
Allen Motor Co, Fostoria, Bucyrus, Columbus, Ohio

The Allen was a popular and well-known 4-cylinder car. In its nine years of production, an estimated 20,000 units in both open and closed models were sold. The engine was a 189ci L-head unit.

ALLEN-KINGSTON 1907–1909
Allen-Kingston Motor Car Co, Kingston, N.Y.

This was a large car with 48hp T-head engine. The four-passenger Gunboat had a boat-tailed body and runningboard-mounted spare tires.

ALLSTATE 1952–1953
Kaiser-Frazer Corporation, Willow Run, Mich.

This was a mail-order car made by Kaiser-Frazer for the famous house

1911 ALCO 60hp touring car. *Alco Products Inc*
1920 ALLEN (ii) touring car. *William S. Jackson*

of Sears Roebuck. It was identical except for trim with the contemporary Henry J compact, and used the same L-head 4- and 6-cylinder Willys engines. The car carried a 90-day guarantee, but the tires were guaranteed for 18 months, and the battery for two years, which may explain why the catalog price was higher than that quoted for the regular Henry J: the differential was $227 in the case of the 6. The Henry J was discontinued at the end of the 1953 season, and the Allstate died with it.

ALL-STEEL 1915–1916
All-Steel Car Co, St Louis, Mo.

The All-Steel, or Alstel, had a conventional 4-cylinder engine, but was unusual in having a narrow platform backbone frame which enclosed the propeller shaft and transmission. The electrically welded body was attached to this frame and rear axle at only three points and could easily be removed. The price was only $465.

ALPENA (ALPENA FLYER) 1910–1914
Alpena Motor Car Co, Alpena, Mich.

The Alpena was a light and inexpensive car, using a water-cooled 4-cylinder engine rated at 34hp. The two open models had 3-speed transmissions.

ALSACE 1920–1921
Automotive Products Co, New York, N.Y.

The short-lived Alsace was a small assembled car built by Piedmont Motor Co for Automotive Products, produced with right-hand drive for export only. It differed from the standard Piedmont only in its Rolls Royce type radiator and right-hand drive. The engine was a 189ci Herschell-Spillman 4-cylinder unit.

ALSTEL see ALL-STEEL

ALTER 1914–1917
Alter Motor Car Co, Grand Haven, Mich.

The 1914 Alter used a 4-cylinder engine of 22hp. In 1916 a five-passenger with a 201ci 6-cylinder engine was built on a chassis of 116in wheelbase. In 1917 this new policy was reversed, with two sizes of Lycoming 4-cylinder engines being used.

AMALGAMATED 1917–1919
Amalgamated Machinery Corp, Chicago, Ill.

The Amalgamated Six used a special engine in which the poppet valves were closed as well as opened positively. Instead of disk cams which lifted only, grooved cylindrical cams of the type familiar in machine tools and other machinery were used. The Amalgamated was otherwise an assembled car and few were produced.

AMBASSADOR (i) 1922–1926
Yellow Cab Manufacturing Co, Chicago, Ill.

The large Ambassador cars of 1922 and 1923 were simply leftover Shaw (i) cars with a new emblem and a Continental engine, Yellow Cab having taken Shaw over in 1922. The 'Drive-Yourself' smaller cars, known as the Model D-1, appeared in mid-1924 and were marketed as Ambassadors until 1926 when the name was changed to Hertz.

AMBASSADOR (ii) see AMERICAN MOTORS

AMCO 1919–1920
American Motors, Inc, New York, N.Y.

The Amco used a 4-cylinder G.B. & S. engine and could be had with either left- or right-hand drive. The radiator was especially designed for tropical climates and most of the cars were marketed in beige.

AMERICA 1911
Motor Car Co of America, New York, N.Y.

The America was available in five models, all with an L-head 4-cylinder engine of 40hp. The torpedo, for two passengers, had a long, low silhouette and rounded aft-section. An unusual feature of these cars was an auxiliary 1½-gallon fuel tank. It is claimed that this company was later associated with McIntyre.

AMERICAN (i) 1902–1903
American Motor Carriage Co, Cleveland, Ohio

This company made a light runabout powered by a 5hp single-cylinder engine, mounted under the seat. Steering was by tiller and the car used single chain drive. The price was $1,000, rather high for such a simple vehicle.

AMERICAN (ii) 1914
American Cyclecar Co, Detroit, Mich.

This car had a 4-cylinder water-cooled engine of 73ci, and was built with a friction transmission and chain drive. The headlights were inserted into the fenders, a design which was later a distinctive feature of the Pierce-Arrow. This make was succeeded by the Trumbull.

1920 ALSACE 19.6 sedan. *Autocar*

1922 AMBASSADOR Model R 34hp touring car. *Keith Marvin Collection*

AMERICAN (iii) 1914
American Cyclecar Co, Seattle, Wash.

The prototype American cyclecar had a 3-cylinder, 2-cycle engine with a friction transmission and chain drive to the front wheels. With a wheelbase of 90in and a tread of 40in, it weighed about 650lb. It was proposed to sell this car for $350.

AMERICAN (iv) 1916–1920
American Motor Vehicle Co, Lafayette, Ind.

Also known as the American Junior, this was an ultra-light two-passenger car with a single-cylinder engine, intended mainly for children.

The makers also hoped to compete with rickshaws in China and to build electric invalid cars.

AMERICAN (v) 1916–1924
1 American Motors Corp, Plainfield, N.J.
2 Bessemer-American Motor Corp, Plainfield, N.J.

The American, an assembled car using Amco, Rutenber, or Herschell-Spillman engines, was never common, although production reached 1,500 units in 1920. The American became amalgamated with the Bessemer Truck Corp, early in 1923 and in October the car and truck interests combined to form Amalgamated Motors, which included the Winther and Northway truck companies. Production of passenger cars ceased early in 1924.

AMERICAN AUSTIN; BANTAM 1930–1941
1 American Austin Car Co, Inc, Butler, Pa. 1930–1934
2 American Bantam Car Co, Butler, Pa. 1935–1941

The Bantam, a child of the American Depression, was an attempt to popularize the European idea of an economy car (in this case the Austin Seven from Britain) in a market that suddenly found itself impoverished. American styling — horizontal hood louvres, fixed disk wheels with detachable rims, larger lights, bumpers and more generous fenders — was grafted onto an otherwise unaltered Austin Seven. List price was $425. However, Americans continued to prefer bigger cars of the native type, and the original manufacturers went into receivership in 1934. The American Bantam Car Company took over on a more ambitious scale, with a large plant capable of turning out 44,000 vehicles a year, but the Bantam was never more than a curiosity. Bantam designed and built the first successful Jeep for the U.S. Army in 1940, but were unable to deliver these in the quantity demanded, thus losing bulk orders to rival Willys designs.

AMERICAN BERLIET see ALCO

AMERICAN ELECTRIC 1899–1902
1 American Electric Vehicle Co, Chicago, Ill. 1899–1902
2 American Electric Vehicle Co, Hoboken, N.J. 1902

This company made a rather high, ungainly looking electric carriage, some with *dos-à-dos* four-passenger bodies. They moved to New Jersey 'to find more wealthy buyers', according to the company's statement, but failed the same year.

AMERICAN JUNIOR see AMERICAN (iv)

AMERICAN JUVENILE ELECTRIC 1907
American Metal Wheel & Auto Co, Toledo, Ohio

As the name implies this was an electrically powered car, with seats for two children. The wheelbase was only 41in, but was complete with 'lights, bells, etc.' and tiller steering for $800.

AMERICAN MERCEDES 1904–1907
Daimler Mfg Co, Long Island City, N.Y.

These cars were built as exact copies of Mercedes, under exclusive U.S. license. Some commercial vehicles, such as ambulances, were also made. American Mercedes were in direct competition with Mercedes Import Co of New York, which handled the imported Mercedes for the whole of the United States, at least in 1906.

AMERICAN MORS see STANDARD (ii)

AMERICAN MOTORS 1968 to date
American Motors Corp, Detroit, Mich.

American Motors was founded in 1954 as a result of the merger between Nash and Hudson interests. Their products were marketed under Nash and Hudson names until the 1958 season when they became Ramblers. In 1968 there appeared the first A.M.C. product to drop the Rambler name; this was the Javelin, a 4-passenger sport coupé to challenge Ford's Mustang and Chevrolet's Camaro. It was available with V-8 engines of 290, 343, and 390ci, as well as a 232ci six. The Javelin was supplemented by the shorter wheelbase 2-passenger AMX coupé, using the same V-8 engines. The Rambler name was still used for the compact 440 and Rogue sedans, while other cars in the American Motors line-up were the medium-sized Rebel and full-sized Ambassador sedans. In the summer of 1969 appeared the Hornet, a compact sedan available with 6-cylinder engines of 199 or 232ci, or a 299ci V-8. The Ambassador, AMX, Javelin, and Rebel continued in the 1970 range, but the Rambler name was dropped except in export markets where it was used for the Hornet. Even smaller than the Hornet was the 'sub-compact' Gremlin introduced in mid-1970; this had a 96in wheelbase and came with 199 or 232ci 6-cylinder engines, and two- or four-passenger bodies. For 1971 the Rebel became the Matador with three body styles and six engine options from a 232ci six to a 330ci V-8. The Ambassador, Gremlin, Hornet and Javelin were continued for 1971, the latter including a high-performance Javelin-AMX with four V-8 engine options up to 401ci (330bhp). The two-passenger

1933 AMERICAN AUSTIN Series 2-75 roadster. *Harrah's Automobile Collection*

1971 AMERICAN MOTORS Javelin SST coupé. *American Motors Corporation*

1910 AMERICAN SIMPLEX 50hp touring car. *Automotive History Collection, Detroit Public Library*

1922 AMERICAN STEAMER touring car. *Keith Marvin Collection*

1914 AMERICAN UNDERSLUNG Model 644 touring car. *Harrah's Automobile Collection*

AMX was dropped, but a new limited production car was the mid-engined AMX-3 with 401ci engine and chassis designed by Giotto Bizzarini. This was built in Italy.

AMERICAN MOTOR SLEIGH 1905
American Motor Sleigh Co

This vehicle was designed for travel on snow with a single-cylinder engine which drove a pronged wheel, and runners in the place of wheels.

AMERICAN POPULAIRE 1904
American Automobile Power Co, Lawrence, Mass.

The American Populaire was a 4-passenger tonneau powered by a 12hp 2-cylinder engine. Final drive was by single chain.

AMERICAN SIMPLEX 1906–1910
Simplex Motor Car Co, Mishawaka, Ind.

This make used 4-cylinder, 2-cycle engines, initially of 40hp. These were later increased to 393ci and rated at 50hp. For 1910, three open models and two closed versions were offered, ranging in price up to $5,400. The name was changed to Amplex in 1910 to avoid confusion with the better-known Simplex of New York. This change coincided with a company reorganization.

AMERICAN STEAM CAR 1929–c.1931
American Steam Automobile Co, West Newton, Mass.

The American Steam Car was built by Thomas S. Derr, a former faculty member of the Massachusetts Institute of Technology. Derr, while specializing in modifications and improvements of the Stanley boiler and servicing and rebuilding Stanley cars, marketed a number of cars under the American Steam Car emblem. These used basic Hudson components, chassis and bodies. The condenser emblem and hubcaps, however, carried the American name.

AMERICAN STEAMER 1922–1924
The American Steam Truck Co, Chicago, Ill.; Elgin, Ill.

Only 16 of these cars were built in 1922, an additional cheaper model being unsuccessfully added to the line a year later. The car featured a 2-cylinder compound double-acting motor and was capable of a speed in excess of 60mph. The prototype was tested as early as 1918 but neither the exhaustive testing nor the Lincoln-appearing condenser saved it from bankruptcy. A touring car, roadster, coupé and sedan were available.

AMERICAN TRI-CAR 1912
Tri-car Co of America, Denver, Colo.

This was a 3-wheeler with drive to the single rear wheel, which was also the only braked wheel. It had a 2-cylinder, 13hp air-cooled engine. A planetary transmission was used. This two-passenger car had a wheelbase of 82in.

AMERICAN UNDERSLUNG 1906–1914
American Motor Car Co, Indianapolis, Ind.

This make achieved its fame from the underslung models, so-called because the frame was slung below the axles, which gave a low appearance and center of gravity, but did not sacrifice good ground clearance. In fact this design was not introduced until 1907, earlier cars having conventional chassis and Renault-based engines. 1908 models used 40 and 50hp 4-cylinder Teetor-Hartley engines. The most rakish models were the roadsters, originally only a two-passenger, but supplemented in 1909 by a long-wheelbase four-passenger. A 70hp 6-cylinder car came in 1910.

AMERICAN WALTHAM 1898–1899
American Waltham Mfg Co, Waltham, Mass.

This was a typical light steam buggy with a 2-cylinder engine under the seat, tiller steering and cycle-type wheels. It was the product of a bicycle firm, and must not be confused with the more famous Waltham or Waltham Orient steamer made by another bicycle firm at the same time.

AMES 1910–1915
1 Carriage Woodstock Co, Owensboro, Ky. 1910–1911
2 Ames Motor Car Co, Owensboro, Ky. 1912–1915
Early Ames models had 4-cylinder engines with a choice of five-passenger touring car or gentleman's roadster body styles. Later models with 2-cycle, 4-cylinder engines of 45hp had friction transmissions and double chain drive. At $850 for the roadster, this was an extremely cheap car for its size.

AMHURST (CDN) 1912
Two in One Co, Amhurstberg, Ont.
The Amhurst 40 was a seven-passenger touring car which could be converted to a pick-up truck. Probably not more than six were made.

AMPLEX 1910–1915
1 Amplex Motor Car Co, Mishawaka, Ind.
2 Amplex Mfg Co, Mishawaka, Ind.
Amplex was a continuation of American Simplex. Both 40hp and 50hp models were produced, with 2-cycle engines. These were expensive, a limousine costing as much as $5,600. This firm clung too long to the obsolete 2-cycle engine, although a 4-cycle design was used unsuccessfully in 1913. Gillette Motor Co took over the manufacturing facilities in 1916, perpetuating this aversion to normal engine-valving by manufacturing a rotary sleeve-valve power unit. There is no evidence of their having been any more successful than their predecessors.

AMS-STERLING *see* STERLING (iii)

AMX *see* AMERICAN MOTORS

1919 ANDERSON (ii) 25.3hp touring car. *Autocar*
1920 APPERSON 33.8hp V-8 touring car. *Autocar*

ANCHOR 1910–1911
1 Anchor Motor Car Co, Cincinnati, Ohio
2 Anchor Buggy Co, Cincinnati, Ohio
This motor buggy, made by a branch of Anchor Carriage Co, while more attractive in appearance than most, was not a financial success, as it lasted less than a year.

ANDERSON (i) 1907–1909
Anderson Carriage Mfg Co, Anderson, Ind.
This Anderson was a typical high-wheeler with 2-cylinder air-cooled engine, solid tires and transverse front suspension.

ANDERSON (ii) 1916–1926
The Anderson Motor Co, Rock Hill, S.C.
This car, built by a former carriage works, was the most successful of all makes built in the southern United States. Utilizing 6-cylinder Continental motors of various sorts, production reached nearly 2,000 units in 1923. Andersons appeared in a large variety of body styles and in unusual color combinations and were particularly highly regarded in the southern states, although they were sold throughout the country.

ANGER *see* A.E.C.

ANGUS *see* FULLER (i)

ANHUT 1909–1910
Anhut Motor Car Co, Detroit, Mich.
The Anhut used 6-cylinder ohv engines of 231ci. Two- and four-passenger open models were made, on a common chassis. In 1910, the company was succeeded by Barnes Automobile Co which failed a month later.

ANNA 1912
The Anna is a motor 'orphan', whose origin and manufacture are unknown. It was a two-passenger, with what was termed a 'Democrat' body on a 100in wheelbase. Its water-cooled 2-cylinder engine was of 173ci. The drive was by planetary transmission and roller-chain.

ANN ARBOR 1911–1912
Huron River Mfg Co, Ann Arbor, Mich.
This was designed as a dual-purpose vehicle which could be converted from a passenger car to a small pick-up truck as required.

ANSTED 1926–1927
Ansted Motors, Connersville, Ind.
The Ansted car was in reality the Lexington with substituted radiator emblem and hubcaps. A few Lexingtons were changed in this way and these were marketed in the Chicago area.

APOLLO (i) 1906–1907
Chicago Recording Scale Co, Waukegan, Ill.
The only model by this manufacturer was a five-passenger with a *Roi-des-Belges* body. Power was provided by a 4-cylinder, water-cooled engine by way of a 3-speed transmission and shaft drive.

APOLLO (ii) 1962–1964
1 International Motorcars, Inc, Oakland, Calif. 1962
2 Apollo International Corp, Pasadena, Calif. 1963–1964
The Apollo was a small-production sports car powered by 215ci or 300ci V-8 Buick engines. The sports two-seater or GT coupé bodies were hand-made in Italy. The name was changed to Vetta Ventura in 1964, and manufacture shifted to Dallas, Texas, where it lasted at least into 1966.

APPERSON 1902–1926
1 Apperson Bros Automobile Co, Kokomo, Ind. 1902–1924
2 Apperson Autumble Co, Kokomo, Ind. 1924–1926

After the brothers Elmer and Edgar Apperson withdrew from the Haynes-Apperson concern, they introduced a front-engined car powered by a 16hp horizontally-opposed twin engine. A 4-cylinder model with horizontal engine followed in 1903, and for the 1904 season the company turned to a conventional vertical 4-cylinder layout. These were 25 and 40hp cars with double chain drive, although a 20/24hp horizontal twin was still made. They were expensive cars, the twin costing $3,500, and the larger four $5,000. By 1907 there were three fours of 24/30hp, 40hp and 50hp, the latter costing $7,500 for a limousine. In this year appeared the Jackrabbit, a 60hp two-passenger speedster with flared fenders, capable of 75mph and costing $5,000. Later, the name Jackrabbit was applied to touring Appersons as well.

A number of lower-priced models appeared in the next few years, the cheapest being a 26hp four at only $1,350 in 1915. In 1914 a 29hp six and a 31hp V-8 were introduced; these had V-radiators, a feature which was continued until 1918. 1916 was the company's peak production year, with 2,000 units sold. In 1917 appeared the Silver-Apperson, an eight with styling by C. T. Silver, the New York dealer who later applied his styling talents to Kissel cars. The Silver-Apperson had an oval radiator, bullet-shaped headlights and very clean, modern body lines. The name Silver-Apperson was dropped in 1919, but the design was continued until 1923, when a new line with cycle-type fenders was introduced. A proprietary engine was now used, in the shape of a 195ci Falls Six, although the 332ci V-8 was still Apperson's own make. These models, together with a range of Lycoming-engined straight-8s, introduced in 1925, were continued until the end of production. In 1924 there was a rumour of a refusion with the Haynes company, but this came to nothing. Front-wheel brakes were introduced on the 1926 models, but production ended in the summer of that year.

APPLE 1917–1918
W. A. Apple Motor Car Co, Dayton, Ohio

The Apple 8 was a conventional-looking touring car with a pointed radiator rather like that of the contemporary Paige. It was priced at $1,150.

ARABIAN c.1917
William Galloway Co, Waterloo, Iowa

This light car was a continuation of the Galloway and like its predecessor was an Argo (ii) built under license. A two-passenger and a four-passenger were offered at $385 and $435 respectively. A 4-cylinder, water-cooled engine of 17.5hp was used. The drive system featured a Bailey transmission which drove each rear wheel separately.

ARBENZ 1911–1918
1 Scioto Car Co, Chillicothe, Ohio 1911–1912
2 ArBenz Car Co, Chillicothe, Ohio 1912–1918

The prototypes of this car were known as Scioto in honor of the Scioto River which runs through Chillicothe. Production cars were always called ArBenz after a defunct furniture company whose plant was used for manufacture. Originally the ArBenz was a medium-large touring car with 48hp 4-cylinder engine, priced at $1,885. By 1917 ArBenz was offering a small touring car powered by a 25hp 4-cylinder Lycoming engine, priced at $750.

ARDSLEY 1905–1906
Ardsley Motor Car Co, Yonkers, N.Y.

This fairly large and expensive car was designed by W. S. Howard, who had been previously connected with Howard Automobile Co also of Yonkers, N.Y. It had a 30/35hp 4-cylinder engine and shaft drive.

ARGO (i) 1912–1914
Argo Electric Vehicle Co, Saginaw, Mich.

Argo electrics used a 60-volt system with Westinghouse motors. These were claimed to be capable of 20mph. Both four- and five-passenger cars, in open and closed versions, were made. All models used wheel steering.

1916 ARGO (ii) 22hp touring car. *Keith Marvin Collection*
1955 ARNOLT-BRISTOL coupé. *Bristol Cars Ltd*

1929 AUBURN (i) 6-80 coupé. *G. N. Georgano Collection*
1934 AUBURN (i) straight-8 phaeton. *Kenneth Stauffer*

ARGO (ii) 1914–1916
Argo Motor Co, Jackson, Mich.

The Argo was originally a cyclecar based on the French Ajax built by the Briscoe brothers in France. It had a 4-cylinder 12hp engine and differed from the Ajax only in not using friction drive. Few cyclecars sold well in America and in 1916 it was replaced by a conventional 22hp assembled touring car. In 1916 the name was changed to Hackett and the company moved to Grand Rapids.

ARGONNE 1919–1920
Argonne Motor Co, Jersey City, N.J.

One of several outstanding sports cars of the period, the Argonne had a Duesenberg 4-cylinder engine and a radiator which closely resembled the Austro-Daimler. In 1920 a smaller engine by Buda was also listed. Less than a hundred of these handsome, fast cars were built, most of them two-passenger roadsters.

ARIEL 1905–1907
The Ariel Co, Boston, Mass.; Bridgeport, Conn. 1905–1906

Ariels were available with either air-cooled or water-cooled engines of 30hp using a single overhead camshaft. Radiators were oval in shape, reminiscent of the Delaunay-Belleville, giving rise to their slogan 'Look for the Oval Front'. In 1907 the make name was changed to Maryland (ii).

ARMAC 1905
Armac Motor Co, Chicago, Ill.

The only car model produced under this name was a light roadster.

ARNOLT 1953–c.1964
S. H. Arnolt, Inc, Chicago, Ill.

The first Arnolts used an M.G. chassis, but the best-known cars were the Arnolt-Bristols which had the 120ci Bristol engine and chassis with Bertone body. Competition, touring and GT coupé models were made, and the prices were from $6,000 up. Arnolt-Bristols achieved a number of sporting successes.

ARROW (i) 1914
National United Service Co, Detroit, Mich.

This was a 4-cylinder friction drive cyclecar selling at $395.

ARROW (ii) 1914
M. C. Whitmore Co, Dayton, Ohio

The manufacturer termed this a 'light car' but the design had the typical cyclecar configuration, being a two-passenger, belt-driven vehicle with a water-cooled, 4-cylinder, 91.5ci engine. It was priced at $395.

ASHEVILLE 1914–1915
Asheville Light Car Co, Asheville, N.C.

This cyclecar used a 7hp Indian air-cooled engine, with drive through a friction transmission and belts to the rear wheels. Wheelbase was 90in and the tread 40in.

ASTON 1908–1909
Aston Motor Car Co, Bridgeport, Conn.

'The Aston built to your order' is the information contained in the only advertisement located for this automobile. At least one model in 1908 was rated at 25hp and one in 1909 at 40hp. No other data are available for this make.

ATLAS 1907–1911
Atlas Motor Car Co, Springfield, Mass.

This was a subsidiary venture of the Knox Motor Truck Co, headed by Harry A. Knox. All models, both 2- and 4-cylinder, were two-cycles. The Atlas was more successful as a taxi than as a passenger car, although one Atlas was entered in the 1909 Vanderbilt race. The design was replaced by the Atlas-Knight.

ATLAS-KNIGHT 1911–1913
Atlas Motor Car Co, Springfield, Mass.

This car was a continuation of the Atlas using the Knight engine to replace the obsolete two-cycle engine of its predecessor. For 1912 the Atlas-Knight was available as either a five- or seven-passenger touring car, the latter selling for $3,750. All cars carried a one-year guarantee.

AUBURN (i) 1900–1937
Auburn Automobile Co, Auburn, Ind.

One of the most famous of all American cars, the Auburn first appeared in 1900 when Frank and Morris Eckhart of the Eckhart Carriage Co, in Auburn, Ind., began experimenting with hand-built cars, selling them in and around Auburn. The first production car appeared in 1903 as a single-cylinder chain-driven runabout with the engine under the body and the fuel tank under the hood. A touring model was added in 1904 and in 1905, 2-cylinder cars were introduced and continued until 1910, in which year a 4-cylinder type with a Mercedes-shaped radiator and a Rutenber engine was introduced. Both open and closed bodies were available on this larger chassis. In 1911 Auburn bought the Zimmerman Mfg Co, which had been producing high wheelers under that name, and continued to manufacture them. Auburn introduced a 6-cylinder car with electric lights as standard equipment in 1912. Right- or left-hand steering was optional in 1914, and from 1914 to 1919, 4- and 6-cylinder cars were available with Teetor, Rutenber and Continental engines. In 1919, the company introduced its Beauty Six model featuring streamlined bodies with bevelled edges on the sides. In 1921 this became the 6-51 sports model with cycle-type fenders, step-plates instead of running-boards, disk wheels and a small luggage compartment behind the front bumper. Nickel trim was also featured, as well as leather upholstery and an abundance of bright color schemes. The Auburns of 1923 were powered by a Continental engine for the 6-43 or a Weidely ohv six for the larger model 6-63, or Supreme. In 1924, balloon low-pressure tires were available on Auburns at extra cost. Up to now production figures had seldom exceeded 4,000 units per year.

In 1924 E. L. Cord bought the Auburn company and from that point on, the Auburn took a leading position in the American automobile business. Cord had the entire range redesigned by J. M. Crawford, and the 1925 line consisted of 4-, 6- and 8-cylinder models. The new cars had two-tone color schemes and a novel belt molding which extended at the cowl over the top of the hood with its apex at the radiator cap. The cars were handsome and well built, although some of the larger models had ugly 6-spoked iron wheels more suited to truck design. These were soon discontinued and normal spoke or wire wheels became standard. The basic lines of the 1925 models were so advanced that the design remained practically the same until 1930. The 4-cylinder car was dropped in 1927 and sales climbed steadily. The 1931 Auburn was perhaps the sleekest car in the company's history and sales reached a peak of 28,103 that year. The 1931 Straight-Eight was augmented in 1932 with a new 391ci V-12, both cars being equipped with a Columbia 2-speed rear axle. This V-12 was the first 12-cylinder car to sell at under $1,000, and probably the only one, too. These lines were continued in 1933. In 1934 a new design replaced the basic 1931 type and a six was added to the range. In 1935 a new and handsome sports design was announced and a supercharged line of Auburns augmented the 653 six and 851 eight. The pointed-tail 150bhp speedster models were guaranteed to have been test driven at more than 100mph. The cars remained unchanged for 1936 and although a new range of Auburns had been planned for 1937, no cars were produced by the company.

AUBURN (ii) 1967 to date
Auburn-Cord-Duesenberg Co, Tulsa, Okla.

After building a small number of Cord replicas, Glenn Pray turned to the 1936 Auburn Speedster. His replica of this, known as the Auburn 866, uses a 427ci Ford V-8 engine giving a top speed of 135mph.

AUBURN-MOORE see MOORE (ii)

AULTMAN 1901–1902
The Aultman Co, Canton, Ohio

The Aultman was a typical light steam buggy of the period with two-passenger body and tiller steering. The firm also experimented with a 4-wheel-drive steam truck.

AURORA (i) 1906–1908
Aurora Motor Co, Aurora, Ill.

This make was represented by 30hp touring cars and runabouts at a price under $1,000. The manufacturer is given variously as Aurora Motor Works, and Aurora Automobile Co. Production may have been resumed in 1909.

AURORA (ii) 1958
Father Alfred Juliano, Bradford, Conn.

A 'safety car' designed by a Catholic priest, the Aurora had one of the most unusual 4-door sedan bodies ever seen. Sculptured fenders flowing from back to front gave the impression that the car was being driven in reverse. The driver sat behind a bulbous windshield, and the general lay-out was distinctive if little else. A choice of Cadillac, Lincoln or Chrysler engines was offered, and the car could be bought for $15,000.

AUSTIN 1901–1921
Austin Automobile Co, Grand Rapids, Mich.

The Austin was known as The Highway King. Despite an output of 50 or less units per year, it was something of a pioneer in a number of ways. The 1902 2-cylinder models were much larger than most contemporary makes and for several years, although colors were optional, most of these big cars were painted either white with tan trim or light brown. By 1911, the cars were equipped with electric lights and left-hand steering. Two years later, Austins featured a highly successful 2-speed axle, with wheelbase up to 142in. After 1915, the company attempted to market smaller and cheaper cars and also introduced a 12-cylinder model in 1917 which was produced until the firm ceased operations. About 1,000 cars were made altogether.

1914 AUSTIN '66' 48 hp touring car. *The Veteran Car Club of Great Britain*

AUTO-BUG 1909–1910
Auto-Bug Co, Norwalk, Ohio

The Auto-Bug had large-diameter wheels and solid rubber tires. It was built in two- and four-passenger models. The drive was by double chains from a 22hp 2-cylinder engine and steering was by wheel.

AUTOBUGGY see A.B.C.

AUTOCAR 1897–1911
1 Pittsburgh Motor Vehicle Co, Pittsburgh, Pa. 1897–1899
2 The Autocar Co, Ardmore, Pa. 1900–1911

The first products of this company were largely experimental and

1906 AUTOCAR 12hp two-passenger car. *Kenneth Stauffer*

included a single-cylinder tricycle and light 4-wheel buggy (1898). Twenty-seven cars were made in 1900, by which date the company had moved to their new Ardmore factory, and in 1901 there appeared a 3½hp 2-cylinder car with shaft drive, the first multi-cylinder shaft-driven car in America. By 1905 large 2- and 4-cylinder cars were being made with gear shift, clutch, spark and throttle all controlled from the steering column. Trucks were introduced in 1907, and after 1911 became the only products of the firm. Autocar is now a division of White Motor Co and still makes heavy trucks.

AUTOCYCLE 1907
Vandergrift Automobile Co, Philadelphia, Pa.

This curious vehicle had four wire wheels arranged in a diamond pattern. It was steered by wheel, which turned the front wheel as well as the middle pair. The rear wheel was chain-driven from a 6hp air-cooled engine.

AUTODYNAMICS 1964 to date
Autodynamics, Inc, Marblehead, Mass.

Headed by Ray Caldwell, Autodynamics is America's largest builder of racing cars, and up to the middle of 1970 had produced over 1,000 competition cars. Most of these have been Formula Vee racing cars, but Caldwell has also built a Can-Am car, the D-7, and a number of Hustler VW-engined fiberglass sports cars. These are available in kit form or as complete cars.

AUTOETTE (i) 1910–1913
Manistee Motor Car Co, Manistee, Mich.

The Autoette was one of the first American cyclecars, with single-cylinder 5hp engine of only 38.5ci capacity. It had friction transmission, final drive by V-belts, and a small diameter wire wheels. The only body style was a two-passenger roadster which cost $300. From 1912 the car was also known as the Manistee.

AUTOETTE (ii) 1913
Autoette Co, Christman, Ill.

This was a short-lived cyclecar with a 9hp air-cooled engine, two speeds and reverse, and shaft drive.

1921 AUTOMATIC (ii) electric light car. *Autocar*

AUTOETTE (iii) to date
Autoette Electric Car Co, Long Beach, Calif.
 This is a small electric used for running errands. This type of car is relatively inexpensive and popular in Long Beach where many retired people live.

AUTOMATIC (i) *see* STURTEVANT

AUTOMATIC (ii) 1921
Automatic Electric Transmission Co, Buffalo, N.Y.
 The Automatic electric was a very small two-passenger car with a wheelbase of only 65in. It had a speed of 25mph, and a creditable range of 60 miles per charge, but the price of $1,200 was very expensive for so small a car.

AUTOMOTOR 1901–1904
Automotor Co, Springfield, Mass.
 Automotor's final model had a *Roi-des-Belges* five-passenger body, with a 4-cylinder 16/20hp engine. The purchaser had a choice of planetary or sliding-gear transmission. This 1,700lb car was claimed to be capable of 45mph.

AUTO RED BUG *see* RED BUG

AUTO-TRI *see* KELSEY (ii)

AUTO TRI-CAR 1914
A. E. Osborn, New York, N.Y.
 This was a 3-wheeled vehicle, classed as a cyclecar. It used a single-cylinder engine with slide valves. This drove the single front wheel through a planetary transmission and a roller-chain. The steering was by tiller. Two models were offered with wheelbases of 96in and 108in respectively. The cost was $350.

AVANTI II 1965 to date
Avanti Motor Co, South Bend, Ind.
 A new lease of life was given this sports car when several South Bend businessmen took over the dies and plant from Studebaker and rejuvenated the marque with some face-lifting and a 323ci Corvette engine for power. For 1970 a 300bhp 350ci Corvette engine was introduced.

AVERAGE MAN'S RUNABOUT 1907–1908
Adams Automobile Co, Hiawatha, Kan.
 This high-wheeler had a 14hp air-cooled engine mounted beneath the body. Wheelbase was 74in, and steering was by tiller.

B

BABCOCK (i) 1906–1912
Babcock Electric Carriage Co, Buffalo, N.Y.

The company was formed by F. A. Babcock who built his first electric car in 1903. The Babcock did not differ greatly from the Buffalo (ii) which it succeeded. In turn it was superseded in 1912 by the Buffalo Electric Vehicle Co.

BABCOCK (ii) 1909–1913
H. H. Babcock Co, Watertown, N.Y.

The Babcock line included a motor buggy with a 2-cylinder engine, as well as conventional cars with larger 4-cylinder engines rated at 35/40hp. The five-passenger touring car was on a 114in wheelbase and weighed 2,500lb.

BACHELLE 1901–1902
Otto Bachelle, Chicago, Ill.

The Bachelle was a two-passenger electric with tiller steering. The rear wheels were individually driven by separate motors. Total weight was 800lb and a full battery charge was sufficient for 35 miles, the manufacturer claimed.

BADGER (i) 1908–c.1910
Four Wheel Drive Auto Co, Clintonville, Wis.

The Badger was an early attempt to make a 4-wheel-drive touring car. It was powered by a 55/60hp 4-cylinder engine, had a large touring body and cost $4,500. Very few cars were made, but the F.W.D. company later became one of America's best-known truck manufacturers.

1909 BABCOCK (i) two-passenger electric car. *Automotive History Collection, Detroit Public Library*

BADGER (ii) 1910–1912
Badger Motor Car Co, Columbus, Wis.

This Badger had a 30hp 4-cylinder engine and Bosch dual ignition. Touring and roadster models were made, priced at $1,600. It should not be confused with Badger (i). The company made 237 Badgers.

BAILEY (i) 1907–1910
Bailey Automobile Co, Springfield, Mass.

This car used a 4-cylinder rotary engine of 20/24hp, and of 254ci capacity. It had a 2-speed selective transmission, shaft drive, and was on a wheelbase of 100in. The hood had a rounded cross-section and the five-passenger body had a peculiar high appearance. There is no known connection with Bailey (ii), also of Massachusetts. Car and company were sometimes listed as Bailey-Perkins.

BAILEY (ii) 1907–1915
S. R. Bailey & Co, Amesbury, Mass.

In 1911 the Bailey electric was available as a Victoria phaeton with wheel-steering at a price of $2,600. For 1913, there was a chain-driven runabout with very advanced styling.

BAKER (i) 1899–1916
Baker Motor Vehicle Co, Baker, Rauch & Lang Co, Cleveland, Ohio

Early Bakers had one ¾hp motor with a maximum speed of 17mph and a 50-mile range on a full battery charge. Later models, such as the 1910 limousine, had a false hood holding batteries, steering-wheel controls and a speed of 30mph, all for $3,000. A Baker-built Torpedo established a 1km speed record in 1902. The company absorbed the R. M. Owen Co, makers of the Owen Magnetic, in 1915. Baker electric car production was among the most important in the US.

BAKER (ii) 1917–1924
Baker Steam Motor Car & Mfg Co, Pueblo and Denver, Colo.

This steam car was more fancy than fact, although roadster and touring models, and also a truck, were produced about 1921. Baker boilers, designed by Dr H. O. Baker, were used successfully, however, as replacements on Stanley cars.

BAKER-BELL 1913
Baker-Bell Motor Co, Philadelphia, Pa.

Hummingbird was the model designation for this obscure make of car. This two-passenger roadster was driven by a 4-cylinder 22.5hp engine and cost $675.

BALBOA 1925
Balboa Motors Corp, Fullerton, Calif.

The Balboa had a supercharged rotary valve ohc engine of its own design and sleek, streamlined bodywork. A five-passenger touring car and a sports brougham were produced but the make lasted only one year.

BALDNER 1901–1903
Baldner Motor Vehicle Co, Xenia, Ohio

This company made a 12hp runabout and a 20hp touring car.

BALDWIN 1899–1902
Baldwin Automobile Mfg Co, Connellsville, Pa.

The Baldwin steamer had a 2-cylinder double-acting vertical engine, with condenser mounted in front on the dash. The body seated two passengers, and final drive was by single chain.

1913 BAILEY (ii) two-passenger electric runabout. *Henry Ford Museum, Dearborn, Mich.*

1910 BAKER (i) two-passenger electric phaeton. *Kenneth Stauffer*

BALL 1902
Miami Cycle and Mfg Co, Middletown, Ohio

The Ball was one of the most luxurious and expensive steam cars made in America. Its engine developed a claimed 60hp, and, complete with seven-passenger body, the weight was over 2 tons. It carried 24 gallons of gasoline and 68 gallons of water, and was good for 40mph over long stretches. Three were planned but only one was completed. Designed by C. A. Ball, it was also known as the Ramapaugh, after an Indian tribe.

BALZER 1894–c.1900
1 Stephen M. Balzer, Bronx, N.Y. 1894–1898
2 Balzer Motor Carriage Co, Bronx, N.Y. 1898–1900

The Balzer car used a 10hp 3-cylinder rotary engine, probably the first application of such a design to a road vehicle. Unlike the later Adams-Farwell, the Balzer's engine was mounted vertically, revolving round a horizontal crankshaft, and driving the rear wheel by gearing. Several cars were made, and the 1894 prototype still exists in the Smithsonian Institution in Washington, D.C. The 1906 Carey used a 5-cylinder engine of Balzer design.

BANKER 1905
A. C. Banker Co, Chicago, Ill.

The Banker had a 294ci 4-cylinder, L-head engine which was water-cooled. The chassis had a tubular front axle and a 100in wheelbase. The five-passenger side-entrance tonneau was priced at $2,250 with wooden body, or $2,500 with aluminum one. A limousine was available at $3,000.

BANKER JUVENILE ELECTRIC 1905
Banker Brothers Co, Pittsburgh, Pa.

A small two-passenger electric roadster intended for use by children. Its 24in × 2in tires on wire wheels, and '25% reduction in scale from standard car measurements' might class this as an early cyclecar.

BANNER BOY BUCKBOARD 1958
Banner Welder, Inc, Milwaukee, Wis.

This car was similar to the Briggs-Stratton Flyer, and in fact used a Briggs-Stratton 2¾hp single-cylinder air-cooled unit. However, instead of the fifth wheel drive of the original, the Banner Boy transmitted its power to the right rear wheel via a centrifugal clutch and V-belt. Supplied as a kit together with plans and instructions, it sold for $399.50.

BANTAM (i) 1914
Bantam Motor Co, Boston, Mass.

The first American car of this name (not to be confused with the later, better-known small car from Pennsylvania), was a short-lived cyclecar with an air-cooled V-twin engine and friction and chain transmission, costing $385.

BANTAM (ii) *see* AMERICAN AUSTIN

BARBARINO 1924–1925
Barbarino Motor Car Corp, New York, N.Y.; Port Jefferson, L.I., N.Y.

Salvatore Barbarino was an automobile designer and engineer who took over the assets of the defunct Richelieu company in 1923 and set out to market a small car embodying his own design. The Barbarino, of which about 10 were made, was a high-grade product, including a 4-cylinder Le Roi engine of Barbarino's design, 4-wheel brakes, a high-rounded radiator, wheelbase of 110in and bodies built to the customer's own order by Chupudy Auto Coach, New York City.

BARLEY 1922–1924
Barley Motor Car Co, Kalamazoo, Mich.

This automobile was named after Albert Barley who headed the firm and who had also started the Roamer car; the Barley company was actually a subsidiary of Roamer. With a Continental 6-cylinder engine and standard components, Barleys were available as sedans, touring cars and taxis. Early in 1925, the name was dropped and the Barley became the Roamer '6-50', except for the taxicabs which were continued through the year under their old name of Pennant.

BARNES 1907–1912
Barnes Mfg Co, Sandusky, Ohio

Barnes Mfg Co succeeded Anhut Motor Co in 1910, and produced both the Barnes and the Anhut. The Barnes was a roadster with a 4-cylinder air-cooled engine.

BARNHART 1905
Warren Automobile Co, Warren, Pa.

The only known model of the Barnhart had a 44hp, 4-cylinder engine with an automatic control 'by which one or more cylinders can be cut out'. The touring car on a 110in wheelbase cost $3,500.

BARRIE (CDN) 1919–1920
Barrie Carriage Co Ltd, Barrie, Ont.

A typical assembled touring car with no distinguishing features.

BARROWS 1897–1898
Barrow's Vehicle Co, Willimantic, Conn.

The Barrows was a two-passenger electric 3-wheeler with drive through the single front wheel. It was claimed that this wheel could be fitted to any 2-wheeled horse carriage.

BARTHOLOMEW *see* GLIDE

BARTLETT (CDN) 1914–1917
Toronto, Ont.

Over 200 touring cars and roadsters were built, all with thin, solid rubber tires and most of them with pneumatic rubber cushions between frame and axles instead of conventional springs. This suspension system was dropped for the last few models. Shortages of parts forced an end to production during World War 1.

BARTON *c.* 1903
Barton Boiler Co, Chicago, Ill.

Though primarily a boiler manufacturer, Barton offered 'special steam tonneau cars' built to order. These used the Barton flash boiler, Burnell kerosene burner, and Mason 2-cylinder slide valve engine.

BASSON'S STAR 1956
This was an ephemeral minicar with three wheels, fiberglass body, and 2-cycle single-cylinder engine. The price was $999.

BATES 1903–1905
Bates Automobile Co, Lansing, Mich.

The Bates car used an 18/20hp 3-cylinder engine, and had 3 forward speeds and shaft drive. With a four-passenger touring body, it cost $2,000. The company's optimistic advertising slogan was 'Buy a Bates and Keep Your Dates'.

BAY STATE (i) 1906–1907
Bay State Automobile Co, Boston, Mass.

The Bay State Forty was a large seven-passenger vehicle with a 354ci 4-cylinder engine. It had a 3-speed selective transmission, and final drive was by shaft.

BAY STATE (ii) 1922–1924
R. H. Long Co, Framingham, Mass.

In three years of production approximately 2,500 units of this assembled car left the factory. Powered by a Continental 6-cylinder engine, the Bay State was designed by a former Winton technician, which accounts for the similarity in radiator appearance.

B.C.K *see* KLINE KAR

B.D.A.C. *see* BUCKMOBILE

1966 BEACH Formula Vee racing car. *Autosport*

BEACH 1962 to date
Competition Components, Inc, Clearwater, Fla.

Eugene Beach was one of the most prolific of the Formula Vee producers, surpassing the 200 mark for kits completed from the commencement of the Formula up to mid-1967. Square-section tubular frames were supplied, with fiberglass bodies and other components as necessary.

BEARDSLEY 1915–1917
Beardsley Electric Co, Los Angeles, Calif.

The Beardsley electric was offered in as many as twelve models, simultaneously. It was claimed that the lightest model was capable of 28mph. The common wheelbase was 92in and the price range was $1,285 to $2,650. Most models were equipped with wire wheels.

BEAU-CHAMBERLAIN *see* HUDSON (i)

BEAUMONT *see* ACADIAN

BEAVER 1916–1923
Beaver State Motor Co, Gresham, Oreg.

Named after the Beaver State (Oregon), this was an assembled car with a 6-cylinder engine and worm drive. Very few were made.

BEEBE 1906
Western Motor Truck & Vehicle Works, Chicago, Ill.

This obscure car used a 2-cylinder, two-cycle engine of 30hp connected to a friction transmission. Two models were offered with wheelbases of 80in and of 100in. It has been claimed that these cars had push-button starting.

BEGGS 1918–1923
Beggs Motor Car Co, Kansas City, Mo.

A typical assembled car, the Beggs used standard components throughout. It was powered by a Continental 6-cylinder motor.

BEISEL 1914
Beisel Motorette Co, Monroe, Mich.

This short-lived cyclecar used a 4-cylinder water-cooled Prugh engine of 95ci. A friction transmission was used, and this was connected to the rear wheels by drive belts. The wheelbase was 96in, the tread 40in, and its cost was $385.

1910 BERGDOLL 30hp touring car. *Kenneth Stauffer*

B.E.L. 1921

Consolidated Motor Car Co, New London, Conn.

A small car of severely limited production, the B.E.L. was built by the company which had earlier produced the Sterling (iii). The B.E.L. was mounted on a 101in wheelbase and powered by a 4-cylinder engine of its own design.

BELDEN 1908–1911

Belden Motor Car Co, Pittsburgh, Pa.

Few of these cars were made. The company issued a catalog in 1907 showing 6-cylinder cars, but in September 1909 admitted that it had just completed its first car.

BELL (i) (CDN) 1916–1918

The Barrie Carriage Co, Barrie, Ont.

About 20 of these light touring cars were built, powered by a 4-cylinder Lycoming engine and using mainly imported parts apparently from the U.S. Bell company.

BELL (ii) 1915–1921

Bell Motor Car Co, York, Pa.

A small, inexpensive car (the Model 16 touring car of 1916 sold for $775) on a 112in wheelbase, which used at first G.B. & S. and Continental engines, and a 4-cylinder Herschell-Spillman engine from 1919 onwards. Although made in limited numbers, at least one still exists.

BELLEFONTAINE 1908

Bellefontaine Automobile Co, Bellefontaine, Ohio

The Bellefontaine Model B-8 had a five-passenger *Roi-des-Belges* body. The engine was a 35hp, L-head, with 4 cylinders of 286ci capacity. It had a selective transmission and was priced at $2,500.

BELMOBILE 1912

Bell Motor Car Co, Detroit, Mich.

This make was available only as a two-passenger roadster on a 100in wheelbase. Its 20hp engine drove through a 3-speed transmission. Full elliptical springs were used in the rear, semi-elliptical in front. There is no known connection with the later Bell automobile.

BELMONT (i) 1909–1912

1 Belmont Motor Car Co, New Haven, Conn.
2 Belmont Motor Vehicle Co, Castleton-on-Hudson, N.Y.

The Belmont 30hp touring car had a complex history, certainly out of proportion to the few vehicles which could have been built between re-organizations. One of the originators was Dr C. Baxter Tiley, who was also connected with Tiley-Pratt.

BELMONT (ii) 1916

Belmont Electric Auto Co, Wyandotte, Mich.

This car was somewhat unusual for an electric, as only four- and six-passenger limousines were offered for sale. The company also produced commercial electric cars.

BENDIX 1907–1910

The Bendix Co, Chicago, Ill.; Logansport, Ind.

The Bendix Co was the successor to the Triumph Motor Car Co who built the Triumph (ii). The Bendix '30' was a motor buggy with a 4-cylinder water-cooled engine of 30hp, selling for $1,500. Distinguishing features were large-diameter wheels with solid tires, and a minute hood. For 1910 a standard size hood was used.

BENHAM 1914–1917

Benham Mfg Co, Detroit, Mich.

Successors to S. & M. (Strobel & Martin), Benham produced approximately 60 units. The Benham had a Continental engine and other standard components and was attractively streamlined for its time.

BEN HUR 1916–1918

Ben Hur Motor Co, Willoughby, Ohio

The Ben Hur used a 303ci 6-cylinder Buda engine, and had a wheelbase of 126in. Only open models were built, sporty two-passenger roadsters being typical.

BENNER 1908–1910

Benner Motor Car Co, New York, N.Y.

This car was powered by a 6-cylinder, 25/30hp ohv Brownell engine. The touring car was priced at $1,750. Nearly 200 were made.

BERG 1902–1905

1 Berg Automobile Co, Cleveland, Ohio 1902–1904
2 Worthington Automobile Co, New York, N.Y. 1905

The original Berg car was made for the Berg company by the Cleveland Machine Screw Co. It had a 4-cylinder engine said to develop 15 to 20hp, a sloping finned-tube radiator and double chain drive. The 1903 model was basically similar, but for 1904 the company introduced a smaller car with 251ci 15/18hp engine, vertical honeycomb radiator and shaft drive. The following year they merged with the Worthington Automobile Co of New York, who were also concerned with the Worthington-Bollée and Meteor (iii) cars. The larger, chain driven car was still made, now of 24hp.

BERGDOLL 1908–1913

Louis J. Bergdoll Motor Co, Philadelphia, Pa.

The Bergdoll Thirty was the model produced during most of the lifetime of this make. In 1911, five different models of 4-cylinder cars were available, from a touring car at $1,500 to a limousine at $2,500. This was one of the outstanding makes of the period from the standpoint of quality.

BERKSHIRE 1905–1913

1 Berkshire Automobile Co, Pittsfield, Mass. 1905–1908
2 Berkshire Motor Car Co, Pittsfield, Mass. 1908–1909
3 Berkshire Auto-Car Co, Pittsfield, Mass. 1909–1912
4 Berkshire Motors Co, Cambridge, Mass. 1912
5 Belcher Engineering Co, Cambridge, Mass. 1912–1913

The pilot model of this make was built as early as 1903. Herschell-Spillman 4-cylinder engines were fitted in 1905 and 1906 Berkshires; later the company built their own 35hp 4-cylinder units of 379ci capacity. An early patented transmission designed to prevent stripping was not successful. In the period 1907–1909 a few rakish speedsters were built.

1911 BERKSHIRE Model E roadster. *G. Marshall Naul*

After the Berkshire Motors Co was sold, Belcher Engineering bought up all spare parts and assembled three more Berkshires from these, bringing total production of this make to an estimated 150 cars.

BERTOLET 1908–1912

1 Dr J. M. Bertolet, Reading, Pa. 1908–1909
2 Bertolet Motor Car Co, Reading, Pa. 1909–1912

The original Bertolet was available with interchangeable bodies, one a two-passenger roadster, the other a five-passenger touring type. Both bodies, with chassis, cost $2,400. Later models were rated at 40hp and had conventional water-cooled 4-cylinder engines.

BERWICK 1904
Berwick Auto Car Co, Grand Rapids, Mich.

The Berwick was a two-passenger electric runabout for which its manufacturers did not claim more than 15mph. It had three speed positions, was tiller-operated and had an abundance of brasswork, all for $750.

BEVERLY *see* UPTON

BIDDLE 1915–1923
Biddle Motor Car Co, Philadelphia, Pa.

A small luxury car, the Biddle featured exquisite coachwork and a wide variety of body variations with an optional choice of either Duesenberg horizontal valve or Buda 4-cylinder engines. Biddle cars were never common, and few were built after 1921. Their design embodied a V-type radiator which closely resembled the German Mercedes.

BIRMINGHAM 1921–1922
Birmingham No-Axle Motor Corp, Jamestown, N.Y.

The Birmingham car featured independent suspension by transverse semi-elliptic springs, while the fabric-covered bodies were a departure from normal American practices. A Continental 6-cylinder motor supplied power. About 20 cars were built, the first few being made in Detroit. Plans were laid to produce the design in Canada under the name of Parker.

BLACK 1903–1909
Black Mfg Co, Chicago, Ill.

The Black company made mainly high-wheelers powered by 10hp 2-cylinder air-cooled engines, and using chain drive and solid rubber tires. In 1909 they sold a number of the 4-cylinder cars made by the Crow Motor Car Company under the name Black Crow.

BLACK CROW *see* BLACK

BLACK DIAMOND *see* BUCKMOBILE

1918 BIDDLE Model K roadster. *Autosport*

1922 BIRMINGHAM 6-cylinder touring car. *Automotive History Collection, Detroit Public Library*

BILLIKEN 1914
Milwaukee Cycle Car Co, Milwaukee, Wis.

The lone model of this cyclecar was a two-passenger with side-by-side arrangement. It was driven by a water-cooled 4-cylinder engine of 71ci displacement. It had a planetary transmission and shaft drive. The tread was 48in and the wheelbase was 96in.

BIMEL *see* ELCO

BINNEY-BURNHAM 1901–1902
Binney & Burnham, Boston, Mass.

This was a steam car available in two- and four-passenger versions, the latter with forward-facing, folding front seat, the driver being at the rear. The engine had two cylinders, and steam was supplied at a pressure of 150psi.

BIRCH 1917–1923
Birch Motor Cars, Inc, Chicago, Ill.

The Birch was a car which was sold exclusively by mail order, largely through magazine advertisements. Both 4- and 6-cylinder models were available with Herschell-Spillman, Lycoming and LeRoi engines of various ratings. Both open and closed body styles were available to suit the customer.

BLACKHAWK 1902–1903
Clark Mfg Co, Moline, Ill

The Blackhawk was a light two-passenger phaeton with tiller steering and chain drive, priced at $750. The name Black Hawk was used for the cheaper line of Stutz from 1930 to 1931, and is sometimes listed as a make in its own right.

BLAKESLEE *see* DE MARS

BLISS (i) 1901
Bliss Chainless Automobile Co, Attleboro, Mass.

This company made an experimental steam car with drive by spur gearing to the rear axle, instead of the more usual chain drive.

BLISS (ii) 1906
E. W. Bliss Co, Brooklyn, N.Y.

The Bliss had a 4-cylinder T-head engine of 382ci. The flywheel and fan were integral. Final drive was by double chain. The only standard body was a five-passenger tonneau, at $5,000; other bodies were built to order. The Bliss was advertised as 'The Finest American Motor Car'.

B.L.M. 1906–1907
Breese, Lawrence & Moulton Motor Car & Equipment Co, Brooklyn, N.Y.

S. S. Breese and Chas. L. Lawrence were of school age when they built their first 12hp racer in 1905. The above company was formed to manufacture the Pirate, a racing runabout similar in appearance to the T-head Mercer, with a 24hp French-built engine. This was probably the first U.S. manufacturer to offer what is now known as a sports car. Despite their slogan 'The Greatest Runabout in the World', the company became bankrupt later in 1907.

BLOMSTROM 1907–1909
Blomstrom Mfg Co, Detroit, Mich.

A five-passenger touring car and a three-passenger runabout made up the complete Blomstrom line. They had 4-cycle 4-cylinder engines developing 30hp. Final drive was by shaft. This manufacturer also built the Gyroscope.

BLOOD 1903–1905
Blood Brothers Auto & Machine Co, Kalamazoo, Mich.

The last model of this car was a five-passenger tonneau with a 2-cylinder opposed engine under the hood. The drive system had a 4-speed transmission and shaft to the rear axle. The wheelbase was 92in and the car cost $1,800. Some ten years later this company built the Cornelian cyclecar.

B.M.C. SPORTS 1952
British Motor Car Co, San Francisco, Calif.

The B.M.C. Sports was a British Singer 1500 chassis fitted with an American-made fiberglass sports body and a Simca grill.

B.M.W. c.1949 to date
Boulevard Machine Works, Los Angeles, Calif.

This company produced electric minicars and golfmobiles for a number of years, and in 1966 introduced a larger electric roadster with two motors and eight 3-cell batteries giving a claimed maximum speed of 70mph.

BOBBI-KAR 1945–1947
1 Bobbi Motor Car Corp, San Diego, Calif. 1945–1946
2 Bobbi Motor Car Corp (Dixie Motor Car Corp), Birmingham, Ala. 1947

One of the more promising minicars that failed to attain production, the Bobbi-Kar was shown in several plastic-bodied prototype forms, variously powered by rear-mounted air-cooled and water-cooled engines. All four wheels were independently sprung. It was succeeded by the Keller in 1948.

BOBSY 1962 to date
C. W. Smith Engineering Co, Medina, Ohio

Small sports-racing cars, with engines by Ford, Osca, Porsche, SAAB or Alfa-Romeo driving through Hewland 5-speed transmissions, achieved numerous class successes in S.C.C.A. races. Single-seaters, with Volkswagen mechanical parts to conform with Formula Vee, also figured in the range.

BOCAR 1958–c.1960
Bocar Mfg Co, Denver, Colo.

Bob Carnes built and tested a number of experimental sports cars before the first XP-4 was marketed. This two-passenger was available with Chevrolet or Pontiac power, Girling brakes and Jaguar wire wheels. In 1959 the XP-5 appeared with a 90in wheelbase and strengthened VW suspension. The further refined XP-6 that followed was on a longer wheelbase and used a supercharged Chevrolet Corvette engine modified to produce 400hp at 6,200rpm. Body structure was of tubing and fiberglass, the brakes were by Buick and suspension was by rigid axles with paired trailing arms and torsion bars. Curb weight with a full tank of fuel was 2,290lb. Acceleration was extremely good. A standing quarter mile was achieved in 14.6 seconds with a speed of 112mph; 120mph was clocked in 16.0 seconds.

BOLIDE 1969 to date
Bolide Motor Car Corp, Long Island, N.Y.

The Bolide Can-Am 2 is a mid-engined sports coupé powered by a 351ci Ford V-8 engine. The prototype Can-Am 1 appeared at the 1969 New York Auto Show, and production of the Can-Am 2 is scheduled for 1971 at a price of $3,500.

BOLTE 1901
T. H. Bolte, Kearney, Neb.

This 4hp car was claimed to attain 20mph with two passengers. Full elliptical springs were used all round and final drive was by double chains. Steering was by tiller and the vehicle was priced at $600.

BORBEIN 1903–1907
1 H. F. Borbein & Co, St Louis, Mo.
2 Borbein Automobile Co, St Louis, Mo.

Borbein was the successor to Brecht. It was available as a four-passenger car but without engine which had to be supplied and installed by purchaser.

BORLAND 1903–1914
Borland-Grannis Co, Chicago, Ill.

Also known as Borland-Grannis, these cars were electrically powered by General Electric motors. The Borland used shaft drive in place of the chain drive then usual for electrics. The last line of cars included one open model and three closed ones, including a limousine at a price of $5,500. The maximum speed claimed was 22mph. In 1914 Borland merged with Argo (i) and Broc.

BOSS 1903–1907
Boss Knitting Machine Works, Reading, Pa.

The Boss steamer was sometimes referred to as Eck after its designer, James L. Eck. The car had a 2-cylinder 7/8hp engine, and was tiller-steered. It weighed 1,400lb and had a separate unsprung underframe for the running-gear. The price was $1,000. (There were two projected cars named Boss, one in 1904, the other in 1911, but neither is known to be connected with this steam car.)

BOSTON 1906–1907
Concord Motor Car Co, Boston, Mass.

This electric car was scheduled for exhibition at the 1907 Boston Auto Show, but did not make it. Further details are lacking.

BOSTON & AMESBURY 1904
Boston & Amesbury Mfg Co, Amesbury, Mass.

The only model built by this manufacturer was a two-passenger roadster powered by a 2-cylinder water-cooled engine. This had an exposed coil radiator in front and was fitted with an early example of left-hand wheel steering.

BOSTON HIGH WHEEL 1907
Boston High Wheel Auto Mfg Co, Boston, Mass.

This vehicle had wheels of 44 and 48in diameter and solid rubber tires. It was driven by a 2-cylinder air-cooled engine of 12hp. The transmission utilized an expanding/contracting sheave system with belts.

BOURASSA 6 (CDN) 1899–1926
Montreal, Que.

H. E. Bourassa was a mechanical genius from rural Quebec who built the first car ever made there, a one-off runabout with the engine under the seat, in 1899. For several years after that he built much larger cars to special order, each one different. His goal was to form a regular production company, and in the mid-1920s he put an engine of his own design into a Rickenbacker chassis, which was to be the Bourassa 6 prototype. However, he could not raise enough capital to continue, and finally destroyed the car.

1919 BREWSTER 26hp town car. *Antique Automobile*

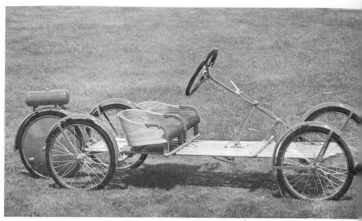

1920 BRIGGS & STRATTON Flyer 2½hp buckboard. *Harrah's Automobile Collection*

BOUR-DAVIS 1915–1922

Bour-Davis Co, Louisiana Motor Car Co, Chicago, Ill.; Shreveport, La.; Detroit, Mich.

This car was a typical assembled make which was built in various places as the result of corporation changes. Production was limited to open body styles and a Continental 6-cylinder engine provided power. The name was changed to Ponder in 1923.

BOWMAN 1921–1922

Bowman Motor Car Co, Covington, Ky.

The Bowman, a short-lived car, was produced primarily if not exclusively as a roadster. This small car used an engine of its own manufacture.

BRADLEY 1920–1921

Bradley Motor Car Co, Cicero, Ill.

The short-lived Bradley was built in limited numbers, a five-passenger touring car being its only model. Lycoming engines were used, a 4-cylinder type for the Model H of 1920 and 1921 and a six for Model F in the final year of production. The wheelbase was 116in and wooden artillery wheels were used throughout.

BRAMWELL 1902–1904

1 Bramwell Motor Co, Boston, Mass.
2 Springfield Automobile Co, Springfield, Ohio

The Bramwell had a two-passenger body on a wooden frame and a 2-cylinder engine. The only unusual feature was a single headlight.

BRAMWELL-ROBINSON 1899–1901

John T. Robinson & Co, Hyde Park, Mass.

This company were makers of paper box machinery who also made some notable cars. The Bramwell-Robinson was a 3-wheeler powered by a horizontal 3hp single-cylinder engine which drove the single rear wheel by chain. It had tiller steering. W. C. Bramwell left to make cars under his own name, while Robinson made a line of expensive 4-cylinder cars, later called Pope-Robinson.

BRASIE 1914–1917

Brasie Motor Car Co, Minneapolis, Minn.

The Brasie was a light roadster powered by a 12hp 4-cylinder engine, with chain drive. The two- or four-passenger open bodies had no doors. Known as the Brasie Packet, the car sold for $450. From 1916 car and company name were changed to Packet.

BRAZIER 1902–1904

H. Bartol Brazier, Philadelphia, Pa.

Brazier was a Frenchman who made a small number of cars to special order. They were mostly heavy-looking vehicles with waggonette bodies and double chain drive. Engines were 18hp 2-cylinders.

BRECHT 1901–1903

Brecht Automobile Co, St Louis, Mo.

Original models, powered by 2-cylinder non-condensing steam engines, were available in four body styles as well as a delivery wagon. Later, electrically-powered cars were built. In 1903 cars were marketed 'ready for power', in other words, engineless. This would indicate some indecision on the part of the manufacturer.

Brecht also built the Rushmobile and was succeeded by Borbein, another manufacturer who disdained to furnish ready-powered cars.

BREMAC 1932

Bremac Motor Car Corp, Sidney, Ohio

An experimental automobile, the Bremac featured an 80hp 8-cylinder engine mounted at the rear of the chassis. A five-passenger sedan was the only body style planned. The Bremac differed from other experimental cars of the era in having no chassis frame or propeller shaft. The car was a failure.

BRENNAN 1907–1908

Brennan Motor Mfg Co, Syracuse, N.Y.

Brennan were engine makers who supplied power units to several manufacturers, including Selden, and made a very few medium-sized 4-cylinder cars.

BREW-HATCHER 1904–1905

The Brew & Hatcher Co, Cleveland, Ohio

Sometimes known as the B & H, this car was powered by a 16hp horizontally-opposed 2-cylinder engine mounted at the front under a hood. It had three forward speeds (direct drive in top) and shaft drive. With a four-passenger rear-entrance tonneau body, the price was $1,750.

BREWSTER

1 Brewster & Co, Long Island City; New York, N.Y. 1915–1925
2 Springfield Mfg Co, Springfield, Mass. 1934–1936

Between 1915 and 1925, the venerable firm of Brewster & Co, carriage builders and makers of custom-built car bodies, produced an expensive and meticulously-built automobile in a variety of open and closed models.

Powered by a 4-cylinder Knight sleeve-valve engine, these compact town-carriage types of cars were widely sought after by the wealthy who did not want the ostentation of a larger custom-built car. Production of the initial Brewsters ceased shortly before the company was absorbed by Rolls-Royce of America, Inc.

The Brewster name re-appeared in 1934 in a series of open and closed Brewster bodies mounted on Ford, Buick and other standard chassis. Approximately 300 of the later Brewsters were built, the cars carrying the Brewster name and costing $3,500.

BRIGGS-DETROITER *see* DETROITER

BRIGGS & STRATTON 1919–c. 1923
Briggs & Stratton Co, Milwaukee, Wis.

To the comfort-loving American motorist, the cyclecar was a bad joke, and the Briggs & Stratton was one of the worst. The Buckboard of 1919 resembled nothing so much as a child's soapbox racer, except that it had rather less bodywork. Two bucket seats sat on a frame with a baby carriage wheel at each corner, while a fifth trailing wheel carried a single-cylinder air-cooled engine that also powered lawn-mowers. In the United States, rough country roads were highly unsatisfactory for the cyclecars which was even less of a commercial success in America than in Europe. Briggs & Stratton went on to make outboard motors, pumps and generators. The design was sold to the Automotive Electric Service Co, who made it as the Auto Red Bug with an electric motor geared directly to the rear axle.

BRISCOE 1914–1921
Briscoe Motor Corp, Jackson, Mich.

The Briscoe car, originally designed in France, was manufactured by Benjamin Briscoe, formerly head of Maxwell. Several thousand of the 4-cylinder cars, using a 155ci engine of his own make, left the factory in nearly eight years of production. There was also an ohv V-8 in 1916. The early cars featured a single or 'cyclops' headlight which was built directly into the radiator cowling. In the autumn of 1921, the car became the Earl, which was outwardly similar to its predecessor.

BROC 1909 1916
Broc Carriage & Wagon Co, Cleveland, Ohio; Saginaw, Mich.

The electric Broc offered three or four models each year. The earlier models had 1hp series motors, with five speed settings, and either shaft drive or double-chain drive. Later models, some with tiller steering, were claimed to reach speeds up to 24mph.

BROCK SIX (CDN) 1921
Brock Motors Ltd, Amherstburg, Ont.

Originally incorporated as Stansell Motors Ltd, the company changed its name to Brock in January 1921. They planned to build 1,000 units per year of the Brock Six, a five-passenger touring car with 55bhp Continental Red Seal engine, but probably not more than one car was made.

BROCKVILLE-ATLAS (CDN) 1910–1915
Brockville Atlas Auto Co, Ltd, Brockville, Ont.

This car was based on the American E.M.F. and was assembled in Canada to be sold at prices up to $2,250. Production was apparently in some quantity as the firm advertised widely and was well-represented by agents in Ontario.

BROGAN 1946–1948
B and B Specialty Co, Rossmoyne, Ohio

A two-passenger, 3-wheeled clutchless machine with an air-cooled, rear-mounted engine of 10hp.

BROOKE-SPACKE 1920–1921
Spacke Machine & Tool Co, Indianapolis, Ind.

The cyclecar in its European form was altogether too crude, drafty,

1915 BRISCOE roadster. *Kenneth Stauffer*
1921 BROOKE-SPACKE cyclecar. *Autocar*

noisy, cramped and uncomfortable for the vast majority of American motorists. By 1916 most of the short-lived makers of these machines in the US were finished and the survivors did not last long thereafter. The Brooke-Spacke was actually a new arrival, even though the market of dedicated enthusiasts was minute and rapidly diminishing. Like most of its breed it had a 2-cylinder air-cooled engine, which was used by many other cyclecar makers, but it catered to American taste with electric lighting and starting, and three forward speeds. Later cars reverted to cyclecar tradition by using 2-speed planetary transmission.

BROOKS (CDN) 1923–1926
Brooks Steam Motors Ltd, Stratford, Ont.

The Brooks Steam Car was second in popularity to the Stanley in the Americas of the 1920s, more than 300 units being delivered in the car's relatively short existence. It used a 2-cylinder steam engine of Brooks design, and only one body style, a 4-door, five-passenger closed model, was available. Brooks cars were all built with fabric-covered bodies.

BROWN 1914
Brown Cyclecar Co, Asbury Park, N.J.

The Brown cyclecar had a track of 44in and a wheelbase of 96in. It was driven by a 2-cylinder Spacke engine, with V-belts to the rear axle. The two-passenger roadster was priced at $375.

BROWNIE 1916–1917
J. O. Carter, Hannibal, Mo.
The Brownie was a light car powered by a 4-cylinder engine of 38bhp. The price was $735.

BROWNIEKAR 1908–1910
Omar Motor Co, Newark, N.Y.
This was an ultra-light two-passenger car with a 3hp single-cylinder engine and belt drive. It cost only $150, and was intended mainly for children, the advertisement claiming that it could be operated by any intelligent child of 8 years or more. It was designed by W. H. Birdsall, chief engineer of the Mora Motor Car Co, who also made the Browniekar, Omar being a convenient anagram of Mora.

BRUNSWICK 1916
Brunswick Motor Car Co, Newark, N.Y.
This was a conventional assembled car powered by a 4-cylinder Wisconsin engine.

BRUSH 1907–1913
1 Brush Motor Car Co, Detroit, Mich.
2 Brush Runabout Co, Detroit, Mich.
The Brush was a popular two-passenger runabout with coil springs all round, and a wooden frame and axles. The initial model had a single cylinder, 12hp engine, with chain drive and solid tires, priced at $780. By the end of 1907 the price was down to $500, and in 1912, a stripped version, the Liberty-Brush, sold for only $350. Brush chassis with an abbreviated landaulette body were marketed in 1912 for taxi use under the name Titan. Later models used a larger engine and pneumatic tires, but the basic design of the car remained unchanged. The car was designed by Alanson P. Brush, and the company was formed by Frank Briscoe. Later, Brush became a division of U.S. Motors Co and ceased production with the collapse of this combine in 1913.

BRYAN 1918–1923
Bryan Steam Motors, Peru, Ind.
The Bryan steam car was a handsome vehicle, its outward appearance closely resembling that of the Apperson. Six of these 4,500lb touring cars were produced in six years of business.

BUCKAROO 1957
The Buckaroo is reported to have been a small air-cooled cyclecar, built in Cleveland, Ohio, with a speed of 18mph and a price of $400.

BUCKEYE *see* LAMBERT

BUCKLES 1914
T. E. Buckles, Manchester, Okla.
This was a two-passenger cyclecar with a 2-cylinder, air-cooled Spacke engine, a friction transmission, and belt drive. Its tread was 36in, with a wheelbase of 96in. The price was $350.

BUCKMOBILE 1903–1905
1 Buckmobile Co, Utica, N.Y. 1903–1904
2 Black Diamond Automobile Co, Utica, N.Y. 1904–1905
Buckmobile was a small two-passenger roadster with a 15hp 2-cylinder engine (either air- or water-cooled) mounted under the seat. In 1904 Black Diamond Automobile Co (B.D.A.C.) bought Buckmobile Co and the plant of Remington Automobile & Motor Co; they continued the manufacture of Buckmobiles, but there is no evidence of a Black Diamond car.

BUFFALO (i) 1900–1902
Buffalo Automobile & Auto-Bi Co, Buffalo, N.Y.
This was a light runabout with 7hp single-cylinder engine which became the Thomas in 1902, and thus can be considered as the ancestor of the great Thomas Flyer, winner of the 1908 New York to Paris race.

1910 BRUSH 10hp roadster. *The Veteran Car Club of Great Britain*
1904 BUFFUM flat-8 racing car. *Autocar*

BUFFALO (ii) 1901–1906
Buffalo Electric Carriage Co, Buffalo, N.Y.
This company built a wide range of electric vehicles, from typical light runabouts to some exceptionally large and expensive cars. The 1903 four-passenger touring car had wheel steering and a small hood under which some of the batteries were housed, the others being beneath the body. It had a range of 75 miles per charge. 1904 models ranged from a two-passenger runabout at $1,650 to a six-passenger touring car at $5,000. After 1906 the cars were renamed Babcock (i). Other cars which bore the Buffalo name include: (a) experimental cars by the Buffalo Gasolene Motor Co, who made engines for the later Selden cars; (b) the 1908 de Schaum. There were also several firms making gasoline and electric commercial vehicles under the name Buffalo.

BUFFALO (iii) 1912–1915
Buffalo Electric Vehicle Co, Buffalo, N.Y.
This car was merely a revival of the Buffalo (ii) and the immediate successor to the Babcock (i), and was formed from Clark Motor Co, Buffalo Automobile Station Co and Babcock.

BUFFUM 1901–1907
H. H. Buffum & Co, Abington, Mass.
This company was a pioneer of the flat engine and of multicylinders. In 1902 they offered a 16hp horizontally opposed 4-cylinder car, and in 1904 a racing car with horizontal 8-cylinder engine and coil springs all round. From 1905 to 1907 they made a V-8 with the same dimensions as the V-8 Hewitt.

BUGETTA 1969 to date
Bugetta, Inc, Costa Mesa, Calif.
In addition to their well-known off-road vehicles, Bugetta offer a sports

car for two or four passengers, powered by a mid-mounted Ford 302ci engine. It has a one-piece fiberglass body and optional top in either fiberglass or cloth. Price is $3,695.

BUGGYCAR 1907–1909
Buggy-Car Co, Cincinnati, Ohio

This was a two-passenger buggy-type car with solid rubber tires. It had an opposed 2-cylinder air-cooled engine under the seat. The drive to the rear axle was by cable.

BUGMOBILE 1909
Bugmobile Co of America, Chicago, Ill.

The Bugmobile was a tiller-steered two-passenger high-wheeler with a 2-cylinder, 4-cycle 15hp engine. The final drive was by belts to the rear wheels. This car was devoid of fenders.

BUICK 1903 to date
1 Buick Motor Car Co, Detroit, Mich. 1903
2 Buick Motor Car Co, Flint, Mich. 1904 to date

David Buick's first car followed conventional American design in having a flat-twin engine mounted amidships under the floor, a 2-speed planetary transmission, and final drive by chain — but unusual were its mechanically-operated full overhead valves, a feature of all cars bearing the name of Buick to the present day. Displacement was 159ci, and it sold for $1,200. By 1907, there was already a companion 286ci four with front-mounted engine, and a 'square' four ($3\frac{3}{4}$in × $3\frac{3}{4}$in) with planetary transmission added to the range. In 1908 W. C. Durant formed General Motors, Buick being one of the original members of the group. In 1909 Bob Burman drove a Buick to victory in the first race ever held at Indianapolis Speedway. Sales had exceeded 30,000 cars by 1910. For the next few years Buicks with English bodywork were sold in Britain first as 'all British Bedfords', and then as 'Bedford-Buicks'. By 1912 planetary transmission had been dropped and 4-cylinder cars were available in 167ci, 201ci and 318ci sizes, still with rhd, but with the brake and gear levers faired into the driver's door. Delco electric lighting and starting were standard on all models by 1914, in which year Buick marketed their first six, the B-55. Nearly 126,000 cars were sold in 1916, and the company entered the post-World War 1 era with a 170ci four and a 238ci six, cars which brought Buick into fourth position in U.S. sales, behind Ford, Dodge, and Chevrolet, all far cheaper vehicles; a Buick Six touring car cost $1,795 in 1921.

Drastic change came in 1924. The cars acquired front wheel brakes as standard equipment, while cylinder heads were now detachable, and the rounded radiator shell gave way to an angular, Packard-like outline that was to continue until 1928. Prices of fours started at $935, and the cheapest six was listed at $1,565. The 6-cylinder cars became the staple in 1925 and the 'back-to-front' gear shift pattern was discarded in 1927. The cars were completely re-styled in 1929, when hydraulic shock absorbers were added, and the capacities of the two basic models were increased to 210ci and 307ci respectively. Prices ran from $1,195 to $2,145, but for Buick customers with thinner wallets there was the Marquette (ii). Buick went over to an all-straight-8 program, still with overhead valves, in 1931. Expanding brakes were now standard at front and rear. Synchromesh was standardized on the more expensive models and available as an extra on all and was then standardized on the 1932 range.

Buick's evolution up to World War 2 followed General Motors policy: cruciform-braced frame and no-draught ventilation in 1933, Dubonnet-type ifs in 1934, and turret-top styling, down-draught carburation and hydraulic brakes in 1936 with the DA-series — one example of which became famous when it took Mrs Ernest Simpson into exile at the time of the British Abdication crisis. Despite Buick's upper middle-class position in the G.M. sales picture, the 1937 range of 248ci and 320ci eights covered everything from a sedan on a 122in wheelbase at $855 up to a seven-passenger C090 limousine at $2,095. 1938 Buicks had coil springing all round, and that year the Division produced GM's first 'dream car', a two-passenger convertible coupé styled by Harley Earl on a Roadmaster chassis. Buicks used the same engines up to 1952, though they came out with a 2-speed Dynaflow automatic transmission in 1948. In 1948 they pioneered the now popular hardtop convertible body with their Riviera. The smaller engines were, however, enlarged to 264ci in 1952, and the following year the Division's first ohv V-8 unit appeared; its displacement was 322ci, and its output 188bhp. All 1954 Buicks used this type of engine.

Sales dropped in 1958, but the 1959 cars were style leaders with the delta tail and fins. Buick's first effort at a compact car in 1961 was the Special with an all-aluminium 155bhp 215ci V-8 engine, replaced the following year by a cast-iron V-6, used also by Oldsmobile. The demand for cars with a sporting flavour resulted in the handsome Riviera sports coupé of 1963, which by 1966 was giving 340bhp from 427ci, and was capable of 120mph. Automatic transmission was, of course, standard. The 1966 Buick range had a more sporting atmosphere than in the past, and embraced the Special with a 115in wheelbase and a choice of V-6 or 300ci V-8 engines; the Skylark with the same chassis dimensions and a 400ci V-8 engine; and the bigger Buicks in the shape of the 340ci Le Sabre, the

1920 BUICK 27hp two-passenger roadster (English-bodied Bedford-Buick). *G. N. Georgano Collection*

1909 BUICK 18hp roadster. *Don McCray*

1926 BUICK Model 50 sedan. *Lucien Loreille Collection*
1937 BUICK Eight convertible. Coachwork by Carlton. *G. N. Georgano Collection*

1961 BUICK Special sedan. *G. N. Georgano Collection*
1971 BUICK Electra Limited sedan. *General Motors Corporation*

425ci Wildcat, the Electra and the top-line Riviera. These models were continued without basic change through 1971, although displacement and output were increased throughout the range, so that the 1971 V-6 engine developed 155bhp from 250ci, and the largest V-8 in the Centurion, Electra, and Riviera ranges developed 370bhp from 456ci.

BURDICK 1909–1910
Burdick Motor Co, Eau Claire, Wis.
   The Burdick was a very large car, with a 166in wheelbase. The 6-cylinder engine of 590ci was linked with a 4-speed transmission and shaft drive to the rear axle. The Model C eight-passenger touring model was listed at $7,000.

BURG 1910–1913
L. Burg Carriage Co, Dallas City, Ill.
   Early Burg cars had 4-cylinder engines. There were five-passenger touring car, two-passenger roadster and runabout versions. The Burg range was later extended to larger cars with 6-cylinder engines developing 40hp.

BURNS 1908–1911
Burns Bros, Havre de Grace, Md.
   This was one of the few makes of high-wheelers built east of the Allegheny Mountains. During its career the Burns used a 2-cylinder air-cooled engine with friction transmission and double-chain drive. Steering was by wheel.

BURROWES 1905–1908
E. T. Burrowes Co, Portland, Maine
   An early model, with the engine under the seat, single-chain drive and tiller steering, had wire wheels and full-elliptical springs. The model E, made in 1908, had a 4-cylinder L-head engine of 30hp and wheelbase of 117in. Probably fewer than a dozen Burrowes were built, two of which still exist.

BURROWS 1914
Burrows Cyclecar Co, Ripley, N.Y.
   This tandem two-passenger cyclecar had a wheelbase of 106in, and a tread of 36in. Its 2-cylinder engine was air-cooled and rated at 9hp. It drove the 715lb car through a friction transmission. The headlights were mounted above the level of the body.

BUSH 1916–1924
Bush Motor Co, Chicago, Ill.
   Like the Birch, the Bush was a mail-order car. Lycoming and Continental units were used for both the 4- and 6-cylinder versions of these vehicles.

BYRIDER 1908–1909
Byrider Electric Auto Co, Cleveland, Ohio
   The Byrider electrics were all small two passenger cars. The only model for 1909 was on a wheelbase of 81in with a tread of only 48in. This vehicle was advertised to sell for $1,800.

B-Z-T 1914
B-Z-T Cyclecar Co, Owego, N.Y.
   This cyclecar had a full set of fenders and a V-twin engine of 12/15hp. It used a friction transmission and final drive was by chain. The only model made was a two-passenger which was priced at $385.

CADILLAC 1903 to date

1 Cadillac Automobile Co, Detroit, Mich. 1903–1905
2 Cadillac Motor Car Co, Detroit, Mich. 1905 to date

The 'Standard of the World' started humbly as a single-cylinder car selling for $750. Henry M. Leland, its creator, had been associated with Henry Ford and had also built engines for Oldsmobile. The Model-A Cadillac was markedly similar to the early Fords in having a horizontal underfloor engine, 2-speed planetary transmission and central chain drive via a spur-type differential, but Cadillac's 98.1ci inlet over exhaust power unit had one cylinder where Ford used two. There was no hood on the early models. This very successful design remained in production until 1908, later improvements including rack-and-pinion steering, transverse front suspension and a dummy hood. The marque was introduced to Britain by F. S. Bennett, who in 1908 conducted a 'standardization test' at Brooklands. Three single-cylinder cars were dismantled and the parts mixed up — they were then reassembled and the vehicles run on the track. The R.A.C. awarded Cadillac the Dewar Trophy for this achievement.

A 30hp 4-cylinder car with separate cylinders and copper water jackets was announced for 1906 and 75,000 of this type were sold before it was discontinued in 1914. The original planetary transmission gave way first to a conventional 3-speed transmission, and finally in 1914 to a 3-speed transmission with 2-speed back axle. Cadillac was one of the firms organized into the General Motors group in 1909 by W. C. Durant, and in 1910, when a 4-cylinder touring car could be bought for $1,600, the company was claiming that tolerances on 112 parts of the car were accurate to one-thousandth of an inch. 1912 saw a most important innovation: the standardization of the Delco system of electric lighting and starting on the Cadillac, now of 286ci displacement and capable of 60mph. The first left-hand drive Cadillac of 1915 was also the first of the company's V-8s, to become as much a hallmark of the breed as were Buick's overhead valves. Inspired by the French De Dion-Bouton of 1910 it had a 314ci engine and sold for $2,700. 13,000 were sold in the first year of production and the model was widely used by the U.S. Army in World War 1. Cylinder heads were detachable from 1917 on, and 1924 versions had Duco cellulose finish and front wheel brakes.

In 1927, when 47,000 cars were sold, a less expensive companion make, La Salle appeared, and the cars were restyled in 1928. The synchromesh transmission made its world debut with the 1929 models, which also featured chromium plating and safety glass, with a price range from $3,295 to $5,995. 1930 saw the advent of the ohv V-16 of 452ci, which gave 185bhp and had a wheelbase of 148in. This sold at an average rate of 500 a year for eight seasons in the $6,000–$9,000 price bracket. It was joined in 1931 by an equally impressive ohv 368ci V-12. Improvements over the next few years included power brakes (1931), ride control (1932), no-draft ventilation (1933), ifs (1934) and 'turret-top' all-steel bodies (1935). 1938 models had column shift as standard, a year ahead of other G.M. products, while the V-12 and V-16 were dropped in favor of a L-head short-stroke 16-cylinder model which was made until 1940. Another new model for 1938, the 8-cylinder Sixty Special, anticipated G.M.'s 1940 styling with its absence of running boards and 4-window sedan bodywork. L-head V-8s in three wheelbase lengths made up the 1941 range, on which Hydramatic transmission was optional for the first time.

The post-war era was to see Cadillac outstrip all its competitors in the top-price class and become an international symbol of wealth. Sales climbed from 66,000 in 1941 to 103,857 in 1950, and to a new record of 165,959 in 1964. Tail fins made their first appearance on the company's 1948 fastback coupé, and in 1949 Cadillac, along with Oldsmobile, adopted overhead valves and oversquare cylinder dimensions, their new 331ci engine developing 160bhp. Cadillacs were raced at Le Mans in 1950 by Briggs Cunningham and the engine was also used in export editions of Britain's J.2 Allard. Power output increased steadily: 190bhp in 1952 (by which time manual transmission was no longer offered), 210bhp in 1953 (when a 12-volt electric system was standardized), and 230bhp in 1954, the year when panoramic wrap-around windshields and power steering became standard.

The expensive Eldorado Brougham of 1957 (it cost over $13,000) was the first car to have air suspension (dropped after a few seasons) as standard equipment, while Cadillac, along with Lincoln, started the fashion

1906 CADILLAC 8hp three-passenger roadster. *Western Reserve Museum, Cleveland, Ohio*

1928 CADILLAC Series 341 town car. *General Motors Corporation*

1935 CADILLAC V-12 town car. *G. N. Georgano Collection*
1953 CADILLAC Eldorado convertible. *General Motors Corporation*

1971 CADILLAC Eldorado coupé. *General Motors Corporation*

for four headlights, that later became universal in the U.S.A. 1966 Cadillacs featured G.M.'s perimeter-type chassis frame, a 340bhp 429ci engine, variable-rate power steering, full air conditioning, electric door locks and seat controls, a time switch for the headlights and a six-position steering wheel. Prices started at $4,650. Cadillac are one of the very few firms still to list a full nine-passenger limousine — the '75' with a wheelbase of 151in and an overall length of 247in. In 1967 Cadillac followed Oldsmobile's lead in adding to the range a big front-wheel-drive car, the Eldorado. Engine displacement of all Cadillacs went up to 472ci for 1970, while the re-styled 1971 Eldorado was offered with a 500ci engine, the largest of any production car in the world.

CALIFORNIA 1913
California Cycle Car Co, Los Angeles, Calif.
   This cycle-car was on a wheelbase of 102in and a tread of 44in. It used a 2-cylinder air-cooled engine of 69ci and had a friction transmission with belt drive and an underslung frame.

CALIFORNIAN 1920–1921
California Motor Car Corp, Los Angeles, Calif.
   The Californian was an assembled car which was first shown in May 1920 in the showrooms of the Gates-Kelly Automotive Co of Los Angeles.

The car was advertised as having been designed for the requirements of the Western motorist, but this shortlived concern had failed by 1921.

CALL c.1911
   This auto appeared in four models with engines of 30 and 36hp. Other information is not available.

CALORIC 1904
Chicago Caloric Engine Co, Chicago, Ill.
   The single model of this car was a closed coupé with a height equal to its length. It was driven by a 3-cylinder, 9hp engine with hot-tube ignition, and a 3-speed transmission.

CALVERT 1927
Calvert Motor Associates, Baltimore, Md.
   A low-priced small car using a 6-cylinder engine of the firm's own manufacture. Calverts were available in three open models only, or as a chassis at $550.

CAMERON 1902–1921
1 United Motor Co, Pawtucket, R.I. 1902–1903
2 James Brown Machine Corp, Pawtucket, R.I. 1903–1904
3 Cameron Car Co, Brockton, Mass.; New London, Conn. 1905–1908
4 Cameron Car Co, Beverly, Mass.; New London, Conn. 1908–1912
5 Cameron Motor Co, West Haven, Conn. 1912–1913
6 Cameron Motor Co, New Haven, Conn. 1914–1916
7 Cameron Motors Corp, Norwalk, Conn. 1917–1918
8 Cameron Motors Corp, Stamford, Conn. 1917–1921
   Few cars can have had so many changes of address and company organization as the Cameron. It began life as a light two-passenger powered by a 6hp single-cylinder air-cooled engine, and using shaft drive. This lasted during the Pawtucket period, but with the formation of the Cameron Car Co, at Brockton, larger cars with 2- or 3-cylinder engines of up to 12hp were made. They had the transmission mounted on the rear axle, a feature that was retained until the end of Cameron production. In 1906 a 20hp 4-cylinder car was introduced, still with air-cooling and a round hood rather like that of the contemporary Franklin. A six was made for a short time in the New London factory, and in 1913 came the first cars with water-cooled engines. Apart from the position of the transmission the later Camerons were conventional cars, though the 1917 models had adjustable cantilever suspension. A 6-cylinder car was built in small numbers until 1921, in the Stamford factory.

CAMPBELL 1918–1919
Campbell Motor Car Co, Kingston, N.Y.
   This was a 4-cylinder car built in small numbers and in touring car form only. Before 1918 the car was sold under the name Emerson.

CANADA CARS *see* GALT

CANADIAN (CDN) 1921
Colonial Motors Ltd, Walkerville, Ont.
   Designed by E. G. Gunn, formerly of Packard, this car had independent front suspension consisting of two semi-elliptic transverse springs linked by short kingpin support arms at the outer ends. The touring version was designed to sell at $2,600 and at least one was built. Advertised as the 'all-Canadian' car, it had a low V-type radiator and curiously flared front fenders, and was powered by a Continental engine.

CANADIAN BABY CAR (CDN) 1914
Montreal, Que.
   A cyclecar, known as the C.B.C., which offered a choice of J.A.P., De Luxe or Wizard engines, all 2-cylinder air-cooled units. Two-speed planetary transmission and drive through V-belts to the rear wheels were standard, as were an 84in wheelbase, 36in tread and wire wheels. The cost was $495.

1904 CAMERON 9hp runabout. *Michael Ware*

CANADIAN MOTORS (CDN) 1900
Canadian Motors Ltd, Toronto, Ont.

This firm built various electric vehicles, apparently one-off models, all to special order, as well as one large 'Tally-Ho' bus which held 14 adults and four children. The firm continued in various fields, eventually becoming Hudson-Essex distributors in Toronto until the Depression.

CANADIAN STANDARD *see* MOOSE JAW STANDARD

CANNON 1902–1906
Burtt Mfg Co, Kalamazoo, Mich.

This maker built several different tonneau models. Both 2- and 4-cylinder engines were used of up to 393ci capacity. Smaller models used a friction transmission, larger ones a sliding-gear type. Both shaft and chain drive were used. This make is shown by most compilers as a steamer, but this is apparently due to confusion with a home-built steam racing car.

CANTONO 1904–1907
Cantono Electric Tractor Co, Canton, Ohio

The Cantono was an Italian design built under license, and despite the similar sound, the name was not in any way connected with the town of Canton where the cars were made. It was an *avant-train*, made either complete or as a 2-wheel attachment for horse-drawn carriages. The batteries were mounted over the axle, and electric motors provided an independent gear drive to each wheel. The after part was also modified to take band brakes on the rear wheels.

CAPITOL 1902
Capitol Auto Co, Washington, D.C.

The Capitol steam car used a 6hp 2-cylinder engine and cost $1,200. Solid tires were fitted, and the body had more opulent curves than most light steamers of the period.

CAPS 1905
Caps Bros Mfg Co, Kansas City, Mo.

The Caps was built as a two-passenger runabout and as a side-entrance tonneau. Both were powered by a 14hp engine. Production had hardly started when the company was taken over by Kansas City Motor Car Co.

CAR DE LUXE (DE LUXE) 1906–1910
1 De Luxe Motor Car Co, Detroit, Mich. 1906
2 De Luxe Motor Car Co, Toledo, Ohio 1906–1910

The company combined with C. H. Blomstrom Motor Car Co in 1906 and moved to Toledo, where they produced the Queen as well as the Car De Luxe. The latter was a 60hp 4-cylinder car with expensive features, such as roller-bearings on the crankshaft. The seven-passenger touring car was priced at $4,750.

CARDWAY 1923–1925
Frederick Cardway, New York, N.Y.

This was an assembled car, using a Continental 6-cylinder engine. A total of six cars, all touring models, were built by Colonel Cardway, of which one was fitted with right-hand drive and exported to Australia.

CAREY 1906
Carey Motor Co, New York, N.Y.

This car used a Balzer type, front-mounted air-cooled 5-cylinder rotary engine and was exhibited at the A.C.A. Show in 1906. It had no known connection with either the Carey Mfg Co of Fairmount, Ind. (1904) or the later Carey Motor Car Co of Detroit (1910).

CARHARTT 1910–1911
Carhartt Automobile Co, Detroit, Mich.

Carhartt offered a choice of two models, the '25–30' and the '30–35' with runabout or touring bodies. Cars were announced for 1912 but probably never produced.

CARNATION (CAR-NATION) 1912–1914
American Voiturette Co, Detroit, Mich.

This was a cyclecar weighing 700lb, powered by a 4-cylinder air-cooled engine. It had a 3-speed transmission and cost $495. The American Voiturette Co was also the last owner of the Keeton make.

CARRIAGE-MOBILE *see* SUMMIT

CARRICO 1909
Carrico Motor Co, Cincinnati, Ohio

This was not a complete car, but a chassis ready for mounting a body. It was complete with a 2-cylinder air-cooled, 122ci engine. The chassis layout was typical of the motor buggy.

CARROLL (i) 1912–1920
Carroll Motor Car Co, Strasburg, Pa.

The Carroll cars featured a 4-cylinder engine with a 393ci displacement. Later cars with a 6-cylinder engine augmented the 4-cylinder line.

CARROLL (ii) 1920–1922
Carroll Automobile Co, Lorraine, Ohio

Few Carrolls were built and all were open models. Although a Duesenberg 4-cylinder engine was announced as the power unit, in fact the cars used a Beaver 6. The cars were distinctive in appearance, fitted with disk wheels and a radiator which was set back behind the front axle.

CARTERCAR 1906–1916
1 The Motor Car Co, Pontiac, Mich. 1906–1908
2 The Cartercar Co, Pontiac, Mich. 1908–1916

This firm employed friction-drive transmission on all models, using a 2-cylinder engine in one model as late as 1909. The Model R for 1912 was a 4-cylinder car, using single chain drive to the rear axle. The Motor Car Co combined with the Pontiac Spring and Wagon Co in 1908 to form the Cartercar Co, which also made the Pontiac (i). They became part of the General Motors Corp in 1909.

1909 CARTERCAR 22hp three-passenger roadster. *Henry Ford Museum, Dearborn, Mich.*

1914 CASE (ii) 30hp touring car. *Montagu Motor Museum*

CARTERMOBILE 1924–1925
Carter Motor Car Co, Washington, D.C.

An unsuccessful assembled car which was built in limited numbers. A 4-cylinder Herschell-Spillman engine was used and open and closed body styles were available.

CARTER TWIN-ENGINE 1907–1908
Carter Motor Car Co, Washington, D.C.; Hyattsville, Md.

The Carter Twin-Engine was an early attempt at complete reliability as it was powered by two independent systems. The car could operate on either of its 24hp 4-cylinder engines singly or on both together. The separate systems were extended to individual radiators, ignition and exhausts. This shaft-driven five-passenger touring car cost $5,000. The same company built the Washington (ii). The Carter Twin-Engine appears to have been preceded by Carter, built at least in 1904 by American Mfg Co of Alexandria, Va.

CASE (i) (CDN) 1907
Lethbridge Motor Car Co, Lethbridge, Alt.

The Case Model A had a 20/24hp 4-cylinder air-cooled engine, friction drive, and what were described as 'Fawkes airless tires'. The price was $2,000.

CASE (ii) 1910–1927
The J. I. Case Threshing Machine Co, Racine, Wis.

The Case was a conventional car made by one of America's best-known makers of threshing machines, steam traction engines and agricultural tractors. The cars were mainly sold through the farm equipment dealers. At first 4-cylinder cars only were made, the 1914 range consisting of a '25', '35', and '40', but a Continental-engined six was offered for 1918. This was available in three body styles, a touring, a sedan, and a 'sport', which was a close-coupled open four-passenger. The engine was rated at 29.4hp (241ci), and this was gradually increased to 31.5hp (303ci) by 1923. These 6-cylinder engines were all by Continental, and usually only one size was offered each year, although in some years (such as 1923) an overlap between models made two sizes available. From 1924 a smaller six of 240ci was made, but in decreasing quantities, and in 1927 car production ceased. The company is still active and well-known in the field of agricultural tractors and other farm equipment. These, like the cars, carry the eagle emblem modelled on 'Old Abe', the famous mascot of the 8th Wisconsin Regiment from 1861 to 1881.

CAVAC 1910
Small Motor Car Co, Detroit, Mich.

The Cavac was built only as a two-passenger roadster, with a 4-cylinder water-cooled engine. Its crankshaft was fitted with two ball-bearings, while the chassis was underslung in the same manner as that of the larger American Underslung.

C.B. 1917–1918
Carter Brothers Motor Co, Hyattsville, Md.

The C.B. was offered in three models, a 28hp four, a 35hp eight, and a 65hp twelve. The latter was priced at only $2,500, a low price for a 12-cylinder car. The name C.B. was also applied to a model of Downing-Detroit, which has been confused with the Maryland car.

C. DE L. 1913
C. de L. Engineering Works, Nutley, N.J.

This was made in two models, one with 20–40hp engine and the other designated as 30–60hp. These had displacements of 192 and 425ci respectively. The pistons were either single- or double-acting 'at the pleasure of the operator'. The smaller chassis had a 118in wheelbase, and the larger was 140in. Prices ranged from $1,500 to $2,800.

CENTRAL 1905–1906
Central Automobile Co, Providence, R.I.

This car used a rotary steam engine, an unusual design for this type of motive power.

CENTURY (i) 1899–1903
Century Motor Vehicle Co, Syracuse, N.Y.

The first car produced by the Century company was a light steamer powered by a 4¾hp 2-cylinder vertical engine. Final drive was by bevel gear instead of the more usual single chain. This model was made until 1903, when it was succeeded by the gasoline-engined Century Tourist. This was also a tiller-steered two-passenger car, but had a single-cylinder engine and chain drive.

CENTURY (ii) 1911–1915
1 Century Motor Co, Detroit, Mich. 1911–1913
2 Century Electric Car Co, Detroit, Mich. 1913–1915

The Century was an electric car with an underslung chassis. It was tiller operated, and the customer had a choice of solid or pneumatic tires. The speed controller gave a choice of six speeds, and the series-wound Westinghouse motor was geared directly to the rear axle.

C.F. *see* CORNISH-FRIEDBERG

CHADWICK 1904–1916
1 L. S. Chadwick, Chester, Pa. 1904–1906
2 Fairmount Engineering Co, Philadelphia, Pa. 1906–1907
3 Chadwick Engineering Works, Pottstown, Pa. 1907–1916

The Chadwick was the first high-performance car of U.S. manufacture to achieve volume production and recognition. The first Chadwick model had a 4-cylinder engine and double chain drive. In 1905 and 1906 this car had 4-speed progressive transmission. With the introduction in 1907 of the Great Chadwick Six with its large 707ci engine, the make began competing successfully in racing events. This engine, designated Type 19, had overhead valves and copper water-jackets. By 1911, the wheelbase had expanded to 133in, and the five-passenger touring model cost $5,500. The 1908 racing cars entered in the Vanderbilt Cup and Savannah Grand Prize employed supercharging, the first recorded instance of this method of increasing power. It was not offered on production Chadwicks.

CHALFANT 1906–1912
Chalfant Motor Car Co, Lenover, Pa.

The Chalfant was built as a five-passenger touring car. Its water-cooled engine was a horizontally opposed 22hp 2-cylinder type. A planetary transmission and double chain drive were used. The 1907 Model C sold at $1,300.

CHALMERS; CHALMERS-DETROIT 1908–1924
Chalmers Motor Car Co, Detroit, Mich.

The Chalmers was one of the most popular automobiles made in the U.S. for more than a decade. It was the successor to the Thomas-Detroit which was built by a company which had been founded in 1906 by E. R. Thomas (builder of the Thomas car in Buffalo, N.Y.), Roy D. Chapin and Howard Earle Coffin; the two latter had previously served at Oldsmobile. The Thomas-Detroit of which some 500 were sold during the first year of production, was marketed through the parent firm in Buffalo which manufactured a larger line of cars under the Thomas emblem. The Thomas-Detroit was a medium priced 4-cylinder car which had been designed by Coffin. In 1907, Hugh Chalmers, vice president of the National Cash Register Co and a noted salesman, entered the firm. Shortly after, he bought a half of E. R. Thomas' stock and became president of the company which became the Chalmers-Detroit Motor Co. The Thomas-Detroit became the Chalmers-Detroit in 1908 and in 1910, the Chalmers. Open and closed models in two lines comprised the Chalmers 4-cylinder cars, with self-starters appearing in 1912. Chalmers (as Chalmers-Detroit) had distinguished itself in road races as early as 1908 when W. R. Burns won the Motor Parkway Sweepstakes at Jericho, N.Y. averaging 48.7mph in the six-lap 140.76 mile run.

In 1913, the Chalmers brought out its first 6-cylinder model, as well as the four and apart from small mechanical and design changes, continued both until 1914. The four was dropped from the 1915 line, however, and sixes were to be used exclusively until the ending of manufacture. By 1915, some 20,000 cars per year were coming off the Chalmers production line and would even exceed that figure before the advent of World War 1. In 1917, an L-head motor replaced the earlier overhead-valve type and on August 4th, Chalmers again headed racing news when Joe Dawson won the 24-hour Stock Car Endurance Run at Sheepshead Bay, N.Y. Sales flagged following the end of the war and Hugh Chalmers, always the salesman, and with the realization that a competitor, Maxwell, wasn't faring well either, arranged to lease his plants to Maxwell, using his salesmanship to promote the two concerns and getting the benefit of Maxwell tooling and manufacturing equipment. By the early 1920s, however, many makes of cars were in financial difficulties due to over-expansion and recession, and Walter P. Chrysler was called in to try and reorganize Maxwell. Chrysler was at this time planning his own corporation and in

1907 CHADWICK Great Six touring car. *Kenneth Stauffer*

1922 Chalmers was taken over by Maxwell which had become a Chrysler subsidiary. The last Chalmers cars were equipped with Lockheed hydraulic brakes but 1923 was the last year of production with some 9,000 units leaving the factories. The Maxwell survived until 1925 when it became the Chrysler Four.

1909 CHALMERS 30hp roadster. *J. Price*
1923 CHALMERS 25hp sedan. *Chrysler Corporation*

CHAMPION (i) 1908–1909
Famous Mfg Co, East Chicago, Ill.

This vehicle was a high-wheeler with front wheels of 36in and rear wheels of 42in. A 10/12hp 2-cylinder engine was located under the seat. The two-passenger roadster had solid rubber tires.

CHAMPION (ii) 1916–1917
Champion Auto Equipment Co, Wabash, Ind.

This car was very similar in appearance to the contemporary Ford. It used a 188ci, 4-cylinder L-head engine. A two-passenger roadster was produced.

CHAMPION (iii) 1917–1923
1 Direct Drive Motor Co, Pottstown, Pa.
2 Champion Motors Corp, Philadelphia, Pa.

Originally sold under the name Direct Drive, early models drove through gearing mounted on the rear wheel rims. Later cars had conventional rear axles. Two nearly identical versions were available, the Tourist with a Lycoming 4-cylinder engine and the Special with a 4-cylinder Herschell-Spillman. The only external difference was in the radiator shape, the Tourist carrying a Packard or Paterson type, while the Special had one resembling the Rolls-Royce. A 6-cylinder Falls engine was used in the 1919 Model C-6. Prices ranged from $1,050 to $1,195.

CHARLES TOWN-ABOUT 1958–1959
Stinson Aircraft Tool and Engineering Corp, San Diego, Calif.

Named after its sponsor Dr Charles H. Graves, the Town-About was an attempt at electric vehicle manufacture. Prototypes resembled the VW-Karmann Ghia in appearance, the experimental layout varying with each car. Several of them had fiberglass bodies and two batteries powering motors adjacent to the rear wheels.

CHARTER 1903
James A. Charter, Chicago, Ill.

The Charter Mixed Vapor car was supposed to run on a half-and-half mixture of gasoline and water, which was injected into the combustion chamber in atomized form. The gasoline exploded in the normal way and the water was converted into superheated steam, which was said to result in a longer and softer explosion. A four-passenger rear-entrance tonneau body was fitted to the car.

CHARTER OAK 1916–1917
Eastern Motors Syndicate, New Britain, Conn.

Named after the famous tree where the 1662 Charter was hidden, the Charter Oak was powered by an old-fashioned 6-cylinder Herschell-Spillman T-head engine. The original factory was at New Britain, but the makers intended to move to Hartford or Waterbury during 1917.

1927 CHANDLER 33hp 8-cylinder sedan. *Autocar*

1966 CHECKER Marathon sedan. *Checker Motors Corporation*

CHANDLER 1913–1929
Chandler Motor Car Co, Cleveland, Ohio

A highly esteemed independent make of American car, the Chandler reached its greatest production in 1920, with an output of approximately 20,000 cars. Design was generally conventional, but the make was noted for its Traffic Transmission, a constant-mesh gear-shift introduced in 1924, and for all-round lubrication effected by the pull of a lever, adopted two years later. Engines were sixes of Chandler's own make, joined in 1928 by two eights. Sales tapered off toward the end of the 1920s, and the company was absorbed by Hupmobile in 1929. Although at least one prototype of the 1930s line was built, the Chandler name ended with the 1929 models. A cheaper line was the Cleveland six, made from 1919 to 1926.

CHAPMAN 1899–1901
Belknap Motor Co, Portland, Me.

The Chapman was a light electric car weighing 360lb designed by W. H. Chapman, who was an electrician employed by the Belknap company. It was also known as the Electromobile.

CHASE 1907–1912
Chase Motor Truck Co, Syracuse, N.Y.

Chase built a 'Business Runabout' or Surrey which could be converted from a four-passenger, high-wheeled car to a light truck. It was powered by an air-cooled 2-cylinder engine and the car had chain drive and solid rubber tires. The main product of this company was commercial vehicles.

CHATAUQUA 1913–1914
Chatauqua Cyclecar Co, Jamestown, N.Y.

This cyclecar had a steering column gear-shift. The only model was a two-passenger car driven by a 2-cylinder air-cooled engine of 12hp.

CHATHAM (CDN) 1907–1908
Chatham Motor Car Co, Chatham, Ont.

About 75 to 100 of these cars were produced, and apparently performed very well. Most are believed to have used a Reeves 4-cylinder air-cooled engine. Wood bodies were built by Wm Gray & Sons Ltd, who later built the Gray-Dort.

CHECKER 1959 to date
Checker Motors Corp, Kalamazoo, Mich.

Although the Checker company has existed since 1923 as a maker of taxicabs, it is only in recent years that passenger cars have been made. The standard cab was offered as a 'pleasure car' in catalogs from 1948 onwards, but officially, passenger car production dates from 1959. Two models were made, the Superba and the Marathon, both differing from the cabs in relatively small ways. High doors allowed easy access, and with the two auxiliary seats, the cars could accomodate eight persons. Until 1965 engines were 226ci Continental sixes, as had been used in Checker cabs for years, but these were replaced by Chevrolet six (230ci) or V-8 (283ci). Styling has remained practically unchanged since 1959. The cars are extremely well built, and mileages of more than 400,000 have been reported. The 1971 Checkers use a 250ci six or V-8 engine of 327 or 350ci. The price of the 120in wheelbase sedan is $3,842, and that of the special 129in wheelbase limousine, $5,510. An eight door 12-passenger Aerobus for airport and hotel work is also made, on a 189in wheelbase.

CHELSEA (i) *see* WELCH

CHELSEA (ii) 1914
Chelsea Mfg Co, Newark, N.J.

This car was classed as a cyclecar despite its standard tread of 56in. Its 4-cylinder engine was water-cooled and developed 12hp. Shaft drive was used. The side-by-side two-passenger car was priced at $390.

CHEVROLET 1911 to date
Chevrolet Motor Co, Detroit, Mich.

Chevrolet, General Motors' least expensive American car and the world's best-seller, was actually started by W. C. Durant at a time when he did not control G.M. In association with racing driver Louis Chevrolet he brought out a 299ci six with side valves in a T-head, selling for $2,150. This was followed by a smaller 6 cylinder model, but the make's first big impact came with the 4-cylinder overhead-valve Baby Grand touring car at $875, and its companion roadster model, the Royal Mail. Electrics were an optional extra on Chevrolets until 1917, but in the meantime the company had come right to the fore with the 171ci 4-cylinder 490, also an ohv, in 1916. The type designation indicated its original list price in dollars, and sales went up from 13,600 to 70,701.

General Motors acquired Chevrolet in 1917, and by 1920 the marque was outsold in the U.S. only by Ford and Dodge. A one-model policy was pursued in 1923, but before this there had been other types of Chevrolet including the FA and FB fours, and a short-lived V-8 with a Mason engine at $1,100. There was also an abortive air-cooled car using the regular chassis and body styles in 1923. The 1925 Superior coach with disk wheels and Duco cellulose finish sold for $650, and two years later Chevrolet outsold Ford for the first time, though this was hardly a fair comparison, since Ford was shut down for a good part of the year during the change-over from the Model T to the Model A. Chevrolet did not have front-wheel brakes until 1928, the last year of the 4-cylinder cars. In 1929 came the 'Cast Iron Wonder', the 194ci ohv International 6 with a 107in wheelbase and detachable disk wheels. More than a million were sold during its first season at $595, and the engine was progressively developed up to 1953.

In 1931 Chevrolet finally went ahead of Ford and stayed there apart from three seasons. 1932 cars resembled scaled-down Buicks or Oldsmobiles and featured rubber engine mountings, synchromesh and free wheeling, all for $495. In 1933 a V-grill was adopted, and displacement went up to 205ci. G.M.'s Dubonnet-type ifs was fitted on the 1934 cars — in that year the ten millionth Chevrolet was delivered. Turret top styling followed in 1935 and hydraulic brakes in 1936. Engine displacement was increased slightly again in 1937. In 1939 came the fifteen millionth car; station wagons were catalogued, column-shift was optional, and prices ranged from $628 upwards. In 1940 Chevrolet was offering a power-top convertible in the low-price field, and Juan Manuel Fangio scored his first big victory in a long-distance race in Argentina at the wheel of one

1912 CHEVROLET Classic Six 30hp touring car. *General Motors Corporation*
1930 CHEVROLET Model AD 26hp sedan. *General Motors Corporation*

1935 CHEVROLET Master EC coupé. *G. N. Georgano Collection*
1968 CHEVROLET Corvette sports car. *General Motors Corporation*

of that year's coupés. Fastback coupés were listed in 1942, but along with most other American makes, the cars were little altered when they reappeared on the market after World War 2. Extensive restyling and lowering took place in 1949, when a sedan cost $1,460, but in 1950 Chevrolet offered the option of a 2-speed Powerglide fully-automatic transmission, as well as a now-fashionable hardtop coupé style. A new sports car, the Corvette, with fiberglass bodywork, featured in the 1953 line with a 160bhp version of the regular 6-cylinder engine.

Chevrolet's lead over Ford was down to a narrow 20,000 margin by 1954. In 1955 they came out with a 265ci ohv V-8 on conventional lines, giving 162bhp with an 180bhp 'power pack' available at extra cost. The displacement of the companion six was now 235ci. By 1957 the Corvette had acquired the 8-cylinder engine, and special SS versions were being tried with 360bhp power units and 4-speed all-synchromesh transmissions listed as a factory option. 1958 V-8 Chevrolets had 348ci engines and air suspension was available, though the idea was soon discarded.

A new departure was the Division's 1960 compact car, the Corvair, a 140ci air-cooled flat-6 with engine at the rear, unitary construction of chassis and body and all wheels independently sprung. It proved a little too advanced for the market at which it was aimed, but by 1966 had entered upon a new lease of life as a specialist semi-sporting machine available with such options as a 4-speed transmission and 180bhp turbo-supercharged engine.

The evolution of subsequent Chevrolets reveals the need of the modern American mass-producer to offer a diversity of products, rather than to concentrate on a single basic model and ring the changes on body styles. In 1962 the company started to bridge the gap between the Corvair and

brakes as standard equipment. 1966 coverage of the market was comprehensive. Besides the specialized Corvair and Corvette there was the Chevy II in three series, the Chevelle with a wide choice of power units and five different types of full-sized Chevrolet from the inexpensive Biscayne up to the luxurious Caprice. Prices ranged from $2,028 for the simplest Chevy II with 90bhp 4-cylinder engine up to the Caprice custom station wagon at $3,347. Chevrolet engines were used by Checker, Avanti, the revived 8/10 Cord, Excalibur, the last Canadian-built Studebakers, the Anglo-American Gordon-Keeble and the Italo-American Iso and Bizzarrini. They were also used in the smallest Oldsmobiles in 6-cylinder form and in Canadian-built Pontiacs and the Acadian, an all-Canadian G.M. product. They are also found in the biggest 8-cylinder Opels. For 1967 the company added to its range a sports coupé model, the V-8, 350ci Camaro with 295bhp and front disk brakes, a belated answer to Ford's Mustang. Camaro displacement was increased to 395ci for 1968, and the Corvette was completely restyled. The Corvair was dropped during 1969. New for 1970 was the Monte Carlo, a prestige coupé on the Chevelle chassis with five engine options, all V-8s, from 350 to 454ci. The 1971 Chevrolet range was the widest ever, starting with the all-new 'subcompact' Vega with 140ci single-ohc 4-cylinder engine and 97in wheelbase. Next in size was the Nova with 250ci six, or 307 and 350ci V-8 engines, followed by the Chevelle and Chevrolet (Biscayne, Bel Air, Impala and Caprice) both with engine options from 250ci six to 454ci V-8, and the Monte Carlo, now with three engines, 350, 402, and 454ci V-8s. Sporting models included the Camaro coupé with four engines, 250 to 402ci, and the Corvette with 350 to 454ci engines, the latter developing 425bhp.

1971 CHEVROLET Vega 2300 coupé. *General Motors Corporation*

1905 CHRISTIE 50hp touring car. Coachwork by Healey. *Keith Marvin Collection*

the inexpensive, but by no means small Impala, Bel Air and Biscayne series (that year's versions were 210in long!) with a 'semi-compact', the Chevy II. This had integral construction, a 110in wheelbase and the choice of three engines of modest dimensions, a 153ci four and a 194ci six and 283ci eight. The slightly bigger Chevelle of 1964 was the first Chevrolet to use G.M.'s perimeter-type chassis frame (standardized on the big cars in 1965) and was available either with the Chevy II six or a 283ci V-8. A new model for 1963 was the Corvette Stingray sports car with retractable headlights, giving 145mph from 360bhp: the following season it had disk

CHICAGO (i) 1905–1907
Chicago Automobile Mfg Co, Chicago, Ill.

This was a steamer with an unusual V-4 engine, 2-speed transmission and shaft drive, with a wooden *Roi-des-Belges* body. The price was $2,500.

CHICAGO (ii) 1915–1916
Chicago Electric Motor Co, Chicago, Ill.

Chicago electric cars were primarily enclosed coupés for four or five passengers, which could be operated from either the front or rear seats. The doors were arched at the top for easier entrance and exit. The speed controls gave five positions, up to 23mph.

CHICAGOAN 1952–1954
Triplex Industries Ltd, Blue Island, Ill.

The Chicagoan sports car used a 6-cylinder Willys engine and had a two-passenger fiberglass body. Not more than 15 were made.

CHICAGO MOTOR BUGGY 1908
Chicago Motor Buggy Co, Chicago, Ill.

This was a typical high-wheeler with a 14hp air-cooled engine. The price was $550.

CHRISTIE 1904–1910
Christie Front Drive Motor Co, New York, N.Y.; Hoboken, N.J.

J. Walter Christie was the first serious proponent of front-wheel drive cars in the U.S. He brought his principle before the public eye with racing cars, the first of which appeared on the race track in January 1904. It had a 30hp 4-cylinder engine mounted transversely, the crankshaft taking the place of the front axle.

Six racers were built in all, of which one had two 60hp engines, one at each end of the car, while the machine entered in the 1907 French Grand Prix had a V-4 engine of 1200ci, making it the largest car ever to take part in a Grand Prix. Two or three touring cars were built in 1905, and a later (1909) Christie vehicle was a taxicab with a 4-cylinder transverse engine. Christie subsequently made front-wheel-drive tractor conversions for fire engines, and tanks.

CHRYSLER 1923 to date
Chrysler Corp, Detroit, Mich.

Walter P. Chrysler, formerly of Buick and Willys, acquired Maxwell-Chalmers in 1923, and the first car to bear his name, the 6-cylinder '70' of 1924, was something of a sensation with its 4-wheel contracting hydraulic brakes and 70mph performance. At $1,645 for a sedan, 43,000 were sold in 1925. The 1926 range was widened to include a 183ci 4-cylinder '58' to replace the Maxwell and the expensive 289ci 6-cylinder Imperial, selling for $3,095. The 6-cylinder roadsters offered an excellent road performance for a modest price, as was shown by their 3rd and 4th places at Le Mans in 1928, behind a Bentley and a Stutz. The 1929 models had internal-expanding brakes and their body styling and ribbon-type radiator shells were widely imitated in Europe over the next few years.

Meanwhile Chrysler had laid the foundations for a motor empire to rival General Motors and Ford by taking over Dodge and launching two new makes, the Plymouth Four in the lowest price sector and the De Soto Six in a slightly higher bracket — all this in 1928. Chrysler sold 98,000 cars in 1929. The 1931 cars featured the long, low look inspired by the Cord of 1929; 4-speed transmissions were offered for a short while and for the first time a brace of straight-8s featured in the range — the medium-priced CD, and the 384ci CG-type Imperial for the carriage trade, often with bodies by Le Baron. 1932 saw fully flexible rubber engine mountings ('Floating Power'), automatic clutches and free wheeling. Synchromesh followed a year later. Automatic overdrive was available in 1934, and regular equipment by 1936. The Chrysler line for 1934 was spearheaded by the revolutionary CU-type 8-cylinder Airflow, with welded unitary construction of chassis and body, all seats within the wheelbase, headlights mounted flush in the fenders, a full aerodynamic shape and concealed luggage accommodation. At $1,345 it was a commercial failure, though it was continued till 1937. Chrysler hurriedly brought out the more conventionally styled Airstream line in 1935, and for the next 20 years the company's styling policy was cautious, though technical progress is represented by the adoption of independent front suspension and hypoid rear axles (1937), steering-column gear-shift (1939) and optional fluid drive from 1939 onward.

The 1942 cars, generally competitive with G.M.'s Buick, embraced two 250ci sixes and three 323ci eights, all L-head, with prices ranging from

1931 CHRYSLER Imperial CG sedan. *Montagu Motor Museum*
1934 CHRYSLER Airflow CU sedan. *Chrysler Corporation*

1946 CHRYSLER Town and Country sedan. *Chrysler Corporation*
1971 CHRYSLER Newport 2-door hardtop. *Chrysler Corporation*

$1,295 for the Windsor up to $3,965 for the big Crown Imperial limousine on the 145½in wheelbase.

Early post-war design followed the 1942 models closely, apart from some interesting 'Town and Country' bodies, basically standard sedans and convertibles with wooden exterior trim in station-wagon style. In 1951, however, Chrysler broke new ground with a 331ci overhead valve oversquare V-8 with hemispherical heads, a fully automatic transmission and the option of hydraulic power-assisted steering. This was at the time America's most powerful car and engines were fitted and raced by Cunningham and by the British Allard. Caliper disk brakes were optional, but were dropped after a few years, while another individual feature of Chrysler Corp products was the push-button layout of controls for the automatic transmission, found on cars made between 1956 and 1965. Chrysler's lag in styling was painfully apparent by 1954, when the group lay a bad third behind G.M. and Ford, and 1955 not only saw the retirement of the old L-head six in favor of a 301ci 188bhp V-8, but also new, lower 'Flight Sweep' lines which put the cars well back in the running. A new range of '300' coupés and convertibles gave Chrysler a 'personal car' competitive with Ford's Thunderbird and the 392ci V-8s used in the 1957 Chrysler developed more bhp than any of their rivals. Alternator ignition and unitary construction of chassis and body were adopted in 1960, while Chrysler, who had had a gas-turbine car running experimentally in 1954, built a series of fifty vehicles using Plymouth running gear in 1964 which were supplied to selected customers for evaluation.

Also in the 1960s the corporation extended its automobile interests into Europe by the acquisition of majority interests in Simca of France and the Rootes Group of Great Britain. Another overseas venture was Chrysler Australia Ltd of Adelaide, who from 1956 to 1963 built a Royal model specially adapted to Australian requirements, with a 305ci V-8 engine in what amounted to the 1954 body and chassis design. This subsequently gave way to a version of Plymouth's Valiant. Chrysler's V-8 engine was also used by Facel Vega in France, and by Bristol and Jensen in Britain. Chrysler's 1968 cars were all V-8s in the $3,000–$4,000 price bracket, with 384 and 440ci power units. The 300 coupé now developed 350bhp. The Newport, New Yorker, and 300 models continued without major change through the 1969, 1970, and 1971 seasons. Output of the 440ci engine was up to 370bhp by 1971.

CHURCH-FIELD 1912–1913
Church-Field Motor Co, Sibley, Mich.

This was an unusual electric car with an underslung chassis. It used 2-speed planetary transmission which, combined with ten electrical selector positions, gave a total choice of 20 speed ranges.

CINCINNATI 1903–c.1905
Cincinnati Automobile Co, Cincinnati, Ohio

The Cincinnati was a two-passenger car which did not differ greatly from the many other steamers of the time, although it had a rather lower build. The 2-cylinder engine was under the seat, final drive was by chain, and steering by tiller.

CINO 1909–1913
Haberer & Co, Cincinnati, Ohio

The Cino had a 4-cylinder engine with overhead valves. The wheel hubs and hub-caps were similar to those of the Packard. Beginning with five body types, including a semi-racer, the line was reduced at the last to a five-passenger touring car and a roadster.

CLARK (i) 1900–1909
Edward S. Clark Steam Automobiles, Dorchester, Mass.

After several years of experimental work at Boston, Edward Clark began manufacture of steam cars at Dorchester. These were of advanced design, using horizontally-opposed 4-cylinder engines of 20hp. These were mounted amidships, with the flash boiler under the hood. Final drive was by shaft. Earlier models were expensive ($5,000 in 1904), but by 1909 the price had been reduced to $2,500. However this was still over

$1,000 more than the price asked for a comparable Stanley Steamer, and very few Clarks were sold.

CLARK (ii) 1910–1912
Clark Motor Car Co, Shelbyville, Ind.

The design of the Clark car was typical for these years, with a 4-cycle water-cooled 4-cylinder engine of 30/40hp. Shaft drive was used, with selective transmission at the axle. This car became the Meteor (v).

CLARK (iii) 1910–1912
Clark & Co, Lansing, Mich.

This Clark was a 3-passenger high-wheeler with sold rubber tires and wheel steering. Its 2-cylinder opposed engine was air-cooled and developed 14hp. Fully-elliptical springs were used.

CLARKE-CARTER see CUTTING

CLARK-HATFIELD 1908–1909
Clark-Hatfield Auto Co, Oshkosh, Wis.

This car was a typical high-wheeler with an air-cooled 2-cylinder horizontally opposed engine of 16hp. This 4-cycle power unit was mounted cross-wise behind the two-passenger seat. No fenders were fitted.

CLARKMOBILE 1903–1906
1 Clarkmobile Co, Lansing, Mich. 1903–1906
2 Deere-Clark Motor Car Co, Moline, Ill. 1906

The 1903 Clarkmobile was a two-passenger roadster, shaft-driven from a single-cylinder, 7hp engine, with steering by wheel. Its cost was $750. In 1906 the car became the Deere-Clark, in turn succeeded by the Deere.

CLASSIC 1916–1917
Classic Motor Car Corp, Chicago, Ill.

Both four- and five-passenger touring models of the Classic were offered at $885. The common chassis had a wheelbase of 114in. The car was powered by a 4-cylinder Lycoming engine of 192ci. Both models had early slanted windshields.

1924 CLEVELAND (iv) 6-cylinder touring car. *Keith Marvin Collection*

CLEVELAND (i) 1899–1901
Cleveland Machine Screw Co, Cleveland, Ohio

The first make to bear the name Cleveland was a light electric two-passenger car with solid rubber tires. In its last year of production it was known as the Sperry.

CLEVELAND (ii) 1904–1909
Cleveland Motor Car Co, Cleveland, Ohio

The second make to bear the name Cleveland was a conventional touring car with a 4-cylinder 18hp engine, priced at $2,800. Later, a larger car costing $4,000 was introduced, this model being responsible for the company's closure as it was too expensive in comparison with other cars of its kind. The only unusual feature of the Cleveland was that the rear axle half shafts could be slid out simply by removing the hub caps.

CLEVELAND (iii) 1914
Cleveland Cyclecar Co, Cleveland, Ohio

The Cleveland was advertised as 'The Aristocrat of Cyclecars'. It seated two passengers, side-by-side, and it had a water-cooled 4-cylinder *en bloc* engine.

CLEVELAND (iv) 1919–1926
Cleveland Automobile Co, Cleveland, Ohio

This car was really a smaller version of the Chandler, produced in a separate factory. It was powered with the firm's own 6-cylinder ohv engine.

CLIMBER 1919–1923
Climber Motor Corp, Little Rock, Ark.

This car was available in both 4- and 6-cylinder models, all open, with Herschell-Spillman engines. The Climber Corp built several hundred cars in its few years of production. Ten distribution agencies, most of them in Arkansas, handled the make.

CLINTON (CDN) 1912
Clinton Motor Car Co Ltd, Clinton, Ont.

Mainly builders of trucks, the Clinton company exhibited a 4-cylinder touring car and a combination car convertible to a light truck at the 1912 Toronto Auto Show.

CLIPPER 1955–1956
Studebaker-Packard Corp, Detroit, Mich.

The former Packard Clipper was marketed as a separate make for the 1956 season only, in an attempt to establish the 'senior' Packards as a luxury make more expensive and exclusive than the medium-priced Clippers. They came in three models, DeLuxe, Super DeLuxe, and Custom, all using 352ci V-8 engines developing 240bhp (275bhp in the Custom model). Wheelbase was 122in, and prices ranged from $2,731 to $3,069. For the 1957 season the Clipper was re-absorbed into the Packard range, and in fact used a Studebaker body shell.

CLOUGHLEY 1902–1903
Cloughley Motor Vehicle Co, Parsons, Kan.

The Cloughley company had made an experimental steamer at Cherryvale, Kansas as early as 1896, but their production cars did not appear until 1902. They used an 8hp 2-cylinder engine, front-mounted and driving the rear axle by chain. Steam was provided at 175psi from a 19in water tube boiler. The only body style was a four-passenger surrey. This car was also available with a 2-cylinder gasoline engine.

CLOYD 1911
Cloyd Auto Co, Nashville, Tenn.

The Cloyd used a 4-cylinder 40hp engine which was water-cooled. Wheelbase was 123in for the five-passenger touring cars and 110in for the runabout and roadster.

CLUB (CLUB CAR) 1910–1911
Club Car Co, New York, N.Y.

The Club Car Co was a unique cooperative organization formed to furnish cars for its members. The cars were actually built by Merchant & Evans Co of Philadelphia, with 4-cylinder 40/50hp engines from the American & British Mfg Co of Bridgeport, Conn. Body styles included a limousine, a seven-passenger touring car, a torpedo and a club runabout, all made by Biddle & Smart of Amesbury, Mass. Prices to members ranged from $2,800 to $3,750.

CLYMER 1908
Durable Motor Car Co, St Louis, Mo.

The only product was a two-passenger motor buggy with a 12hp engine and a one-year guarantee. This period was longer than the Clymer was produced.

COATES-GOSHEN 1908–1910
Coates-Goshen Automobile Co, Goshen, N.Y.

This car had 4-cylinder Rutenber engines of 25 or 32hp, and appears to have been a pioneer of the modern dropped frame. A fire in the plant contributed to the early demise of this make after only 32 cars had been made. Later Coates Commercial Car Co (1912–1914) attempted a comeback with a 3-wheeled parcel truck.

COATS STEAM CAR 1922–1923
Coats Steam Motors, Sandusky, Ohio

Despite wide publicity, few Coats Steamers were marketed. The car was powered by a 3-cylinder engine of Coats design, and, unusually for a steam car, it had a 2-speed and reverse shift with floor change. A touring car was the only model available.

COEY 1913–1917
Coey Motor Co, Chicago, Ill.

The Coey was available in two versions, the Bear, which was a cyclecar, or a full-sized model, the Flyer. The Flyer had a 6-cylinder engine of 380ci displacement. The company was absorbed by the Wonder Motor Truck Co in 1916 and the 1917 Flyer was a smaller car with 22hp engine.

COGGSWELL 1911
Coggswell Motor Co, Grand Rapids, Mich.

This firm built at least some pilot models as five-passenger touring cars which had a wheelbase of 112in. The 4-cylinder, 218ci engine had a single overhead camshaft with valves at 45° to the head. It was provided with dual ignition and was to be sold for $1,600.

1913 COEY Flyer Model A touring car. *Harrah's Automobile Collection*

COLBURN 1906–1911
Colburn Automobile Co, Denver, Colo.

Early models were roadsters and racers, the 1909 model advertised as having a top speed of over 70mph. Their 4-cylinder engines were rated at 40hp and the cars weighed 2,600lb. Colburn also built large touring cars with radiators behind the engine, and a sloping hood similar to early Renaults.

COLBY 1911–1914
Colby Motor Car Co, Mason City, Iowa

With a 40hp L-head engine, the Colby five-passenger 'foredoor' model sold for $1,750. Its selective transmission gave three forward speeds, and final drive was by shaft.

COLE 1909–1925
Cole Motor Car Co, Indianapolis, Ind.

The first Cole, possibly a reflection of the company's history of horse-drawn carriage manufacture, was a primitive high-wheeler with solid tires, powered by a 14hp air-cooled flat twin engine that appeared in 1909. It was soon dropped in favor of large, conventional fours and sixes, which had electric lighting and starting, in 1913. The V-8 model, the best-known Cole, was an expensive car introduced in 1915 and combined the conservative feature of a cone clutch with unit construction of 346ci Northway engine and transmission. By 1923, the accent of this Aero Eight was on comfort. This was achieved by balloon tires, which Cole pioneered in America, and the use of the unsightly Westinghouse air springs.

In fact the tires were held to justify the Cole's slogan of 'the World's Safest Car', but this was arguable, as they led to wheel wobble and heavy steering. The well-appointed bodies, with light, handsome lines, were better than the excruciating names — 'Tourosine', 'Sportosine', etc. — they were given.

1921 COLE Aero Eight 39.2hp touring car. *Automotive History Collection, Detroit Public Library*

COLEMAN 1933
Coleman Motors, Littleton, Colo.

The Coleman was an unsuccessful attempt to interest the public in a low-priced car with straight body sides and all-enveloping shape, rather in the manner of 1960s design. The engine was mounted under the sharply-arched front axle. The closed model, the only one offered by the company, was listed to sell at less than $1,000.

COLLINET 1921
Collinet Motor Co, Garden City, Long Island, N.Y.

This car was displayed in chassis form at the 16th Auto Salon in New York. Despite a chassis price of $5,500, it had a 4-cylinder Wisconsin engine. It is not known whether this make ever got into production.

COLLINS 1920
Collins Motors, Inc, Huntington, Long Island, N.Y.

The Collins Country Club Six used a 29hp 6-cylinder engine, and was made in two wheelbases. Very few were sold under the name Collins, but it has been suggested that the design was sponsored or taken over by Peerless, who made it as the Peerless Six.

COLONIAL (i) 1912
Colonial Electric Car Co, Detroit, Mich.

This electric car was built as a five-passenger closed model and as a two-passenger roadster. The steering was by tiller. It was claimed that the top speed was 25mph and that it could travel 75 miles on a single charging. The wheelbase was 93in. The closed models included a cut-glass flower vase, and a toilet set.

COLONIAL (ii) 1917–1921
Colonial Automobile Co, Indianapolis, Ind.

Few of these assembled cars were produced in the four years during which they were presumably manufactured. The cars, mostly touring models, were powered by a 6-cylinder overhead-valve engine. The wheelbase was 116in and prices started at $995.

COLONIAL (iii) 1920
Mechanical Development Corp, San Francisco, Calif.

Although only one of the West Coast Colonial cars was built, it is important as being presumably the first car built, at least in the U.S., with

1922 COLONIAL (v) 29hp roadster. *Keith Marvin Collection*

four-wheel hydraulic brakes, appearing even before the similarly equipped Duesenberg and Kenworthy. The car had a straight-8 engine with a bore and stroke of $2\frac{1}{2}$in × $4\frac{1}{2}$in which developed 60bhp. Besides a unique hard-top touring body, readily convertible into a closed car, it featured disk wheels with two side-mounted spares. The prototype, which probably cost $30,000 to construct, was to have sold for $1,800.

COLONIAL (iv) *see* SHAW (i)

COLONIAL (v) 1921–1922
Colonial Motors Co, Boston, Mass.

The Colonial was a disk-wheeled, attractive sporting-type of car which the prospectuses claimed would be produced 'in excess of 100' units in its first year of production. Probably no more than ten units — if that — ever got on the road. With a high, rounded radiator and a 130in wheelbase, the Colonial was powered with a 6-cylinder Beaver engine with a $3\frac{1}{2}$in × $5\frac{1}{4}$in bore and stroke. Five body styles were offered but probably only the open models were actually ever constructed.

COLT (i) 1907
Colt Runabout Co, Yonkers, N.Y.

This car was built only as a two-passenger runabout, using a 40hp 6-cylinder engine, and sold for $1,500. With a weight of 1,800lb their 'Mile-a-Minute' slogan was probably realistic.

COLT (ii) 1958
Advertised as 'Built in America by Americans' the Colt was a two-passenger fiberglass minicar with a single-cylinder air-cooled engine.

COLUMBIA (i) 1897–1913
1 Pope Mfg Co, Hartford, Conn. 1897–1899
2 Columbia Automobile Co, Hartford, Conn. 1899
3 Columbia & Electric Vehicle Co, Hartford, Conn. 1900
4 Electric Vehicle Co, Hartford, Conn. 1901–1909
5 Columbia Motor Car Co, Hartford, Conn. 1909–1913

The detailed organizational history of this make is complex, and its ancestry includes such pioneers as Riker and Morris & Salom. The initial models were electrically powered and this source was used at least as late as 1907. They were sold in England under the name City and Suburban,

1901 COLUMBIA (i) electric dog cart. *The Veteran Car Club of Great Britain*
1919 COLUMBIA (iv) Six touring car. *Keith Marvin Collection*

and in France as l'Electromotion. Gasoline models were introduced in 1899, known then as the Pope-Columbia, and were designed by Hiram Maxim. These gasoline cars were advanced for their time, with left-hand steering wheel, full elliptical springs, a coil radiator in front, and a 2-cylinder engine. The 1903 Type XLI showed definite European influence, with a sloping hood, double chain drive, and its 14hp engine drove it at 45mph.

In 1907, an electric transmission was introduced, giving 7 forward speeds, with a 4-cylinder engine of 48hp. In 1911 a Knight sleeve-valve engine was used in one model known as the Columbia-Knight. This had a 410ci engine, and was continued to 1913.

The Columbia Motor Car Co was absorbed by United States Motor Co in 1910, and the make ended when this company collapsed in 1913.

COLUMBIA (ii) 1914
Seattle, Wash.

This was a side-by-side two-passenger cyclecar. It used a 2-cylinder engine with overhead valves, combined with a friction transmission and belt drive. Its wheelbase was 96in, with a tread of 40in. The name of the manufacturer is not known.

COLUMBIA (iii) 1914–1918
Columbia Electric Vehicle Co, Detroit, Mich.

This electric car was made in open two-passenger, three-passenger 'coupelette', and four-passenger brougham form and was furnished with wire wheels. The price-range of this model, with various options, was $785 to $985. Soon after its introduction the name was changed to Columbian.

COLUMBIA (iv) 1916–1924
Columbia Motors Co, Detroit, Mich.

The Columbia was a well thought of assembled car of its era and its low price attracted a considerable number of buyers. Two basic models were offered, both sixes and both powered by Continental engines. As many as 6,000 units were sold in 1923, principally the roadster at $995 (disk wheels were extra). Planning to expand its manufacturing activities, Columbia purchased the Liberty in 1923, but both makes failed a year later.

Noteworthy was Columbia's use of thermostatically-controlled radiator shutters, as early as 1920, which opened as radiator temperature increased. This was one of the first automobiles to use this device and doubtless it aided Columbia sales.

COLUMBUS (i) *see* IMPERIAL (i)

COLUMBUS (ii) 1903–1913
Columbus Buggy Co, Columbus, Ohio

The Columbus cars were either electric or gasoline, and it appears that they were not always offered simultaneously. Four-cylinder, 4-cycle engines, with 3-speed transmissions in chassis of 110in were built in 1909, with one open electric car. For 1913, large 6-cylinder cars were built. Also for 1913, four closed electric models were made with General Electric motors, and six speed ranges.

COMET (i) 1906–1908
Hall Auto Repair Co, San Francisco, Calif.

This car had a 25hp 4-cylinder engine with square dimensions (4in × 4in) and overhead valves. The two-passenger runabout had a wheelbase of 102in, and the few cars made did well in West Coast races. Probably not more than five cars were made. Mr Hall achieved greater fame subsequently with the manufacture of Hall-Scott engines which were used in railcars, trucks, buses, and airplanes.

COMET (ii) (CDN) 1907–1908
Comet Motor Co, Montreal, Que.

The Comet was the first car to reach production in Montreal and was undoubtedly the most successful. It was backed by a number of Quebec businessmen, and probably reached the height of its fame when a Comet was used to drive the Prince of Wales during a visit to Quebec.

The Comet was well-promoted and production is believed to have been at least 50 units and possibly as high as 200. Bodies were made locally, but most of the mechanical components were imported from Europe — a majority from France. Fours and sixes were planned but most if not all production was of fours. Engine castings were bought from Clément-Bayard and the clutch was a Hele-Shaw. Shaft drive was used. Doors were fitted only to the tonneau and the wooden body was covered with fabric. When the company found itself unable to expand it ceased car production and turned to selling other makes, eventually the Packard.

COMET (iii) 1914–1915
1 Economy Cyclecar Co, Indianapolis, Ind. 1914
2 Comet Cyclecar Co, Indianapolis, Ind. 1915
The Comet was a tandem two-passenger cyclecar with an air-cooled 2-cylinder engine and final drive by belt.

COMET (iv) 1914
Continental Motors Corp, Buffalo, N.Y.
The information on this make is sparse. The two models, a roadster and a five-passenger touring car, were listed at $750 and $950 respectively. These were both powered by a 4-cylinder 25hp engine.

1908 COMET (i) 25hp roadster. *Warren K. Miller*

COMET (v) 1917–1922
Comet Automobile Co, Decatur, Ill.
An assembled car with a Continental 6-cylinder engine (6-cylinder Lewis engines on 1917 models), the Comet sold in small but consistent numbers. Open models as well as closed cars were available but sales were generally restricted to the area of manufacture.

COMET (vi) 1946–1948
General Development Co, Ridgewood, Long Island, N.Y.
Weighing 175lb, this 3-wheeler had a 4½hp air-cooled engine in the rear. The plastic body was mounted on a tubular frame and Comet claimed a fuel consumption of 100mpg. An odd aspect of the Comet distributing plan was that the company asked potential dealers to produce their Marvel delivery car on a royalty basis in no less than one hundred units per year.

COMMERCE 1924
Commerce Motor Truck Co, Detroit, Mich.
This well-known truck manufacturer offered briefly a Model 20 De-Luxe sedan, powered by a 4-cylinder engine.

COMMONWEALTH 1917–1922
Commonwealth Motors Co, Joliet, Ill.
Formerly the Partin-Palmer, this typical assembled car used a 4-cylinder engine throughout its existence, except for a Victory Six model in 1919. Commonwealth's Checker taxicab model ultimately became the famous Checker taxi.

COMPOUND 1904–1908
Eisenhuth Horseless Vehicle Co, Middletown, Conn.
The Eisenhuth company gained its name from a Mr Eisenhuth who built an experimental car in San Francisco in 1896. The company later moved to New Jersey where they experimented with cars using the Graham-Fox compound engine. This was a 3-cylinder unit in which the center cylinder ran solely on the pressure of exhaust gases from the other two. It was claimed to be very smooth-running and silent. A Graham-Fox 60hp car was shown at the Madison Square Gardens Show in 1903, but the first cars to be put into production were made at Middletown, and called Compounds. Their 3-cylinder engines were of 12/15hp and 24/28hp, and they were of conventional design apart from their power units.

1920 COMMONWEALTH 20hp touring car. *Autocar*

CONOVER 1906–1908
Conover Motor Co, Paterson, N.J.
This was a massive-looking car, available as a five-passenger tonneau or runabout. It was powered by a 4-cylinder 35/40hp engine. The transmission was of the sliding-shift type, with three forward speeds, and drive to rear axle was by shaft.

CONRAD 1900–1904
1 Conrad Motor Carriage Co, Buffalo, N.Y. 1900–1903
2 Lackawanna Motor Co, Buffalo, N.Y. 1904
The Conrad company made mainly steam cars, light 2-cylinder vehicles with side-tiller steering and single chain drive. In 1903 they introduced two gasoline engined cars of 8 and 12hp, both with 2-cylinder engines, three speeds and single chain drive. They were out of business by the end of 1903, but one of their gasoline engined models was exhibited by the

Lackawanna Motor Co at the 1904 New York Show. However, this latter company concentrated mainly on engines.

CONTINENTAL (i) 1907
Continental Motor Car Co, Chicago, Ill.

This was a two-passenger roadster with an oval hood, on a wheelbase of 90in. It was equipped with a 2-cylinder, 12hp engine, with a choice of air- or water-cooling. A planetary transmission and shaft drive were used.

CONTINENTAL (ii) 1907–1909
University Automobile Co, New Haven, Conn.

This make was available in the form of a three-passenger runabout, or a six-passenger touring car. Both used a 4-cylinder engine with Apple ignition. The transmission had four forward speeds.

CONTINENTAL (iii) 1909–1914
Indiana Motor & Mfg Co, Franklin, Ind.

A touch of elegance was added to this car by a mahogany dash panel. The only model available was a five-passenger touring car weighing 2,200lb. Power was furnished by a 4-cylinder L-head engine of 338ci.

CONTINENTAL (iv) 1914
Continental Engine Mfg Co, Minneapolis, Minn.

The power for this cyclecar was furnished by an air-cooled T-head engine of 4-cylinders and of 66.5ci displacement. This engine was of their

1933 CONTINENTAL (vi) Beacon roadster. *Keith Marvin Collection*

The Continental Mark II was introduced for the 1956 season as a luxury car which would be a spiritual descendant of the much-prized Lincoln Continentals of 1940–1948, and a rival to the best imported automobiles. It was a four-passenger coupé powered by Lincoln's 368ci V-8 engine, and costing $8,800 compared with $4,064 for the Lincoln Premiere. The Continental Mark II remained basically unchanged during its 20-month life, although a convertible was listed for the 1957 season, and prices were increased that year to $9,695. Production was discontinued in

1906 COMPOUND 16hp touring car. *Harrah's Automobile Collection*

own manufacture. The final drive was a choice of belt or chain. The tread was unusually narrow at 32in with a wheelbase of 92in. The price was $360 for the two-passenger tandem model.

CONTINENTAL (v) *see* MOOSE JAW STANDARD

CONTINENTAL (vi) 1933–1934
Continental Automobile Co, Detroit, Mich.

Sold in one 4- and two 6-cylinder models, the Continental was an unsuccessful attempt by the famous engine-building concern to market the defunct De Vaux under the Continental name. Prices started as low as $335. The car was also sold in Canada under the Frontenac emblem.

CONTINENTAL (vii) 1955–1957; 1968 to date
Ford Motor Co, Continental Division, Detroit, Mich.

1956 CONTINENTAL (vii) Mark II coupé. *G. N. Georgano Collection*

June 1957 after 3,012 Continentals had been built. The name Continental was continued for a model of Lincoln after 1957, but in early 1968 it was revived once more for a separate range, known as the Continental Mark III. This used Lincoln's 460ci V-8 engine in an individually-styled coupé body. The price was $6,800. As with the Mark II, annual changes were not envisaged for the Mark III, and 1971 models are similar, except for small details, to the 1968 cars.

CONVAIRCAR 1947
The Consolidated-Vultee Aircraft Corp, San Diego, Calif.

The Convaircar was an interesting project that combined a car with an aircraft. The wings and engine assembly were built as an entirely separate unit that could be attached to a small Crosley-powered 2-door sedan of Convair design. Flight and road tests were conducted but the plan was later abandoned.

c. 1910 CORBIN 32hp touring car. *Kenneth Stauffer*
1931 CORD (i) L-29 sedanca de ville. Coachwork by Murphy. *Montagu Motor Museum*

CORBIN 1903–1912
Corbin Motor Vehicle Co, New Britain, Conn.

Early Corbins had 4-cylinder engines air-cooled by two fans set above the cylinders. Water cooled models appeared in 1908, but air-cooling was continued as an alternative until 1910. The 1905 cars pioneered metal brake-shoes, but this feature was not continued. Later models, all with 4-cylinder engines, were rated at either 32 or 36hp. A distinctively peaked radiator shell and hood was a feature of all Corbins. The parent company (American Hardware Corp) is still in business.

CORBITT 1912–1913
Corbitt Auto Co, Henderson, N.C.

The 4-cylinder Corbitt came in three body styles, on a chassis with 120in wheelbase. Model A, a two-passenger roadster cost $1,750 and Model C, a five-passenger touring car cost $1,800. The name Corbitt continued until the early 1950s on trucks.

CORD (i) 1929–1937
Auburn Automobile Co, Auburn, Ind.

The first American front-drive car to win popular approval, the Cord was one of a trio of distinctive cars (the others being the Auburn and the Duesenberg) that made up Erret Lobban Cord's empire. The first Cord was the Model L-29, powered by a 301ci straight-8 engine made by Lycoming, another Cord subsidiary. The L-29 was much lower than most contemporary American cars and was made in open and closed models,

as well as being given special coachwork by such firms as Murphy, Hayes, and in England, Freestone & Webb. However, the price of over $3,000 was against the car in the Depression years, and production ended in 1932 after some 4,400 cars had been sold.

The name re-emerged later in 1935 with the strikingly modernistic Model 810. Designed by Gordon Buehrig, this car had originally been intended as a small model of Duesenberg. Like the L-29 the new car was front-driven and Lycoming-powered, although by a slightly smaller V-8 engine of 289ci. The body was of a very advanced design, and featured retractable headlights and a wrap-around grill. Body styles were the Westchester and Beverly sedans (identical except for upholstery pattern), two-passenger Sportsman and four-passenger Phaeton convertibles. In 1937 the Model 812 series was introduced, featuring a long-wheelbase Custom berline with chauffeur division, while an optional supercharger boosted power to 195bhp. Prices ranged from $1,995 for the early models to $3,575 for the 1937 Supercharged Custom berline, and this drastically restricted sales. Only 2,320 examples of 810 and 812 were made.

CORD (ii) 1964 to date
1 Auburn-Cord-Duesenberg Co, Tulsa, Okla. 1964–1967
2 Elfman Motors, Inc, Philadelphia, Pa. 1967–1968

1937 CORD (i) Model 812 Custom Beverly sedan. *G. N. Georgano Collection*

3 S.A.M.C.O., Inc, Tulsa, Okla. 1968 to date

By the mid-1960s the Model 810/812 Cords had become such popular classic cars that Glenn Pray put on the market a scaled-down 8/10ths version of the two-passenger convertible using a Chevrolet Corvair engine and Royalex plastic bodywork. It was priced at $4,700, and about 85 cars were made. Like the original Cords, the 8/10 had front-wheel drive, but the next attempt at Cord revival turned to rear-wheel drive and Ford V-8 power and abandoned the retractable headlights which had been such a feature of the pre-war Cords. Cords for 1971 come in two models, the Warrior powered by a 302ci Ford V-8 engine, and the Royale with 440ci Chrysler Magnum V-8 engine. Prices are from $7,000 up.

CORINTHIAN 1922–1923
Corinthian Motors Co, Philadelphia, Pa.

An assembled car of short duration, the Corinthian was available as a medium-priced car with a Herschell-Spillman 4-cylinder engine and a large and expensive version with a 4-cylinder Wisconsin T-head power plant.

CORNELIAN 1914–1915
Blood Bros Machine Co, Allegan, Mich.

The Cornelian cyclecar had a 4-cylinder Sterling engine and the unusual feature for the time of independent rear suspension. About 100 were made, after which the makers devoted themselves to producing universal joints. A racing version, driven by Louis Chevrolet, ran at

Indianapolis in 1915. At 115ci its engine was the smallest of any Indy car at that time.

CORNISH-FRIEDBERG (C.F.) 1908–1909
Cornish-Friedberg Motor Car Co, Chicago, Ill.

A three-passenger roadster and a five-passenger touring car were built by this manufacturer. The engine used was a water-cooled, 4-cylinder one, developing 35hp at a speed of 1,000rpm. The final drive was by shaft, and both models were priced at $2,250.

CORREJA 1908–1915
Vandewater & Co, Iselin, Elizabeth, N.J.

The chief model was a 'speed runabout' for which was claimed a speed of more than 60mph. This car used a 35hp engine and 3-speed transmission and sold for $1,450. Manufacture may have begun before 1908.

COSMOPOLITAN (HAYDOCK) 1907–1910
D. W. Haydock Automobile Mfg Co, St Louis, Mo.

The Cosmopolitan was a spindly high-wheeler with a single-cylinder, air-cooled engine mounted in front of the body. The car had wheel steering and double-chain drive. It lacked fenders and was priced at $350.

1920 COTAY 11hp roadster. *Autocar*

COTAY 1920–1921
Coffyn-Taylor Motor Co, New York, N.Y.

The Cotay designers attempted a compromise between the cyclecar and the full-sized car. A 4-cylinder, in-line engine (albeit air-cooled) by Cameron, coil ignition, unit construction of engine and 3-speed sliding-pinion transmission, shaft drive, cantilever rear springs and electric lighting and starting were combined with the 'cyclecar' features of a wooden frame integral with a wood and aluminum body, and wooden disk wheels. The weight was 1,512lb. E. S. Cameron, the designer and manufacturer of the engine, which had horizontal overhead valves, was in fact a member of the company.

COTTA 1901–1903
1 Cotta Automobile Co, Lanark, Ill. 1901–1902
2 Cotta Automobile Co, Rockford, Ill. 1902–1903

In appearance the Cotta was similar to many other light steam cars of the period, but it was the only one to feature 4-wheel drive and steering. The 6hp 2-cylinder engine was mounted exactly in the center of the chassis and power was transmitted to all four wheels by compensating chain gear.

COUNTRY CLUB 1904
Country Club Car Co, Boston, Mass.

The Country Club was distinguished by a 3-speed sliding-gear transmission operated by compressed air. Its horizontal 2-cylinder engine produced 16hp and had a Longuemare carburetor.

1904 COVERT 6½hp runabout. *Henry Ford Museum, Dearborn, Mich.*

COURIER (i) 1904
Sandusky Automobile Co, Sandusky, Ohio

The Courier was a light open two-passenger car, powered by a single-cylinder engine with 4¾in bore and 5¾in stroke. A sliding-gear transmission was used with a single chain for final drive.

COURIER (ii) 1909–1912
1 Courier Car Co, Dayton, Ohio
2 United States Motor Co, Dayton, Ohio

Made by a subsidiary of Stoddard-Dayton, the Courier was similar in design to the product of the parent company, but a cheaper and smaller car. Originally a 25hp 4-cylinder engine of 198ci displacement was used, followed in 1912 by a 30hp of 222ci. Roadsters and touring cars were made, 1912 models being known as Courier Clermont. When Stoddart-Dayton was acquired by the United States Motor Co, Courier was naturally included in the combine, and the name disappeared with the failure of the United States Motor Co.

COURIER (iii) 1922–1924
Courier Motor Co, Sandusky, Ohio

Successor to the Maibohm, the Courier had a 6-cylinder Falls engine with full-pressure lubrication.

COVERT 1901–1907
1 Byron V. Covert & Co, Lockport, N.Y. 1901–1904
2 Covert Motor Vehicle Co, Lockport, N.Y. 1904–1907

The 1901 Covert range consisted of a light steam runabout with 2-cylinder engine and chain drive, and a 3hp gasoline car that weighed only 350lb. Later shaft-driven Coverts used gasoline engines of 6½hp single-cylinder (Model A) and 24hp 4-cylinder (Model B).

COYOTE 1909–1910
Redondo Beach Car Works, Redondo Beach, Calif.

A two-passenger roadster which was apparently powered by a 50hp engine of eight cylinders. It had very rakish fenders, presumably to denote speed.

C.P.T. 1906
Chicago Pneumatic Tool Co, Chicago, Ill.

Although they made commercial trucks for some years, the only passenger car venture of the Chicago Pneumatic Tool Co was a 22hp runabout, with solid tires, which they built only for the use of their salesmen.

1915 CRANE-SIMPLEX Model 5 46hp touring car. *Don McCray*

1922 CRAWFORD Six touring car. *Robert H. Kohl*
1902 CRESTMOBILE 8hp runabout. *Montagu Motor Museum*

CRAIG-TOLEDO 1906–1907
Craig-Toledo Motor Co, Dundee, Mich.; Toledo, Ohio

This company offered a three-passenger runabout for 1907 at $4,000. The company was still in existence in 1909 but there is no evidence of manufacture after 1907.

CRANE 1912–1915
1 Crane Motor Co, Bayonne, N.J. 1912–1915
2 Crane Motor Car Co, New Brunswick, N.J. 1915

The Crane Motor Car Co was a successor to Crane & Whitman Automobile Works of Bayonne, N.J. which went out of existence in 1908 after building several experimental cars. The Crane had a 4-cylinder engine of 563ci rated at 46hp. It had a 4-speed transmission and its wheelbase was 133in. The chassis was priced at $8,000. The Crane became the Crane-Simplex when the Simplex Automobile Co took over the company.

CRANE & BREED 1912–1917
Crane & Breed Mfg Co, Cincinnati, Ohio

For 1912 this company listed a 48hp 6-cylinder car with six body styles, at prices from $3,000 to $4,500. However, most of their subsequent production was devoted to ambulances and hearses.

CRANE-SIMPLEX 1915–1924
Simplex Automobile Co, New Brunswick, N.J.; Long Island City, N.Y.

One of America's outstanding prestige cars of any time, the Crane-Simplex (or Simplex, Crane Model No. 5), with its $10,000 chassis, succeeded the earlier Simplex after Henry M. Crane had taken control of operations. It was powered by a 6-cylinder engine of over 563ci displacement designed by the firm, and was sold in many body styles with coachwork by a variety of America's finest custom builders. In 1922, after the purchase of Crane-Simplex by Hare's Motors, who already owned Locomobile, a new Simplex was announced with 245ci single ohc 6-cylinder engine. It was to be built in the Locomobile factory at Bridgeport, Conn.

CRAWFORD 1905–1923
Crawford Automobile Co, Hagerstown, Md.

This car was built under the aegis of M. P. Möller, a successful builder of pipe organs. Only limited numbers were built, chain drive being used up to 1907, with transaxles on 1911–1914 models. Later models featured disk-covered artillery wheels and were powered by Continental 6-cylinder engines in 60 and 70bhp forms. The company afterwards made the Dagmar car.

CRESCENT (i) 1907
Crescent Motor Car Co, Detroit, Mich.

This firm was said to be building a large factory to carry on the touring car business of the Reliance Motor Car Co, and the runabout business of the Marvel Car Co, but they probably never actually turned out cars.

CRESCENT (ii) 1913–1914
Crescent Motor Co, Cincinnati, Ohio

Two models of this make were advertised, the Ohio and the Royal. The former was a continuation of Ohio (i) and was the smaller of the two, with a 270ci 4-cylinder engine, on a chassis of 116in wheelbase. This was built as a five-passenger car. The Royal model, with a wheelbase of 132in used a 6-cylinder engine of 454ci. This manufacturer may have moved to St Louis, Mo., late in 1914.

CRESTMOBILE 1900–1905
Crest Mfg Co, Cambridge, Mass.

The first cars made by this company were called simply Crest, and had a De Dion engine mounted in front of a straight dash, with no hood. Final drive was by single chain. By 1903 the engine was enclosed in a neat hood, and four-passenger models were being made as well as two-passenger runabouts. The 1904 Crestmobile had an 8hp air-cooled engine of the company's own manufacture, planetary transmission, and shaft drive. It was sold in England by O'Halloran Brothers under the name OHB.

CRICKET 1914
Cricket Cyclecar Co, Detroit, Mich.
A small cyclecar driven by a 2-cylinder engine with 2-speed transmission which cost $385. This company combined late in 1914 with the Motor Products Co, manufacturers of motor cycles.

CROESUS JR 1907
1 Croesus Motor Car Co, Kansas City, Mo.
2 W. L. Bell, Kansas City, Mo.
This very obscure brand of auto was represented by both a two-passenger roadster and a seven-passenger touring car. The latter had a wheelbase of 108in and was powered by a 318ci, 4-cylinder engine. Final drive was by shaft.

CROFTON 1959–1961
Crofton Marine Engine Co, San Diego, Calif.
This company built small vehicles including the Bug, a 1,100lb 4-wheeled utility machine using a 35hp 4-cylinder, overhead cam engine based on the Crosley Cobra.

CROMPTON 1903–1905
Crompton Motor Carriage Co, Worcester, Mass.
The Crompton steam car used 24 separate fire-tube boilers mounted in two groups on each side of the 4-cylinder horizontal engine. Drive was by vertical shaft to the rear axle. A two-passenger body with curved dash in the style of the Oldsmobile was fitted, but steering was by wheel.

CROSLEY 1939–1952
Crosley Motors, Inc, Cincinnati, Ohio
The radio pioneer Powel Crosley developed this small car and succeeded in competing on the American market where few other cars of this type had. Although not as inspired in appearance as many of its overseas contemporaries, sound engineering did go into its production; its postwar water-cooled engine was particularly notable.
Before World War 2 the Crosley had been an air-cooled 35.4ci twin, but the opportunity to power the vehicle with the 44ci ohc 4-cylinder Cobra engine presented itself when production was resumed. This engine was the result of a U.S. Navy project. The block was originally made of oven-brazed copper and sheet steel with a fixed cylinder head. Later this was replaced by the CIBA engine which was of cast iron for greater economy and strength. Pistons, pumps, intake manifold and oilpan were of aluminum and the crankshaft ran in five main bearings. The CIBA engine developed 26.5hp at 5,400rpm and was used in Crosley sports cars with great success.
At the peak of its post-war boom Crosley was making a wide range of vehicles including sedans, station wagons, delivery trucks and several sports models. Mention should be made of the Hotshot in particular, for it out-performed anything in its class and is still cherished by many collectors as an outstanding machine.

CROUCH 1897–1900
Crouch Automobile Mfg & Transportation Co, New Brighton, Pa.
The Crouch was a conventional-looking steam carriage with an 8hp V-twin engine and a boiler providing super-heated steam at a working pressure of 275psi.

CROW (CDN) 1915–1918
Canadian Crow Motor Co Ltd, Mount Brydges, Ont.
Though allied with the U.S. Crow-Elkhart Motor Car Co, this firm was mainly backed by local residents in an agricultural community. Most parts were imported from the American company but some were Canadian, and all bodies were built in the firm's factory. About 100 open cars were built before the concern went bankrupt.

1949 CROSLEY Hotshot sports car. *Autosport*
1916 CROW-ELKHART 15/20hp roadster. *Autocar*

CROWDUS 1901–1903
Crowdus Automobile Co, Chicago, Ill.
The Crowdus was a light electric runabout with a tubular frame. The steering tiller also operated speed changing and braking. The car had a range of 50 miles per charge.

CROW-ELKHART 1909–1924
Crow-Elkhart Motor Car Co, Elkhart, Ind.
The Crow-Elkhart was a conventional car made originally as a 30hp 4-cylinder touring car, although by 1911 no less than ten different body styles were available, including closed models. Production reached its peak in about 1915, when prices were at their lowest, the 25hp touring car or coupé costing only $725. On the whole Crow-Elkhart styling was angular and uninteresting, but the 1918 Clover-Leaf Tourer and Roadster featured V-radiators and dual-tone color schemes. In 1919, 6-cylinder cars were available as well as the fours, but had been dropped by 1922 when the company was standardizing on one 4-cylinder model with a Herschell-Spillman engine. Also in 1919 they built the prototype of a car intended for export to Great Britain, to be called the Morriss-London. This was later made by a new company, Century Motors Co, but few Morriss-Londons were actually built.

CROWN (i) 1905
Detroit Auto Vehicle Co, Detroit, Mich.
The Crown was a side-entrance five-passenger car with wheelbase of 98in. The engine was a 4-cycle, 4-cylinder one of 208ci, with overhead valves. The final drive was through a friction transmission and shaft.

1910 CROXTON-KEETON 40hp touring car. *Keith Marvin Collection*
1912 CUNNINGHAM (i) 40hp limousine. *Keith Marvin Collection*

1928 CUNNINGHAM (i) V-8 sedan. *Harrah's Automobile Collection*
1951 CUNNINGHAM (ii) C-1 sports car. *B. S. Cunningham Co.*

CROWN (ii) 1907–1910
1 Crown Motor Vehicle Co, Amesbury, Mass. 1907–1909
2 Graves & Congdon Co, Amesbury, Mass. 1909–1910
    The Crown two-passenger high-wheeler had tiller-steering and air-cooled 2-cylinder 12hp engine, mounted cross-wise under the seat. The chassis had a 'reach' frame and platform springs. Double chains drove the rear wheels.

CROWN (iii) 1913–1914
1 Crown Motor Car Co, Louisville, Ky. 1913–1914
2 Hercules Motor Car Co, New Albany, Ind. 1914
    The Crown was a two-passenger cyclecar, priced at $385. It had a 4-cylinder engine of 106ci and a friction transmission. Its wheelbase was 90in. This make was succeeded by the Hercules (ii).

CROWTHER ; CROWTHER-DURYEA 1915–1916
Crowther Motors Co, Rochester, N.Y.
    This was a light car, powered by a 4-cylinder engine of 188ci. The two-passenger model was on a wheelbase of 112in and sold for $450.

CROXTON 1911–1914
1 Croxton Motor Co, Massilon, Ohio 1911
2 Croxton Motor Co, Cleveland, Ohio 1911–1912
3 Croxton Motors Co, Washington, Pa. 1912–1914
    In 1911 F. M. Keeton left the Croxton-Keeton company to return to Detroit where he took up again manufacture of the Keeton car. The conventional Croxton-Keeton with 40hp 4-cylinder Rutenber engine was continued, known in 1912 as the 'German 45' and in that year it was joined by cars of Renault origin. These had dashboard radiators, and were known as the 'French Six', and 'French 30', with 6- and 4-cylinder engines respectively. In 1911 H. A. Croxton merged his company with Royal Tourist of Cleveland, but in less than a year this merger was dissolved and a new company was formed to make the cars at Washington, Pa. The same designs were made in small numbers, also a new six. In 1914 the company foundered in an effort to launch a $475 cyclecar.

CROXTON-KEETON 1909–1910
Croxton-Keeton Motor Co, Massilon, Ohio
    H. A. Croxton who had made the Jewel joined forces with F. M. Keeton of Detroit to make the Croxton-Keeton car. Two models were listed, the 'German type' which was based on the Rutenber-engined Jewel 40, and the 'French type' which sported a dashboard radiator and all seating between the axles.
    In 1910 the two partners separated, and made cars under their own names.

CRUISER 1917–1919
Cruiser Motor Car Co, Madison, Wis.
    This was an attempt to sell a car and camping outfit as a single package, the roadster model carrying such gear as bed, chairs, ice-box, tent, stove and cooking utensils. There was also portable plumbing in the form of a toilet and hot and cold running water in four large storage compartments, two on each running board. Prices were from $1,175. Several of the Cruisers were used experimentally by the U.S. Army.

CRYSTAL CITY 1914
Troll & Manning, Corning, N.Y.
    The Crystal City, named after the famous American glass center, was a small 2-passenger car with 4-cylinder water-cooled engine, and 3-speed selective transmission.

CUB 1914
Szekely Cyclecar Co, Richmond, Va.
    The Cub was a cyclecar with a tubular frame and a 2-cylinder De Luxe V-type air-cooled engine. The drive to the rear axle was by belt. The weight of the vehicle was 550lb and its price $350.

CUBSTER 1949
Osborn Wheel Co, Doylestown, Pa.
    This was a home assembled 6.6hp chain-driven car, also available as a chassis assembly only.

CULVER (i) 1905
Practical Automobile Co, Aurora, Ill.

This typical high-wheeler had wheel-steering, with a tilting column for ease of entry. The 2-passenger car had an under-the-seat, 2-cylinder air-cooled engine. A planetary transmission and double chains completed the power system.

CULVER (ii) 1916
Culver Mfg Co, Culver City, Calif.

This vehicle was a youth's car selling for $225. The single-cylinder engine was built by Culver and was air-cooled. The wheelbase was 66in.

CUNNINGHAM (i) 1907–1936
James Cunningham Son & Co, Inc, Rochester, N.Y.

The first Cunningham cars were made in 1907 by an old-established manufacturer of carriages. At first they were assembled vehicles. Before World War 1, Cunninghams were powered by 4- and 6-cylinder engines made by Buffalo and Continental, and by a 40hp four of Cunningham's own manufacture. The first completely Cunningham-built car appeared in 1910. Until 1915 carriages continued to be made alongside the cars, but from that year cars only were offered, in a single model. This V-8 Cunningham was one of the handsomest cars to come out of America in its period and in 1916, its first production year, it was of extraordinarily modern lines. Mechanically, it was generally conventional, although the V-8 engine was one of the early examples of its type. This 440ci power unit gave around 100bhp at 2,400rpm. The Cunningham was a finely-made luxury car, built a few at a time, and selling at up to $9,000 in open touring form. Owners included Marshall Field (the store tycoon), William Randolph Hearst, Mary Pickford and Harold Lloyd. It was still being offered as late as 1933. From then until 1935 only bodies were made (for other manufacturers' cars) and also ambulances and hearses on the original chassis. Like Brewster, they offered a town car version of the Ford V-8.

CUNNINGHAM (ii) 1951–1955
B. S. Cunningham Co, West Palm Beach, Fla.

The racing and sports car driver Briggs Cunningham set out to produce an American sports car that would surpass European machines of the same class, but though his cars scored some successes in American events he was never able to achieve his goal of victory at Le Mans. Six different models were made beginning with the C-1, containing stock Cadillac and Chrysler engines in a tubular chassis. The C-2 was nearly identical in appearance but was powered by a 180hp Chrysler unit. It came in 18th at Le Mans and 1st at Watkins Glen in 1951. The C-3 was a Vignale-bodied coupé of Michelotti design with an automatic transmission and a 220hp Chrysler engine. The C-4 was available as a coupé or roadster with 200hp. C-5s with a 310hp engine and a SIATA transmission finished 3rd, 5th and 10th at the 1954 Le Mans. The final model, the C-6, was driven by a 16-valve, 4-cylinder Offenhauser engine of 260hp but lacked the speed of previous machines.

The cars sold in small numbers and were costly to produce but they represented a valiant attempt in the field of sophisticated motorcar design.

1910 CUTTING Model A-40 roadster. *William S. Jackson*

CURTIS 1921
Curtis Motor Car Co, Little Rock, Ark.

The Curtis (sometimes listed as Curtiss) was a minor assembled car which used a 4-cylinder Herschell-Spillman engine.

CUTTING 1909–1912
1 Clarke-Carter Automobile Co, Jackson, Mich. 1909–1911
2 Cutting Motor Car Co, Jackson, Mich. 1911–1912

The Cutting was a powerful, good-quality car using engines by Milwaukee, Model or Wisconsin of 30, 40, 50 and 60hp. Cuttings were entered at Indianapolis in 1911 and 1912, their best performance being 10th place in the 1911 event. Prices were modest, ranging from $1,200 to $1,500. The company failed in 1912 because of insufficient capital.

C.V.I. (or C.VI) 1907–1908
C.V.I. Motor Car Co, Jackson, Mich.

The C.V.I. was built as either a touring car or a roadster with a common chassis. A 4-cylinder 377ci engine was used in this car. With 3-speed selective transmission and shaft drive, these cars sold for $4,000.

CYCLEPLANE 1914–1915
The Cycleplane Co, Westerly, R.I.

A bridge type frame and body support (used much later by Maserati) was one feature of this cyclecar. Its appearance was distinguished by the use of a one-piece horizontal fender running the full length of the hood and body (except at the single entrance). Three models used single- and 2-cylinder De Luxe engines.

CYCLOMOBILE 1920
Cyclomobile Mfg Co, Toledo, Ohio

This lightweight automobile with a 90in wheelbase was available either as a two-passenger roadster or a light-delivery truck. It was powered by a 2-cylinder air-cooled V-type Spacke engine of 68ci. It used friction drive, power being transmitted to the rear axle by a heavy chain.

D

D.A.C. 1922–1923
Detroit Air-Cooled Car Co, Detroit, Mich.

This air-cooled V-6 was first shown to the public in late 1922, but only a few touring cars were actually produced.

DAGMAR 1922–1927
Crawford Automobile Co, M. P. Möller Car Co, Hagerstown, Md.

The Dagmar, one of the most distinctive sporting cars in the U.S., first appeared in 1922 in both open and closed models which featured straight-line fenders and all-brass trim instead of the then-conventional nickel. The Dagmars were actually the basic Crawford car with sport treatment and were named for the daughter of M. P. Möller, a Hagerstown pipe organ manufacturer who had many years before acquired the Crawford Automobile Co. Powered by a Continental 6-cylinder engine, additional body styles were added in 1923 and a year later, conventional fenders were available as an alternative to the straight type. By 1925, a smaller Dagmar was placed on the market, also powered by Continental, of smaller specifications.

The final year for general production was 1926 and the last car built, an enormous seven-passenger sedan, was made in 1927 for Mr Möller when he returned for a visit to his native Denmark with his family. Although only a few hundred Dagmars were built over a six-year-period, the Möller interests also produced the Crawford and Standish cars as well as the Paramount, Luxor, Astor, Five Boro, 20th Century and Möller taxicabs.

DALTON 1911–1912
Dalton Motor Car Co, Flint, Mich.

Hubert K. Dalton, former manager of the Whiting Motor Car Co, planned to build a car basically similar to the Whiting under his own name. It had a 20hp 4-cylinder engine and a 96in wheelbase. Only three were made.

D & V 1903
DeVigne & Van Sickle, Paterson, N.J.

The only known model of this car was a tonneau of 'simplified French type'. The engine was claimed to deliver 16hp from the three cylinders of 226ci displacement.

DANIELS 1915–1924
Daniels Motor Car Co, Reading, Pa.

G. E. Daniels had been President of Oakland before turning to manufacture on his own account. The Daniels was a big, expensive and short-lived luxury car made in very small quantities, mostly to order, and best-known in its powerful speedster form. All were powered by L-head V-8 engines. The Herschell-Spillman was used up to 1919, giving way to their own 404ci unit. The Submarine Roadster and the starker Submarine Speedster of 1919 were extremely handsome sports cars. They disappeared with the decline of the speedster market in the middle 1920s.

DARBY 1909–1910
Darby Motor Car Co, St Louis, Mo.

The Darby high-wheeler used solid rubber tires. The steering was by wheel and power came from a 2-cycle 2-cylinder engine somewhat optimistically rated at 20hp. The four-passenger model sold for $800.

DARLING 1917
Darling Motor Co, Dayton, Ohio

The Darling was built as a five-passenger touring model of pleasing lines. It was powered by a 6-cylinder Continental engine of 303ci. The wheelbase was 130in and wire wheels were standard equipment.

DARRIN 1946; 1953–1958
Howard A. Darrin Automotive Design, Los Angeles, Calif.

Besides designing for other firms, including the Kaiser and Frazer

1924 DAGMAR 6-70 34hp petite sedan. *Keith Marvin Collection*

1922 DANIELS 39.2hp sedan. *Keith Marvin Collection*

sedans, Howard Darrin made several attempts at building cars. A convertible shown in 1946 had one of the earliest examples of a fiberglass body. In 1953 Darrin re-entered the market with a two-passenger sports car designed for Kaiser. The Kaiser-Darrin KD-161 was of fiberglass and had doors that slid forward into the front fenders. On his own again in 1956, Darrin powered the KD-161 with a 305hp Cadillac motor. From 1957–1958, Darrin sold the Flintridge DKW Darrin Mark II sports with a six-passenger steel body and a removable top on a DKW chassis.

DARROW 1902–1903
Darrow Motor Vehicle Co, Owego, N.Y.

The Darrow light runabout used a 3½hp Thomas engine, and in two-passenger form cost $550.

DART (i) 1914
Automatic Registering Machine Co, Jamestown, N.Y.

The Dart two-passenger cyclecar, built by the world's biggest voting machine maker, had a 2-cylinder engine. Its wheels had slab-like spokes similar to the later Bugatti Type 35.

DART (ii) (CDN) 1914
Dart Cyclecar Co, Toronto, Ont.

This typical cyclecar, based on the U.S. Scripps-Booth, was assembled under license for a short time. All parts were made in Detroit. The company later became body builders.

DART (iii) see MARTIN (iii)

DAVIS (i) 1908–1930
George W. Davis Motor Car Co, Richmond, Ind.; Baltimore, Md.

George Davis, a builder of buggies and wagons, entered the automobile business with a successful 4-cylinder touring model and subsequently added a six, a twin six and, in 1927, an eight. Most of these cars had Continental engines. Davis cars through the years were sold with a variety of body styles and two-tone color schemes at a time when the latter were unusual. Noteworthy were the Fleetaway touring car and the Man-o'-War roadster of the early 1920s characterized by sporting lines.

The company was acquired by the Automotive Corp of America in 1928 which continued the Davis Eight and the New York Six, both available with a patented Parkmobile device which lifted the cars into tight parking places. After 1930 the company's activities at Richmond were concentrated on the production of aircraft, lawn-mowers and power machinery.

DAVIS (ii) 1914
Davis Cyclecar Co, Detroit, Mich.

The Davis cyclecar used the familiar 2-cylinder, air-cooled Spacke engine. This was connected with a 3 speed selective transmission and a double chain drive. The tandem two-passenger car cost $425.

DAVIS (iii) (CDN) 1924
Davis Dry Dock Co Ltd, Kingston, Ont.

This was a luxury car project initiated by a shipyard firm to utilize their expanded wartime facilities. The car resembled the current Locomobile and all components were imported from the U.S. Only two cars were produced, both with custom-built bodies.

DAVIS (iv) 1947–1949
Davis Motor Co, Van Nuys, Calif.

The Davis three-wheeler was one of the more spectacular attempts to produce a small car in America. The original model had an all-aluminum body, tubular frame, Kinmont disk brakes (all the designers were in some way connected with the aircraft industry), coil springing at the rear and a 133ci 4-cylinder Hercules engine. Later cars (only seventeen were made altogether) were rather more conventional and used a channel frame, Bendix hydraulic brakes and semi-elliptic springs. The engine was a

162.4ci 4-cylinder Continental as used in the contemporary Del Mar. The wrap-around coupé body seated four abreast, not five as has been claimed.

DAWSON (i) 1900–1902
Dawson Mfg Co, Basic City, Va.

The Dawson was a typical tiller-steered steam runabout with a 2-cylinder engine and single chain drive. Two passengers could be accommodated in addition to the driver on a wide bench seat.

DAWSON (ii) 1904–1905
J. H. Dawson Machinery Co, Chicago, Ill.

This car was built only as a four-passenger touring car. Its power came from a 2-cylinder, 16hp engine. It had a peculiar 2-speed transmission and a very long single chain drive to the rear axle.

DAYTON (i) 1909–1911
W. D. Dayton Automobile Co, Chicago, Ill.

The Dayton was a high-wheeler with a water-cooled ohv 2-cylinder engine. The steering was by wheel, and the car had solid tires and full fenders.

DAYTON (ii) 1911–1915
Dayton Electric Car Co, Dayton, Ohio

This company made electric cars in small numbers, although they listed as many as six different models each year. Prices ranged from $2,000 to $3,000.

1948 DAVIS (iv) 3-wheeled coupé. *Montagu Motor Museum*

DAYTON (iii) 1913–1915
1 Dayton Cyclecar Co, Joliet, Ill. 1913–1914
2 Crusader Motor Car Co, Joliet, Ill. 1914–1915

This was a cyclecar available in either side-by-side or tandem arrangement for two passengers. The frame was of ash wood and the engine was a 2-cylinder air-cooled Spacke of 9/13hp. The price was $375.

DAYTONA 1956
Randall Products, Hampton, N.H.

The $495 Daytona minicar was an ultra-light two-passenger car with no doors or weather protection, powered by a 2hp Briggs & Stratton engine. The makers claimed that the rear-mounted engine could be used as a 1,000 watt power generator, or for scores of jobs about the house.

DAY UTILITY 1911–1914
Day Automobile Co, Detroit, Mich.

The Day utility car used a conventional 4-cylinder engine and shaft drive, but was unusual in offering a body which could be converted from five-passenger touring car to light truck in one minute. There should have been a wide market for such a vehicle among farmers and small tradesmen, but even so, the Day only lasted for three years.

DEAL 1905–1911
Deal Motor Vehicle Co, Jonesville, Mich.

This was a small four-passenger motor buggy, with solid rubber tires, but it had wheel steering even in 1905.

DECKER 1902–1903
Decker Automatic Telephone Exchange Co, Owego, N.Y.

The Decker was a light roadster with a single-cylinder 7hp engine mounted in front driving the rear wheels by shaft. Radiator and hood were on the Renault pattern.

DE CROSS 1913–1914
De Cross Cyclecar Co, Cincinnati, Ohio

The De Cross was a freakish cyclecar, with tandem arrangement and driver's controls in the rear seat. Its engine, of 69.5ci, had two cylinders and air-cooling. The final drive was by belts.

DEERE 1906–1907
Deere-Clark Motor Car Co, Moline, Ill.

Succeeding Clarkmobile and Deere-Clark, the Deere Type B for 1907 was a four-passenger car driven by a 4-cylinder engine of 25/30hp. It cost $2,500.

DEERING MAGNETIC 1918–1919
Magnetic Motors Corp, Chicago, Ill.

Designed by Karl H. Martin, designer of Roamer and Kenworthy and later builder of the Wasp automobile, the Deering Magnetic was a prestige motorcar in every sense of the word. It had a Dorris 6-cylinder engine and an Entz electric transmission, which eliminated the functions of the electric starter, flywheel, clutch and transmission. A 132in wheelbase allowed for luxury coachwork and prices for the closed models approached $7,000.

DELCAR 1947–1949
American Motors Inc, Troy, N.Y.

Although the short-lived Delcar was initially built as a delivery truck, one, and possibly more station wagons were produced. With a 60in wheelbase and a 4-cylinder engine located forward under the floor, it could seat six in relative comfort.

DE LEON 1905–1906

This puzzling make was exhibited at the 1905 New York show by Archer & Co, which also exhibited the Hotchkiss, so the De Leon may have been imported, although dimensions were not given in the metric system. It was described as a seven-passenger car weighing 2,400lb and priced at $5,500. It had a 4-cylinder engine of 293ci, 4-speed transmission and double chain drive.

DELLING 1923–1927
Delling Steam Motor Co, West Collingwood, N.J.; Philadelphia, Pa.

The Delling Steamer was developed by Eric H. Delling, who had designed Mercer cars and was later associated with Stanley. Both open and closed models were shown, powered by a 2-cylinder engine of Delling design mounted, with the boiler, under the hood. Few cars were produced.

DEL MAR 1949
Del Mar Motors, Inc, San Diego, Calif.

The Del Mar was an early post-war compact car, using a 4-cylinder

Continental engine, of about 162.4ci, developing 63hp. It had a 3-speed Warner transmission and the price was to be $1,200 for a 2-door five-passenger sedan or convertible. There were ambitious plans to set up factories at Chicago, Philadelphia and Fort Worth, but only a few prototype cars were made.

DELTA c.1923–1925

Of unknown origin, the Delta car was presumably a pilot model for a line of cars which never materialized. A 6-cylinder Continental engine and standard components were used. Whether more than a single car was built is not known.

DE LUXE see CAR DE LUXE

DE MARS 1905–1906
De Mars Electric Vehicle Co, Cleveland, Ohio

This was an electric car driven by a 1½hp motor. One distinguishing feature was a single electric headlight. Final drive was by double chains. Changes of ownership resulted in the cars being called Blakeslee from 1906 to 1907, and Williams from 1907 to 1908.

DEMOT 1909–1911
Demot Car Co, Detroit, Mich.

The Demot was a light (800lb) two-passenger roadster with a 2-cylinder water-cooled engine. It was driven through a 2-speed planetary transmission. Brake-linings were of asbestos and camel's hair.

DE MOTTE 1904
De Motte Car Co, Valley Forge, Pa.

In one year of operation, De Motte offered a 10hp runabout and a 4-cylinder chain-driven touring car, as well as several models of commercial vehicles.

DERAIN 1908–1911
1 Simplex Mfg Co, Cleveland, Ohio 1908–1910
2 Derain Motor Co, Cleveland, Ohio 1910–1911

The Derain used 4-cylinder, two-cycle engines which were air-cooled. These, it was claimed, had a range of 100 to 2,000rpm. The larger models, for seven passengers, used a wheelbase of 125½in, and weighed up to 3,600lb.

DERBY (CDN) 1924–1926
Derby Motor Cars Ltd, Saskatoon, Sask.

Under the slogan 'Built of the Best', the Derby was assembled in coach and sedan bodies. The design was similar to that of the U.S. Davis (i). The company is believed to be connected with the earlier Winnipeg Motor Cars firm.

DESBERON 1903–1904
Desberon Motor Car Co, New York, N.Y.

The 1903 model of this car used a 4-cylinder engine of 382ci. It was a five-passenger with left-hand drive, a 3-speed transmission and double-chain drive. In 1904, a smaller model with a 12hp engine was also built.

DE SCHAUM 1909
De Schaum Motor Syndicate Co, Buffalo, N.Y.

The appearance of the De Schaum high-wheeler was somewhat more attractive than the majority of this type. The horizontal engine was of two cylinders and was air-cooled. The car had a friction transmission and double chain drive.

DE SHAW 1906–1909
1 Charles De Shaw, Brooklyn, N.Y. 1906–1907
2 De Shaw Motor Co, Evergreen, Long Island, N.Y. 1907–1909

This was essentially a built-to-order car. The engines used were 3-cylinder, 2-cycle types of 12/14hp. These were very light power units weighing only 119lb. A planetary transmission was used and the car had a distinctive oval hood.

DE SOTO (i) 1913–1916
De Soto Motor Car Co, Auburn, Ind.

The De Soto appears to have succeeded the Zimmerman. This was a large car with a 55hp, 6-cylinder engine, which was furnished with a compressed-air starter. The model Six-55 five-passenger touring car sold for $2,185.

DE SOTO (ii) 1928–1960
Chrysler Motors Corp, Detroit, Mich.

The De Soto was launched in 1928 as a 175ci L-head six to compete with Oldsmobile, Pontiac and the cheaper Nashes. Styling and general design were in line with the 1929 Chryslers, and at $885 for a sedan 90,000 were sold in the first twelve months. A 208ci straight-8 on a 114in wheelbase was announced for 1930 as the world's cheapest 8-cylinder car. However, De Soto suffered badly in the Depression, and in 1932, when flexible rubber engine mountings and free wheeling were made available, sales dropped to 26,000 cars.

The De Soto disappeared from the British market about this time, though certain 'Chrysler' models listed in England (the Mortlake, Croydon, and some of the Richmonds) were in fact De Sotos in all but name. A 6-cylinder version of Chrysler's advanced unitary-construction Airflow, the SE-type with a 241ci engine, was brought out in 1934, but was as unsuccessful as its bigger sister. Later De Sotos followed regular Chrysler lines closely, though in later years there was a tendency to move into a higher price class than Dodge; by 1952 De Sotos started $300 higher than the companion make.

By 1939 the cars were being made with independent front suspension, hypoid rear axles and column shift. There was a choice of two 6-cylinder engines and three wheelbase lengths, the longest of these being reserved for seven-passenger bodywork — De Soto continued to offer a really roomy family car right up to 1954. A 4-speed semi-automatic Vacumatic transmission became an option in 1941, but De Soto's big post-war change of models did not take place until 1952, when the division followed Chrysler's lead in adopting the oversquare ohv V-8; their version was of 276ci displacement and developed 160bhp. With the advent of Chrysler's 'flight sweep' styling in 1955, the L-head sixes were dropped and the standard engine was now a 291ci eight, giving 185bhp in Firedome guise, and 200bhp in Fireflite form. Though this redesigning saved Chrysler sales generally, the slump in the medium-price class had an adverse effect on De Soto and in 1959 the division was merged with Plymouth. Last of the De Sotos were the 1961 models, unitary-construction cars with a 361ci V-8 engine developing 265bhp. Production ceased in December 1960 after only a few had been delivered.

DE TAMBLE 1908–1913
1 Speed Changing Pulley Co, Indianapolis, Ind. 1908–1909
2 De Tamble Motors Co, Anderson, Ind. 1909–1913

The initial De Tamble model was a small runabout with a flat 2-cylinder engine which sold for $650. From 1909, larger conventional 4-cylinder cars were made. Four body types were offered, the largest being Model K, a seven-passenger touring car with a 120in wheelbase.

DETROIT (i) 1899–1902
Detroit Automobile Co, Detroit, Mich.

Although very few cars were made, this company is significant as it was the predecessor of the Cadillac Automobile Co, and because its chief engineer was Henry Ford. Although formed in 1899, the company did not turn out any cars until 1901 when a Ford-designed car with 2-cylinder engine, planetary transmission and single chain drive appeared. The engines were built by Henry M. Leland's company, Leland & Faulconer, and in 1902 Leland took control of the Detroit Automobile Co. He changed the name to Cadillac, and the first Cadillac car to be made on a production basis left the works in March 1903.

1932 DE SOTO (ii) Model SC convertible. *Chrysler Corporation*
1942 DE SOTO (ii) Model S-10 sedan. *Chrysler Corporation*

1958 DE SOTO (ii) Fireflite convertible. *Chrysler Corporation*
1909 DE TAMBLE 36hp roadster. *Automotive History Collection, Detroit Public Library*

DETROIT (ii) 1904
Wheeler Mfg Co, Detroit, Mich.

This Detroit was a five-passenger tonneau with rear entrance. Its 15hp opposed 2-cylinder engine was claimed to give 35mph. It was furnished with a removable wooden top, and the standard colors were red and green with yellow drive-shaft and axles.

DETROIT (iii) 1904–1908
Detroit Auto Vehicle Co, Detroit, Romeo, Mich.

This car was built as a two-passenger runabout, or a five-passenger tourer. The final models of this make were shaft-driven and had 2-cylinder engines of 22/24hp. These had a complex hood and radiator outline.

DETROIT (iv) 1913–1914
Detroit Cyclecar Co, Detroit, Mich.

This was a cyclecar, at 850lb somewhat heavier than was normal for its type, which used a 4-cylinder water-cooled engine of 91.5ci displacement. The price was $375.

DETROIT-DEARBORN 1910–1911
Detroit-Dearborn Motor Car Co, Dearborn, Mich.

A touring torpedo, designated the Minerva model, and a roadster termed Nike were the two models of this make. They used a 4-cylinder engine of 35hp.

DETROIT ELECTRIC 1907–1938
1 Anderson Carriage Co, Detroit, Mich. 1907–1910
2 Anderson Electric Car Co, Detroit, Mich. 1911–1918
3 Detroit Electric Car Co, Detroit, Mich. 1919–1938

One of the best-known electric automobiles built in the U.S. as well as one of the most long-lived, the Detroit Electric car reached its peak in production and sales between 1912 and 1920. Its success was largely due to the demand by women for a simple car for urban use. More than 1,000 units per year were sold up to World War 1, but production tapered off in the 1920s. A few Detroits with Renault-type hoods were made under license in Scotland by Arrol-Johnston in 1913–1914. In 1920, the old-fashioned appearance of the cars was modified by the introduction of false fronts which made the Detroit look more like a conventional car. In the early 1930s, production was cut to individual orders, and bodies for the more conventional-looking cars were obtained from Willys-Overland, complete with the horizontal hood louvres. The earlier design, however, with rounded battery covers, fore and aft, was also available. Only a handful of Detroit Electric cars were produced annually after 1935. Some of the last cars used the Dodge hood and grill.

DETROITER; BRIGGS-DETROITER 1912–1917
Briggs-Detroiter Motor Car Co, Detroit, Mich.

The Detroiter was a popular light car sold in large quantities. The early models were powered by a 32hp, L-head engine. For 1915 a five-passenger touring car was produced with a V-8 engine of 214ci. This car weighed less than 2,300lb and sold for $1,295. In 1917 a Detroiter with 6-cylinder Continental motor was listed.

DETROIT-OXFORD; OXFORD 1905–1906
Detroit-Oxford Mfg Co, Oxford, Mich.

This car used a 16hp 2-cylinder (opposed) engine with water cooling. It had shaft drive and was of conventional design except that the five-passenger touring car was doorless.

DETROIT STEAM CAR 1922–1923
Detroit Steam Motors Corp, Detroit, Mich.

The Detroit Steamer initially appeared as the Trask-Detroit. Very few of these touring cars were actually built. All of them had a 2-cylinder engine of their own design. A handful of prototype models carrying the Windsor name were also built for the company's projected sales in Canada.

1909 DETROIT ELECTRIC brougham. *The Veteran Car Club of Great Britain*

1914 DETROIT ELECTRIC brougham. *Gilltrap's Auto Museum*

1931 DE VAUX Model 6-75 coupé. *Keith Marvin*

DE VAUX 1931–1932
De Vaux-Hall Motor Corp, Oakland, Calif.; Grand Rapids, Mich.

The De Vaux was an economy car with a 6-cylinder engine and a full line of body styles which failed after 14 months in business. The 1931 cars were called the Model 6-75. By January 1932, sales were poor and the De Vaux was in financial trouble. Its assets were taken over by the Continental Motor Co of Detroit, Mich. and subsequent cars produced during 1932 were known as the De Vaux Model 80 or the De Vaux Continental. As Continentals they were sold until 1934.

DE-VO 1936
De-Vo Motor Car Corp, Hagerstown, Md.

Norman De Vaux, builder of the De Vaux car in 1931 and 1932, set up a corporation in Maryland late in 1936 with the idea of manufacturing a 4-cylinder, full-size five-passenger sedan for the export market. The prototype car was shown at the Waldorf-Astoria Hotel in New York City late in 1936 or early in 1937 with production scheduled for early 1937. It was displayed by the M. P. Möller Co of Hagerstown, Md., which had previously built the Crawford, Dagmar, Standish and other cars, and resembled the 1933–1934 Continental with a 1935 Reo-style grill.

DEY 1917
Dey Electric Corp, York, Pa.

This company made a short-lived three-passenger electric runabout.

DEY-GRISWOLD 1895–1898
Dey-Griswold & Co, New York, N.Y.

Invented by Harry E. Dey, the Dey-Griswold was probably the only car to combine an electric motor with a fluid drive system whereby oil was forced through turbines attached to the rear wheels. After three years of experiments, the system was abandoned as there was too much slippage in the turbines for the limited power available.

DIAMOND (i) 1910–1912
Diamond Automobile Co, South Bend, Ind.

The Diamond was a continuation of the Ricketts. The 50hp 6-cylinder Diamond was produced in three body types, including the five-passenger touring car at $2,200. During 1911 and 1912, this car was referred to as R.A.C., apparently in memory of the Ricketts Automobile Co.

DIAMOND (ii) 1914
Cyclecar Co of Wilmington, Wilmington, Del.

This two-passenger cyclecar, with side-by-side seating, weighed 500lb. It had a 4-cylinder air-cooled engine and a 2-speed transmission.

DIAMOND T 1905–1911
Diamond T Motor Car Co, Chicago, Ill.

Diamond Ts were all large cars with 4 cylinder engines of 286 to 432ci with ratings up to 70hp. They were all equipped with sliding gear transmission and shaft drive. As many as five body types were offered in one year. The name Diamond T survives on large commercial vehicles to the present day.

DIANA 1925–1928
Diana Motors Co, St Louis, Mo.

The Diana company was a subsidiary of the Moon Motor Car Co. The cars, powered by a 244ci 8-cylinder Continental engine, carried a radiator which was an almost exact copy of the Belgian Minerva and, on one model of sports roadster, was offered in bronze instead of nickel, with bronzed wire wheels to match. Steel windshield posts on the closed models afforded the driver increased visibility. Prices for Dianas ranged from $1,595 to $2,895 and a rarely seen town car was offered at $5,000.

DIEBEL 1901
Diebel Cox Mfg Co, Pa.

The Diebel was a light runabout with a 7hp 2-cylinder engine which was air-cooled by toothed-edge fins projecting from the cylinders. The price was $650.

DIEHLMOBILE 1962–1964
H. L. Diehl Co, South Willington, Conn.

A 'spare car' that folded to fit in the trunk of a car. When assembled it was a 3-wheeled conveyance with a 3hp Briggs and Stratton engine and a canopy top.

DILE 1914–1916
Dile Motor Car Co, Reading, Pa.

This make of light car appears to have been made only as a two-passenger roadster. It had an 86.5ci 4-cylinder engine, sliding-gear transmission and wire wheels.

DINGFELDER 1902–1903
Dingfelder Motor Co, Detroit, Mich.

The Dingfelder was a typical motor buggy with a horizontal water-cooled, 2-cylinder engine of 3.5hp. Price for this two-passenger car was $500.

DIRECT DRIVE *see* CHAMPION (iii)

DISBROW 1917–1918
Disbrow Motors Corp, Cleveland, Ohio

Louis Disbrow, a noted racing driver, designed this two-passenger speedster from the engine up. Its appearance was similar to the racing cars of the time, with the addition of cycle-type fenders. The car was fitted with wire wheels but no running boards. A choice of Wisconsin-built 453 or 605ci 4-cylinder, T-head engines was available. The larger engine would drive the car to 90mph, it was claimed.

DISPATCH 1911–1922
Dispatch Motor Co, Minneapolis, Minn.

The first Dispatch cars had 2-cycle engines, but these were replaced by a conventional L-head Wisconsin unit of 23hp. Roadster, touring and coupé models were made, at prices from $935 to $1,210. An unusual feature of the cars was that they used chain drive until at least 1918.

DIXIE; DIXIE JR. 1908–1909
Southern Motor Car Factory, Houston, Tex.

The Flier, the roadster model of the Dixie, had a 4-cylinder water-cooled engine of 24hp with a 2-speed transmission and shaft drive. The Dixie Jr. was a high-wheeler with an air-cooled, 2-cylinder under-seat engine of 10/12hp, with friction transmission and double-chain drive.

1926 DIANA roadster. *Automobile Manufacturers Association*

DIXIE FLYER 1916–1923
Kentucky Wagon Mfg Co, Vincennes, Ind.; Louisville, Ky.

The Dixie Flyer was an assembled car which used various engines by

Lycoming or Herschell-Spillman at different times and was available in numerous body types. In 1922, with the Jackson car, the Dixie Flyer was absorbed by National and became the National Model 6-31.

D.L.G. 1906–1907
St Louis Automobile & Supply Co, St Louis, Mo.

The initials of this car stood for Dyke, Leibert and Givens, the first named being A. L. Dyke who had sold cars for home assembly a few years earlier. The D.L.G. had a 4-cylinder 35hp engine with overhead inlet valves, and was sold as a two-passenger runabout.

DOBLE 1914–1931
1 Abner Doble Motor Vehicle Co, Waltham, Mass. 1914–1915
2 General Engineering Co, Detroit, Mich. 1916–1918
3 Doble Steam Motors Corp, Emeryville, Calif. 1924–1931

Steam as a means of propulsion for passenger cars persisted longer in America than elsewhere because of the degree of flexibility it afforded, and the finest by far of steam cars in America or anywhere else was the Doble. As far as the public was concerned, the major snag of steam cars was the time they took to start from cold, but in its final, 1923 form the Doble, the most sophisticated of the breed, got up steam automatically in less than one and a half minutes after the electric ignition switch lit the burner. There was also a really efficient condenser, which gave a range of up to 1,500 miles on 24 gallons of water. A horizontal 4-cylinder engine fed from a flash boiler developed something like 76bhp, providing acceleration and hill-climbing ability out of the ordinary even among steamers.

1925 DOBLE Model E touring car. *Henry Ford Museum, Dearborn, Mich.*

With all this went an elegance and luxury that was even rarer, a price of about $8,000 and a three-year guarantee.

After experimental vehicles had been made, the first Doble to be offered for sale appeared in 1917, and allegedly 11,000 orders were received, but war priorities stopped the project. Plans were made to restart production in 1924, 1,000 cars a year being the target. In addition, a line of cheaper steamers costing $2,000 was to be made. In fact Abner Doble was a perfectionist who could never produce on such a scale, and not more than 45 Dobles were ever made. These came from a succession of companies and factories. The General Engineering Co of Detroit was to have made the 1917 car as the Doble-Detroit. Then Doble moved west to California, where a big new factory at Emeryville was to have coped with the expansion of 1924, but this dream never became reality.

DODDSMOBILE (CDN) 1947
Only one prototype was built of the Doddsmobile 3-wheeler. It had a small air-cooled engine driving the rear wheel, open two-passenger molded plywood body, and automatic transmission.

DODGE (i) 1914 to date
1 Dodge Brothers, Detroit, Mich. 1914–1928
2 Chrysler Corp, Detroit, Mich. 1928 to date

The brothers John and Horace Dodge, early Ford shareholders and builders of engines for the Ford Motor Co, produced their first car in November 1914. It was a conventional L-head monobloc four of 212ci, developing 35bhp. It was noted for its 12-volt electrics, and 'back-to-front' gear shift, features that were not discarded until 1926. The tough Dodge 4 won early acceptance by the American army after being used in General Pershing's punitive expedition to Mexico in 1916, and the type was widely used in World War 1 as a staff car and ambulance. Also in 1916 Budd all-steel touring bodywork was adopted; some sedans were also made in this year, using the same construction. The price of open cars was $785, and Dodge was fourth in overall U.S. sales in 1916 with 70,700 cars delivered, following this up with a second place in 1920. The 4 was still the staple product in 1924, when 1,000 cars were being made a day. A new departure for 1927 was a 224ci L-head six with internal-expanding hydraulic brakes.

In July 1928, Walter P. Chrysler paid $175,000,000 for the company. Discontinuation of the 4, now developing 40bhp and fitted with front-wheel brakes, followed almost immediately, but for the next three years Dodges preserved their individual appearance. Though their cars were reckoned more expensive than De Sotos, Dodge offered a very cheap Standard 6 at $765 in 1929, their other models being the Victory at about $1,000, and a big Senior which paralleled Chrysler's 75 at $1,675. A straight-8 was listed from 1930 to 1933. Free wheeling were among the regular Chrysler improvements which appeared on the scene in 1932, followed by synchromesh transmissions in 1933. In this year Dodge again took fourth place in sales, with 86,062 cars delivered. There were no Dodge versions of the Chrysler Airflow, but 1935 cars had the Airstream styling and L-head 6-cylinder engine of 218ci displacement. Overdrive, hypoid rear axles and independent front suspension made their appearance in the later 1930s, and Dodges of the 1940s were hard to distinguish from De Sotos or the de luxe Plymouths.

The expected ohv V-8, publicized under the name Red Ram, materialized in 1952; it was a modest-sized 241ci unit, and in 1955, when Chryslers were largely restyled, the cars were available both with the old 230ci L-head six and with V-8s in three ratings up to 193bhp. By 1959 — the last year of the L-head 6-cylinder — the most powerful eight disposed of some 345bhp, from 383ci. Dodge has continued to offer more potent alternatives to the regular sedans, with a brisk Charger fastback coupé available in 1966. A 'compact' car, the Lancer, was listed in 1961, but this was

1915 DODGE (i) sedan. *Dodge Division, Chrysler Corporation*

1934 DODGE (i) sedan. *Montagu Motor Museum*
1941 DODGE (i) Custom sedan. *Dodge Division, Chrysler Corporation*

1971 DODGE (i) Challenger 2-door hardtop. *Dodge Division, Chrysler*

virtually indistinguishable from the Plymouth Valiant. Regular 1967 Dodges had Chrysler's unitary construction and alternator ignition, introduced in 1960. Three basic types were produced: the semi-compact Dart with a 111in wheelbase; the bigger Coronets with 6- or 8-cylinder overhead valve engines; and the full-size Polara and Monaco V-8s on a 121in wheelbase, offered with 383ci and 440ci engines, and ratings up to 375bhp. For 1970 the Challenger line was introduced, with a choice of six engines from a 225ci six to a 440ci V-8, though the most powerful engine in this, and the Coronet and Charger ranges, was the 425bhp 426ci hemi-head unit. For 1971 the overall range was pruned from 49 to 37 models, but a newcomer was the sub-compact Demon 2-door coupé with four engine options from a 198ci six to a 340ci V-8.

DODGE (ii) 1914–1915
A. M. Dodge Co, Detroit, Mich.

This was considered a cyclecar despite its standard track and 102in wheelbase. It had a 4-cylinder 25hp water-cooled engine, with a friction transmission, and was designed by George Wahl of Wahl Motor Co. The company was sued in 1915 by Dodge Bros who successfully claimed that their name had been infringed.

DODGESON 1926
Dodgeson Motors, Detroit, Mich.

The Dodgeson was designed and engineered by John Duval Dodge, son of John F. Dodge, builder of the Dodge Brothers car. It had a straight-8 rotary valve engine with a $2\frac{1}{2}$in × 5in bore and stroke (187ci) producing 72bhp at 3,000rpm. The engine was placed in a 4-point suspension position, being supported between a channel section of side rails by rubber shock insulators set in brackets. Only prototype models were built and series production was never started.

DOLPHIN 1961
This California-built space-framed vehicle, with a Ford 105E engine and fiberglass body, was offered to West Coast Formula Junior enthusiasts. The designer was John Crosthwaite, who had worked in Britain with Lotus and Cooper.

DOLSON 1904–1907
1 J. L. Dolson & Sons, Charlotte, Mich.
2 Dolson Automobile Co, Charlotte, Mich.

The Dolson was a large car with a 60hp engine. In 1907 a seven-passenger touring model cost $3,250. It was advertised as the 'Mile-a-Minute' car. There were also smaller chain- and shaft-driven 20hp flat-twins, and a shaft-driven four of 28/30hp.

DOMINION (i) (CDN) 1911
New Dominion Motor Co, Windsor, Ont.

In 1910 Dominion Motors Ltd was organized to build engines and a car, styled after the U.S. Regal, to be known as the Royal Windsor. After a company reorganization the projected car was renamed the Dominion, but this effort failed too and the firm was liquidated. In 1911 the assets were bought by Detroit principals, who formed the New Dominion Motor Co, and apparently did produce some cars called Dominions.

DOMINION (ii) (CDN) 1914
Dominion Motor Car Co, Coldbrook, N.B.

This firm was organized largely with U.S. capital to take over the remains of the Maritime Motor Car Co of Saint John, N.B. It bought new machinery and more land, and produced a few pilot models before going out of business.

DORCHESTER 1906–1907
Hub Automobile Co, Boston, Mass.

The Dorchester was an obscure runabout, with a choice of single- or 2-cylinder air-cooled engines. The engine was exposed and was mounted in front of the dashboard. The final drive was by chain and steering was by tiller.

DORMANDY 1903–1905
1 United Shirt & Collar Co, Troy, N.Y.
2 Troy Carriage Works, Troy, N.Y.

Four Dormandy automobiles were built, all of them powered by 4-cylinder air-cooled engines. In the last car, certain Frayer-Miller components were used.

DORRIS 1905–1926
1 St Louis Motor Carriage Co, St Louis, Mo. 1905–1906
2 Dorris Motor Car Co, St Louis, Mo. 1906–1926

Cars built by George P. Dorris between 1897 and 1905 were known as St Louis automobiles; thereafter the Dorris name was used. The cars were of advanced design. The earlier 4-cylinder Dorris models gave place to sixes in 1916 and Dorris engines were used throughout production. Later cars were prestige vehicles with prices approaching $7,000 for closed

1906 DORRIS 30hp touring car. *Automotive History Collection, Detroit Public Library*
1923 DORRIS 38hp sedan. *Jacques Kupélian Collection*

models. The Pasadena phaeton with ohv engine was well thought of in the 1920s. The complete range of Dorris models was available until the end of 1926, although production actually ceased in late 1923.

DORT 1915–1924
Dort Motor Car Co, Flint, Mich.

Joshua Dallas Dort had been building carriages for many years when he decided to go over to car manufacture. His 1915 Model 5 was the first

1918 DORT touring car. *Court Myers*

car he produced, and he went on to sell some 107,000 cars altogether. During 1916–1917 Dorts were similar to the Model 5, but there were 4 doors now instead of 3 on the five-passenger touring cars. A fleur-de-lys roadster and a center-door sedan were added and prices ranged from $695 to $1,065. The engine, a 4-cylinder L-head 166ci Lycoming, had thermo-syphon cooling and the axle was of the three-quarter-floating type. All Dorts were equipped with cantilever rear and semi-elliptic front springs.

Lycoming's famous 4-cylinder L-head Model K engine was adopted in 1918 — displacement was 192ci — but the old clutch and service brake controls were retained, both on the same pedal: the other pedal operated the 'emergency' brake. Open cars cost $865, the sedan and a coupé $1,265. A 'sedanette' was introduced at $1,000; this had removable sides. 1919 Dorts were similar but higher in price. 1920 brought such improvements as conventional pedal controls, a hand-brake lever, and the removal of the gasoline tank to the rear. Although prices had risen to $985–$1,535, this was probably the firm's most successful period and more than 30,000 cars were sold.

A new phase began in 1921, with Rolls-Royce-type radiators and longer bodies. In 1922 an unusual 9-window sedan and a delivery truck joined the range. Improvements included a disk instead of cone clutch, spiral bevel gears, S.S. tires and, later, Lynite pistons which, with a heavy 2-bearing crankshaft, provided good torque; maximum rpm were 2,000 and engine rating was 19.6hp. Prices ranged from $865 to $1,445. Dorts were little changed in 1923, when sports models were given disk wheels. A six with a Falls ohv power unit was added to the range. The popular Dort fours were abandoned, surprisingly, in 1924. The six, a smooth, powerful car with forced lubrication, was given new body styles, but retained its 2-wheel brakes. Dort ceased production in this same year and another make passed into history. See also Gray Dort.

DOUGLAS 1918–1922
Douglas Motors Corp, Omaha, Neb.

Formerly the Drummond car, the Douglas (sometimes erroneously spelt 'Douglass') was announced in May 1918 'with the idea of supplying the Middle-West with a high-powered car at a reasonable price . . .' The Douglas, with an 8-cylinder Herschell-Spillman engine, was available in roadster and touring car forms at prices ranging from $2,000 to $2,150. Production was limited but the cars were highly regarded in their own district.

DOWAGIAC *see* LINDSLEY

DOWNING 1913–1915
Downing Cycle Car Co, Cleveland, Ohio

Despite the manufacturer's name, this was a light car with a 'standard' track of 56in and a wheelbase of 98in. It was furnished with a 4-cylinder Farmer engine with overhead valves and a displacement of 95ci. It had a selective transmission, and the two-passenger roadster cost only $400.

DOWNING-DETROIT 1913–1915
Downing Motor Car Co, Detroit, Mich.

This cyclecar was made in two models. One was driven by a conventional air-cooled V-twin engine of 13hp and carried two passengers in tandem. The more advanced model was akin to a light car with a water-cooled, 4-cylinder engine and a 3-speed transmission.

DRAGON (i) 1906–1908
1 Dragon Automobile Co, Philadelphia, Pa. 1906–1907
2 Dragon Motor Co, Philadelphia, Pa. 1908

This car was built in two- and five-passenger touring models with 25hp and 35hp 4-cylinder engines. These were all equipped with sliding-gear transmissions and shaft drive. The last models included a very sporty runabout on a 96in wheelbase.

DRAGON (ii) 1921
Dragon Motors Corp, Chicago, Ill.

A short-lived and attractive car produced in very limited numbers.

Featuring wire wheels, individual door steps and a high, pointed radiator quite similar to the ReVere, the Dragon was available as a speedster, and as four- and six-passenger touring models.

DREXEL 1916–1917
Drexel Motor Car Co, Chicago, Ill.

The Drexel succeeded the Farmack (1916). Two models were built. Model 5-40 was a five-passenger touring car with a 4-cylinder Farmer overhead camshaft engine at a surprisingly low $985. Model 7-60 was available either as a four-passenger roadster or as a seven-passenger touring car. The '7-60' had a remarkable 192ci, 4-cylinder engine with double overhead camshafts operating four valves per cylinder. This engine developed 65hp at 3,600rpm; a very high speed for that time.

DRIGGS 1921–1923
Driggs Ordnance & Mfg Co, New Haven, Conn.; New York, N.Y.

The Driggs was a small car with a 4-cylinder engine of its own design which, according to the company was 'Built With the Precision of Ordnance'. Driggs cars were relatively expensive for their size and production never exceeded a few units per day. Closed and open models were available.

1922 DRIGGS 11hp sedan. *Floyd Clymer Publications*

DRIGGS-SEABURY 1915–1916
Driggs-Seabury Ordnance Corp, Sharon, Pa.

The initial model of this make was an open two-passenger cyclecar, with underslung chassis and a water-cooled 4-cylinder engine. This model was succeeded by the Sharon late in 1915. Later Driggs-Seabury cars included both open and closed models which were small but well-proportioned, with wire wheels. This manufacturer was also involved in building Driggs, Ritz, Twombly (iii) and Vulcan cars.

DRUMMOND 1915–1918
Drummond Motor Car Co, Omaha, Neb.

The Drummond was an assembled 4-cylinder car which sold in limited quantity with bodies ranging from a roadster and touring car at $1,095 to a 'town car with detachable top' at $1,445. In 1917 a larger model was introduced, using a Herschell-Spillman V-8 engine which was claimed to develop 70bhp at 2,400rpm. The next year the name of company and car was changed to Douglas.

DUAL-GHIA 1955–1964
Dual Motors Corp, Detroit, Mich.

The original Dual-Ghia Firebomb used a convertible body by the Italian coachbuilders Ghia and a 315ci Dodge V-8 engine in a Dodge chassis shortened to 115in. A total of 117 Firebombs were made between 1955 and 1958, at prices which reached $8,000 by the latter year. In 1962 a new model, the L6.4, with 383ci Chrysler engine and convertible or coupé bodies was announced. Assembly was completed in Italy, and the price was $15,000 when the cars reached the U.S. Among the most prominent customers for Dual-Ghias was Frank Sinatra.

DUDLY; DUDLY BUG 1913–1915
Dudly Tool Co, Menominee, Mich.

This ash-framed cyclecar at first had a 2-cylinder air-cooled engine and final drive was by V-belts. A two-passenger open model was the only type offered. The 1914 Dudly had a 4-cylinder engine of 72.1ci displacement.

DUER 1907–1908
Chicago Coach & Carriage Co, Chicago, Ill.

The Duer was a two-passenger high-wheeler. It was tiller-steered and the 1907 model had its 2-cylinder, 12/15hp engine under the seat. In 1908 the engine was moved to a hood in front. The final drive was by rope to the rear wheels.

DUESENBERG 1920–1937; 1966
1 Duesenberg Motor Co, Indianapolis, Ind. 1920–1937
2 Duesenberg Corp, Indianapolis, Ind. 1966

Fred Duesenberg began by making bicycles and designed his first car, the Mason, in 1904. He and his brother August made engines with horizontal overhead valves for the 1912 Mason racing cars, and founded Duesenberg Motors in the following year in order to produce marine engines and complete racing cars bearing the Duesenberg name. The most famous of the latter appeared in 1920: a 183ci Bugatti-inspired straight-8 with single overhead camshaft and three (vertical) valves per cylinder. It won the 1921 French Grand Prix. In the 1920s the racing cars were the great rivals of the Millers at Indianapolis, and victory was assured in 1924 by the adoption of a centrifugal supercharger. Though a 2-cycle 91.5ci 8-cylinder racing engine capable of 7,000rpm was made in 1926, this was not proceeded with. The horizontal-valve Duesenberg engine was taken over in 1920 by the Rochester Motor Mfg Co, Inc, and was used in various sporting and luxury cars.

Meanwhile, at the end of 1920, the first Duesenberg production car made its debut. This Model A was an extremely expensive, very advanced, luxurious car, embodying an 8-cylinder in-line engine — the first to be seen in an American production car — of 260ci, basically similar to the racing unit, but with only two valves per cylinder and developing about 100bhp. There were also hydraulically-operated front wheel brakes — another 'first' as far as America was concerned. The Model A was current until 1926. A handful of its little-altered successor, the Model X, were made in 1926–27, but in the former year E. L. Cord of Auburn acquired control of the company. He was an excellent businessman with advanced ideas of styling and publicity. He stipulated that Fred Duesenberg's next car should be completely new, and a quite exceptional machine. In fact, the Model J, which made its bow at the end of 1928, was the most remarkable automobile in America: bigger, faster, more elaborate and more expensive than any other, yet also superior to them in refinement and good looks. Its 420ci, 8-cylinder engine, made by Lycoming (a firm which Cord had also bought), had two chain-driven overhead camshafts operating four valves per cylinder; a layout of racing type unique among American cars at the time and said to develop 265bhp at 4,250rpm — more than double the output of any rival. Although the complete car weighed more than 4,980lb, it was claimed to be capable of 116mph in top gear and 89mph in second. Only chassis were made for which $8,500 was asked in 1929. Immensely long and strong and low-built, Duesenbergs were very popular with all the leading coachbuilders. The company preferred to sell cars complete with bodies designed by them but made by approved builders, such as Murphy, Bohman & Schwartz, Judkins, Derham and Le Baron. In this form, catalogued models cost up to $17,950. The transmission — apart from the double dry-plate clutch — was conventional, as was the suspension by half-elliptic springs and hydraulic shock absorbers.

c. 1926 DUESENBERG Model A roadster. *G. Marshall Naul*
1933 DUESENBERG Model J roadster. *Kenneth Stauffer*

The brakes, of course, were hydraulic, with vacuum servo assistance from late 1929.

In 1932 a supercharged version of the Model J, the SJ, was added. To cope with the 320bhp now alleged to be available, bearings, reciprocating parts and valve springs were strengthened. Usually, the shortest J chassis was used, with the highest axle ratio and stronger front springs. A maximum speed of 129mph was attributed to the SJ, with an acceleration figure of 0–100mph in 17 seconds. Naturally, the most spectacular American motor car attracted similar buyers, among them Mayor Jimmy Walker of New York, William Randolph Hearst, Tommy Manville, Elizabeth Arden, Mae West, Gary Cooper and Clark Gable. In Europe, the Kings of Spain and Italy bought Duesenbergs, but few crossed the Atlantic for the chassis was more expensive than its European counter-

1937 DUESENBERG Model J convertible sedan. Coachwork by Rollston. *A. J. Hoe*

parts by the time freight and duty had been added, and was neither as quiet nor as well-finished. The make survived the Depression, but died in the collapse of the Cord Corp in 1937. Attempts to revive the name were made in 1947 and in 1966. The first was unsuccessful, and in 1966 only one car was actually made, powered by a 440ci V-8 Chrysler engine with push-rod overhead valves, developing 431bhp at 5,000rpm. Transmission was automatic, front suspension was independent, and there were disk brakes. Body styling was by Ghia. This venture, too, collapsed.

DUMONT *see* SANTOS DUMONT

DUMORE 1918
American Motor Vehicle Co, Lafayette, Ind.

This was a late cyclecar and was built for a short time only. It appeared as a two-passenger roadster selling for $410. The 4-cylinder engine had a displacement of 67ci and either a chain or belt drive. The manufacturer built the American Junior from 1916 to 1920.

DUNN 1914–1918
Dunn Motor Works, Ogdensburg, N.Y.

This car maker persisted with the cyclecar design to a later date than most. The Dunn had a 2-speed transmission and shaft drive connecting its 4-cylinder engine to the rear wheels. With wire wheels, this two-passenger model cost $295.

DUPLEX (i) 1909
Duplex Motor Car Co, Chicago, Ill.

The Duplex was so named for its unusual drive system which consisted of two friction transmissions each with its own drive-shaft and separate differential on the rear axle. The transmissions were driven, one at each end of the crankshaft, by a 2-cylinder 20hp engine mounted transversely. The manufacturer neglected to point out any advantage of this complex drive, which was also used on the French Dumont cyclecar.

DUPLEX (ii) (CDN) 1923
United Iron Works Co, Montreal, Que.

The main feature of this car, built on a Hudson chassis, was its unique 4-cylinder engine with two pistons per cylinder. The company claimed a record for gasoline economy. The sedan was priced at $1,750 but hardly any were produced, doubtless through lack of capital.

du PONT (i) 1915
du Pont Motor Car Co, Wilmington, Del.

The du Pont was assembled in Wilmington, the bodies being built in Reading, Pa. It was powered by a 166ci 4-cylinder engine, driving through a 3-speed Covert transmission. The touring model cost $595. There is no known connection with the better-known du Pont (ii).

du PONT (ii) 1920–1932
1 du Pont Motors, Inc, Wilmington, Del. 1920–1923
2 du Pont Motors, Inc, Moore, Pa. 1923–1932

E. Paul du Pont's company built quality cars in limited numbers, total production being 537 vehicles of all types. First of the line was a 249ci L-head four with their own engine, selling for $2,600, but this gave way to proprietary-engined sixes, initially powered by Herschell-Spillman. The 1925 Model D had a 6-cylinder 268ci Wisconsin engine with overhead valves that developed 75bhp, a constant-mesh transmission, and Lockheed hydraulic brakes to all four wheels. Its successor, the Model E, could be had with a supercharger, but the best-known, and best, du Pont was the Model G speedster introduced in 1928. With its narrow straight wings copied from the Amilcar, Woodlite headlights and grill concealing the radiator, the last a pioneering feature, the Model G was not a good-looking car, but it was a very effective one. Like all the du Pont speedsters it had four forward speeds. The 322ci L-head straight-8 engine, by Continental, gave 114bhp at 3,600rpm with catalogued modifications. With the latter, 100mph was guaranteed. In the 1929 Le Mans 24 Hours Race

1929 du PONT (ii) Model G speedster. *Don McCray*

the Model G proved itself faster than the other American entries, Stutz and Chrysler. Touring bodywork was, of course available, and in 1931 came the long wheelbase (146in) Model H, built in a Stearns Knight frame. The later cars were assembled in the Indian motorcycle factory at Springfield, after E. Paul du Pont had acquired this concern. By 1932 the make had gone, killed by the Depression.

DUQUESNE (i) 1903–1906
Duquesne Construction Co, Jamestown, N.Y.

The Duquesne was a medium-sized air-cooled 4-cylinder touring car with a circular dummy radiator and hood in the style of the Hotchkiss. It featured a 'self-starter' by foot-operated ratchet mechanism operating on the flywheel, and a device whereby the rear doors opened when either of the front seats was tilted forward.

DUQUESNE (ii) 1912–1913
Duquesne Motor Car Co, Pittsburgh, Pa.

This Duquesne was made in two models; the smaller on a wheelbase of 124in used a T-head 4-cylinder engine of 390ci. The larger model had a 6-cylinder 364ci engine and a longer wheelbase. Prices ranged from $2,600 to $2,700 for five-passenger models.

DURANT 1921–1932
Durant Motors, Inc, New York, N.Y.; Lansing, Mich.; Muncie, Ind.; Oakland, Calif.; Elizabeth, N.J.; Long Island City, N.Y.; Toronto and Leaside, Ont.; Syracuse, N.Y.

The Durant was, with the Star, Eagle, Flint, Princeton, Rugby and Locomobile, one of several makes comprising William C. Durant's automobile empire. It was introduced as a 4-cylinder car and used its own ohv engine. The first models in 1921 had disk or wooden spoke wheels and a five-passenger touring car cost $850. In 1922, the peak year of production, 55,000 units were sold, the figure falling to 39,000 in 1923 and fluctuating thereafter. The 4-cylinder model remained basically the same through 1926 with various modifications added in keeping with the times. A car with a 6-cylinder Ansted engine was built in 1922 and 1923 at the Muncie plant. In 1927 Durant suspended production, but started again in 1928 with a completely redesigned line of 4- and 6-cylinder cars which were continued in 1929. Another new line was brought out in 1930 and the 4-cylinder car was dropped. The 1930 range included two sixes, with wire wheels as standard equipment for the larger of the two.

The 1931 models were unchanged except for the engines, which were Continentals. Sales had dropped severely, however: the 43,951 cars sold in 1928 fell to 20,261 in 1930. In 1931, only 7,270 Durants were sold and early in 1932, the firm went out of business. The Canadian Durant cars were called Frontenac from 1931, and were sold until 1933.

DUROCAR 1907–1909
Durocar Mfg Co, Los Angeles, Calif.

This early Western car used a 2-cylinder water-cooled 4-cycle engine of 26hp, placed horizontally under the front seat. The drive to the rear axle was by 3-speed selective transmission and drive-shaft. Surrey, runabout and touring body types were offered.

DURYEA (i) 1895–1913
1 Duryea Motor Wagon Co, Springfield, Mass. 1895–1898
2 Duryea Mfg Co, Peoria, Ill. 1896–c.1898
3 Duryea Power Co, Reading, Pa. 1899–1908 (licensees at Waterloo, Iowa; Coventry, England; and Liège, Belgium, during part of this period)
4 Duryea Motor Co, Saginaw, Mich. 1908–1913

These four firms represented the commercial endeavours of Charles E. Duryea, who with his brother Frank constructed one of America's very first cars in 1892–1893. It was a powered horse buggy, with single-cylinder

1923 DURANT Four 24hp touring car. *Montagu Motor Museum*

4hp engine and friction drive. A second prototype was the work of Frank, who won America's first motor race, from Chicago to Evanston on Thanksgiving Day, 1895. There was only one other finisher, a Benz, and Frank Duryea took nine hours to cover the 50 miles. Charles Duryea then set up the first company formed in America expressly for the purpose of making gasoline motor cars, and 13 vehicles were made with horizontal engines, 3-speed belt transmissions and low-tension ignition. Two of these took part in the original British Emancipation Run from London to Brighton in 1896. Three-wheelers were in production at Peoria in 1898, followed in 1900–1901 by cars with transverse front suspension and flat-twin engines. By this time Frank was engaged in the development of the Stevens-Duryea car for the Stevens Arms and Tool Co, and all subsequent Duryeas were entirely Charles's work. In the 1902–1906 period he made 3- and 4-wheeled vehicles powered by rear-mounted transverse 3-cylinder engines of square dimensions with water-jacketed heads, a 2-speed crypto gear mounted in a 'power drum' alongside the engine and tiller steering. Much was made of the single-lever control whereby the tiller also served as gear selector and throttle. In 1902 Henry Sturmey organized a British Duryea Co, which made the cars under license in Coventry; their engines were the work of Willans and Robin-

1896 DURYEA (i) 4hp motor buggy. *Kenneth Stauffer*

1911 DURYEA (i) 12hp motor buggy. *Jackson Products*

1916 DURYEA GEM 10hp 3-wheeler. *Automotive History Collection, Detroit Public Library*

1903 DYKE 12hp tonneau. *Automotive History Collection, Detroit Public Library*

son, and they had moiv and high-tension ignition. In 1906 Charles Duryea listed a 3-wheeler at $1,200, a 12/15hp 4-wheeler with similar mechanics at $1,300 and a big 25hp car, still with three cylinders, at $2,000. By this time the British Duryeas had faded out, the factory being used for the manufacture of the Lotis car but Charles Duryea made a 3-cylinder rotary-valve model in 1907, before turning his attention to the high-wheeler in 1908. His version, the Buggyaut, was powered by a 2-cylinder horizontally-opposed 2-cycle engine at the rear, drive being by twin grooved rollers on the crankshaft which engaged with the rims of the rear wheels. A centrally-mounted tiller enabled it to be controlled from either seat, and it cost $750, pneumatic tires being extra. This car survived most of its competitors, as it was still listed in 1913.

DURYEA (ii) 1914–1915
Cresson-Morris Co, Philadelphia, Pa.

This short-lived cyclecar was designed by Charles E. Duryea. It used the same rim drive as his Buggyaut car, had a 4-cycle flat-twin engine and side-by-side seating. The price was $400.

DURYEA GEM 1916
Duryea Motor, Inc, Philadelphia, Pa.

This 3-wheeler cyclecar with single front wheel used the same basic transmission as the Buggyaut and the Duryea (ii). It sold at $425 and was no more successful than Charles E. Duryea's other cyclecar venture.

DYKE 1901–1904
A. L. Dyke Auto Supply Co, St Louis, Mo.

The Dyke was one of the first kit cars sold in component form for home assembly. A variety of designs were offered, with engines from a 5hp single to a 12hp twin, two-, four- or five-passenger bodies, and solid or pneumatic tires. All components were available from A. L. Dyke, whose prices ranged from $700 to $1,000.

DYMAXION 1933–1934
The Dymaxion was an experimental car in teardrop aerodynamic design conceived by Buckminster Fuller and initially tested by Capt Al Williams, a stunt aviator. The 3-wheeled car, with the single wheel at the rear, was largely constructed of balsa wood and duraluminum and built in the old Locomobile plant at Bridgeport, Conn. Power was supplied by a Ford V-8 engine. The 1,850lb Dymaxion achieved 120mph when tested in July 1933. A later crash killed two passengers. Two more Dymaxions were subsequently built.

E

EAGLE (i) 1904–1905
The Eagle Auto Co, Buffalo, N.Y.

Two models of this car were produced, both five-passenger rear-entrance tonneaus. The smaller used an opposed 2-cylinder engine of 12hp, the larger model a 24hp 4-cylinder unit. These were both air-cooled. Final drive was by roller-chain.

EAGLE (ii) 1905–1906
Eagle Automobile Co, Rahway, N.J.

The Eagle had a 4-cylinder air-cooled engine of 20/24hp and chain drive. A five-passenger touring body was the only model offered.

EAGLE (iii) 1908
Eagle Motor Carriage Co, Elmira, N.Y.

The Eagle high-wheeler had solid tires and a rope drive. The engine was a 4-cycle type with two opposed cylinders. Single cantilever springs were used on each side of the body extending from front to rear axles. Steering was by a wheel.

EAGLE (iv) 1909
Eagle Automobile Co, St Louis, Mo.

This roadster with solid rubber tires sold for $650. It was powered by a 2-cylinder air-cooled 4-cycle engine of 14hp. A 3-speed selective transmission and shaft drive were used.

EAGLE (v) 1914–1918
Eagle-Macomber Motor Co, Sandusky, Ohio

This cyclecar was also known as the Eagle-Macomber. Macomber was the name of its unusual air-cooled 5-cylinder engine, which was a West Coast product. The five cylinders were mounted horizontally in a cylindrical pattern so that each operated against a wobble-plate cum flywheel. This 77.4ci engine developed about 13hp. In 1918 a larger car was made, with 252ci 5-cylinder engine.

EAGLE (vi) 1923–1924
Durant Motors, Inc, New York, N.Y.

This Eagle was a 6-cylinder car produced by William C. Durant for a very short time, ostensibly to fill a gap between the Star Four and Durant Four cars in the Durant line. A Continental engine was used and the Eagles were priced at $820. Few were marketed and a touring car was the only model.

EARL (i) 1907–1908
1 Earl Motor Car Co, Milwaukee, Wis. 1907–1908
2 Earl Motor Car Co, Kenosha, Wis. 1908

This was a light (1,200lb) roadster on an 100in wheelbase with an early 'rumble' or folding seat. The car was driven by a 2-cylinder engine of 15hp. Power to the wheels was by friction transmission and chain drive. The Earl was succeeded by the Petrel.

EARL (ii) 1921–1923
Earl Motors, Inc, Jackson, Mich.

The Earl was the continuation of the Briscoe. Both open and closed

models of this 4-cylinder car were available, and approximately 2,000 were produced.

EASTMAN 1899–1902
Eastman Automobile Co, Cleveland, Ohio

The Eastman Electro Cycle was a 3-wheeler steered by a very long tiller to the single front wheel. It had a one passenger body which was said to be the first all-steel body in America, a tubular frame, and bicycle wheels.

The company later specialized in making steel bodies for other firms.

EATON 1898
Eaton Electric Motor Carriage Co, Boston, Mass.

The Eaton company showed a light electric two-passenger car at the 1898 Boston Motorcycle Show.

ECLIPSE (i) 1900–1903
Eclipse Automobile Co, Boston, Mass.

The Eclipse steam runabout was powered by an 8hp 3-cylinder engine. Unlike the average chain-drive steamer, it used shaft drive to the rear axle. In other ways it was typical of its kind, with a two-passenger body, tiller steering and wire wheels.

ECLIPSE (ii) 1905
Kreuger Mfg Co, Milwaukee, Wis.

The small Eclipse had an attractive appearance and a single-cylinder engine of 103ci. This was fitted with a planetary transmission and shaft drive. The single model, designated A, was a five-passenger car with rear entrance. This company also made a car called the Kreuger.

ECONOMY (i) 1914
Economy Car Co, Indianapolis, Ind.

The Economy cyclecar used coil springs in front and quarter-elliptical springs in the rear. It had a 2-cylinder Spacke engine, a planetary transmission and chain drive. The two-passenger model sold for $375.

ECONOMY (ii) 1917–1921
Economy Motor Co, Tiffin, Ohio

This was an assembled car, offered with either 4- or 8-cylinder engines on a standard chassis. Prices for roadsters and touring models ranged from $985 to $1,395. In 1920 a Continental-engined six was introduced.

ECONOMYCAR 1913–1914
Economycar Co, Providence, R.I.

The Economycar was a two-passenger tandem cyclecar with belt drive and a 2-cylinder air-cooled engine. The front axle was pivoted for steering by capstan cable. The address is sometimes given as New York City and Indianapolis, but the factory was at Rhode Island.

EDSEL 1957–1959
Ford Motor Co (Lincoln-Mercury-Edsel Divn), Detroit, Mich.

The Edsel was introduced for the 1958 season by Ford's Lincoln-Mercury Division to fill the supposed gap between Ford and Mercury lines. Despite vast sums spent on customer-research and public relations, the

1917 ECONOMY (ii) touring car. *Kenneth Stauffer*
1958 EDSEL Citation hard top. *Ford Motor Co*

1925 ELCAR 20hp touring car. *Automotive History Collection, Detroit Public Library*

project backfired. The gap did not exist, and only 35,000 Edsels found customers during the first six months of production. The car itself was typical of its period, with coil-and-wishbone independent front suspension, wraparound windshield, and a choice of two V-8 engines, both oversquare ohv units with displacements of 361 and 410ci. The smaller one offered 303bhp. The cheaper Ranger and Pacer series were available with manual, overdrive or automatic transmission, but only push-button automatic was listed on the costlier Corsair and Citation. A distinctive feature of the car was its curious, horse collar-shaped radiator grill. An attempt was made to widen the make's appeal with a low-cost ohv 223ci 6-cylinder engine in 1959, but the Edsel was dropped shortly after the announcement of the 1960 models.

EDWARDS 1953–1955
E. H. Edwards Co, South San Francisco, Calif.

A Ford V-8-engined prototype appeared in 1949 but in its production form the Edwards sports car used a cut-down Ford chassis with a fiberglass body and a 205bhp Lincoln engine. The f.o.b. price of $4,995 made it something of a bargain.

EDWARDS-KNIGHT 1912–1914
Edwards Motor Co, New York, N.Y.

This car with a Knight engine became the Willys-Knight after 1914. It was a fairly large car powered by a 276ci 4-cylinder engine rated at 25hp. The 4-speed transmission was direct in third gear, giving overdrive in fourth. Built as a five-passenger touring car, it cost $3,500.

E.H.V. *see* COMPOUND

E.I.M. 1915
Eastern Motor Car Co, Richmond, Ind.

This was a very late entrant into the American cyclecar market. The single model had a two-passenger body on an underslung chassis, with a 95ci 4-cylinder engine.

EISENHUTH *see* COMPOUND

ELBERT 1914
Elbert Car Co, Seattle, Wash.

For a cyclecar, this make had a very shapely body. The cross-section of this tandem two-passenger car was similar to an inverted bell. It had a 4-cylinder engine of 95ci, a 2-speed transmission and what was called a 'gearless' differential. The price was very low at $295.

ELCAR 1915–1931
1 Elkhart Carriage & Motor Car Co, Elkhart, Ind.
2 Elcar Motor Co, Elkhart, Ind.

From 1909 to 1915 the products of the Elkhart Carriage & Motor Car Co were known as Sterlings, but for the 1916 season the car's name was changed to Elcar. The first model was a conventional car made in two- and five-passenger versions, powered by a 20hp 4-cylinder Lycoming engine of 192ci. This engine was used until the mid 1920s, but the range was increased by a 6-cylinder car with 224ci Continental engine in 1918. A conventional range of cars was built during the 1920s, all using the 4-cylinder Lycoming or 6-cylinder Continental engine, a number of the former being made as taxicabs. In 1925 the company branched out into the 8-cylinder field, with a car powered by a 299ci straight-8 Lycoming engine. In its final form this engine developed 140bhp, making it the third most powerful car engine in America at the time. Production of Elcars was never large, reaching a peak in 1919 with 4,000 units sold. Experiments with the Powell Lever engine came to nothing, though a Lever-powered Elcar 6 with 8in cycle appeared at the 1930 New York show. In their last year, 1931, the Elcar factory was used for the construction of the revived Mercer, which used an Elcar chassis and a 140bhp Continental engine. However, only two of these cars were made.

ELCO 1915–1916
Bimel Buggy Co, Sidney, Ohio

The Elco 30 was fitted with a 4-cylinder Davis L-head engine of 113ci. The only model was a five-passenger touring car on a wheelbase of 102in. The weight was 1,750lb, the price $585, with speedometer $15 extra.

1966 ELECTRA KING two-passenger runabout. *B & Z Electric Car Co*

1918 ELGIN (ii) Six 21hp convertible sedan. *The Veteran Car Club of Great Britain*

ELDREDGE 1903–1906
National Sewing Machine Co, Belvedere, Ill.

The Eldredge was a light two-passenger runabout, with an early example of left-hand wheel steering. It had an 8hp under-seat engine connected to the rear axle by jackshaft and chain drive. From 1904 there was a larger tonneau with 16hp flat-4 engine. The sales slogan of the Eldredge, 'Just what it ought to be', was not very informative.

ELECTRA 1913–1915
Storage Battery Power Co, Chicago, Ill.

The Electra was driven by a 2½hp electric motor geared to the rear axle. It was a closed two-passenger car which weighed only 750lb.

ELECTRA KING 1961 to date
B and Z Electric Car Co, Long Beach, Calif.

Small and of simple construction, this electric is built in 3- and 4-wheeled models for running errands or for use by the handicapped. Four 6-volt batteries power the 1hp D.C. motor giving up to 45 miles on a charge. The 4-wheeled model, discontinued in 1967, was resumed in 1971.

ELECTRIC SHOPPER c.1960 to date
Electric Shopper, Long Beach, Calif.

A small car similar to the Electra King with a plastic body, which is made for short local journeys.

ELECTRO MASTER c.1962 to date
Nepa Mfg Co, Pasadena, Calif.

With a 40-mile driving range, the little Electro Master is built of steel and fiberglass and weighs 680lb. A 2hp motor and six 6-volt batteries push it along at 20mph.

ELECTROMOBILE see CHAPMAN

ELECTRONIC LA SAETTA 1955
Electronic Motor Car Corp, Salt Lake City, Utah

Referred to as a 'turbo-electric' car, the Electronic used an 80-cell battery system that was regenerated by a gasoline or diesel turbogenerator. The fiberglass bodied La Saetta two-passenger sports was exhibited in Salt Lake City in 1955. Announced at the time, but not completed, were a sedan, station wagon, panel truck and children's La Saetta. After a promising start nothing came of this interesting project.

ELECTRONOMIC see HOOD

ELGIN (i) 1899–c.1901
Elgin Automobile Co, Elgin, Ill.

This company made a very simple single-cylinder runabout with a 5hp engine. It was sometimes known as the Winner, but had no connection with the later car made under this name at St Louis. Elgin also made an electric runabout.

ELGIN (ii) 1916–1925
1 Elgin Motor Car Corp, Argo, Ill. 1916–1923
2 Elgin Motor Car Corp, Chicago, Ill. 1924–1925

The Elgin was a conventional car built originally in 4-cylinder form, but using the 6-cylinder ohv Falls engine in 1918. The most interesting model was the six introduced in 1922, with Cutler-Hammer preselector, and double transverse rear springs. The body featured a built-in trunk which, although small in comparison with today's equivalents, was an advanced feature for its day.

ELITE 1901
D. B. Smith & Co, Utica, N.Y.

The Elite was a typical American light steam car, differing only from the general run by its ornate bodywork and profusion of brass on lights, dash, hubs and steering tiller. It used a 2-cylinder engine, and a gasoline car with similar body was also listed.

ELKHART 1908–1909
1 Elkhart Carriage & Mfg Co, Elkhart, Ind. 1908
2 Elkhart Motor Car Co, Elkhart, Ind. 1908–1909

The Elkhart was a medium-sized five-passenger touring car which weighed 2,400lb. Its 4-cylinder 30/35hp engine had a displacement of 270ci.

ELLIS see TRIUMPH (i)

ELLSWORTH 1907
J. M. Ellsworth, New York, N.Y.

This car offered a choice of shaft or double-chain drive. Its 4-cylinder engine had a single overhead camshaft operating T-head valves. The crankshaft journals were the same diameter as the crank throws. Twin ignition was used as well as a 4-speed transmission.

ELMORE 1900–1912
Elmore Mfg Co, Clyde, Ohio

Elmore were the most persistent advocates of the 2-cycle engine in

1904 ELMORE 5hp runabout. *Henry Ford Museum, Dearborn, Mich.*

1912 E.M.F. 30hp touring car. *Kenneth Stauffer*

America, and never made a 4-cycle engined car. From 1900 to 1904 they made a light runabout with a 5hp single-cylinder engine under the seat, three speeds, single chain drive and tiller steering. The first models had vertical engines, but from about 1902 they were horizontal. In 1903 a 2-cylinder model was added, and in 1904 the larger car had a dummy hood, although the engine was still under the seat. For 1906 a completely new range was introduced, with front-mounted engines of 22/24hp (2-cylinder) and 32/35hp (4-cylinder), shaft drive and side-entrance touring bodies. A 24hp 3-cylinder model appeared in 1907, and was made for several years. In 1909 the Elmore company was absorbed by General Motors, and production ended three years later. The last models were 4-cylinder cars of 30 and 50hp, still with 2-cycle engines.

EMANCIPATOR 1909
Emancipator Automobile Co, Aurora, Ill.

The two models of the Emancipator (three- and five-passenger cars) had 2- and 4-cylinder opposed engines placed crosswise under the hood. Drive was by planetary transmission with shaft drive to the rear axle.

EMBREE 1910
McLean Carriage Co, St Louis, Mo.

In 1910, the Embree had an engine rated at 35hp. Other details are lacking.

EMERSON (i) 1907
1 V. L. Emerson, Cincinnati, Ohio
2 American Auto Car Co, Cincinnati, Ohio

The short-lived Emerson 'Military' model was an $8,000 three-passenger car weighing 1,500lb and with a 96in wheelbase. Steering was described as being through 'toggle movement'. Its 6-cylinder, 650ci engine had rotary valves. It had only two forward speeds. Performance, though unknown, must have been unusual.

EMERSON (ii) 1916–1917
Emerson Motors Co, Kingston, N.Y.

The Emerson was a conventional car with a 22hp 4-cylinder engine and five-passenger touring body. It sold for $545 which was reduced to $395 for 1917. It was succeeded by the Campbell, which was a similar design, also selling for $395.

E.M.F. 1908–1912
Everitt-Metzger-Flanders Co, Detroit, Mich.

The E.M.F. was a slightly larger car than its companion make, the Flanders, both makes being marketed by Studebaker. Throughout its existence the E.M.F. used a 226ci water-cooled, 4-cylinder engine. This

was coupled with a 3-speed transmission and shaft drive. The wheelbase remained constant at 106in. Both runabout and touring models were built for sale in the range of $900 to $1,100. The name disappeared when Studebaker started to build as well as act as a selling organization.

EMPIRE (i) 1901–1902
Empire Mfg Co, Inc, Sterling, Ill.

Also known as the Sterling Steamer, this was a typical light steam buggy in appearance, but was unusual in using a V-twin engine. A water-tube boiler produced superheated steam at a pressure of 400psi, and maximum speed of the two-passenger car was 30mph.

1914 EMPIRE (iii) Model 31 touring car. *Antique Automobile*

EMPIRE (ii) 1904–1905
William T. Terwilliger & Co, Amsterdam, N.Y.

This steamer had an opposed 2-cylinder engine of 15hp rating. This was 'hung pivotally from rear axle' and the 'cylinder end was suspended from boiler'. It had tubular steel wheels and its rear-entrance tonneau body carried five passengers.

EMPIRE (iii) 1909–1919
1 Empire Motor Car Co, Indianapolis, Ind. 1909–1912
2 Greenville Metal Products, Greenville, Pa. 1912–1919

A two-passenger car with a 4-cylinder, 20hp G.B.S. engine with pair-cast cylinders was produced with little change from 1909 to 1912. It was known as The Little Aristocrat and cost $950. In 1912 operations moved to Pennsylvania, and for one season the car was known as the Fay. Although sold by the Empire Automobile Co of Indianapolis, all subsequent cars were made in Greenville. After 1912, a large line of cars in two-, four- and five-passenger models was made, with wheelbases up to 120in. These were powered by 4-cylinder Teetor and 6-cylinder Continental engines and prices ranged to $1,360.

EMPIRE STATE 1900–1901
Empire State Automobile Co, Rochester, N.Y.

This company made a light runabout with wire wheels, tiller steering, chain drive, and the engine under the seat. There was also an Empire State Motor Wagon Co, of Catskill, N.Y. who operated one of America's first used car lots, and may have made one or two light runabouts.

ENDURANCE 1923–1924
Endurance Steam Car Co, Los Angeles, Calif.

A short-lived steamer built on conventional lines, the Endurance was produced only as a five-passenger touring car. Disk wheels were standard equipment and the price was $1,885.

ENGER 1909–1917
Enger Motor Car Co, Cincinnati, Ohio

The first Enger was a 2-cylinder high-wheeler, but rapidly evolved through the 1910 40hp model to the Twin Six of 1915. This engine was designed and built by Enger and the car was one of the earliest 12-cylinder models in America. The 1916 model had an overhead-valve engine which could be converted to work as a 6-cylinder unit, by operating a lever which stopped the flow of fuel and opened the valves of one bank of cylinders. This engine developed 55hp at 3,000rpm.

ENGLER 1914–1915
W. B. Engler Cyclecar Co, Pontiac, Mich.

This two-passenger cyclecar used a De Luxe air-cooled, 2-cylinder engine of 71ci, driving through friction transmission and belts. The price was $385.

ERIE 1916–1919
Erie Motor Co, Painesville, Ohio

The Erie was built as a five-passenger sedan, roadster and tourer designated Model 33 because the 4-cylinder engine developed 33hp.

ERSKINE 1926–1930
Studebaker Corp, South Bend, Ind.

This compact car by Studebaker was named after the company President, Albert R. Erskine. It had a 140ci L-head 6-cylinder engine, and prototypes exhibited in Europe in 1926 had two unusual features: fixed wire wheels with demountable rims and fuel feed by electric pump; both of these were discarded on production machines in favor of wood wheels and vacuum feed respectively. Though it sold well enough on the export market, the Erskine was never successful at home, even when restyled in 1929, in which form a sedan cost $945. In 1930, its last year, it had grown up into a 207ci car with a 114in wheelbase and was nothing more than a small Studebaker.

ESHELMAN SPORTABOUT 1953–1958; 1960
The Eshelman Co, Baltimore, Md.

With its top speed of 30mph and a fuel consumption of 50mpg, the tiny Sportabout was built for errand running and golf-course transport. An 8.4bhp air-cooled engine powered it. A snowplough attachment was optional. This design was abandoned after four units had been built but in 1960 a dozen fiberglass-bodied models were produced.

1928 ERSKINE Six Type 50 sedan. *G. N. Georgano Collection*

ESS EFF 1912
Ess Eff Silent Motor Co, Buffalo, N.Y.

This car was built only as a cheap ($350) two-passenger runabout. It used a 2-cycle, 2-cylinder, air-cooled engine of 82.5ci and had a friction transmission and out-dated double-chain drive.

ESSEX (i) 1906
Essex Motor Car Co, Boston Mass.

This was a steamer with a single-acting, 4-cylinder engine. Cylinders were of 3.25in bore and 4in stroke. Poppet valves were used. The side-entrance tonneau was similar in appearance to the French Serpollet, and was priced at $3,500.

1921 ESSEX (ii) roadster. *American Motors Corporation*

ESSEX (ii) 1918–1932
Hudson Motor Car Co, Detroit, Mich.

The Essex, introduced as a low-priced line at $1,595 by Hudson in 1918, featured a 179ci F-head 4-cylinder engine developing 55bhp, which gave it a top speed of 60mph in standard form. It was recognizable by its angular lines and radiator shutters and the very cheap coach (2-door

1929 ESSEX (ii) Super Six coach. *G. N. Georgano Collection*

1971 EXCALIBUR SS roadster. *SS Automobiles Inc*

sedan) available at $1,295 in 1922 made it a best-seller. In 1924 the rapid four was supplanted by a 145ci L-head six, later enlarged to 153ci. This model pushed Hudson sales up to over 300,000 in 1929, in which year the company ranked third in the U.S. with 6.6 per cent of total registrations. Four-wheel brakes were an optional extra in 1927, and standard in 1928. In 1930 the new 18.2hp Challenger with ribbon radiator and 60bhp engine was introduced. In 1932 the Essex grew up into a 193ci car with V-radiator, detachable wire wheels, free wheeling and Startix automatic starter, but it was supplanted the following season by the Terraplane.

ETNYRE 1910–1911
Etnyre Motor Car Co, Oregon, Ill.

The initial Etnyre had a 4-cylinder 471ci engine. The 4-speed selective transmission gave direct drive in third gear. A seven-passenger touring car, a five-passenger closed coupé and a four-passenger roadster were the body styles built.

EUCLID (i) 1904
Berg Automobile Co, Cleveland, Ohio

The Euclid had a 'domestic' appearance, while the Berg (by the same manufacturer) had a 'European' flavor. The Euclid was a five-passenger touring car, weighed 1,650lb, cost $2,750 and was powered by a 4-cylinder 200ci engine of 18hp.

EUCLID (ii) 1907–1908
Euclid Automobile Co, Cleveland, Ohio

The 3-cylinder Euclid engine was a 2-cycle type, but with separate compression chamber, operated by the pistons, lower in the cylinder wall than the combustion chamber. It was air-cooled and was claimed to produce 20hp. A planetary transmission and double-chain drive were used. The models available were a roadster and a light touring car.

EUCLID (iii) 1914
Euclid Motor Car Co, Cleveland, Ohio

The manufacturer described the Euclid as a 'cycle-light car'. It used a 99ci, 4-cylinder air-cooled engine. The weight was 775lb and the price $445.

EUREKA (i) 1899
Eureka Automobile & Transportation Co, San Francisco, Calif.

The Eureka four-passenger surrey was powered by a horizontal 3-cylinder engine mounted under the rear seats. It had four forward speeds and reverse, and final drive was by single chain. Plans were announced to make cars and trucks in 'a very large factory', but apparently nothing came of this.

EUREKA (ii) 1907–1914
Eureka Motor Buggy Co, St Louis, Mo.

This was a high-wheeled buggy with solid rubber tires. It had wheel steering and a 2-cylinder horizontally opposed air-cooled, 4-cycle engine. The wheelbase of this two-passenger vehicle was only 80in and the gross weight was 1,000lb.

EUREKA (iii) 1908–1909
Eureka Motor Buggy Co, Beavertown, Pa.

This was yet another high-wheeled motor buggy with solid rubber tires which used a 2-cycle Speedwell engine of two cylinders, giving 10–20hp. The two-passenger car had a wheelbase of 79in. This became the Kearns.

EUREKA (iv) 1909
Eureka Co, Rock Falls, Ill.

This was a high-wheeler with 40 and 42in wheels and solid rubber tires. The 2-cylinder engine was mounted under the hood. A planetary transmission connected with shaft drive and steering was by wheel.

EVANSVILLE 1907–1909
Evansville Automobile Co, Evansville, Ind.

This make was available with either 20hp or 30/35hp 4-cylinder engines. A 3-speed selective transmission drove the rear wheels through double roller chains.

EVERITT 1909–1912
Metzger Motor Car Co, Detroit, Mich.

This company was founded by Everitt and Metzger who had previously launched the Flanders and the E.M.F. The last model of the Everitt was a 6-cylinder, 38hp five-passenger car. This had a self-starting device, and sold for $1,850. In 1912 there was also a model with a 25.6hp 4-cylinder Continental engine.

EVERYBODY'S 1907–1909
Everybody's Motor Car Mfg Co, St Louis, Ill.; Alton, Ill.

This was a light runabout powered by an air-cooled flat-twin 10hp engine. The price was $400.

EXCALIBUR J 1952–1953
Beassie Engineering Co, Milwaukee, Wis.

This sports car used a modified Henry J chassis and engine (although one prototype used an Alfa Romeo '1900') with an aluminum body designed by Brooks Stevens. Three prototypes were to be raced during the 1953 season to see if it was worth going into production, but apparently it was not. The intended price was $2,000.

EXCALIBUR SS 1964 to date
SS Automobiles, Inc, Milwaukee, Wis.

This handsome car designed by Brooks Stevens superficially resembles the 1930 Mercedes-Benz SSK but uses modern components. The SS has a 350hp Chevrolet Corvette engine (originally a Studebaker engine with optional supercharger) and is available in two- or four-passenger form. SS Automobiles, Inc, also distribute the Brooks Stevens designed, Italian-built, Excalibur 35X, a Bugatti-styled replica.

EXCEL 1914
Excel Distributing Co, Detroit, Mich.

At 1,000lb this two-passenger cyclecar was heavier than most of its kind. It had a 91.5ci water-cooled engine of four cylinders. The drive was by friction transmission and belts.

1912 EVERITT 38hp touring car. *The Veteran Car Club of Great Britain*

F

FAGEOL 1916–1917
Fageol Motors Co, Oakland, Calif.

The few passenger cars produced by this well-known bus and truck company were among the largest and most expensive ever built in America. An enormous 6-cylinder, 825ci Hall-Scott engine of 5in × 7in bore and stroke giving 125hp at 1,300rpm, powered these cars, which had wheelbases measuring up to 145in. Closed and open models were available. Prices were from $9,500 for a chassis to $17,000 complete.

F.A.L. 1909–1913
1 Fal Motor Co, Chicago, Ill. 1909–1913
2 Fal Auto Co, Chicago, Ill. 1913

With a 4-cylinder, L-head engine of 281ci, this medium-sized car was available in three body sizes: a two-passenger, 'toy' tonneau and a seven-passenger touring car. Selective transmission gave three forward speeds.

1917 FAGEOL touring car. *The Veteran Car Club of Great Britain*
1928 FALCON-KNIGHT 20hp Gray Ghost roadster. *Autocar*

FALCON (i) 1909
Falcon Engineering Co, Chicago, Ill.

This monster, with 156in wheelbase, was powered by a 6-cylinder engine of 90hp and 642ci displacement. The nine-passenger touring model was priced at $12,500. The Falcon had two reverse speeds in addition to three forward ones.

FALCON (ii) 1914
Falcon Cyclecar Co, Cleveland, Ohio

The Falcon was an attractive cyclecar with a typical air-cooled 2-cylinder engine rated at 10hp. The vehicle weighed only 325lb and its price was $385.

FALCON (iii) 1922
Halladay Motors Corp, Newark, Ohio

This Falcon was a small car produced by a company which had just discontinued a model bearing its own name of Halladay. Powered by a 4-cylinder engine developing 20bhp at 2,200rpm, the make was distinguished by high, rounded radiators and beautifully-appointed bodies by Healey & Co. Standard size cars with 4- and 6-cylinder engines were also listed.

FALCON-KNIGHT 1927–1928
Falcon Motor Corp, Detroit, Mich.

Although the Falcon-Knight was theoretically an independent car, it was placed on the market by John North Willys as a companion car to the smaller Whippet Six and the Willys-Knight 70. Powered by a 6-cylinder Knight sleeve-valve engine, the car had a 109½in wheelbase and was equipped with artillery wheels, although wire wheels were used in the Gray Ghost roadster. A complete line of closed and open models constituted the catalog, with prices from $995 for the coupé and brougham to $1,250 for the Gray Ghost roadster. The Falcon-Knight was officially taken over by the Willys-Overland Corporation late in 1928 and then discontinued.

FAMOUS 1908–1909
Famous Mfg Co, East Chicago, Ill.

The Famous had an air-cooled, overhead valve 2-cylinder opposed engine under the seat. The rear wheels were larger than the front ones. There were several two-passenger models ranging in price from $450 to $600.

FANNING 1902–1903
The F. J. Fanning Mfg Co, Chicago, Ill.

The Fanning had a 9hp 2-cylinder vertical engine under a short hood, and single chain drive. A two-passenger runabout was the standard body, but a four-passenger tonneau was also available.

FARMACK 1915–1916
Farmack Motor Car Co, Chicago, Ill.

The Farmack was available with a five-passenger touring body, or in two-passenger roadster form for $885. The engine was a Farmer 4-cylinder with overhead camshaft. The Farmack was superseded by the Drexel.

FARNER 1922–1923
Farner Motor Car Co, Streator, Ill.
A short-lived assembled car using a 6-cylinder Falls motor. Few were built.

FAUBER 1914
W. H. Fauber, New York, N.Y.
This two-passenger cyclecar was priced at $285. It was powered by a 2-cylinder, 8hp air-cooled engine, had a friction transmission and final drive by belts.

FAULKNER-BLANCHARD 1910
Faulkner-Blanchard Motor Car Co, Detroit, Mich.
This little-known make offered a five-passenger touring car for $2,500 in 1910. It was powered by a 6-cylinder engine of 33hp.

FAULTLESS 1914
The Faultless was one of the many ephemeral cyclecars, and not even the name of the manufacturer is known. It was a two-passenger car with staggered seats, on a wheelbase of 100½in. The 2-cylinder engine was air-cooled and drove through friction transmission.

FAWICK FLYER 1910 1912
Fawick Motor Car Co, Sioux Falls, S.Dak.
This make has been entered in many rosters as Fwick. This was built in five-passenger touring models with 4-cylinder 40hp Waukesha engines.

FEDELIA 1913–1914
J. H. Sizelan Co, East Cleveland, Ohio
A boat-tailed body distinguished this cyclecar which was driven by a 67ci De Luxe engine. It had a narrow track of 38in.

FEDERAL (i) 1901–c.1903
Federal Motor Vehicle Co, Brooklyn, N.Y.
The Federal was a typical light steam buggy with a 10hp 2-cylinder engine, tiller steering and single chain drive.

FEDERAL (ii) 1907
Federal Motor Car Co, Chicago, Ill.
This was a very crude-looking runabout with a 12hp 2-cycle engine, friction transmission and steering by wheel. No fenders were supplied with this vehicle. It may have become the Federal (iii).

FEDERAL (iii) 1907–1909
1 Federal Automobile Co, Chicago, Ill. 1907–1908
2 Rockford Automobile & Engine Co, Rockford, Ill. 1908–1909
The Federal was a typical motor buggy or high-wheeler of the period, designed for two passengers. Its engine was air-cooled and had two opposed cylinders giving 14hp. A friction transmission and belt drive were used.

FENTON *see* SIGNET

FERGUS (i) (GB/US) 1915–1922
1 J. B. Ferguson Ltd, Belfast 1915–1916
2 Fergus Motors of America, Newark, N.J. 1921–1922
3 O.D. Cars Ltd, Belfast 1921
The Fergus was a remarkably advanced concept that emanated from the works of J. B. Ferguson, bodybuilder and machine-tool maker of Belfast, in 1915. A 4-cylinder 159ci, single ohc engine was installed in a rigid boxed frame that had cantilever springs at each corner; the modern combination of an efficient engine in a stiff frame with soft suspension. Furthermore, the engine was rubber-mounted, the earliest recorded instance of this anti-vibration practice. There was an engine-driven tire inflator and fully automatic chassis lubrication to ease maintenance, and the standard of workmanship was very high. The designer was J. A.

McKee. World War 1 prevented Ferguson from putting his car into production in Ireland, so its manufacture was transferred to the U.S. However, wartime restrictions caught up with it there as well, and the Fergus appeared not in 1917, as planned, but in 1921. By then it had acquired the additional refinements of six cylinders (a modified Northway engine was used) and front wheel brakes, but it was too expensive for a fairly small car. Just one was made in Ireland in 1921. Its new name was to be O.D., for owner-driver, stressing its ease of maintenance, but this third attempt to sell it also came to nothing.

FERGUS (ii) 1949
Fergus Motors, Inc, New York, N.Y.
The same company who developed the Fergus (i) built a prototype sports car using Austin A40 components and an all-enveloping body rather like that of the English Austin A40 sports. The Fergus did not go into production.

1909 FEDERAL (iii) 14hp buggy. *The Veteran Car Club of Great Britain*
1921 FERGUS (i) 6-cylinder sedan. *Autocar*

FERRER-VW-GT 1966 to date
Ferrer Motor Corp, Miami, Fla.

Built of fibreglass and reinforced steel, the Ferrer is a smartly styled sports car on the Volkswagen chassis. There is a choice of a more powerful engine of 70hp and the body is also available in kit form.

FERRIS 1920–1922
Ohio Motor Vehicle Co, Cleveland, Ohio

The Ferris was an assembled car of high quality which used a Continental 6-cylinder engine and other standard components. The makers placed great emphasis on perfection of coachwork. Disk wheels were standard, and open and closed models were available. A high, rounded radiator was a distinguishing factor of this expensive car. Less than 1,000 were produced.

FIAT 1910–1918
Fiat Motor Co, Poughkeepsie, N.Y.

This was an independent concern, formed with American capital to manufacture Fiat cars under license. It handled only the bigger models

1908 FIRESTONE-COLUMBUS motor buggy. *Antique Automobile*

1915 FIAT Light 30 roadster. *Michael Sedgwick*

1966 FITCH PHOENIX sports car. *Autocar*

of the '50' series with 4-cylinder L-head monobloc engines, shaft drive, multi-plate clutches and 4-speed transmissions, starting in 1910 with the 360ci Tipo 54. In 1914 came the big 556ci Tipo 55 and later in the year the Light 30, which was in fact the short-chassis 207ci Tipo 53, which cost $3,750 with full electrical equipment. Peculiar to America was the 348ci Tipo 56, a 4-cylinder machine on similar lines, but with all brakes on the rear wheels. It sold for $4,650. From 1914 onwards the later pear-shaped radiator was generally found on American Fiats. In 1917 a one-model policy was pursued with an improved Tipo 55, the E-17 on a 140in wheelbase. One of the last American cars to have right-hand drive, it sold for $5,500. Production ceased in March 1918, when the factory was sold to Rochester-Duesenberg for airplane-engine manufacture.

FINA-SPORT 1953–1955
Perry Fina, New York, N.Y.

The Fina-Sport was a convertible with bodywork by Vignale, built on a modified Ford chassis with a Cadillac engine and Hydramatic transmission.

FINCH LIMITED *see* PUNGS-FINCH

FIRESTONE-COLUMBUS 1907–1915
Columbus Buggy Co, Columbus, Ohio

The Firestone-Columbus made in 1907 and 1908 was a high-wheeled

buggy. For the years 1909–1911, a 'Mechanical Greyhound' roadster was built as well as a five-passenger touring car. The two-passenger roadster had a 26hp engine and a 106in wheelbase. Some closed models were offered in 1913 and 1914.

FISCHER 1914
G. J. Fischer Co, Detroit, Mich.

This was a light car rather than a cyclecar, as it had standard track and a 104in wheelbase. It was built in two- and four-passenger versions, including a sedan, powered by Perkins 4-cylinder, water-cooled engines of 97.6ci. It had a selective transmission and shaft drive. The two-passenger cost $525, the sedan $845.

FITCH PHOENIX 1966
John Fitch and Co, Inc, Falls Village, Conn.

The Phoenix, with an Italian-built body, was Fitch's first fully original sports car after some years of marketing Corvair modifications. Appointments included spare tires in enclosed mountings, fog lights and reclining leather seats. A Chevrolet Corvair engine tuned to 170hp provided power.

FLAGLER 1914–1915
Flagler Cyclecar Co, Sheboygan, Wis.

The Flagler was one of the few cyclecars with a positive (geared) transmission, and shaft drive, rather than a chain or belt. It was powered by a

4-cycle water-cooled 4-cylinder engine. The weight of this car was 900lb and its price $450: a very low cost-to-weight ratio, even for a cyclecar.

FLANDERS (i) 1909–1912
Everitt-Metzger-Flanders Co, Detroit, Mich.

The Flanders 20 was a light car which was marketed by Studebaker and remained virtually unchanged throughout its life. It used a 4-cylinder engine of 155ci. In 1909, a 2-speed transmission was employed, but this was changed to one with three forward speeds for the succeeding models. Two-passenger and five-passenger open models were offered as well as a two-passenger closed coupé. The E.M.F. was a companion make.

FLANDERS (ii) 1912–1915
1 Flanders Mfg Co, Pontiac, Mich. 1912–1913
2 Tiffany Electric Co, Detroit, Mich. 1913–1914
3 Flanders Electric Co, Pontiac, Mich. 1914–1915

The Flanders Electric was a typical electric car made in open and closed form, with rather attractive flowing lines. From October 1913 to March 1914 only, the car was known as the Tiffany.

engine had 4-cylinders with 149ci displacement and overhead valves. Along with this was a 3-speed transmission and shaft drive. Such a car was displayed at the 1905 Denver auto show, but further information is lacking.

FLYER 1913–1914
Flyer Motor Car Co, Mt Clemens, Mich.

The Flyer had a monobloc 4-cylinder water-cooled engine with selective transmission. It should be classed as a small car as it had standard tread and a 100in wheelbase.

FORD 1903 to date
Ford Motor Co, Detroit, Mich.

Henry Ford built his first experimental car in a workshop behind his home in Bagley Avenue, Detroit, in 1896. It had a twin-cylinder engine with chain-cum-belt drive, and attained 20 mph. A second car was made and tested in 1898. In 1899 he left his employment with Edison to help organize the Detroit Automobile Co. He was replaced there by H. M. Leland, and his third experimental machine had certain similarities with

1925 FLINT (ii) 24/40hp touring car. *Montagu Motor Museum*

1906 FORD Model K roadster. *The Veteran Car Club of Great Britain*

FLINT (i) 1902–1904
Flint Automobile Co, Flint, Mich.

The Flint was a light two-passenger runabout with a rear-mounted single-cylinder engine and no fenders. It was designed by A. B. C. Hardy, who was later general manager of Marquette (i) and then Chevrolet. It is sometimes erroneously called the Hardy after the designer.

FLINT (ii) 1923–1927
Locomobile Co of America, Long Island City, N.Y.; Flint, Mich.; Bridgeport, Conn.

Fitted with a 7-bearing crankshaft and a steel tube for added reinforcement, the Flint occupied an important niche in William C. Durant's car empire. With its 6-cylinder Continental engine and a price of less than $2,000 for the closed models, it was popular in its class and as many as 3,000 were sold in a year. Lockheed hydraulic 4-wheel brakes came with the 1925 model, and during the company's last two years there were two sixes of 196ci and 268ci, as well as the 171ci Junior, a compact six with rear wheel brakes only.

FLINTRIDGE *see* DARRIN

FLINT-LOMAX 1905
Flint-Lomax Electric & Mfg Co, Denver, Colo.

This was a light five-passenger touring car with side entrance. Its 14hp

Leland's Cadillac, notably the basic layout, wheel steering, and planetary transmission. The first production Ford, the Model A of 1903, had a flat-twin underfloor-mounted engine, central chain drive, and rear-entrance tonneau bodywork, and sold for $850, or $100 more than the Cadillac. 1,708 were sold in the first season, and from the outset Ford elected to fight both Seldon's alleged master patent and the Association of Licensed Automobile Manufacturers set up by those makers who were willing to recognize the patent's validity. Ford and the other rebels were not finally vindicated until 1911. During these early years Ford built a number of experimental racing machines, of which the most famous was the 999, a vast 4-cylinder affair without clutch or gears, in which Henry himself recorded 91.4mph on the frozen Lake St Clair in 1904. That year the company offered Model C, a development of the original A with the now-mandatory dummy hood, and the first of their fours, Model B at $2,000. Both these models had the 2-speed planetary transmission, and this was applied in 1905 to a 430ci six, the Model K, selling at $2,500. The transmission proved the big car's Achilles' heel, and no more 6-cylinder cars were marketed until 1941. In 1906 Ford undercut Oldsmobile with the 4-cylinder Model N runabout at $500, and this led logically to the immortal Model T announced for the 1909 season.

The Tin Lizzie put the world on wheels during its 18-year production run; for its day it was very advanced, with a 177ci monobloc L-head 4-cylinder engine, detachable head, a top speed of 40–45mph, and a fuel consumption of 25–30mpg. Original list price was $850, but this was

c. 1913 FORD Model T touring car. Coachwork by Sanders of Hitchin.
Bernard Sanders

1929 FORD Model A roadster. *Ford Motor Co*

1937 FORD V-8 De Luxe sedan. *Ford Motor Co*

1948 FORD V-8 Super De Luxe sedan. *Ford Motor Co*

progressively cut until a roadster could be bought for as little as $260 in 1925. The car retained Ford's pedal-controlled transmission with two forward speeds, and some American states were, as a result, to issue two categories of driving license — one for ordinary cars, and others for planetary types, i.e. the Ford. More than 15 million were made between October 1908, and May 1927. It formed the basis for a farm tractor (1916) and a one-ton truck (1917), and in 1919 41 per cent of all motor vehicles registered in Great Britain were Fords. Production figures soared: more than 100,000 were made in 1913, the 300,000 mark was passed in 1914, and more than half a million left the works in 1916. The first 'million year' was 1922, and the Model T reached its production peak a year later, with more than two million cars delivered. A British factory was opened in Manchester in 1911, and subsequently French and German plants were to produce their own individual species of Ford. Black was the only color offered from 1914 to 1925, and a painted black radiator shell replaced the original brass type in 1917; 4-wheel brakes were never available, but electric starters were, from 1920, though it was possible to buy an open car with hand starting only and magneto-driven headlights as late as 1925.

With the demise of the Model T in 1927, the factory was idle for six months pending the changeover to the Model A, which turned out to be a conventional 200ci 4-cylinder L-head machine with 3-speed sliding-type transmission, 4-wheel brakes, and pleasing lines inspired by the Lincoln (iv) which had been under Ford control since 1922. The price was $450, and four-and-a-half million were sold in four seasons despite the Depression, Ford outselling Chevrolet two-to-one in the peak year, 1930. The Model A was also sold in station-wagon versions from 1929, the first large-scale production of a style of body that is now a *sine qua non* in an American manufacturer's range. In 1932 Ford again broke new ground with a mass-produced 221ci V-8 offering 70bhp for $460. It used the 4-cylinder chassis, and as in roadster form it weighed only one ton, the performance was exciting and sometimes lethal. A revised four, the Model B, was made for a short while, but was dropped once V-8 production got into its stride. Inherited from both the T and the A was the all-round transverse-leaf suspension of the B and all V-8s up to 1948. The V-8's first million year was 1935. The Rumanians Zamfirescu and Cristea won the 1936 Monte Carlo Rally for Ford, a success repeated by the Dutchman Bakker Schut in 1938. A smaller companion V-8, the 136ci Model 60, came out for 1937, but it was not a great success, and disappeared after 1940. V-8s acquired hydraulic brakes in 1939, and column shift in 1940, and a companion 226ci six was listed in 1941.

After World War 2, the 1942 Fords were continued for three seasons with little change, but the 1949 line, though it used the same power units, was entirely new, with a longer and lower silhouette, and coil-spring independent front suspension. Automatic transmission became available during 1950, and in 1952 a 'square' 218ci ohv six was introduced. Two years later the old L-head V-8 at long last gave way to a new 130bhp ohv engine in the modern idiom, and another unusual departure was the sporting two-passenger Thunderbird, described by its makers as a 'personal car'. Engine options were 292 or 312ci, the latter giving a speed of 113mph, but by 1958 it had grown up into a bulky five-passenger convertible with unitary construction. Fords were further restyled in 1955, and from 1957 to 1959 there was a fully-convertible hardtop, the Skyliner. In 1958 the most powerful V-8 engines extracted 300bhp from 308ci. The 50 millionth Ford was delivered in 1959, and along with G.M. and Chrysler the company had a compact ready for the 1960 season, in the shape of the ohv 6-cylinder 144ci Falcon. A step toward the semi-compact was achieved in 1962, when the big Fairlane models were listed with two modest-sized engines, a 170ci six and a short-cycle eight of 221ci, the exact displacement of the original 1932 V-8.

Since 1962 there has been an increasing emphasis on competition; the big Galaxies with 427ci engines finally ousted the Jaguars from their domination of British sedan racing, and the adoption of the V-8 engine by A.C. Cars Ltd for their Cobra model brought Ford back into the sports car field as well. A team of Falcon Sprints was entered in the 1963 Monte Carlo Rally and dominated the big-car class. 1964 brought the Mustang, a compact semi-GT with close-coupled four-passenger body-

1955 FORD Thunderbird sports car. *Ford Motor Co*
1967 FORD Mustang 2 × 2 fastback coupé. *Ford Motor Co*

work, sold for $2,480 with a 289ci V-8 engine giving a top speed of over 110mph; a cheaper model used a 120bhp six. This car achieved a sensational success, with half a million sold in less than eighteen months. By 1971 the Mustang was available with seven engine options from a 250ci six to a 429ci V-8 with ram air induction. The compact Maverick, introduced in mid-1969, was joined in the fall of 1970 by the sub-compact Pinto, a 2-door sedan with choice of 97.6ci 4-cylinder engine built by Ford of Britain or 122ci overhead cam engine built by Ford of Germany. Other cars in the comprehensive Ford line-up for 1971 included the intermediate Torino in fourteen models, the full-sized Ford in eleven models, and the Thunderbird personal luxury car in three models.

1971 FORD Pinto sedan. *Ford Motor Co*

FOREST 1905–1906
Forest Motor Car Co, Boston, Mass.

The Forest five-passenger tourer was powered by a 20hp flat-twin engine, and had a wheelbase of 86in.

FORSTER (CDN) 1920–1922
Forster Motor Mfg Co, Montreal

The Forster was a distinguished-looking Canadian assembled car with a streamlined body showing British influence, and Herschell-Spillman 6-cylinder engine. All Forsters were produced with right hand drive.

FORT PITT 1908–1909
Fort Pitt Mfg Co, New Kensington, Pa.

The Fort Pitt had a 6-cylinder, 559ci engine of 70hp. Three body models were available on a standard chassis with a 121in wheelbase. The cars were shaft-driven. After 1909 the cars were known as Pittsburghs.

FOSTER 1900–1905
1 Foster Automobile Co, Rochester, N.Y. 1900–1903
2 Artzberger Automobile Co, Allegheny, Pa. 1903–1905

These steamers, of which there were three models, operated with boiler pressure of 250psi. The rear axle was chain-driven and the frame was of the 'reach' type. The manufacturer proudly claimed the 'best performance' in several endurance runs against internal combustion engines, but they also offered a short-lived gasoline car from the Rochester factory in 1903.

FOSTLER 1904–1905
Chicago Motorcycle Co, Chicago, Ill.

This was a flimsy two-passenger car with a single-cylinder water-cooled engine with radiator in the rear. Chain drive was used to the rear wheels, which were on a dead axle consisting of two lengths of angle-iron.

FOSTORIA 1916–1917
Fostoria Light Car Co, Fostoria, Ohio

The Fostoria, a light four-passenger car was powered by a Sterling ohv 4-cylinder engine of 127ci. It weighed 1,910lb and cost $675.

FOURNIER *see* SEARCHMONT

FOX 1921–1923
Fox Motor Co, Philadelphia, Pa.

The luxurious Fox provided the Franklin with its only serious competition among American air-cooled cars. It was bigger, both in dimensions and engine (249ci against 199ci), lower-built and better-looking. Like the Franklin, the Fox had overhead valves, but they were actuated by an overhead camshaft and there were aluminum pistons. With its 50bhp, this was the more efficient engine, making the Fox the faster car. Speed, combined with a comparative freedom from overheating, gave the Fox a certain vogue among bootleggers. The method of cooling was similar to that of the Franklin: six separately-cast cylinders cooled by a fan super charger.

1922 FOX sedan. *Kenneth Stauffer*

FRANKLIN 1901–1934

1 H. H. Franklin Mfg Co, Syracuse, N.Y. 1901–1917
2 Franklin Automobile Co, Syracuse, N.Y. 1917–1934

Probably the world's most successful air-cooled car before the advent of the Volkswagen, the Franklin inspired an intense make-loyalty. H. H. Franklin had founded a factory for the manufacture of die castings in 1895, and in 1901 he was introduced to John Wilkinson's air-cooled designs by Messrs Brown and Lipe, later well-known as manufacturers of proprietary transmissions. The New York Motor Co had already made three prototypes before the first Franklins went on sale in 1902. These featured transversely-mounted 108ci 4-cylinder air-cooled engines — the valves were overhead, with mechanically operated inlet valves from 1905 — float-feed carburetors, 2-speed planetary transmission, full-elliptic suspension and the wooden frames which became standard on Franklins to the end of 1927. A push-on handbrake was used until 1906. A version with water-jacketed engine was projected, but the company remained faithful to air-cooling until they closed down. Sales rose from 13 in 1902 to 184 in 1903, when wire wheels gave way to the wood artillery type, and in 1904 a Franklin broke the San Francisco–New York record. The transverse-engined cars were catalogued until the end of 1906, but from 1905 onwards new models with conventionally-located engines made their appearance. These had auxiliary exhaust valves, shaft drive, 3-speed sliding-type transmissions and round hoods modelled on the Delaunay-Belleville. A 4-cylinder sold for $1,800, but there was also a 6-cylinder Model H with a 7-bearing crankshaft and a 114in wheelbase for $4,000: all subsequent 6-cylinder Franklins had seven main bearings. A straight-8 appeared without success in the 1905 Vanderbilt Cup Eliminating Trials. Franklin's full-elliptic suspension was continued. This gave an excellent ride and resulted in tire mileages in the region of 20,000: this is why the company was refusing to fit detachable rims as standard equipment as late as 1922! In 1907 an automatic spark advance-and-retard was fitted and in 1908 a gear-driven fan. The 1910 cars used a suction-driven sirocco fan incorporated in the flywheel. Smallest of the 1909 range was the 18hp Model G, a 108ci 4-cylinder car with quadrant shift sold at $1,850. Selective shift was used on the bigger fours and sixes which had oversquare cylinder dimensions and cost $2,800 and $3,750 respectively. With the 1912 models came a Renault-type hood and full pressure lubrication, and a 4-cylinder was still available at $2,000, or $1,500 less than the big 38.4hp 6-cylinder.

In 1914 only a 6-cylinder car, the '6-30', was offered, and Franklin fell into line with the rest of the American industry by going over to left-hand drive, central shift and full electrical equipment. A year later aluminum

1905 FRANKLIN 12hp runabout. *Henry Ford Museum, Dearborn, Mich.*

1928 FRANKLIN 26hp sedan. Formerly owned by Col Charles Lindbergh. *Henry Ford Museum, Dearborn, Mich.*

pistons were adopted. A stunt drive from Walla Walla, Washington, to San Francisco in bottom gear demonstrated the car's ability to keep cool. The 1917 models had electric chokes, while imitators arose in the industry to try and cash in on Franklin's success with air-cooling. One of these firms, Holmes, was headed by a former vice-president of the Franklin Automobile Co. By the end of World War 1 a 6-cylinder Franklin could be bought for $2,050, reduced two years later to $2,000. 8,648 cars were sold in 1920. Late in 1922, came a redesigned car with a 'horse-collar' hood allegedly modelled on the Fiat, pressure air-cooling with frontal supercharger, unit transmission, single dry-plate clutch, 6-volt instead of 12-volt electric system and detachable rims. Sales rose to 11,000 and the company which had pioneered series-production closed cars as early as 1913 was offering a sedan at $2,850. During 1925 the design was face-lifted once again and the De Causse-styled Series 11 introduced. Cylinder displacement remained a modest 199ci, but appearance was entirely changed with a 119in wheelbase and a vertical-barred 'radiator'. This revolutionary step so appalled John Wilkinson that he resigned from the company forthwith! Some of the semi-custom body styles — especially the boat-tailed sports coupé at $3,150 — were remarkably attractive. Subsequently some excellent and expensive custom bodywork was designed for Franklin by such firms as Derham, Willoughby, Holbrook, and (especially) Dietrich. Over 13,000 Series 11s were sold between mid-1925 and the end of 1926, among those who favored Franklins being Colonel Charles Lindbergh. Yet even the '11B' of 1927 retained the wooden frame, full-elliptic suspension and foot transmission brake. Front-wheel brakes did not arrive until the introduction of the 1928 236ci Airman, which boasted internal-expanding Lockheed hydraulics at a time when the contracting type were generally favored in America. In 1928 long-chassis models were given steel frames, standardized in 1929, and a standard sedan sold for £885 in England. All but the cheapest Franklins now had silent 2nd gears. This was the period in which Dietrich introduced their delightful speedster (actually a 4-door convertible sedan) and a 274ci 6-cylinder Franklin engine actually took to the air in a Waco biplane. Prices were generally in the $2,200–$3,500 range, with custom models running up to $7,200.

The 1930 Series 14 introduced a new radiator and side-blast cooling, and the elegant Pirate models had concealed running-boards as well. The unconventional, however, could no longer sell in America, and only 2,851 Franklins were delivered in 1931. In 1932 came synchromesh, free wheeling and 'Startix' devices, as well as a magnificent Dietrich-styled 415ci supercharged V-12 (Series 17) on a 144in wheelbase. Unfortunately this was re-engineered to incorporate proprietary axles and semi-elliptic suspension, and in production form it weighed nearer three tons than the two tons of the prototype. It combined elegance, 95mph, and 150bhp for $4,400, but few were sold, though a drastic price cut to $2,885 was made for 1933.

The last new Franklin was the Olympic, an inexpensive 6-cylinder using a Franklin engine wedded to a Reo chassis and body. The factory closed down in 1934. The patents were, however, taken over by the Air-Cooled Motors Corps (now Franklin Engine Co), whose Syracuse factory has specialized in light horizontally-opposed aircraft engines: a 6-cylinder Franklin helicopter engine, converted to water cooling, drove the Tucker of 1947. Two-, 4-, and 6-cylinder engines of up to 348ci displacement were being produced in 1966.

FRANTZ 1901–1902
The Reverend H. A. Frantz, Cherryville, Pa.

In 1900 an announcement appeared in the English motoring press that 'The Revd H. A. Frantz of Cherryville, Pa. believes he has received a call to the motor trade, and will henceforth make gasoline cars in place of sermons.' No details of the cars were given, and shortly afterwards a further notice said 'the Revd H. A. Frantz, who retired from the ministry to build automobiles, has resumed his former calling, an intimation the significance of which depends entirely upon your point of view.'

FRAYER-MILLER 1904–1910
Oscar-Lear Automobile Co, Springfield, Ohio; Columbus, Ohio

This make featured air-cooling, via a rotary supercharger which forced

1908 FRAYER-MILLER touring car. *Kenneth Stauffer*

air through aluminum jackets surrounding the cylinders. In other respects, including appearance, the cars were conventional, with side valves in a T-head, cone clutch, 3-speed sliding-type gear, and bevel drive. Front suspension was by transverse leaf spring. A 24hp 4-cylinder sold for $2,500 in 1905, and the following year it was joined by a 398ci six. Three 110hp 4-cylinder cars with oversquare engines and left-hand drive were entered for the 1906 American Vanderbilt Cup Eliminating Trials, but only Lawwell's car was chosen to compete in the event and it retired during the race.

FRAZER 1946–1951
Kaiser-Frazer Corp, Willow Run, Mich.

The Frazer was the Kaiser's more expensive running mate — the original list price was $2,152, as against $1,967 — and unlike the Kaiser it was never intended to have front-wheel drive. The specification was straightforward: box-section frame, coil-spring independent front suspension, 3-speed synchromesh transmission, a 226ci L-head 6-cylinder Continental engine, and Howard Darrin's slab-sided styling; it was distinguishable only from the cheaper cars by its rather better appointments. Up to 1949, evolution paralleled the Kaiser line, with a 4-door convertible listed in that year, but when Kaiser-Frazer's cars were redesigned for 1951 the Frazer received less drastic attention, retaining its slab sides and the old type of chassis. A dual-purpose Vagabond model was offered, but there were no Frazers in the 1952 production, their prestige Manhattan model, at $2,094 each, being assigned to Kaiser for the rest of the company's effective life.

FREDERICKSON 1914
Frederickson Patents Co, Chicago, Ill.

This was a two-passenger (tandem) cyclecar with an air-cooled 2-cylinder engine. It had friction transmission, weighed 650lb and cost $375.

FREDONIA 1902–1904
Fredonia Mfg Co, Youngstown, Ohio

The Fredonia was built in two- and five-passenger versions. It used a

1949 FRAZER Manhattan 4-door convertible. *Kaiser-Jeep Corporation*

1904 FREDONIA 9hp tonneau. *Keith Marvin Collection*

single-cylinder engine of a hybrid type. An annular chamber was used to pre-compress the fuel mixture before introduction to the cylinder, an arrangement which dispensed with valves. The final drive was by a single chain.

FREMONT 1921–1922
Fremont Motors Corp, Fremont, Ohio

The Fremont was a typical assembled car powered by a 6-cylinder Falls engine. The bodywork was attractive, with separate step plates and no running-board.

FRIEDMAN 1900–1903
Friedman Automobile Co, Chicago, Ill.

The Friedman was a runabout powered by a 2-cylinder engine under the seat. It had single chain drive, tiller steering, and cost $750. There was also a Friedman steamer, but it was probably not a production car.

FRIEND 1920–1921
Friend Motors Corp, Pontiac, Mich.

The Friend was built in limited numbers. It was equipped with artillery wooden wheels and its own make of 4-cylinder engine. The price of the five-passenger touring car was $1,285.

FRITCHLE 1904–1917
Fritchle Auto & Battery Co, Denver, Colo.

The Fritchle company achieved some renown in 1908 when they challenged other makers of electric cars to a race from Lincoln, Nebraska, to New York. No one took up the challenge, so the Fritchle made the journey alone, completing the 1,800 miles in 28 days. It was helped by lightweight batteries which gave it a range of over 100 miles per charge, a very high figure then, or now. Encouraged by this sporting success, Fritchle included a two-passenger roadster in their range for subsequent years, in addition to the usual coupés and broughams with prices up to $3,600. In 1916 Fritchle announced a gasoline-electric car on the lines of the Woods Dual Power, with a 4-cylinder air-cooled engine. They sold very few of them, and the following year abandoned car production.

FRONT DRIVE 1906
Automobile Front Drive Mfg Co, St Louis, Mo.

This car was powered by a 16hp Streite engine driving by chain to the front axle. It had a crude-looking four-passenger body, and solid tires. The company invited inquiries for financing manufacture, but apparently the car did not go into production.

FRONTENAC (i) 1906–1913
Abendroth & Root Mfg Co, Newburgh, N.Y.

This car was built in several body types from a two-passenger roadster

1915 F.R.P. 4-cylinder touring car. Non-standard radiator. *Keith Marvin Collection*

1910 FULLER (ii) 2-cylinder motor buggy. *Montagu Motor Museum*

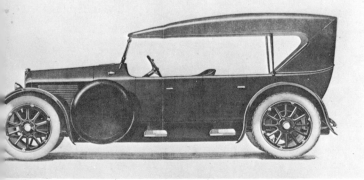

1922 FREMONT Six touring car. *Keith Marvin Collection*

to a seven-passenger limousine. Chassis were large, none having less than a 120in wheelbase. All models had selective transmission and shaft drive. The runabouts were of particularly racy design.

FRONTENAC (ii) 1922
Frontenac Motor Corp, Indianapolis, Ind.

This was an advanced touring car designed by Louis Chevrolet, who had built racing cars called Frontenac, and C. W. van Ranst. It was backed by Stutz officials, and was sometimes called the Stutz-Frontenac. The engine was a 197ci single-ohc 4-cylinder unit with thermo-syphon cooling, unusual on an American high-performance car at this date. Because of financial troubles, production never started.

FRONTENAC (iii) (CDN) 1931–1933
Dominion Motors Ltd, Toronto, Ont.

Several thousand of these were produced as the last corporate gasp of the firm which had been the Canadian builder of American Star and

Durant cars. The Frontenac, a well-made car, was to some extent an outgrowth of the last Durants and also the U.S. De Vaux. It used Continental engines and other purchased components. Bodies, however, were produced in Canada by the Canadian Top & Body concern, and were largely of all-steel construction. Frontenac prices ranged from $1,200 to $1,500. There was limited production of a De Luxe model called the Ace, with a somewhat longer hood.

FRONTENAC (iv) (CDN) 1959–1960
Ford Motor Co of Canada Ltd, Oakville, Ont.

This was identical to the Falcon except for its special grill and trim. The Frontenac was sold only in Canada to widen Mercury-Lincoln agents' coverage of the market.

FRONTMOBILE 1917–1918
1 Bateman Mfg Co, Grenlock, N.J.
2 Safety Motor Co, Camden, N.J.

As the name implies, this roadster had front-wheel drive. The transmission was placed between the 4-cylinder engine and the front axle, necessitating a complex mechanism for shifting the gears. It was accomplished by the use of two straight-line levers. Transverse springs were used and the frame dropped abruptly behind the engine to give a very low center of gravity.

F.R.P. 1914–1918
The Finley-Robertson-Porter Co, Port Jefferson, Long Island, N.Y.

Finley Robertson Porter, designer of the T-head Mercer, constructed a handful of the revolutionary F.R.P. cars which featured a 170bhp engine and a chassis priced from $5,000. A V-shaped radiator distinguished the car, and bodies were custom built by well-known coach-builders.

F-S 1911–1912
F-S Motors Co, Milwaukee, Wis.

This car, by the makers of the Petrel, was offered with three different chassis, powered by 4-cylinder Beaver engines of 22hp, 30hp and 40hp respectively. Friction transmission and double-chain drive were used.

FULLER (i) 1908
Angus Automobile Co, Angus, Neb.

This company built conventional touring cars in three models, two with 4-cylinder engines of 22/26hp and 35/40hp, and a 60hp six. The make has sometimes been listed as the Angus.

FULLER (ii) 1909–1910
Fuller Buggy Co, Jackson, Mich.

The Fuller company offered high-wheelers as well as models of normal design. The high-wheeler had double-chain drive, while the others had shaft drive. The standard models used 4-cylinder water-cooled engines of 30hp. Full-elliptical springs were used on all Fuller cars.

FULTON 1908
Connecticut Motor Works, New Haven, Conn.

The Fulton was a light car using a 10/12hp 2-cylinder air-cooled engine, which used a combination flywheel and fan. Had it appeared a few years later it would have been called a cyclecar, and might have proved more successful, but in fact it never went into production.

F.W.D. see BADGER (1)

G

GADABOUT 1915

Gadabout Motor Corp, Newark, N.J.

The Gadabout was a two-passenger cyclecar with a water-cooled 4-cylinder engine. An unusual feature was its wickerwork body. This was claimed to excel in riding comfort, but it cannot have been very durable.

GAETH 1902–1911

Gaeth Motor Car Co, Cleveland, Ohio

Paul Gaeth was a bicycle maker who added stationary engines to his business, and made an experimental steam car in 1898. His gasoline cars were unusual in using a large 3-cylinder horizontal engine of 25/30hp. Although the car had a dummy hood, the engine was mounted under the front seat, from where it drove by a planetary transmission and chain

final drive. This car, known as the Gaeth Triplex, was made until about 1908, when a conventional car with a front-mounted vertical 4-cylinder engine was introduced. At $3,500 it was nearly $1,000 more expensive than the Triplex, and it did not sell well. In 1911 Gaeth's company was absorbed by Stuyvesant.

GALE 1904–1910

Western Tool Works, Galesburg, Ill.

The Gale car began as a light runabout with an 8hp single-cylinder horizontal engine mounted under the seat, planetary transmission and shaft drive. In 1905 a 16hp 2-cylinder model was added. Both these cars had bodies which were hinged at the rear, so that the whole body could be lifted up when the engine needed attention. This was the best-known

1915 GADABOUT Model G 10hp cyclecar. *The Veteran Car Club of Great Britain*

1910 GAETH 30hp touring car. *Automobile Manufacturers' Association*

1904 GALE 8hp runabout. *Herbert de Garis*

1930 GARDNER roadster. *Kenneth Stauffer*

feature of Gale cars. In 1907 a 26hp 4-cylinder car was added to the range; in this car the engine was mounted vertically under a hood.

GALLOWAY 1908–1910; 1915–1917
The William Galloway Co, Waterloo, Iowa

This famous wagon-building firm made a number of vehicles which could do double duty, as load carriers on weekdays, and as passenger cars at weekends. They had 2-cylinder engines mounted under the seat, solid tires and chain drive. In 1915 Galloway advertised a 4-cylinder light car which was made for them by the Argo Motor Co of Jackson, Mich., and seems identical with Argo's own light roadster. In 1917 this car was sold by Galloway under the name Arabian.

GALT (CDN) 1911–1915
Canadian Motors Ltd, Galt, Ont.

Equipped with Hazard engines and other U.S. parts, the Galt was available in touring and roadster styles as well as a light truck. The 1911 30hp model was well received and found about 50 buyers. It was sold outside the Galt area as the Canada Tourist and the Canada Roadster, and a life-time guarantee was offered. The 1912 Galt had an electric starter which gave so much trouble that it cut sales to the point of bankruptcy. All remaining parts were sold to the Galt Motor Company which in 1915 turned out a gas-electric roadster. This car used a tiny gasoline engine to charge batteries, which powered the car through an electric motor. It ran well but sales were poor.

GARDNER 1919–1931
Gardner Motor Co Inc, St Louis, Mo.

Russell E. Gardner made the horse-drawn Banner Buggy before turning to motorcars in 1916. At first his works was the local assembly plant for Chevrolets and also made bodies for them. Then, in 1919, the first Gardner car appeared. It was an assembled, but well-made machine with a 4-cylinder, 192ci, L-head engine specially built for it by Lycoming, who supplied all the Gardner power units. The four was replaced by a 209ci six and a 276ci straight-8 for 1924. From 1926 to 1929, only eights were offered. The largest came into the luxury category, with a price of $2,295. So far the Gardner had run true to American form, except for its 'tailor-made' engines, but the new six of 1929 not only lost cylinders when other makers were adding them — its hydraulic brakes were internal expanding, a great rarity at the time in America. The make went out in a spectacular fashion, with the exceptionally low-hung front-wheel-drive six exhibited at the New York Show of 1930.

GAREAU 35 (CDN) 1909–1910
Montreal, Que.

This well-built car featured a 4-cylinder engine of its own design and bodies built by a local carriage maker. Only three cars, all touring, were built but they performed well. Inability to raise enough capital caused the firm to close down.

GARFORD 1906–1912; 1916
Garford Mfg Co, Elyria, Ohio

The Garford was a large car made originally in 4-cylinder 40hp form, replaced later by a 6-cylinder engine of 447ci displacement. Some of the later models had a single headlight mounted in the top of the radiator, as on the Briscoe. As well as their own cars, Garford made chassis for Studebaker from 1904 to 1911, when they were acquired by Willys-Overland. They were also well-known makers of trucks. From 1913 to 1915 they built Willys-Knight cars, but, for 1916 they again offered a range of cars under their own name.

GARY 1916–1917
Gary Automobile Mfg Co, Gary, Ind.

This company made a short-lived car with a 34hp 6-cylinder engine. It was made in roadster and touring car form, and cost $2,300.

GAS-AU-LEC 1905–1906
1 Vaughn Machine Co, Peabody, Mass.
2 Corwin Mfg Co, Peabody, Mass.

This was a gasoline-electric vehicle with a 4-cylinder engine of over 470ci displacement. The engine had electromagnetically operated valves whose timing could be varied by the operator. The electric generator was directly connected to the engine. Storage batteries were used for reserve and for very slow speeds. This was called 'The Simple Car'.

GASLIGHT 1960–c.1961
Gaslight Motors Corp, Detroit, Mich.

One of several attempts to offer a replica veteran car, this time based on the 1902 Rambler. Built on a 77in wheelbase and weighing 640lb, the Gaslight was powered by a modern air-cooled, single-cylinder engine of 4hp. At $1,495 it can have had little appeal to the true enthusiast.

GASMOBILE 1900–1902
Automobile Company of America, Marion, N.J.

This company began manufacture of cars and tricycles in 1899, under the name Automobile Voiturette, but the name Gasmobile was not applied until 1900. The cars originally had rear-mounted 3-cylinder horizontal engines, and chain drive. By 1902 two lines of design were being followed: the horizontal rear-engined models made in 9 and 12hp form, and a front vertical-engined car with 20hp 4-cylinder engine which was said to be a close copy of the Panhard. There was also listed a 35hp horizontally-opposed six, but whether this was actually made is uncertain.

1908 GARFORD 40hp touring car. *Automotive History Collection, Detroit Public Library*

1955 GAYLORD (ii) 'Gentleman' V-8 coupé. Designer Brooks Stevens at the wheel. *Lucien Loreille Collection*

GATTS 1905
Alfred P. Gatts, Brown County, Ohio

Only five examples of this car were built, one of which is extant in an Indiana collection. These were powered by a single-cylinder air-cooled engine with integral flywheel and fan. Starting was by a crank in the rear of the body.

GAYLORD (i) 1910–1913
Gaylord Motor Car Co, Gaylord, Mich.

The Gaylord was one of several makes of this era which was convertible from a four-passenger car to a utility vehicle, with rear space for packages. Four-cylinder ohv engines of 20, 30, 35, and 40hp were used, the latter in 1912–13 only.

GAYLORD (ii) 1955–1956
Gaylord Cars Ltd, Chicago, Ill.

A two-passenger coupé, the Gaylord 'Gentleman' used a Chrysler engine and sold for $10,000. The German-built Spohn body was designed by Brooks Stevens. A Cadillac-engined car at $17,500 was listed for 1956.

GEARLESS (i) 1907–1909
1 Gearless Transmission Co, Rochester, N.Y. 1907–1908
2 Gearless Motor Car Co, Rochester, N.Y. 1908–1909

The 1907 Gearless cars had large engines of 50hp (2-cycle) 60 and 75hp (4-cycle), friction transmission and double chain drive. In 1909 came the Gearless 35, a much cheaper car selling at $1,500 compared with the $3,500 to $4,000 of the larger cars. Also in the 1909 range was the Olympic 35, which used a similar engine to the Gearless 35 but had a conventional transmission.

GEARLESS (ii) 1921–1923
Gearless Motor Corp, Pittsburgh, Pa.

The Gearless, produced as a roadster and touring car at $2,650 and $2,550 respectively, had two separate 2-cylinder double-acting side-valve steam engines for power, and was available with either wood or wire wheels. The company failed when four of its officials were charged with mail frauds and conspiring to sell more than $1,000,000-worth of company stock fraudulently.

G.E.C. 1898; 1902
1 General Electric Co, West Lynn, Mass. 1898
2 General Electric Co, Schenectady, N.Y. 1902

The only cars to be made by the vast General Electric Company were both experimental. The earlier was an electric carriage, while the later model was a gasoline-electric car with a 4-cylinder engine. The Philadelphia-built General Electric car had no connection with G.E.C.

GEM 1917–1919
Gem Motor Car Co, Jackson, Mich.; Grand Rapids, Mich.

The Gem was a light, assembled car using a 4-cylinder G.B. & S. engine. Only two models were made, a touring car, selling at $845, and a light delivery truck.

GENERAL see HANSEN

GENERAL ELECTRIC 1898–1899
General Electric Automobile Co, Philadelphia, Pa.

These cars had no connection with the famous G.E.C., but were a product of the Brill Company, makers of trolleys and electrical equipment. The cars were light runabouts with especially light batteries which permitted a long range per charge.

GENESEE 1912
Genesee Motor Co, Batavia, N.Y.

This extremely large car, with a wheelbase of 148in, was driven by a 6-cylinder engine of 564ci displacement. Tire size was 43 × 5. It featured electric lights, compressed-air starter, two spare tires, clock, rear-view mirror and a gradometer. The eight-passenger torpedo touring model cost $8,000 and a limousine was listed at $10,000.

GENEVA (i) 1901–1904
Geneva Automobile & Mfg Co, Geneva, Ohio

This was a 2-cylinder steamer with its engine connected directly to the differential. The smaller of the two models produced was tiller-operated, while the larger one was steered by wheel. It is sometimes stated that Genevas were also built with internal-combustion engines.

GENEVA (ii) 1916–1917
Schoeneck Co, Chicago, Ill.

This was a large car with a wheelbase of 139in. It used a 415ci 6-cylinder engine by Herschell-Spillman. The two-passenger speedster had a sporty appearance, with vents on top of the hood and cycle-type fenders, with two spare tires mounted flat on the tail of the body. There may be a connection with the elusive Owen Schoeneck car of 1915–1916.

GENIE 1962 to date
British Motor Car Importers, San Francisco, Calif.

Rear-engined Formula Junior cars, with multi-tubular space frames designed by J. Huffaker, were the initial product of this firm. Later, sports-racing cars were assembled, using various American engines.

GERMAN-AMERICAN 1902
German-American Automobile Co, New York, N.Y.

This company announced a 24hp 4-cylinder car which, it was said, 'closely followed the general lines of the Daimler (i.e. Mercedes), but incorporated some novel features to make the car more suitable for American roads'. Probably it followed Mercedes lines too closely, for little was heard of it after the announcement.

GERONIMO 1917–1920
Geronimo Motor Co, Enid, Okla.

Named after the famous Red Indian chief, the Geronimo began its existence as a 4-cylinder assembled car, but changed its power plant to

1901 GENEVA (i) 2-cylinder steam car. *Henry Ford Museum, Dearborn, Mich.*

a 6-cylinder Lycoming engine in 1918. Less than 1,000 were built, and only open models were available.

GHENT 1917–1918
Ghent Motor Co, Ottawa, Ill.

This was an assembled car without distinguishing features, on a 125in wheelbase. The Model 6-60 was a five-seater with a 187ci 6-cylinder engine.

GIBSON 1899
C. D. P. Gibson, Jersey City, N.J.

The Gibson was powered by a horizontal 2-cylinder engine designed to run on carbonic acid gas, which was stored in batteries at a pressure of 6,000psi. It was said to develop 12bhp at 500rpm, and to have a maximum speed of 60mph, which would have almost gained it the Land Speed Record in 1899! There were plans to form a syndicate to manufacture it, but they came to nothing.

GILLETTE see AMPLEX

GILSON (CDN) 1921
Gilson Mfg Co, Guelf, Ont.

The Gilson company were makers of horse-drawn vehicles, stationary engines and agricultural tractors. They built at least three small 4-cylinder touring cars, but serious production never started.

G.J.G. 1909–1911
G.J.G. Motor Car Co, White Plains, N.Y.

The various models of the G.J.G. had imaginative names such as Scout, Pirate, Comfort and Carryall. With 4-cylinder, 354ci engines and 3-speed selective transmissions, it was claimed these cars could attain 65mph. G.J.G. hoods had a peculiar 'cupola' running the full length. The designer was G. J. Grossman.

GLASSIC 1966–1968
Glassic Industries, Inc, West Palm Beach, Fla.

Styled in the manner of the Ford Model A, this fiberglass-bodied phaeton was built on the International Scout chassis, which contained an IHC 93.4hp 4-cylinder engine. A 3-speed transmission and 3.73 rear axle were standard equipment. The Glassic's cruising speed was given as 70mph and its top speed as 90mph.

GLEASON 1909–1914
Kansas City Vehicle Co, Kansas City, Mo.

The Gleason, which succeeded the Kansas City, was a high-wheeler, although later models used pneumatic tires. Two-cylinder, water-cooled engines were used, and final drive was by shaft.

GLEN (CDN) 1921
Scarboro Beach, Ont.

The Glen was an odd-looking 3-cylinder cyclecar that resembled a scaled-down American Essex with a kennel-shaped hood and a Rolls-Royce style of radiator. The engine was air-cooled. Passengers sat side by side in the plywood body. Production was limited.

GLIDE 1903–1920
The Bartholomew Co, Peoria, Ill.

Also known as the Bartholomew, the first Glide had an 8hp single-cylinder engine mounted horizontally under the seat, and single chain drive. Similar to the early Cadillac in appearance, it was made until 1907, by which time it had been joined by a 14hp 2-cylinder horizontal model, and a 30hp 4-cylinder vertical model with shaft drive. The latter had a Rutenber engine, and this make was used in all 4- and 6-cylinder Glides until the end of production. Touring and roadster bodies were available,

including a four-passenger roadster on a short wheelbase. From 1915 to the end of production, Glide used a 40hp 6-cylinder Rutenber engine, and was a conventional design.

GLOBE 1921–1922
Globe Motors Co, Cleveland, Ohio

The Globe was a conventional assembled car powered by an 18.2hp 4-cylinder Supreme engine, and using a Warren 3-speed transmission. Body styles were a five-passenger touring car or two-passenger roadster.

GLOVER (GB/US) 1920–1921
Glovers Motors Ltd, Leeds, Yorks.

Like the Alsace, Amco and others, the Glover was an American-assembled car intended for export to England. In this case the design also was English; it had a 15.7hp 4-cylinder engine, 3-speed transmission and a two-passenger body with a rumble seat. The radiator was of Rolls-Royce pattern, and the car was intended to sell at £550 ($2,720).

GOLDEN GATE 1894–1895
A. Schilling & Sons, San Francisco, Calif.

This company was well-known for its Golden Gate gas engines. In 1894 a 3-wheeled, two-passenger car with 2hp engine was sold to a customer in Santa Maria. This was probably the first gasoline car built for sale in California.

GOODSPEED 1922
Commonwealth Motors Co, Chicago, Ill.

The Goodspeed was an abortive attempt to market a luxury car under the direction of Commonwealth Motors' personnel after production of the Commonwealth had ceased. Two of the aluminium-bodied sports phaetons carrying the Goodspeed name were built, with plans for subsequent production. The two $5,400 open cars, however, constituted the entire Goodspeed output. They were shown at both the New York and Chicago Shows.

GOVE 1921
Gove Motor Truck Co, Detroit, Mich.

Gove trucks were built from 1920 to 1922, and during this period the company built a few prototypes of a small 4-cylinder car with an air-cooled engine.

GRAHAM-FOX see COMPOUND

GRAHAM MOTORETTE 1902–1903
Charles Scfrin & Co, Brooklyn, N.Y.

This auto had a single-cylinder, 3hp air-cooled engine with a friction transmission. It was a two-passenger car with tiller steering. Final drive was by a single chain. Price was $475, with $50 extra for a top.

GRAHAM-PAIGE ; GRAHAM 1927–1941
Graham-Paige Motors Corp, Detroit, Mich.

The Graham brothers, Joseph, Robert and Ray, acquired the old Paige concern in 1927. Their Graham-Paiges were conventional machines noted for their internal-expanding hydraulic front-wheel brakes and 4-speed 'twin-top' transmissions, and 78,000 were sold in their first year of production. The range embraced three sixes and two eights, the biggest of these being the '835' with a 137in wheelbase and a 322ci engine. One of these straight-8 Graham-Paiges won the last race ever held on Britain's Brooklands Motor Course in August 1939. The name of the make was simplified to Graham for the 1931 season, though design underwent little alteration until the arrival of the 1932 Blue Streaks, headed by a 245ci eight which introduced skirted front fenders to the American market and was immortalized in the 'Tootsie Toys' found in many a nursery of the 1930s. For 1934 8-cylinder cars were available with a centrifugal super-

1929 GRAHAM-PAIGE Model 621 tourer. *Montagu Motor Museum*
1938 GRAHAM supercharged sedan. *Autocar*

1914 GRANT 12hp roadster. *Montagu Motor Museum*

charger rotating at 5¾ times the engine speed, which gave them a top speed of 95mph. After 1935 only sixes were made, the 218ci Cavalier being listed in 80bhp unsupercharged and 112bhp supercharged versions, both with aluminum cylinder heads — this chassis formed the basis of the Anglo-American Lammas. Despite an attempt to compete in the lowest-priced field with the 170ci Crusader at $595, Graham achieved little beyond three successive outright wins in the Gilmore-Yosemite Economy Run, though these small sixes were copied by Nissan of Japan. An ugly concave nose and enclosed rear wheels characterized the 1938 and 1939 Grahams, which were 218ci cars available with or without superchargers. The company's final fling was the 1940 Hollywood, which made use of the body dies from Cord's 810/812 series. Like Hupmobile's very similar Skylark, this was not a commercial success, and after World War 2 Graham-Paige joined forces with Henry J. Kaiser to build the Kaiser and Frazer cars: the latter were named after Graham-Paige's President Joseph A. Frazer.

GRAMM (CDN) 1913
Gramm Motor Truck Co, Walkerville, Ont.

Mainly known as a truck builder, Gramm made a few cyclecars with 2-cylinder air-cooled engines, tandem seating and belt drive.

GRANT 1913–1922
Grant Motor Car Corp, Findlay, Ohio

The first Grant was a 12hp 4-cylinder light car made in two-passenger form, and sold in England as the Whiting-Grant, by Whiting Ltd of Euston Rd, London. In 1915 the Grant company changed their policy and introduced a 44bhp 6-cylinder touring car. A 1917 model of this could be converted from touring car to sedan by the addition of a 'winter top'. In 1920 a smaller six was introduced, of 20hp.

GRAVES & CONGDON *see* CROWN (ii)

GRAY (i) 1920
Gray Light Car Corp, Longmont, and Denver, Colo.

This concern with a splendid-sounding title in fact only built two cars, both of them cyclecars of what sounds like a particularly spidery kind. One was powered by a single-cylinder motor-cycle engine and the other by a twin, both made by Harley-Davidson. Motor-cycle wheels were fitted.

GRAY (ii) 1922–1926
Gray Motor Corp, Detroit, Mich.

During the 1920s, two new makes, Star and Gray, tried to win a share of the mass market dominated by the Ford Model T. The Gray was in fact made by former employees of Ford, who included the head of the Gray Corporation, F. L. Klingensmith, and was similar to the Ford in several features of engine and chassis. An L-head, 4-cylinder, 161ci engine was used. Unlike the Ford, the Gray's springing was by conventional quarter-elliptics at front and rear. Front-wheel brakes were offered in 1926, but that year was its last. The company's grandiose plans, which included making nearly a quarter of a million cars in the first full year of production, at $490 for the touring car and $760 for the coach, were never fully realized.

GRAY-DORT (CDN) 1915–1925
Gray-Dort Motors Ltd, Chatham, Ont.

The Gray-Dort was undoubtedly one of the most successful and popular cars built by a Canadian company. Production was about 26,000 units, and at one time the company outsold the much-cheaper Chevrolet in Ontario. The Gray-Dort was based on the American Dort car, and the Canadian company only went out of business after the American firm closed down. The U.S. Dort never matched the success that the Gray-Dort achieved in Canada.

The Canadian firm originated in a carriage and sleigh-making concern, Wm. Gray-Sons-Campbell Ltd of Chatham. The 1915 Gray-Dorts were

1922 GRAY-DORT 19.6 hp touring car. *Hugh Durnford*
1909 GREAT WESTERN 40hp roadster. *Keith Marvin Collection*

almost all American-built cars with such items as emblems and hub caps changed, or were assembled in Chatham from American-made parts. Real production began in 1916 with Canadian-made components. While the cars were similar to the American Dorts, the Canadian company did produce several de luxe sports models including a 1922 Special which was claimed to have the industry's first automatic back-up light as standard equipment. A previous sports car, the 1918 Special, was so well received that 200 of them were exported to the U.S. The 4-cylinder Lycoming engine proved well-suited to the harsh Canadian climate and Gray-Dort kept it in production right until the end, although it was dropped in America shortly after introduction of the six in 1923. Gray-Dort prices were in the medium range, but generally increased over the years. The 1917 touring car cost $885 while closed cars in the 1920s were about $2,000. The company also imported the American Gray car for a very short time in the 1920s and continued selling 1924 Gray-Dorts into 1925 while winding up operations.

GREAT EAGLE 1910–1918
U.S. Carriage Co, Columbus, Ohio
These were big cars, mostly seven-passenger machines, with large wheels, and 4- or 6-cylinder engines. The wheelbase on several models was greater than 132in.

GREAT SMITH *see* SMITH

GREAT SOUTHERN 1910–1914
Great Southern Automobile Co, Birmingham, Ala.
The Great Southern was made as a five-passenger touring car or two-passenger roadster. These were available with either 30hp or 50hp 4-cylinder engines. The 50hp models had engines of 515ci.

GREAT WESTERN 1908–1916
1 Model Automobile Co, Peru, Ind. 1908–1909
2 Great Western Automobile Co, Peru, Ind. 1909–1916
This make started out with a seven-passenger touring car with a 50hp engine, and a smaller touring car with a 2-cylinder engine. In 1910 a 4-cylinder 40hp engine in a standard chassis of 114in wheelbase was adopted. As many as five models of this Great Western Forty were available. The Great Western had an elaborate radiator insignia, with a winged 'W'.

GREELEY 1903
E. N. Miller, Greeley, Colo.
This was an unlikely location for the building of two-passenger cars with 4-cylinder engines, planetary transmission and chain drive. The weight of this vehicle was put at 1,345lb, for which the cost was $1,150.

GREENLEAF 1902
Greenleaf Cycle Co, Lansing, Mich.
The Greenleaf was a light surrey powered by a 2-cylinder horizontal engine developing 10hp at 700rpm.

GREGORY (i) 1918–1922
Front Drive Motor Co, Kansas City, Mo.
Ben F. Gregory built about 10 cars, all using fwd. Some were touring cars, including one exhibited at the 1921 Kansas City Auto Show. He also built a few racing cars. His own demonstration racing car was powered first by a Curtis OX-5 and later by a Hispano-Suiza airplane engine. Some of Gregory's ideas were used by Harry Miller in his fwd racing cars. After World War 2 Gregory returned to auto manufacture with the Gregory (ii).

GREGORY (ii) 1949; 1952
Ben Gregory, Kansas City, Mo.
Ben Gregory exhibited a sedan in 1949 with a 40hp 4-cylinder Continental engine mounted in the rear, driving the front wheels. In 1952 he constructed a front-wheel-drive Porsche-engined sports car but neither of these prototypes entered production, and Gregory went on instead to success in designing military vehicles.

GREMLIN *see* AMERICAN MOTORS

GREUTER *see* HOLYOKE

GREYHOUND 1914–1915
Greyhound Cyclecar Co, Toledo, Ohio
This was a two-passenger (tandem) cyclecar with driving controls in the rear seat. It had a sliding-gear transmission, shaft drive and electric starting. It was succeeded by the States.

GRIFFITH-TVR ; GRIFFITH 1964–1968
1 Griffith Motors, Syosset, Long Island, N.Y. 1964–1965
2 Griffith Motors, Plainview, Long Island, N.Y. 1965–1968

The Griffith was originally a British TVR sports coupé with a Ford Fairlane 271hp engine. It sold well on its reputation for smart acceleration until the supply of bodies ceased with the failure of Grantura Engineering in 1965. The company moved to a large factory, redesigned the car completely and had the bodies built in Italy. Chrysler was to supply V-8 engines for the new model. Production plans were continuing in 1967 and the 1968 model was known as the Omega.

GRINNELL 1912–1913
Grinnell Electric Car Co, Detroit, Mich.

The Grinnell electric was claimed to travel 90 miles per battery charge. The five-passenger closed coupé was on a wheelbase of 96in and cost $2,800. This succeeded the Phipps-Grinnell.

GRISWOLD 1907
Griswold Motor Car Co, Detroit, Mich.

This car was designed by the well-known J. P. La Vigne. It offered three different chassis, all with 2-cylinder water-cooled engines. These were of 10hp, 15hp and 20hp. The longest chassis had a wheelbase of 110in. The track was an unusual 55in.

GROUT 1899–1912
1 Grout Bros, Orange, Mass. 1899–1903
2 Grout Bros Automobile Co, Orange, Mass. 1903–1908
3 Grout Automobile Co, Orange, Mass. 1909–1912

The Grout company began manufacture with a typical light steam buggy with a 2-cylinder 4hp engine and single chain drive. An unusual model was the New Home Coupé, a completely enclosed coupé on a very short wheelbase, which looked like a mobile sentry box. From about 1903 the steamers began to look more like ordinary cars, although the hood was circular and had a single headlight mounted in the center, locomotive style. One model continued the locomotive appearance with an enormous cow catcher to act as a bumper.

The last steamer, a 12hp 2-cylinder model, appeared in 1905, and a year earier the company had introduced a gasoline-engined car with a 30hp 4-cylinder engine and shaft drive. Few of these were made as the company was often in financial difficulties from 1905 onwards.

GURLEY 1901
T. W. Gurley, Meyersdale, Pa.

The Gurley was a typical two-passenger motor buggy using a gasoline engine, and a tubular reach frame. Bicycle-type wire wheels and tiller steering completed this undistinguished vehicle.

GUY (CDN) 1911
Mathew Guy Carriage and Automobile Co, Oshawa, Ont.

1901 GROUT 4hp steam runabout. *G. N. Georgano Collection*

A 30hp touring car and a 1-ton truck were the basis of this carriage company's venture into car manufacture, but only a few were built.

GUY VAUGHAN 1910–1913
Vaughan Car Co, Kingston, N.Y.

This make was also known as the Vaughan and was apparently confined to five-passenger touring models, powered by 280ci 4-cylinder engines. A 3-speed selective transmission was used. The 1913 Vaughan Model 5 cost $2,500.

GYROSCOPE 1908–1909
1 Blomstrom Mfg Co, Detroit, Mich. 1908
2 Lion Motor Car Co, Adrian, Mich. 1909

The Gyroscope was so named because of the horizontal, opposed 2-cylinder engine, which, with its horizontal flywheel, was claimed to increase stability and prevent skidding. Many other cars of this period had similar engines, but made no such claims. The 16hp engine connected with a friction transmission and shaft drive. Three body styles were marketed.

H

HAASE 1904
Northwestern Automobile Co, Milwaukee, Wis.
  The two models of the Haase were tiller-steered, with 2-cylinder engines of 6 or 8hp. An optimistic 40mph was claimed for the more powerful model, which weighed 1,400lb. Speed control was accomplished by the lifting of the inlet valves.

HACKETT 1916–1919
Hackett Motor Car Co, Jackson, Mich.
  The Hackett was an assembled car using a 4-cylinder G.B. & S. engine and was the successor to the earlier Argo. The catalog for 1916 to 1918 listed both a touring car and a closed model; 1919 Hacketts were available only as touring cars and roadsters. Following a reorganization, operations were transferred to Grand Rapids, Mich., where the car was continued as the Lorraine (ii).

H.A.L. 1916–1918
1 H. A. Lozier Co, Cleveland, Ohio 1916
2 H.A.L. Motor Car Co, Cleveland, Ohio 1916–1918
  These were the initials of H. A. Lozier who had previously built the Lozier car. The H.A.L. was one of several makes which introduced the 12-cylinder, valve-in-head Weidely engine in 1916. This 389ci power unit developed 87hp. Two-, four- and seven-passenger models were built, as well as a limousine. The seven-passenger weighed 3,550lb and was priced at $2,600; the limousine cost $4,500.

HALL (i) 1904
Hall Motor Vehicle Co, Dover, N.J.
  This was a four-passenger rear-entrance tonneau with a 2-cylinder, 20hp engine, in the rear of the chassis. The weight was 2,400lb and the price $3,000.

HALL (ii) 1914–1915
1 Hall Cyclecar Mfg Co, Waco, Tex. 1914
2 Hall Motor Car Co, Waco, Tex. 1915
  This two-passenger tandem cyclecar had a rear section which could be removed to make a light delivery truck. Its underslung frame allowed a very low center of gravity. A 95ci 4-cylinder engine furnished 18hp. It had a 2-speed Fuller transmission with shaft drive, and with wire wheels it cost $395.

HALLADAY (i) 1907–1916
1 Streator Motor Car Co, Streator, Ill. 1907–1913
2 Barley Mfg Co, Streator, Ill. 1913–1916
  The first model of the Halladay was a five-passenger touring car with a 4-cylinder 35/40hp engine of 336ci. In later years, models were made with 4-cylinder engines of 30, 40 or 50hp, in three different chassis sizes. In 1916, 6-cylinder Rutenber engines were used, and prices of the various models offered ranged from $1,085 to $2,285.

HALLADAY (ii) 1918–1922
Halladay Motors Corp, Warren and Newark, Ohio.
  The Halladay was an assembled car equipped with a Rutenber 6-cylinder engine. Probably less than 500 units were turned out in the five years of production, during which both open and closed models were listed. Halladay Motors remained on the list of automobile manufacturers as builders of the small Falcon car throughout 1922.

HALVERSON 1908
A. Halverson, New York, N.Y.
  This juvenile auto used a 4-cylinder FN engine which was air-cooled. Wheelbase was a diminutive 46in with tread of only 26in. Total weight was given as 223lb.

HAMILTON 1909
Columbia Carriage Co
  The Hamilton was a high-wheeler with a 16hp air-cooled opposed 2-cylinder engine. A planetary transmission was used and the 34in wheels were fitted with solid rubber tires.

HAMLIN-HOLMES; HAMLIN 1919–1930
1 Hamlin-Holmes Motor Co, Chicago, Ill.
2 Hamlin Motor Co, Harvey, Ill.
  The Hamlin-Holmes prototype, which initiated a grandiose scheme to manufacture front-wheel-drive cars, was produced in 1919 in a touring model which was powered by a Lycoming 4-cylinder engine. It looked rather like a Model T Ford. Thereafter, pilot models appeared annually in various styles and using various engines, all of them for test purposes. In 1923, Hamlin-Holmes advertised a touring car as a production car, but production failed to materialize. A racing car was entered in the 1926 Indianapolis event, and 1930 a Hamlin (the Holmes name had been dropped) was advertised. The car had two axle systems allowing all weight to be carried on a dead axle. An exceptionally low centre of gravity was the selling-point of the Hamlin; it was achieved by placing the axles very low. The prototype of the Hamlin Front-Drive car was a 4-door club sedan. The radiator was slanted and hood louvres were horizontal; in appearance, it closely resembled the Gardner Front-Drive prototype of the same year. The concern failed before subsequent models could be manufactured.

1908 HALLADAY (i) 35/40hp roadster. *The Veteran Car Club of Great Britain*

HAMMER 1905–1906
Hammer Motor Co, Detroit, Mich.

This was a light car which in 1905 used a 2-cylinder engine of 12hp. In 1906, a 24hp 4-cylinder engine was used to power an 1,800lb five-passenger tonneau. There was a choice of planetary or sliding-gear transmission and final drive was by shaft. The Hammer Motor Co was formed from part of the Hammer-Sommer Auto Carriage Co, which became defunct in 1905.

HAMMER-SOMMER 1902–1904
Hammer-Sommer Auto Carriage Co Ltd, Detroit, Mich.

This car was made only in a five-passenger, detachable tonneau model. The opposed 2-cylinder engine, mounted beneath the body, developed 12hp and a planetary transmission was used. The car was claimed to reach 35mph. This company split up and manufactured Hammer and Sommer cars separately.

HANDLEY-KNIGHT; HANDLEY 1921–1923
Handley Motors, Inc, Kalamazoo, Mich.

This make was first known as the Handley-Knight and it used the sleeve-valve 4-cylinder Knight engine from its inception until early 1923. Thereafter, the Models 6/60 and 6/40 used Midwest and Falls 6-cylinder engines exclusively. The 6/60 used a conventional radiator whereas its smaller counterpart, the 6/40, was built with a V-type. On both models, small handle attachments, or loops encircled the upper sections of the headlights and helped enthusiasts to recognize the make — 'If it carries handles, it's a Handley' (as a matter of fact, the Reo of this period had the same novel loops). Checker Cab bought up the Handley interests in May 1923.

HANOVER 1921–1924
Hanover Motor Car Co, Hanover, Pa.

The Hanover cyclecar was unusual in that its promoters intended it primarily for export, which was a sensible idea in view of the unpopularity of the type on its home ground. This helped it to be more successful than other American cyclecars: 800 were made, of which many were exported to Japan. The engine was a 2-cylinder, air-cooled unit.

HANSEN 1902
Hansen Automobile Co, Cleveland, Ohio

The Hansen was a light runabout with a fenderless two-passenger body, and a rear-mounted single-cylinder engine. For 1903 the same design was continued by the General Automobile Co, who called the car the General.

HANSEN-WHITMAN 1907
Hansen Auto & Machine Works, Pasadena, Calif.

It is claimed that ten of these were built as five-passenger touring cars. They used a 2-cylinder, 2-cycle water-cooled engine. The drive was through a friction transmission and chains to the rear wheels. An unusual feature was the wicker seat backs.

HANSON 1917–1923
Hanson Motor Co, Atlanta, Ga.

One of the few cars built in Georgia, the Hanson was an assembled vehicle which used Continental 6-cylinder engines in both its Model 50 and larger Model 66 forms. Several hundred Hansons were produced in both open and closed models and sales, unlike many other cars built in the Southern United States, were not confined to the immediate area of manufacture.

HARDING (i) (CDN) 1911
Harding Machine Co, London, Ont.

This two-passenger runabout used a 20hp 4-cylinder G.B. and S. engine. It was also offered with a torpedo body, and was based on the American Hupmobile.

HARDING (ii) 1916–1917
Harding Motor Car Co, Cleveland, Ohio

The Harding Twelve was made only as a seven-passenger touring car. It was one of the earliest 12-cylinder cars on the American market. The engine, of 713ci displacement, was constructed from two 6-cylinder engine blocks which were mounted on a common crankshaft.

HARPER 1907–1908
Harper Buggy Co, Columbus City, Ind.

This car was a small two-passenger runabout, but not a high-wheeler. It was driven by a water-cooled 2-cylinder opposed engine of 14hp. A planetary transmission was used.

HARRIS 1923
Wisconsin Automotive Corp, Menasha, Wis.

A 6-cylinder assembled car, of which very few were produced.

HARRISON 1905–1907
1 Harrison Wagon Co, Grand Rapids, Mich. 1905–1906
2 Harrison Motor Car Co, Grand Rapids, Mich. 1907

The Harrison became a large car through several model changes and ended with a wheelbase of over 120in. The 1906 and 1907 models featured a self-starting system which introduced acetylene into the proper cylinder for starting 'on the spark'. These cars used a 4-cylinder engine of 354ci with overhead valves. Push-rods for the exhaust valves had a ring-shaped section so that they straddled the exhaust piping.

HARROUN 1917–1922
Harroun Motor Sales Corp, Wayne, Mich.

Named after the racing driver Ray Harroun, who distinguished himself in 1911 by winning the first Indianapolis 500 Sweepstakes, the Harroun was a low-priced car ($595) using its own make of 174ci 4-cylinder ohv engine. The only body styles available were open models.

HARTMAN 1914
George V. Hartman, Red Bluff, Iowa

George Hartman built a small number of two or four-passenger cars powered by 4-cylinder Model engines. Most were $3\frac{5}{8} \times 4\frac{3}{4}$in units, but one or two cars had $3\frac{1}{2} \times 5$in engines.

HARVARD 1915–1920
1 Pioneer Motor Car Co, Troy, N.Y.
2 Adirondack Motor Car Co, Hudson Falls, N.Y.
3 Harvard Motor Car Co, Hyattsville, Md.

The Harvard car, powered originally by a 4-cylinder Model engine, appeared only as an open two-passenger car. From 1917 to 1920 a Sterling engine was used.

All Harvards were made with right-hand drive, built for export to New Zealand. They featured a hidden compartment for the spare wheel at the bottom of the rear deck.

HASBROUCK 1899–1901
Hasbrouck Motor Co, Newark, N.J.

The Hasbrouck was a light car with a large single-cylinder engine mounted in the center of the chassis, driving through a 2-speed planetary transmission and chain final drive. The engine had two 18in flywheels.

HASSLER 1917
Hassler Motor Co, Indianapolis, Ind.

A small car of short life and limited production, the Hassler was available only as a two-passenger roadster at a price of $1,650. It was powered by a 4-cylinder Buda engine of $3\frac{3}{4}$in $\times 5\frac{1}{8}$in bore and stroke. Houk wire wheels were standard equipment. Front suspension was by two semi-elliptic springs clipped at mid-point. Rear suspension was by two semi-elliptic transverse springs with radius rods extending from the axle housing to the transmission.

HATFIELD (i) 1906–1908
Hatfield Motor Vehicle Co, Miamisburg, Ohio

This car was a high-wheeler also called the Buggyabout. It was designed for two passengers and had an air-cooled 4-cycle, 2-cylinder opposed engine. A friction transmission was used, with double chain drive. Steering was by wheel.

HATFIELD (ii) 1917–1924
Cortland Car & Carriage Co, Sydney, N.Y.

The Hatfield was a conventional car powered originally by a 4-cylinder G.B. and S. engine. An early example of station wagon body was offered on this chassis. Later Hatfields had 4- or 6-cylinder Herschell-Spillman engines. For the last year or two of production, the open two-passenger car and touring car were available with sports style bodies, the most noticeable features of which were wire wheels and individual step plates.

HAVERS 1908–1914
Havers Motor Car Co, Port Huron, Mich.

Most Havers cars were powered by 6-cylinder engines. They were conventional in design, except for their long chassis. During the last year of manufacture a 55hp engine was used, of 377ci displacement. In 1914 the Model 6-55 Speed Car for two passengers was priced at $2,250.

1915 HARVARD 14.4hp roadster. *Keith Marvin Collection*
1917 HATFIELD (ii) Suburban station wagon. *Keith Marvin Collection*

1912 HAYNES 25hp touring car. *Kenneth Stauffer*

HAWK 1914
Hawk Cyclecar Co, Detroit, Mich.

The Hawk was a belt-driven cyclecar with a 9/13hp V-twin engine. It was advertised at $390 and could seat two passengers side by side. Its only distinctive feature was a sloping hood line.

HAWKINS *see* XENIA

HAWLEY 1907
Hawley Automobile Co Ltd, Constantine, Mich.

The Hawley was made in two models: a two-passenger runabout on a 84in wheelbase, and a four-passenger tonneau on a 96in wheelbase. The same 2-cycle, 2-cylinder engine was used for both. A friction transmission and final chain drive was common to both models.

HAY BERG 1907–1908
Hay Berg Motor Car Co, Milwaukee, Wis.

The only model of the Hay Berg was a three-passenger roadster. It was powered by a 4-cycle, 4-cylinder water-cooled engine of 269ci displacement. This had a 3-speed transmission with shaft drive. The weight of this vehicle was 2,000lb.

HAYDOCK *see* COSMOPOLITAN

HAYNES (1894) 1904–1925
1 The Haynes-Apperson Co, Kokomo, Ind. 1898–1904
2 Haynes Automobile Co, Kokomo, Ind. 1905–1925

Elwood Haynes built his original single-cylinder car of buggy type in 1894. In 1898, with the Apperson brothers, he formed the Haynes-Apperson Automobile Co. In 1902, the Appersons and Haynes separated, although both companies remained in Kokomo. From June 1904 the cars were called either Haynes-Apperson or Haynes, while the company name was still Haynes-Apperson. This was officially changed to Haynes Automobile Company in September 1905.

The first production models of the Haynes (in 1904) were powered by 2- and 4-cylinder engines, sliding-gear transmissions and shaft drive. Only 4-cylinder engines were used in the years 1905–1913. In 1912, three chassis were built, with a total of eight body types. In 1914, Model 26 was fitted with a 6-cylinder engine, and in 1915 an electric gear shift was standard on the larger chassis. For 1916, Haynes advanced to a 12-cylinder engine of 356ci. This large engine was made by Haynes and continued to be manufactured through 1922, with no changes in bore or stroke. The chassis varied in wheelbase during the post-World War 1 period from 120 to 132in. The prices for the various models dropped from $4,200 for a seven-passenger limousine in 1920, to $2,300 in 1925 for a five-passenger sedan. Body styles in the Haynes range were conservative, although one close-coupled four-passenger coupé with distinctive lines was made in 1923, and a Special Speedster, a two-passenger roadster with wire wheels and attractive styling was introduced in 1921.

HAYNES-APPERSON 1898–1904
The Haynes-Apperson Co, Kokomo, Ind.

Although Elwood Haynes had built his first car in 1894, none was made for sale until he joined forces with the Apperson brothers. By the end of 1898 Haynes-Apperson cars were being made in two-, four-, and six-passenger models, all powered by a rear-mounted horizontally-opposed 2-cylinder engine of 190ci. The cars had three forward speeds, spur gear transmission, and tiller steering. For three years this design was made without great change, although the straight dash gave way to a sloping version. In November 1901 the Appersons left the firm to make cars under their own name, but the Haynes-Apperson name continued on the cars for nearly three years longer. By 1903 the left-hand tiller steering had been replaced by a wheel, but this was still mounted on the left side, an unusual feature at the time on American cars. On 1904 models

1923 HAYNES 31hp roadster. *Montagu Motor Museum*

1923 H.C.S. touring car. *Kenneth Stauffer*

the engine was moved to the front under a conventional hood, although it was still a horizontally-opposed twin. Prices ranged from $1,450 for a two-passenger runabout to $2,550 for a five-passenger tonneau. From June 1904 the cars began to be referred to as Haynes, and the 1905 cars with vertical 4-cylinder engines were always known under this name. The company name was not changed until September 1905.

H-B (H. BROTHERS) 1908
H. Brothers, Chicago, Ill.

This high-wheeler for two passengers was priced at $500, or at $400 with 'complete instructions for assembly'. It was of typical high-wheeler design with a 2-cylinder, air-cooled engine, 36in diameter wheels with solid rubber tires, planetary transmission and single chain drive.

H-C 1916
H-C Motor Car Co, Detroit, Mich.

This obscure make was marketed in roadster and touring versions at prices of $600 and $650 respectively. Both had a 4-cylinder, 28hp engine. Production was limited to a very few units.

H.C.S. 1920–1925
H.C.S. Motor Co, Indianapolis, Ind.

Harry C. Stutz sold his interest in the Stutz Motor Car Company of Indianapolis in 1919 and went on to make cars on his own account, in the same city. The H.C.S. was an expensive assembled machine (1921 price was $2,975), like its predecessor, but its engines were by Weidely — a 4-cylinder, 243ci, overhead-valve unit — or else sixes by Midwest. For a while, the H.C.S. sold reasonably well on the strength of its promoter's name, but the firm died making taxicabs. The H.C.S. cars raced at Indianapolis in 1923 were thinly disguised Millers.

HEINE-VELOX 1906–1909; 1921
1 Heine-Velox Motor Co, San Francisco, Calif. 1906–1909
2 Heine-Velox Engineering Co, San Francisco, Calif. 1921

The first Heine-Velox was a high-priced 45hp, 4-cylinder machine that was made for three years. After World War 1, Heine-Velox went into the ultra-luxury market, seeking absolute quality in all respects. Their 1921 offering had a V-12 engine, its chassis was furnished with hydraulically-operated 4-wheel brakes and the complete car was the most expensive in America at the time, costing $17,000. Very few were made.

HENDERSON 1912–1915
Henderson Motor Car Co, Indianapolis, Ind.

This car was built in open two-passenger and five-passenger forms, powered by an L-head, 4-cylinder engine of 281ci. Standard equipment included a Stutz transmission and McCue wire wheels. The roadster was priced at $1,300 and the five-passenger touring car at $1,400. The sons of the founder of this company were responsible for the famous Henderson motorcycle.

HENNEGIN 1908
Commercial Automobile Co, Chicago, Ill.

This was a high-wheeler with solid rubber tires and wheel steering, powered by a 4-cycle, air-cooled 2-cylinder engine. Two models were produced, one on a wheelbase of 75in, the other on one of 87in.

HENNEY 1921–1931
Henney Motor Car Co, Freeport, Ill.

An estimated 50 custom-built sports touring cars were made by this well-known manufacturer of funeral cars. A small number of closed sedans and limousines were also produced during the remainder of the decade, powered by Continental 6 or Lycoming 8 engines. In 1960 the Henney Company produced an electric conversion of the Renault Dauphine, known as the Henney Kilowatt. It had 36 2-volt batteries, a 7.2hp motor, and a range of 50 to 60 miles. Only experimental models were made.

1921 HEINE-VELOX V-12 touring car. *Harrah's Automobile Collection*
1951 HENRY J sedan. *Kaiser-Jeep Corporation*

HENRY 1910–1912
Henry Motor Car Co, Muskegon, Mich.

The first model of this car was a 35hp, five-passenger tonneau which sold for $1,750. For 1911, both 40 and 20hp engines were available, with a choice of five body styles. The 1911 two-passenger roadster had running-board mounted toolboxes.

HENRY J 1950–1954
Kaiser-Frazer Corp, Willow Run, Mich.

Named after its sponsor, this short-lived product of the Kaiser automobile empire was an ill-timed attempt at a 'compact'. It had the same 100in wheelbase as Nash's more successful Rambler, but it was an ugly little 2-door fastback sedan with *fleur-de-lys* grill, and a conventional Detroit specification. On the 1951 models, there was no external access to the trunk, and though preliminary announcements indicated the use of F-head engines, the production vehicles had L-head Willys units — either the 68bhp 134ci 4-cylinder as used in the Jeep, or a 161ci 6-cylinder developing 80bhp. The latter version sold for $1,566 at a time when Chevrolet prices started at $1,428, and it made little impression. In 1952 came the Vagabond, described as a 'sport car' — it had an exposed spare wheel at the rear, and no other deviations from standard specification, though a Henry J chassis was used for Brooks Stevens's experimental Excalibur J sports two-passenger announced that year. Henry J's were assembled in Mexico and Japan, and also built in Israel by Ilin of Haifa. After the Kaiser-Willys merger in the spring of 1953, the Henry J was

continued for one more season, and then dropped in favor of Willys's Aero range; even these cars were no longer marketed after 1955.

HERCULES (i) c.1907
James Macnaughton Co, Buffalo, N.Y.

The Hercules was an electric-powered car made in two- and four-passenger models. The enclosed Model 141 landaulet had a wheelbase of 75in. Drive to the rear wheels was by a single chain.

HERCULES (ii) 1914
Hercules Motor Car Co, New Albany, Ind.

This make succeeded the Crown (iii). It was a four-passenger car costing $495, or $550 with electric starting. It had a 4-cylinder L-head engine of 133ci, and a 2-speed selective transmission. The car was designed by R. W. Fishback who, it was claimed, had been the designer of at least one European make.

HERFF-BROOKS 1914–1916
Herff-Brooks Corp, Indianapolis, Ind.

The Herff-Brooks was a light car, with 4- or 6-cylinder L-head engines of 40 and 50hp respectively. The Six-50 roadster with 3-speed transmission cost $1,375.

HERMES 1920
Tsacomas Desmos, New York, N.Y.

This was a light 4-cylinder four-passenger car built by a Greek in New York and intended for export to Greece only. The radiator bore the name ΕΡΜΗΣ. At least two cars were made, but it is not certain whether either of them ever reached Greece.

HERRESHOFF 1909–1914
1 Herreshoff Motor Co, Detroit, Mich. 1909–1914
2 Herreshoff Light Car Co, Troy, N.Y. 1914

The Herreshoff began as a small car with a 24hp 4-cylinder engine, produced in three models. Later models used 4- and 6-cylinder engines up to 242ci. A 16hp light car was introduced in 1914.

HERSCHELL-SPILLMAN 1904–1907
Herschell-Spillman Co, North Tonawanda, N.Y.

An early model (1904) was a five-passenger tonneau. This was driven by a 4-cylinder engine of 16/18hp and final drive was by chain. The main activity of the manufacturer was engine building.

HERTEL 1895–1900
1 Max Hertel, Chicago, Ill.
2 Oakman Motor Vehicle Co, Philadelphia, Pa.; Greenfield, Mass

1914 HERRESHOFF 16hp roadster. *The Veteran Car Club of Great Britain*

1903 HOFFMAN (i) 8hp tonneau. *Kenneth Stauffer*

The first Hertel was a very light car with bicycle-type frame, and the front wheels carried in bicycle forks. It was powered by two 3½hp engines. The designer, Max Hertel, afterwards made the Impetus cars at Pornichet in France. The Greenfield factory of Oakman made engines for some early Locomobile gasoline cars.

HERTZ 1925–1928
Yellow Cab Mfg Co, Chicago, Ill.

The Hertz car was the result of John Hertz' plan to rent out cars for self-drive. Hertz took over the old Shaw Livery Company of Chicago and marketed the remaining stock of large Shaw cars as Ambassadors. He redesigned the latter make in mid-1924 as the Ambassador Model D-1, a $1,695 sedan intended for car-hire operations. Late in 1925, the D-1 was renamed the Hertz and a touring model was added to the sedan to complete the line. The cars closely resembled contemporary Buicks. The car was withdrawn early in 1928 and since then standard makes have been used by the Hertz Drive Yourself concern.

HESELTINE 1916–1917
Heseltine Motor Corp, New York, N.Y.

This light car, with a choice of 96 or 106in wheelbase, had a 138ci 4-cylinder engine by Lycoming. Both two-passenger and four-passenger cars were priced at $695, including wire wheels.

HEWITT 1906–1907
Hewitt Motor Co, New York, N.Y.

The Hewitt can claim the first true V-8 engine in an American production car as the earlier Buffum had a flat, opposed 8-cylinder engine. The 453ci engine was probably of French manufacture. The Hewitt had selective transmission and shaft drive. The price of the chassis was $4,000. Also offered in 1907 was a model with a 10hp single-cylinder engine, on which the British Adams was based. After 1907, the Hewitt Motor Co concentrated on manufacturing heavy trucks.

HEWITT-LINDSTROM 1900–1901
Hewitt-Lindstrom Electric Co, Chicago, Ill.

This company built mainly heavy electric trucks and buses, but they also made a few electric cars for town use, and a light two-passenger runabout.

HEYMANN 1898; 1904
1 Heymann Motor Vehicle & Mfg Co, Melrose, Mass. 1898
2 Heymann Motor Vehicle & Mfg Co, Boston, Mass. 1904

The first Heymann car was a two-passenger carriage with tiller steering. The second, Boston-built, car was an unconventional machine with a 5-cylinder rotary engine mounted under a hood. Rated at 40hp, it had a displacement of 315ci. Final drive was by shaft, and the price was $4,000.

HIDLEY 1901
Hidley Automobile Co, Troy, N.Y.

The Hidley steamer was rated at 8hp. This was a two-passenger runabout weighing 850lb. A multi-passenger trap was also built.

HIGHLANDER 1921
Midwest Motor Co, Kansas City, Mo.

The Highlander, the name of which frequently appears in trade journals as 'Hylander', was a typical assembled car powered by a Continental 6-cylinder engine. A conventional touring car and a sports version were available during the short life of the make.

HILTON 1921
Motor Sales & Service Corp, Philadelphia, Pa.

The Hilton was a 4-cylinder car which was offered only in coupé form. Designed by Hilton W. Sofield, president of the Motor Sales & Service Corporation, the car was powered by a Herschell-Spillman engine and wire wheels were standard equipment. The factory itself was at Riverton, N.J.

HINES 1908–1910
National Screw & Tack Co, Cleveland, Ohio

This car was designed by and named after William R. Hines, chief plant engineer of the manufacturer. The only model which was marketed was a five-passenger touring car on a 106in wheelbase. It had a 4-cylinder engine of 254ci.

HITCHCOCK 1909
Hitchcock Motor Car Co, Warren, Mich.

This was a small car with power supplied by a 2-cylinder, 2-cycle Speedwell engine of 20hp. Apparently very few cars of this name were manufactured.

HOBBIE 1908–1909
Hobbie Automobile Co, Hampton, Iowa

This make was also known as Hobbie Accessible. It was a high-wheeler with solid rubber tires, powered by a typical 2-cylinder, air-cooled engine mounted under the body. The car was tiller-steered and had double chain drive.

HOFFMAN (i) 1903
Hoffman Automobile & Mfg Co, Cleveland, Ohio

The Hoffman was a light steam car using a 6hp 2-cylinder engine and single chain drive. The firm also made a single-cylinder gasoline car of similar external appearance, and from 1904 onwards the firm concentrated on the manufacture of gasoline cars, which they sold under the name Royal Tourist.

HOFFMAN (ii) 1931
R. C. Hoffman, Detroit, Mich.

Two prototypes of the Hoffman Front Drive car were built. The cars were powered by a Lycoming straight-8 engine and the wheels were carried on a solid load-bearing axle. Semi-elliptic springs were used and torque arms aided the front axle in taking the power.

HOLLAND 1902–c.1905
Holland Automobile Co, Jersey City, N.J.

This company made engines of 6 and 12hp, and chassis with planetary gearing and single chain drive, ready to receive bodies. A steam car was attributed to this firm in 1905, but no details are known.

1918 HOLMES (ii) 29hp touring car. *Keith Marvin Collection*

HOLLEY 1903–1904
Holley Motor Co, Bradford, Pa.

This small car had an attractive appearance with more than the normal amount of brass work. It was a two-passenger car with a single-cylinder water-cooled engine, and a coil radiator. It was steered by wheel and was priced at $650.

HOLLIER 1915–1921
Lewis Spring & Axle Co, Chelsea; Jackson, Mich.

Also known as Vincent-Hollier, this car was available originally with a V-8 engine of its own design, although a companion model powered by a 6-cylinder Falls engine was introduced for 1917. Only open models were built.

HOLLY 1914–1916
Holly Motor Co, Mount Holly, N.J.

The Holly was made in a single chassis using a 60hp 6-cylinder engine. The two models, a roadster and a touring car, were listed at $1,000 for 1916.

HOLMES (i) 1906–1907
1 Charles Holmes Machine Co, East Boston, Mass. 1906
2 Holmes Motor Vehicle Co, East Boston, Mass. 1906–1907

This car was made in two five-passenger touring models. The smaller car used a 2-cylinder opposed engine. The larger model had a 4-cylinder 201ci engine. Both models had a Reeves friction transmission.

HOLMES (ii) 1918–1923
The Holmes Automobile Co, Canton, Ohio

Second in sales only to Franklin among air-cooled cars of the period, the Holmes Six was a highly regarded, if unbelievably ugly car. The louvred front with its series of horizontal slits in a herringbone pattern was generally described as looking like a caterpillar head. Holmes cars cost slightly more than Franklins. Approximately 500 units per year

were sold in a full range of open and closed models. Holmes planned to launch a 4-cylinder car to augment their line of sixes, but by 1922 they were in financial difficulties and the company was declared bankrupt in May 1923.

HOLSMAN 1902–1909
Holsman Automobile Co, Chicago, Ill.

The Holsman was a high-wheeler which was sold in considerable numbers in the Mid-West. In construction it had the typical 2-cylinder opposed engine and a peculiar rope drive. Its large diameter wheels had steel tires and the crude brakes acted directly against the tires.

HOL-TAN 1908
Hol-Tan Co, New York, N.Y.

While the Hol-Tan Co was the sales agent for this make, these cars were built in St Louis, Mo. by the Moon Motor Car Co. Prior to 1906, Hol-Tan had imported European cars including Fiats for the New York market.

The larger model of the Hol-Tan had a long wheelbase (121in) for these years, with a 4-cylinder engine. Its selective, 4-speed transmission was an early overdrive type, with a direct drive in third gear.

HOLYOKE 1901–1903
Holyoke Automobile Co, Holyoke, Mass.

The Holyoke was designed by the Swiss-born engineer, Charles R. Greuter, whose name is sometimes given to the make of car. It was made in single- and twin-cylinder form, and was notable for having overhead valves. In fact it is said to have inspired the 1903 ohv Welch design. The first Holyoke was a large touring surrey with the 2-cylinder engine under the rear seats, but later a single-cylinder runabout was made.

In 1903 the Holyoke assets were acquired by the Matheson Motor Car Co, Grand Rapids, Mich., who used the Holyoke factory for their own products until 1906.

HOMER-LAUGHLIN 1916
Homer Laughlin Engineers' Corp, Los Angeles, Calif.

This car was a combination of innovations and obsolete ideas. It had front-wheel drive, with a friction transmission, and was powered by a 119ci V-8 engine. The wheelbase was 112in with a turning circle of 22ft. The rear springs were a patented combination of two cantilever springs. Only one roadster was made.

HOOD 1900–1901
Simplex Motor Vehicle Co, Danvers, Mass.

Also known as the Electronomic, the Hood steam car looked little different from its many contemporaries, but embodied one or two unusual ideas. The engine had four single-acting cylinders and magnetically operated inlet valves, three small batteries being provided for the purpose. A flash boiler supplied superheated steam at a pressure of 200psi. A simple two-passenger body was standard; the price was $1,000.

HOOSIER SCOUT 1914
Hoosier Cyclecar Co, Indianapolis, Ind.

The Hoosier (the nickname for Indiana) was a tandem cyclecar, with a typical 2-cylinder, air-cooled engine. The drive was by a friction transmission and belts to the rear wheels. The only distinguishing feature of the body was its boat-tail.

HOPPENSTAND 1948–1949
Hoppenstand Motors Inc, Greenville, Pa.

The Hoppenstand was a short-lived American minicar using a 21.4ci flat-twin air-cooled engine just in front of the rear axle, hydraulic transmission, and independent suspension all round by coil. Coupé and convertible models were available.

HORNET *see* AMERICAN MOTORS

1910 HOUPT-ROCKWELL 90hp touring car. *Automobile Manufacturers' Association*

1904 HOWARD (ii) 24hp six-passenger touring car. *Keith Marvin Collection*

1914 HUDSON (ii) Model 54 40hp sedan. *American Motors Corporation*

HOUPT; HOUPT-ROCKWELL 1909–1910; 1910–1912
1 Harry S. Houpt Mfg Co, New Britain, Conn. 1909–1910
2 New Departure Mfg Co, New Britain, Conn. 1910–1912
 The Houpt was a large car powered by a 4-cylinder engine rated at 60hp, or a 6-cylinder unit of 90hp. Later models, known as Houpt-Rockwell from 1910, included a limousine and landaulet and prices ranged up to $7,500.

HOWARD (i) 1900–1901
Howard Automobile Co, Trenton, N.J.
 One of 19 new makes of steam buggy in 1900, the Howard was typical of its kind. A 2-cylinder vertical engine, single chain drive, tubular frame, tiller steering, wire wheels — all these features were found on other designs, including the most successful of the breed, the Locomobile.

HOWARD (ii) 1903–1905
1 W. S. Howard, Troy, N.Y. 1903
2 Howard Automobile Co, Yonkers, N.Y. 1903–1905
 This car was of modest size, but expensive. With a four-passenger *Roi des Belges* body and a 25/30hp, 4-cylinder engine it cost $5,000. Smaller models with a 2- or 3-cylinder engine were also produced. This company was succeeded by Gas Engine & Power Co, in 1905, but apparently the Howard was not continued.

HOWARD (iii) 1913–1918
A. Howard Co, Galion, Ohio
 This car used a 303ci, 6-cylinder engine. It had a 3-speed transmission and shaft drive. Apparently the only body style offered was an open five-passenger touring car.

HOWARD (iv) 1913–1914
1 Howard Motor Car Co, Connersville, Ind. 1913
2 Lexington-Howard Co, Connersville, Ind. 1913–1914
 This manufacturer also built the Lexington. The Howard was a large car with a wheelbase of 130in. Its L-head 6-cylinder Continental engine of 425ci was rated at 60hp and used an early example of dual exhaust system. The five-passenger touring model cost $2,375.

HOWARD (v) 1929–1930
Howard Motor International Corp, New York, N.Y.
 The Howard 'Silver Morn' was announced as a revolutionary development in low-cost motors, but was, in fact, a conventional assembled car which was probably never made in any numbers at all. It was powered by a Continental Red Seal 6-cylinder engine, although advertisements spoke of an 8-cylinder chassis as well. Lockheed hydraulic brakes were featured, and the car had wire wheels and a ribbon-type radiator. With a complete range of smart body styles, prices ran from $695 to $2,395.

HUB (i) 1899–1900
Hub Motor Co, Chicago, Ill.
 The Hub Electric was so called because of the four electric motors mounted in the wheel hubs. The cars were marketed by the Hub Company, and built by the Westinghouse Company of Pittsburgh, Pa. Maximum speed was 15mph.

HUB (ii) 1907
Hub Automobile Co, Boston, Mass.
 The Hub was a very light two-passenger car with a tubular steel frame. Its engine was a single-cylinder, air-cooled unit of 10hp. It had steering by wheel and used a planetary transmission.

HUDSON (i) 1901–1902
Beau-Chamberlain Mfg Co, Hudson, Mich.
 The first car to bear the name Hudson was a light steamer with a vertical 2-cylinder engine, single chain drive and tiller steering. It bore no relationship to the later Hudson car.

1939 HUDSON (ii) Six coupé. *American Motors Corporation*
1950 HUDSON (ii) Commodore Eight sedan. *American Motors Corporation*

HUDSON (ii) 1909–1957

1 Hudson Motor Car Co, Detroit, Mich. 1909–1954
2 American Motors Corp, Kenosha, Wis. 1954–1957

The Hudson was created by Roy D. Chapin, and financed by J. L. Hudson, head of Detroit's famous department store of that name. The first product was a 20hp 4-cylinder car of conventional design, capable of 50mph, of which 4,000 were sold in its first season. These fours, one of which was entered in the 1914 Tourist Trophy were first supplemented and then supplanted by a 6-cylinder line. The first of these was the heavy (3,696lb) and fairly expensive ($2,350) Model 54 with a 4-speed overdrive transmission, but the 274ci Super Six of 1916, with its high-compression L-head engine, really made the company's name, and marked the first of a line of engines of this type which lasted almost to the end of production, giving generous outputs while still burning commercial-grade gasoline. A Super Six made the first two way transcontinental trip — New York to San Francisco and back — in 1916; Ira Vail took 9th place in the Indianapolis 500 Mile Race in 1919, and this model formed the backbone of New Zealand's 'service car' network in the 1920s.

Though Hudson's booming sales in the 1920s were largely due to the inexpensive companion make the Essex, the company also pioneered modestly-priced closed cars, and in 1922 their 'coach' (a 2-door sedan) sold for only $100 more than a touring car. Until 1929, the Super Six remained the staple Hudson model, and during its last three years of production it was powered by a 289ci F-head unit derived from the original Essex Four of 1918. In 1930 it was replaced by a 214ci straight-8, later increased to 254ci in 1932 — this tough and well-liked unit remained in production until 1952, and powered such Anglo-Americans as the Railton and Brough Superior. These firms also used Hudson's 211ci six.

The 1930s were less favorable to Hudson, except in Britain, where the breed's popularity warranted the manufacture of a small-bore 166ci 'export' six rated at only 16.9hp, which was still being made in 1940. The regular Hudson Six was a bigger machine of 211ci and was offered with independent front suspension in 1934 and 1935; in the latter year Electric

Hand gear shift became available. Fencer's mask radiator grills followed in 1936, and steering-column shift in 1939. The first post-war Hudsons were a continuation of the 1942 models, but 1948 brought the revolutionary Step-Down series with the company's high-compression L-head in-line engines. These low-built cars had unitary construction of chassis and body, rear wheels mounted *inside* the chassis frame, and coil-spring independent front suspension. The 308ci 145bhp 6-cylinder Hornet engine, introduced for 1951, proved a great success in stock-car events, but before this the company had reached its post-war sales peak, with nearly 145,000 units delivered in 1950. Competition in the medium-price bracket was too strong, and Hudson's venture into the compact car market in 1953, with the 202ci 6-cylinder Jet at $1,833 (this was also the first Hudson to abandon the wet-plate clutch) was not successful.

In 1954 Hudson amalgamated with Nash to form the American Motors Corporation. Though all production was transferred from Detroit to Kenosha, and the Hudson range now shared its unitized hulls with the bigger Nash models, sales did not prosper. These last Hudsons had initially the old L-head 6-cylinder units or Packard-built V-8s, while both Nash's Rambler and the British Austin-built Metropolitan were sold by Hudson agents. The name was dropped at the end of the 1957 season.

HUFFMAN 1920–1925

Huffman Bros Motor Co, Elkhart, Ind.

The Huffman was a typical assembled car of its time. A possible 3,000 units left the factory in six years of manufacture. A Continental 6-cylinder engine provided power and the cars were available in open and closed models. Sales were mainly confined to the Middle Western area of the United States. During the last few months of Huffman production, cars were equipped with Lockheed 4-wheel brakes and these later models frequently appeared with disk wheels in contrast to the standard artilleries used earlier.

HUGHES 1899–1900

Hughes & Atkin, Providence, R.I.

The Hughes was a light two-passenger buggy with wire wheels and tiller steering. Only 18 were built.

HUMMINGBIRD c.1946

Talmadge Judd, Kingsport, Tenn.

A small convertible coupé built for possible marketing, the Hummingbird was a one-off with a 20bhp 4-cylinder engine providing 50mpg.

HUPMOBILE 1908–1940

Hupp Motor Car Corp, Detroit, Mich.; Cleveland, Ohio

Robert and Louis Hupp, the founders of this company, started with a 112ci 4-cylinder light runabout, with two bucket seats and a bolster tank, distinguished by a 2-speed sliding-type transmission. It sold for $750 and was joined in 1911 by a touring car with three forward speeds and a longer wheelbase of 110in, listed at only $900. Hupmobile, like Dodge and Chevrolet, adhered to the 4-cylinder L-head unit for many years and made nothing else until 1924, though their cars acquired electric lighting and starting in 1914. A version with a 126in wheelbase was made available for seven-passenger bodywork in 1916. Sales were good: 12,000 in 1913, and climbing up to 38,000 by 1923. By 1918 a rounded cowl and hood line had replaced the original angular configuration and fuel feed was by vacuum from a tank at the rear. Open models were listed at $1,250. Aluminum pistons were featured in 1924 and balloon tires in 1925, the last year of the four. Interestingly enough, Hupmobile's 247ci straight-8 appeared in 1925, a year before the first six. It was a conventional machine with contracting Lockheed hydraulic brakes, mechanical actuation being used on the 6-cylinder cars. The company stayed in the medium-price field, sixes selling at $1,295 in 1929, and prices of the M series L-head eight started at $1,825. In 1929 Chandler's plant in Cleveland was acquired and was used for the manufacture of the less expensive Hupps. Like most of America's independent makes, the Hupmobile was hit hard

1914 HUPMOBILE 15/18hp limousine. Coachwork by Zimmermann of Berlin. *Montagu Motor Museum*
1933 HUPMOBILE New Century Six coupé. *Musée de l'Automobile, Le Mans*

1939 HUPMOBILE Junior Six sedan. *Autocar*

made in 245ci, 6-cylinder and 304ci straight-8 forms, but sales were poor and the factory closed down halfway through the 1936 season. It was reopened, but the 1937 and 1938 models were of little interest apart from the standardization of automatic overdrive on the eights. Like Graham, Hupmobile tried to stay in business by adapting the body dies of the discontinued 810/812 Cord series to their conventional running gear. These Skylarks were built in the Graham factory; the last cars were completed in July 1940, but were sold as 1941 models.

HUPP-YEATS 1911–1918
1 R. C. H. Corp, Detroit, Mich. 1911–1912
2 Hupp-Yeats Electric Car Co, Detroit, Mich. 1912–1918

These electric cars seated four passengers, in both open and closed versions. The motors were built by Westinghouse and had five selective speeds. Standard tires were of solid rubber.

HYDROMETER 1917
Automobile Boat Mfg Co, Seattle, Wash.

This was an early attempt at building an amphibian car and was the invention of William Mazzei. Built along the lines of a boat, and rather resembling the German Rumpler car of the 1920s, the Hydrometer was said to be able to reach 60mph in speed on land and 25mph in water. A Continental engine was used and propeller and rudder were mounted at the rear of the car. A two-passenger roadster was the only model shown. The steering wheel operated both the front wheels and the rudder.

HYLANDER *see* HIGHLANDER

HYSLOP 1915
Hyslop & Clark, Toledo, Ohio

By the time the Hyslop was marketed, the cyclecar had become rather more advanced in design. This make had semi-elliptical springs all round, with a 4-cylinder water-cooled engine and a V-shaped radiator shell.

by the Depression, sales dropping from 50,374 in 1929 to 17,450 in 1931, although in the next two years, in 1932 and 1933 some very handsome cars were made.

In 1934 the Aerodynamic range with three-piece wrap-around windshields and headlights faired into the hood sides appeared. An experimental fwd version was not proceeded with. The aerodynamic cars were

I & J

IDEAL (i) 1902–1903
B. & P. Co, Milwaukee, Wis.

This was a light two-passenger car with a 5hp single-cylinder horizontal engine and 3-speed transmission. Maximum speed was 25mph. The company also made steam engines for heavy trucks, but did not manufacture a steam vehicle themselves.

IDEAL (ii) 1909–1914
Ideal Electric Co, Chicago, Ill.

The Ideal electric car was built principally in closed models, most of them for four-passengers. The controller allowed four forward speeds. This car weighed 2,500lb and was priced in the $1,800–$1,900 range.

IDEAL (iii) 1914
The Ideal Shop, Buffalo, N.Y.

This cyclecar was built as either a single-passenger or as a two-passenger with tandem arrangement. The power was from a 2-cylinder Spacke engine, which drove the vehicle through a planetary transmission and belts to the rear wheels.

I.H.C. 1911
Independent Harvester Co, Plano, Ill.

The I.H.C. was a farmers' utility vehicle which could be used either for passengers or as a delivery car. It was powered by an air-cooled 24hp engine — mounted under the seat, despite the presence of a hood in front. It was a tiller-steered high-wheeler with drive by what was termed a 'V-chain belt'. The name I.H.C. was also applied to the earlier products of the International Harvester Corp [see International (ii)].

ILLINOIS 1910–1914
Overholt Co, Galesburg, Ill.

This car was produced as either a five-passenger touring car, or as a baby tonneau. The 4-cylinder, 40hp engine was of 270ci. The Model K of 1911 was quoted at $2,000.

IMP (i) 1913–1914
W. H. McIntyre Co, Auburn, Ind.

The Imp was a cyclecar with a V-twin air-cooled engine, friction transmission and belt drive. Double cantilever springs were used in front and there was a single headlight. With a 36in track, 100in wheelbase and a weight of 600lb, this tandem two-passenger car was priced at $375. The company also built the McIntyre.

IMP (ii) c.1955
International Motor Products, Glendale, Calif.

Only 120in long, the two-passenger Imp was made of fiberglass and contained a 7½hp Gladden air-cooled rear engine.

IMPERIAL (i) 1903–1904
Rodgers & Co, Columbus, Ohio

Four models of the Imperial were made, fitted with opposed 2-cylinder, air-cooled engines. The drive system comprised a sliding-gear transmission and shaft to the rear axle. The steering column was hinged for ease of entrance to the driver's seat. The cars were also known as Columbus or Rodgers.

IMPERIAL (ii) 1906–1907
Imperial Motor Car Co, Williamsport, Pa.

The Imperial four-passenger roadster had a 4-cylinder Rutenber engine with dual ignition. This was water-cooled and had a displacement of 334ci. A 3-speed transmission was used with shaft drive. The chassis had a wheelbase of 108in and the complete car weighed 2,400lb

IMPERIAL (iii) 1907–1916
Imperial Automobile Co, Jackson, Mich.

This Imperial company seems to have specialized in touring cars, having five models in one year (1910). In 1914, four chassis were offered with 4-cylinder engines of 298ci and 318ci, and 6-cylinder 348ci and 427ci units. The 44hp six cost $2,000 in its five-passenger touring car form.

IMPERIAL (iv) 1954 to date.
Chrysler Corporation, Detroit, Mich.

The name of Imperial, used by the Chrysler Corporation for their luxury-car line from 1926 onwards, became a make in its own right in 1954. The object of this move was to put the Imperial on a par with Cadillac and Lincoln in the public mind, but the cars remained large

1913 IMP (i) 12hp cyclecar. *David Burgess Wise*

1955 IMPERIAL (iv) sedan. *Chrysler Corporation*

1971 IMPERIAL (iv) LeBaron 4-door hardtop. *Chrysler Corporation*

Chryslers, with overhead-valve V-8 oversquare engines and automatic transmission as standard equipment. Year-to-year improvements followed those of Chrysler's other products, with 'flight-sweep' styling in 1955 and alternator ignition in 1960. 1955 Imperials had Chrysler's caliper disk brakes as standard. Since 1957 the name of Le Baron, a custom coachbuilder whose work often appeared on the Chrysler Imperials of the 1920s and 1930s, has been associated with the costliest models. In 1966 the Imperial had an engine of 440ci displacement developing 350bhp; prices, at $5,733 upwards, were comparable with Cadillac's De Ville series and the Lincoln Continental. There were no major annual changes except that unitary construction was used from 1967 onwards, and 1971 models introduced the option of a 4-wheel anti-skid brake system, the first on any American car.

INDIAN 1928–1929
Indian Motorcycle Co, Springfield, Mass.

Only three Indian cars were built, these being experimental cars constructed under the direction of Jack Bauer, son of the president of the concern. A roadster, a coupé and one other type were constructed. One of these was powered with an Indian motorcycle engine; the other two with Continental fours. All used wire wheels and were a little larger than the later American Bantam car.

INGRAM-HATCH 1917–1918
Ingram-Hatch Motor Corp, Staten Island, N.Y.

This freakish car used a kerosene-burning, single overhead camshaft 4-cylinder engine. It was air-cooled and developed 40hp. Twin drive shafts transmitted the torque to a friction transmission, one for each axle half. Finally the wheels had a combination of air and mechanical springs in place of spokes.

INNES 1921
American Motor Export Co, Jacksonville, Fla.

The short-lived Innes was a small assembled car powered by an 18.2hp 4-cylinder Supreme engine and using Columbia axles and Grant-Lees transmission. Body styles were a five-passenger touring car, two-passenger roadster, and light truck.

INTERNATIONAL (i) 1900
International Motor Carriage Co, Stamford, Conn.

This company showed a light car with a 2-cycle engine designed to run on kerosene at the Madison Square Garden show in 1900, but it did not go into production.

INTERNATIONAL (ii) (I.H.C.) 1907–1911; 1961 to date
1 International Harvester Co, Chicago, Ill. 1907
2 International Harvester Co, Akron, Ohio 1907–1911
3 International Harvester Co, Chicago, Ill. 1961 to date

The International was a popular high-wheeler built as a two-passenger surrey or as a light delivery truck. It was powered by a horizontally-opposed 2-cylinder engine of 15hp. Friction transmission was used, with two forward speeds. The car was normally fitted with solid rubber tires but a number of touring cars with standard wheels and pneumatic tires were built in 1910 and 1911. These models had 4-cylinder air-cooled engines made by International, with the exception of the model J-30, which used a water-cooled 4-cylinder British-American engine.

After 1911 the high-wheelers were made only in truck form, and although one or two passenger car bodies were built on the small C-line chassis of the 1930s, no more passenger vehicles were made by International until 1961. Then the 4-wheel-drive 'Scout' cross-country vehicle was introduced, now available with a wide range of open or closed bodywork. This was supplemented by the Travelall, a station wagon with 2- or 4-wheel-drive, and 6 or V-8 engines of up to 392ci displacement developing 235bhp.

1907 INTERNATIONAL (ii) motor buggy. *International Harvester Co*
1971 INTERNATIONAL (ii) Travelall station wagon. *International Harvester Co*

INTER-STATE 1909–1918
1 Inter-State Automobile Co, Muncie, Ind. 1909–1914
2 Inter-State Motor Co, Muncie, Ind. 1914–1918

The first models of this make used 4-cylinder engines of 284ci. In 1912, specifications included electric lighting and starting, with an electric fuel pump. In 1912, eight models were offered on three different chassis. The 4-cylinder Model 45 was introduced for 1913, but the company was reorganized in October 1913 and a cheaper model introduced. This was the Model T with 4-cylinder Beaver engine, which remained in production until 1918 when the plant was sold to General Motors for their production of the Sheridan.

INTERURBAN 1905
F. A. Woods Auto Co, Chicago, Ill.

This was a one-passenger, front-wheel-drive electric vehicle. The body served as the frame. The electric motor could be exchanged for an 8hp 2-cylinder internal-combustion engine. This could be done 'in ten minutes' for use on long trips. The car was steered by pivoting of the entire front axle.

INTREPID see ROTARY (i)

IROQUOIS 1904–1908
1 J. S. Leggett Mfg Co, Syracuse, N.Y. 1904
2 Iroquois Motor Car Co, Seneca Falls, N.Y. 1905–1908

In 1904, the Iroquois was a small car of advanced design, having sliding-gear transmission and shaft drive, with a 20hp 4-cylinder engine. In later years, model choices included 25/30hp and 35/40hp, 4-cylinder T-headed engines.

IVANHOE (CDN) 1903
Canada Cycle and Motor Co, Toronto, Ont.

This was an electric car designed by Hiram Percy Maxim. Batteries were carried over the front and rear wheels to balance weight: this was claimed to be a Canadian invention widely copied in the U.S. A Westinghouse motor was suspended from the sprung body, propelling the 30in wheels by chain drive.

IZZER 1911
Model Gas Engine Co, Peru, Ind.

Only three Izzers were built and only as three-passenger roadsters. This whimsical name was dreamed up by a Dr Bissell who wanted an up-to-date car, not a has-been or 'was-er'. Wheelbase of this 4-cylinder car was 98¾in. One of the three is extant in Illinois.

JACKSON 1903–1923
Jackson Automobile Co, Jackson, Mich.

For their first year of production this company made both steam and gasoline cars, both called Jaxon. The steamer used a 3-cylinder vertical engine of 6hp, chain drive and a folding seat. It was out of production by 1904. The gasoline car had a single-cylinder engine, and generally resembled the Curved Dash Oldsmobile. A 2-cylinder car was introduced in 1904, and a 4-cylinder in 1906, in which year there were three models, an old type 20hp 2-cylinder with engine under the seat, and chain drive, and two front-engined, shaft-driven cars, a 20hp 2-cylinder and a 30/35hp 4-cylinder. From then on, the Jackson followed conventional lines, a Northway-engined six being introduced in 1913, and V-8 with ohv Ferro engine from 1916 to 1918.

Later cars had a Rolls-Royce type radiator, but the last model, made in 1923, was a very ordinary looking car made by the Associated Motors combine, who had also acquired Dixie Flyer and National. The 1923 Jackson Six was sold in its final models as the National Model 6–51.

JACQUET FLYER 1921
Jacquet Motor Corp of America, Belding, Mich.

The Jacquet Flyer was a relatively high-priced sports car built in limited numbers for a few months. The car had a 4-cylinder engine with a capacity of 341ci. Wire wheels were standard.

JAEGER 1932–1933
Jaeger Motor Car Co, Belleville, Mich.

The Jaeger car was characterized by the elimination of spring shackles by substituting coil for semi-elliptic springs. In appearance, however, the

1909 JACKSON 30/35hp touring car. *Kenneth Stauffer*

car resembled most other low-priced cars of the period. It was powered by a 6-cylinder Continental engine, credited with 70bhp. The Jaeger sold at $700. Wire wheels were standard and a V-radiator grill and three diagonal groups of four louvres on each side of the hood identified it. Only a few coupés and convertible coupés were actually produced.

JAMES 1909
J. & M. Motor Car Co, Laurenceburg, Ind.

The James was an obscure two-passenger high-wheeled buggy. It had an air-cooled engine with two opposed cylinders.

JAMIESON 1902
M. W. Jamieson & Co, Warren, Pa.

This was a light two-passenger car with a 7hp 2-cylinder engine, single chain drive and tiller steering. Few were made, but one survives today.

JANNEY 1906
Janney Motor Co, Flint, Mich.

The Janney was a light 4-cylinder experimental car which never got beyond the prototype stage. This company was formed by Wm. C. Durant, and occupied the old Buick plant at Flint. A total of four cars were built before the company was absorbed by Buick. The Janney became the 1908 Buick Model E-10, after being redesigned.

JARVIS-HUNTINGTON 1912
Jarvis Machinery & Supply Co, Huntington, W. Va.

This was a very large car with seven- and eight-passenger bodies. The larger model had a wheelbase of 142in. Its engine was a 6-cylinder monster of 572ci. The drive to the rear wheels was by double chains and the price was $5,000.

JAVELIN see AMERICAN MOTORS

JAXON see JACKSON

JEANNIN 1908–1909
Jeannin Automobile Mfg Co, St Louis, Mo.

The Jeannin was a high-wheeler with solid rubber tires, and a 10/12hp air-cooled engine. Steering was by wheel and the car had shaft drive. This was produced only as a two-passenger runabout with a surrey top.

1966 JEEP Wagoneer station wagon. *Kaiser-Jeep Corporation*

1968 JEEPSTER Commando convertible. *Kaiser-Jeep Corporation*

4-cylinder engines, with 5½in stroke and cylinder diameter gradually increased from 4.8in to 4.9in. The cars had peculiarly peaked hoods.

JEWEL 1906–1909
1 Forest City Motor Co, Cleveland, Ohio 1906
2 Forest City Motor Co, Massillon, Ohio 1906–1909
3 Jewel Motor Car Co, Massillon, Ohio 1909

For 1906 and 1907 this make offered only a two-passenger car with a 2-cycle, single cylinder engine of 8hp. During these years, the make was spelled 'Jewell'. In 1908, the Jewel 40 was introduced, powered by a Rutenber engine of four cylinders and 354ci. Roadster and seven-passenger touring models were mounted on a chassis of 120in wheelbase. The Jewel was replaced by the Croxton-Keeton.

JEWETT 1923–1926
Paige-Detroit Motor Car Co, Detroit, Mich.

The Jewett, named after H. M. Jewett, president of the Paige-Detroit Motor Car Co, was in reality a smaller Paige, but was sold as a make of its own, much as the Cleveland was sold as a smaller Chandler. It was a well-liked car and many of its models, particularly the open phaetons, appeared with exceptionally fine and sporty lines. Nevertheless, Jewett sales diminished and after more than 40,000 had been sold, the car was marketed as a Paige. Early cars had 249ci engines but there was a small 152ci version, with fwb in 1925, and the last cars had hydraulic brakes.

JOHNSON 1905–1912
Johnson Service Co, Milwaukee, Wis.

The original Johnson was a 4-cylinder steamer with an enormous hood

1916 JEFFERY 20/30hp sedan. *American Motors Corporation*

1907 JEWEL 8hp runabout. *Keith Marvin Collection*

JEEP 1963 to date
Kaiser-Jeep Corp, Toledo, Ohio

Although the Jeep first appeared during World War 2, and was the sole product of Willys-Overland after 1956, it has been regarded as a make only since the formation of Kaiser-Jeep in 1963. At that time, the range consisted of 2- and 4-wheel-drive station wagons with 4- and 6-cylinder engines as well as updated versions of the original wartime Jeep. For 1965 these engines were supplemented by a 327ci Rambler V-8 unit, used in the Wagoneer station wagon. The Jeep Universal utility vehicle was available with 192ci 4-cylinder Perkins Diesel or 225ci V-6 Buick engines, as well as the 134ci 4-cylinder Jeep engine. Kaiser-Jeep merged with American Motors early in 1970, but the range continued unchanged. For 1971 there were utility and sporting versions of the Universal, with 4-cylinder or V-6 engines (the latter now manufactured by Kaiser-Jeep at Toledo), the more luxurious Jeepster series in station wagon, roadster and convertible forms, and the Wagoneer station wagon with options of 145bhp V-6 or 230bhp, 350ci V-8 engines.

JEFFERY 1914–1917
Thos. B. Jeffery Co, Kenosha, Wis.

The Jeffery was the Rambler (ii) renamed after the founder of the company. It was made for four seasons in conventional 4- and 6-cylinder guises, with L-head monobloc engines, the sixes giving about 60bhp. 1916 prices were $1,000 and $1,350 respectively. After the purchase of the company by Charles W. Nash, the cars were again renamed and went over to push-rod-operated overhead valves.

JENKINS 1907–1912
1 J. W. Jenkins, Rochester, N.Y. 1907
2 Jenkins Motor Car Co, Rochester, N.Y. 1908–1912

The model changes in the Jenkins were very few. These cars all had

1903 JONES-CORBIN 8hp runabout. *Kenneth Stauffer*

and ornate enclosed body. The steam engine was a single-acting type of 30hp. After 1907, Johnson adopted internal combustion engines of three sizes, up to 50hp. This company also produced a large variety of commercial vehicles.

JOHNSONMOBILE 1959
Horton Johnson, Inc, Highland Park, Ill.

Only one of this prototype 1904 Antique Runabout was produced. A 3hp Clinton air-cooled engine powered it, and the two-passenger body was of marine plywood.

JOMAR c.1954–1955
Ray Saidel, Manchester, N.H.

The first Jomar was a small sports car powered by the British Ford Anglia engine of 71¼ci displacement. It had a full-width aluminum two-passenger body. Later the name was applied to the British T.V.R. sports car when sold in the United States.

JONES 1915–1920
Jones Motor Car Co. Wichita, Kan.

The Jones was a thoroughly conventional 6-cylinder car made mainly in open touring models. At first a 21.6hp engine was used, but this was replaced by a 29.4hp Continental for 1917 to 1920 models. The company also made trucks of up to 2½ tons capacity.

1930 JORDAN Speedway Eight sports sedan. *Autocar*

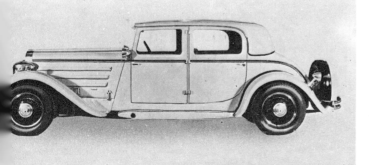

JONES-CORBIN 1902–1907
1 Jones-Corbin Co, Philadelphia, Pa. 1902–1904
2 Jones-Corbin Automobile Co, Philadelphia, Pa. 1904–1907

The early model of this make offered single, 2- and 4-cylinder 'genuine De Dion' engines of 8 to 30hp. This make used double-chain drive and its appearance revealed considerable European influence. A 45hp 4-cylinder car was listed at $4,500 in 1906.

JONZ 1908–1911
1 Jonz Auto Co, Beatrice, Neb. 1909–1910
2 American Automobile Mfg Co, Beatrice, Neb. 1910
3 American Automobile Mfg, Ohio Falls, Ind. 1911

The Jonz used a poorly-explained air/vapor cooling system for its 2-cycle engines. These were of 2, 3 and 4 cylinders, with ratings of 20, 30 and 40hp respectively. Two- to five-passenger open cars were offered, as well as a three-passenger coupé and a taxicab. There is no evidence that this company was ever located in Kansas City, Mo., as is sometimes stated.

JORDAN 1916–1931
Jordan Motor Car Co, Inc, Cleveland, Ohio

Edward S. Jordan will be remembered as the man who broke away from 'nuts and bolts' advertising and introduced the element of emotional appeal into the sale of the automobile. (Indeed his advertising copy has become more famous than his cars). These were among the best of the assembled creations, handsomely proportioned, and always powered by Continental engines. Wire wheels were standard on the first models, which had 303ci 6-cylinder power units: 1918 prices started at $1,995. A year later coil ignition was standardized, and hydraulic fwb were introduced during 1924. 1925 was the first year of straight-eights, a 269ci version being joined a year later by a small model with a 116in wheelbase. 1926 was Jordan's best year, with 11,000 cars sold, but they were unlucky in 1927 with their 'Little Custom', a luxury compact six with worm drive and a wheelbase of 107in, which failed to catch on. A handsome new radiator characterized the 1929 line, priced from $1,295 up. Like many American firms, Jordan's last effort was their greatest. This was the 1930 'Speedway' model, a 322ci, 114bhp eight with a 4-speed transmission, aircraft-type instrument panel, oddly shaped Woodlite headlights, and European styling. Unfortunately at over $5,000 there were very few takers, and at the depth of the Depression there was little market for the cheaper Jordans, either. The company closed down in 1931.

JPL; LA VIGNE 1913
J.P.L. Cyclecar Co, Detroit, Mich.

The JPL cyclecar was designed by J. P. La Vigne who was an early and ubiquitous engineer in the industry. The car used a 4-cylinder air-cooled engine with sliding-gear transmission. It was claimed that gasoline consumption was 30–40mpg, and that the top speed was 50mph.

JULES 30 (CDN) 1911–1912
Jules Motor Car Co Ltd, Guelph, Ont.

This small torpedo touring car used a 30hp engine and carried four passengers. Only two complete cars were built. A unique feature was the placing of the horn button in the middle of the brake pedal.

JULIAN 1922
Julian Brown, Syracuse, N.Y.

Although its designer intended to produce this unusual coupé, only one car was made. Radical in design, it featured a tubular frame, and a 60hp aircraft-type radial engine mounted at the rear. All moving parts were combined in a single unit and these were automatically lubricated.

K

KAISER 1946–1955
1 Kaiser-Frazer Corp, Willow Run, Mich. 1946–1953
2 Willys Motors, Inc, Willow Run, Mich. 1953–1954
3 Willys Motors, Inc, Toledo, Ohio 1954–1955

Probably the last attempt to break into the 'closed shop' of the American car industry, the Kaiser was sponsored by millionaire shipbuilder Henry J. Kaiser and Joseph Frazer of Graham-Paige. Howard Darrin was engaged to style the car, and Kaiser took over the vast Willow Run plant created by Henry Ford for wartime manufacture of the B-24 bomber. Plans embraced two makes — the low-medium-priced Kaiser and the rather more expensive Frazer. As first shown to the public in 1946, the former broke with convention in boasting unitary construction, front-wheel drive, and independent torsion-bar suspension at front and

rear; the slab-sided styling was unlike any other Detroit production. By the time the make went on sale, however, the Kaiser Special was an entirely conventional motorcar with box-section frame, coil-spring independent front suspension, and hypoid final drive to the rear wheels. The engine was a 226ci, 6-cylinder L-head Continental developing 100bhp. In 1947 Kaiser acquired from Continental the plant in which this engine was built. The firm tried hard, but never produced a best-seller. In 1949 Kaisers had 110bhp, and some interesting body styles included the Vagabond (a sedan-cum-station wagon with two-piece tail-gate), a 4-door power-top convertible, and a hardtop version of this which set a fashion in the American industry. The principal feature of the 1951 program was the introduction of a new cheap car, the Henry J, but the Kaiser proper was given a complete face-lift, emerging with narrow pillars, an individual look, a cruciform frame, and the option of automatic transmission. The 1952 versions had crash-padded dashboards, and with the demise of the Frazer, that make's Manhattan model became the head of the Kaiser line at $2,094. In spite of this it was found necessary to lay off 3,000 workers at Willow Run that May.

Even the merger with Willys a year later could not save the situation, though Kaisers generally became more exotic, the 1953 offerings including the Dragon, at $3,628 inclusive of radio, air conditioning, and automatic transmission, and Darrin's handsome KD-161 sports convertible with fiberglass bodywork, sliding doors, and 3-carburetor engine. The 1954 Manhattan sedans were 216in long, and the old Continental engine was stepped up to 140bhp by the addition of a McCulloch clutch-controlled supercharger. It was this year, too, that IKA started to build Kaisers in Argentina, but the company had nothing new to offer in 1955 — the last year of the make.

KAISER JEEP *see* JEEP

K&M 1908
Kreider Machine Co, Lancaster, Pa.

This was a high-wheeler with an air-cooled engine beneath the seat. A 2-speed selective transmission was used along with chain drive. This vehicle was transformable into a 1½ ton truck, and furthermore had a power take-off for driving other equipment.

KANE-PENNINGTON *see* PENNINGTON

KANSAS CITY 1905–1909
1 Kansas City Motor Car Co, Kansas City, Mo. 1905–1909
2 Wonder Motor Car Co, Kansas City, Mo. 1909

The Kansas City succeeded the Caps. As many as six models were introduced in one season, ranging from a two-passenger roadster with a 2-cylinder, 24hp engine to a seven-passenger touring car which used a 6-cylinder, 619ci engine and cost $4,500.

KATO 1907–1908
Four-Traction Auto Co, Mankato, Minn.

The initial Kato had 4-wheel drive via shafts fore and aft from the 2-cylinder, 24hp engine. The five/seven-passenger car was on a wheelbase of 104in and was priced at $1,800. A later model used a 40hp engine.

1947 KAISER Custom sedan. *Kaiser-Jeep Corporation*
1954 KAISER Manhattan sedan. *Motor*

KAUFFMAN 1909–1912
Advance Motor Vehicle Co, Miamisburg, Ohio
The Kauffman four-passenger roadster was powered by an air-cooled 4-cylinder, 254ci engine with overhead valves.

KAVAN 1905
Kavan Mfg Co, Chicago, Ill.
The Kavan was a light runabout with a single-cylinder engine under the seat, and chain drive. The most remarkable point about the Kavan was its price — $200.

1915 KEARNS Model L 12hp roadster. *Keith Marvin Collection*

1913 KEETON Six-48 touring car. *Floyd Clymer Publications*

1950 KELLER sedan. *Autocar*

K-D 1912
K-D Motor Co, Brookline, Mass.
The K stood for Margaret E. Knight and the D for Mrs Anna F. Davidson, the founders of the company. Miss Knight designed the sleeve valve engine used in this car. Its valving differed from Charles Knight's version in the use of a single split-sleeve working outside the cylinder wall, instead of the better-known type with double concentric sleeves. The engine was a 4-cylinder, 301ci unit. The five-seater K-D was on a wheelbase of 137in and had wire wheels. Production of this car, which cost $6,000, was very limited.

KEARNS 1909–1915
1 Kearns Motor Buggy Co, Beavertown, Pa.
2 Kearns Motor Truck Co. Beavertown, Pa.
Known as the Eureka buggy from 1908 to January 1909, this high-wheeler used 2-cycle Speedwell engines of 10/12hp (2-cylinder) or 15/18hp (3-cylinder). They had double friction drive and solid tires, but unlike many of the high-wheelers, had conventional hoods. From the end of 1910 the company concentrated on trucks, but in 1915 they introduced a light car with 18hp 4-cylinder engine, 3-speed transmission, and shaft drive. They also made the Lu-Lu cyclecar in 1914. This had a 13.7hp 4-cylinder engine and shaft drive.

KEETON 1908: 1910–1914
1 Keeton Taxicab and Town Car Works, Detroit, Mich. 1908
2 Keeton Motor Co, Detroit, Mich. 1910–1913
3 American Voiturette Co, Detroit, Mich.; Washington, Pa. 1914
The Keeton had a complex history, intertwined with that of the Croxton-Keeton. The original car had a Renault-like radiator behind the 256ci 4-cylinder engine. Its principal body-type was a landaulet on a wheelbase of 107in. The last model (after the separation from Croxton) used a 365ci 6-cylinder engine and had a wheelbase of 132in. The transmission had four forward speeds. Three body styles were offered at prices from $2,500 to $2,850. This firm built the Car Nation Cyclecar in 1914 and 1915.

KELLER 1948–1950
George D. Keller Motors, Huntsville, Ala.
An offshoot of the ill-fated Bobbi Kar, the Keller Chief and Super Chief were similarly short-lived but offered the buyer the unique choice of front engine on the sedan or rear engine on the convertible. 4-cylinder Continental or Hercules units were available and models shown were a three-passenger and a five-passenger sedan and station wagon with independent suspension using rubber torsion bars. By the summer of 1949 only 18 pilot models had been built, and few cars, if any, were made after that.
The original plans had envisaged an eventual production of 6,000 cars per month, and an assembly plant in Belgium. Some Keller-designed station wagons were assembled in Antwerp in 1954/1955, and sold under the name P.L.M.

KELLER KAR 1914–1915
Keller Cyclecar Corp, Chicago, Ill.
The Keller Kar was a tandem, two-passenger cyclecar. It used a conventional 2-cylinder air-cooled engine with belt drive. It was supplied in standard colors of black and red and sold for $375.

KELSEY (i) 1913–1914
Kelsey Car Corp, Connersville, Ind.
This Kelsey was an ephemeral, completely conventional 6-cylinder car of moderate price. It had no connection with other machines bearing the same name.

KELSEY (ii) 1921–1924
Kelsey Motor Co, Newark, N.J.; Belleville, N.J.
C. W. Kelsey built the first Kelsey car, called the Auto-Tri in 1898 and subsequently constructed several other one-of-a-type models. Between

1910 and 1912 he built the 3-wheeled Motorette. In 1921, he began manufacture of a friction-driven assembled car, augmenting this with a standard version in 1922. Gray and Lycoming engines were used in these 4-cylinder cars, though a 6-cylinder Falls-engined car was offered in 1921.

KENMORE 1909–1912
Kenmore Mfg Co, Chicago, Ill.

This was an unattractive car with large-diameter wheels and pneumatic tires. Early models used 2-cylinder 127ci engines and planetary transmissions. Later versions, with either air- or water-cooled engines, were said to be capable of 30mpg.

KENNEDY (i) (CDN) 1909–1910
Kennedy Mfg Co, Preston, Ont.

The 1909 models were high-wheelers with De Tamble engines and shaft drive. A runabout and a surrey were offered. In 1910 the wheels were changed to 30in though everything else remained unaltered. About 50 of these cars were produced each year.

KENNEDY (ii) 1915–1918
W. J. Kennedy, Los Angeles, Calif.

This Kennedy was a four-passenger coupé with a dashboard radiator and Renault-type hood, also known as the Petite. It used a 4-cylinder gasoline engine, but had very much the appearance of an electric car.

KENSINGTON 1899–1904
Kensington Automobile Co, Buffalo, N.Y.

The Kensington company made cars powered by gasoline, steam and electricity. The steam and electric cars had a similar appearance, both being very simple two-passenger runabouts, the steamer using a 2-cylinder 4hp engine and single chain drive. In 1902 a gasoline car with an 11hp 2-cylinder Kelecom engine was introduced, and for one season all three motive powers were used. Steamers were dropped in 1903, and all manufacture ceased the following year.

KENT 1916–1917
Kent Motors Corp, Belleville, N.J.

This was an assembled car using a 4-cylinder Continental engine of 221ci. Four- and five-passenger models were sold, complete with dash clock, for $985.

KENWORTHY 1920–1922
Kenworthy Motor Co, Mishawaka, Ind.

The Kenworthy shared with the Duesenberg the honor of being America's first production car to have a straight-8 engine and 4-wheel braking. The 'Line-o-Eight' engine, as it was called, used overhead inlet and side exhaust valves. Unlike Duesenberg, the company also offered a more normal six and a 4-cylinder sports model.

1921 KENWORTHY Line-o-Eight touring car. *Floyd Clymer Publications*

KERMATH 1907–1908
Kermath Motor Car Co, Detroit, Mich.

The only model of this make was a small four-passenger runabout with a tear-drop shaped radiator and hood. It used a 26hp 4-cylinder engine with 3-speed transmission and shaft drive. The front axle was tubular. Because of lack of capital, only one Kermath was made.

KESSLER 1921–1922
Kessler Motor Car Co, Detroit, Mich.

The Kessler Four was an assembled car using a 4-cylinder 122ci engine of the firm's own design. A five-passenger touring car with artillery wheels was the only model. At least one example was made of the Kess-Line-Eight, with straight-8 engine designed by William H. Radford. This was later reworked into the Balboa engine, when Radford became vice-president and chief engineer of Balboa Motors Corp.

KEYSTONE (i) 1899–1900
Keystone Motor & Mfg Co, Philadelphia, Pa.

This was an unconventional steamer which had a 3-cylinder engine in each rear wheel hub, fed by steam from a tubular boiler mounted in the body. The company planned to make light cars and heavy trucks using this system.

KEYSTONE (ii) 1909–1910
1 Munch-Allen Motor Car Co, Dubois, Pa. 1909
2 Munch Motor Car Co, Yonkers, N.Y. 1910

The Keystone Six-Sixty model was driven by a 6-cylinder, 477ci engine. A two-passenger roadster and two touring cars were made, all priced at $2,250.

KEYSTONE (iii) 1915
H. C. Cook & Bros, Pittsburgh, Pa.

This Keystone used a 55hp Rutenber 6-cylinder engine and a 4-speed transmission. Electric lighting and starting was advertised for all models.

KIBLINGER 1907–1909
W. H. Kiblinger Co, Auburn, Ind.

The Kiblinger was a high-wheeled buggy with a 2-cylinder, air-cooled engine of 12hp under the seat. Nine different models were offered, the cheapest of which was a two-passenger roadster for $450. This car was succeeded by the McIntyre.

KIDDER 1900–1901
Kidder Motor Vehicle Co, New Haven, Conn.

The Kidder steam carriage used two separate cylinders of 3hp each, mounted horizontally on each side of the boiler. Drive to the rear axle was direct. A two-passenger was the only body style (apart from a delivery car), and the car used tiller steering. The price was $1,000, or rather more than the cheapest of the steam buggies.

KIMBALL 1910–1912
C. P. Kimball & Co, Chicago, Ill.

This small electric car was made in both two-passenger and four-passenger models. Two motors operating at 80 volts drove the rear wheels by double chain drive. Steering was by wheel, and solid rubber tires were standard.

KING 1910–1924
1 King Motor Car Co, Detroit, Mich. 1910–1923
2 King Motor Car Co, Buffalo, N.Y. 1923–1924

Charles B. King built the first car in Detroit in 1896, with a 4-cylinder horizontal engine, and later designed 2- and 4-cylinder cars for Northern. He formed his own company in 1909 and its first product was a 4-cylinder 35hp car with central gear shift. This and a companion 30hp model were made up to 1915, when a small V-8 of under 24hp was introduced. From 1916 onwards only 8-cylinder cars were made, there being two models, of

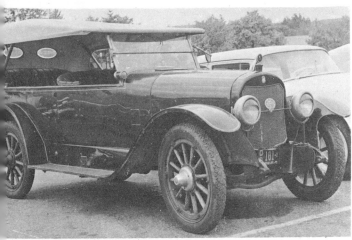

1918 KING 29hp V-8 touring car. *Kenneth Stauffer*
1965 KING MIDGET 9¼hp light car. *Midget Motors Corporation*

1914 KISSEL 6-cylinder touring car. *Montagu Motor Museum*

1925 KISSEL Gold Bug 8–75 speedster. *E. E. Husting*

26 and 29hp. Prices ranged from $1,400 for a 1917 touring car to $4,235 for a 1921 sedan. This inflation, although general in the industry, hit King sales, which slumped from a maximum of 3,000 per year in 1916 to only 240 in 1923, the year that King moved to a smaller plant at Buffalo. A number of Kings were sold in England before and after the war. They were handled by Salmons of Newport Pagnell, who fitted some of them with their own coupé bodies.

KING MIDGET 1946 *to date*
Midget Motors Corp, Athens, Ohio

The sole survivor of the post-World War 2 minicar boom in the United States, the Midget was a small two-passenger car of steel and aluminum construction. Early models contained a single-cylinder 8½hp Wisconsin air-cooled engine with manual transmission. Late cars used a 9¼hp Kohler engine with a unique automatic 2-speed-and-reverse transmission that was simple and dependable. Independent suspension was used and the chassis was made of perforated girders and tubing. Optional extras include doors, top, side curtains, speedometer, golf bag, racks, heater and hand controls for the handicapped. Since the beginning of manufacture approximately 5,000 King Midgets have been produced.

KING-REMICK 1910
Autoparts Mfg Co, Detroit, Mich.

The King-Remick was a two-passenger roadster, with racy lines. Its power was furnished by a 404ci, 6-cylinder engine. It had shaft drive and a wheelbase of nearly 120in.

KIRKSELL 1907
Dr James Selkirk, Aurora, Ill.

Dr Selkirk built a 50hp 4-cylinder car which he planned to sell at $3,000. It is unlikely that more than one was made.

KISSEL 1906–1931
Kissel Motor Co, Hartford, Wis.

At first the name of Kissel was associated with agricultural equipment, then with stationary gas engines. A conventional shaft-driven 35hp 4-cylinder automobile called, rather unfortunately, the Kissel Kar (originally the Badger), was offered from 1906. It was made almost entirely by the company; few parts were purchased. A six with 'square' dimensions (4¾in × 4¾in) appeared in 1909, electric starting came in 1913, and there was a short-lived V-12 powered by Weidely built from 1917 to 1918. None

111

of these had any sporting pretensions. From 1918, however, the policy of the company changed rapidly. The metamorphosis had begun in the previous year, when the Kissel Kar Silver Special Speedster was unveiled. It was named after its designer, C. T. Silver. At the New York Show of January 1918 the firm's new speedster policy was taken a step further with the Gold Bug, a development of the Silver Special Speedster. It earned its name because from 1919 chrome yellow was the make's standard color. It had a Kissel-made 6-cylinder L-head engine at first, of 246ci, later 284ci. More touring Kissels were offered as well, such as the Coach-Sedan and Tourster, which used the same engines as the Gold Bug. In 1924 external contracting Lockheed hydraulic brakes were a listed option. In that year, too, the alternative of a straight-8 with a modified Lycoming engine could be had. 1928 was the last year of Kissel-built engines. The handsome 1929 White Eagle with 185ci 6-cylinder and 247 and 299ci straight-8 engines, as well as internally expanding hydraulic brakes, could not compete at prices ranging from $1,595 to $3,885, and only 1,531 were sold. In 1930 Kissel assembled a few Ruxton cars on contract to New Era Motors, and in 1933 a reorganized company was hired to build Lever engines in order to demonstrate them to a large manufacturer for possible mass production. This venture came to nothing.

KLEIBER 1924–1929
Kleiber Motor Truck Co, Los Angeles, Calif.; San Francisco, Calif.

The Kleiber company was well-known on the American West Coast for its commercial vehicles. For six years it produced a small number of passenger cars which were marketed on the Pacific Coast only. These used a Continental 6-cylinder engine and other standard components.

1925 KLEIBER 6-cylinder sedan. *Lucien Loreille Collection*

KLINE KAR 1910–1923
1 B.C.K. Motor Co, York, Pa. 1910–1911
2 Kline Motor Car Corp, York, Pa. 1911–1912
3 Kline Motor Car Corp, Richmond, Va. 1912–1923

James A. Kline was designer and general manager of the Pullman Motor Car Company up to 1909, when he founded the B.C.K. Company, with S. E. Bailey and Joseph C. Carrell. The first Kline Kars used 6-cylinder engines designed and built in the works, but following the formation of a new company, and the move from New York to Richmond, the engines were bought out from the Kirkham Machine Company of Bath, N.Y., who built them to Kline's design. Four- and 6-cylinder units of 30 to 60hp were made, and the general design of the car was thoroughly conventional.

The post-war 6-55 model used a Continental engine. By 1922 sales had

slumped badly from the 800 to 1,000 per annum of the company's best years, and the following year they closed down.

KLINK 1906–1909
Klink Motor Car Mfg Co, Dansville, N.Y.

The 30hp Klink was available as a five-passenger touring model or as a two-passenger roadster at a standard price of $2,000. The 4-cylinder 270ci engine had a 3-speed selective transmission. For 1909 a choice of a 30 or 40hp engine was offered.

1920 KLINE KAR 6-55 touring car. *Automotive History Collection, Detroit Public Library*
1912 KNOX 40hp touring car. *Kenneth Stauffer*

KNICKERBOCKER 1901–1903
Ward Leonard Electrical Co, Bronxville, N.Y.

This was a small 2-cylinder gasoline car made by a well-known electrical equipment company. They also made an electric car under their own name.

KNIGHT *see* SILENT KNIGHT

KNIGHT SPECIAL 1917
Watson & Stoeckle, New York, N.Y.

This car used a Moline-Knight 4-cylinder engine and Entz magnetic transmission. The chassis cost $4,000, and custom bodies were available. One car was made, and plans were going ahead for modest production, but America's entry into World War 1 put an end to the project.

KNOX 1900–1915
Knox Automobile Co, Springfield, Mass.

These cars were known as the Knox Waterless, or more familiarly as the Old Porcupine, from the fact that air-cooling was by means of 2in pins screwed into the cylinder jackets instead of the more common fins. The first car was a 3-wheeler with a rear-mounted 4hp single-cylinder engine, and planetary transmission. This was made until 1903, but the first 4-wheeler appeared in 1901, and had long springs extending from front to rear axle. Single chain drive was used until 1905, when double chains were introduced for the larger cars, these being replaced by shaft drive in 1907. In 1906 a Knox came through the Glidden Tour without losing a single point.

Water-cooling was optional from 1908, and the later Knoxes though luxurious and expensive, had lost the individuality of Old Porcupine. Large 4- and 6-cylinder cars were made, with prices ranging up to $6,400 for the 1915 66hp 6-cylinder limousine. Harry A. Knox, the founder, had left the company in 1904 to make Atlas and Atlas-Knight cars, also in Springfield.

KOEB-THOMPSON 1910–1911
Koeb-Thompson Motors Co, Leipsig, Ohio

This car was based on engine patents obtained by the founders, R. P. Thompson and Emil Koeb. Apparently the only model produced was a large five-passenger car with a 4-cylinder, 2-cycle engine. The car had rear platform springing.

KOEHLER 1910–1914
H. J. Koehler Co, Newark, N.J.

This make was built by a sporting goods company which ventured into car and truck manufacture. The Montclair was a five-passenger touring model with a 4-cylinder, 318ci 40hp engine.

KOMET see STERLING (i)

KOPPIN 1915
Koppin Motor Co, Fenton, Mich.

This two-seater cyclecar used a 2-cylinder air-cooled De Luxe engine of 71ci. It had friction transmission and its price was $375. It is sometimes claimed that this make succeeded the Signet cyclecar.

KRASTIN 1902–1903
Krastin Automobile Co, Cleveland, Ohio

This company made a 'tonneau touring wagon' with a 2-cylinder engine. The body could be converted from passenger to parcel carrying.

KREUGER 1904–1905
Kreuger Manufacturing Co, Milwaukee, Wis.

This was a light touring car with a 2-cylinder air-cooled engine and shaft drive. The price was $1,000.

KRIM-GHIA 1966 to date
Krim-Ghia Import Co, Detroit, Mich.

These cars were Ghia-bodied versions of the Fiat 1500 and Plymouth Barracuda built to Krim specifications. The Fiat sports model used a 4-cylinder 86hp engine while the Barracuda roadster contained a 245hp Plymouth power plant.

KRIT (K.R.I.T.) 1909–1916
Krit Motor Co, Detroit, Mich.

Early models of the Krit were small three- and four-passenger cars with 4-cylinder engines. For 1911, a roadster with an underslung chassis was built. The last models of this make were classed as light cars, with a

1953 KURTIS racing and sports cars, with Frank Kurtis. *Associated Press Ltd*

221ci 4-cylinder engine. The price was $850 for either the roadster or touring version, and the cars used a swastika badge.

KUNZ 1902–1906
J. L. Kunz Machinery Co, Milwaukee, Wis.

This was a small, rather attractive two-passenger runabout with a single-cylinder engine. Although this car had a hood, the engine was in fact mounted under the seat. A 3-speed transmission was used, described as operating by 'a sliding wedge'. The price was given as $675.

KURTIS 1949–1955
1 Kurtis-Kraft, Inc, Glendale, Calif. 1949–1950
2 Kurtis Sports Car Corp, Glendale, Calif. 1953–1955

Frank Kurtis, prominent sports and racing car designer, tried his hand at marketing his own cars on several occasions. A Kurtis-Kar, planned in 1948 with an 80hp engine, never materialized, but in 1949 the Kurtis Sports appeared with a distinctive two-passenger body and Ford running gear. Bodies were built partially of fiberglass and 36 of this custom-made car were produced before Muntz Motors took over the design in 1950 to continue it as the Muntz Jet. In 1954 came the Kurtis 500-S competition car, which was similar to the Indianapolis 500 racing model, except for some additions including fenders and lights. Thirty of this model were assembled, the engines available including the Mercury. A prototype of this machine delivered to a Hudson dealer in 1953 contained a 6-cylinder Hornet engine, transmission and axle. A 500-KK tubular chassis, adaptable to metal or fiberglass bodies, was also available during 1954–1955.

With the completion of 18 500-M sports cars in 1955, Kurtis turned to other fields of activity, including building airport servicing vehicles for jets and rocket sleds for Cook Electric Research Labs. The 500-M had a fiberglass body with scooped side panels, torsion-bar suspension and a 4-cylinder ohv supercharged engine. The capabilities of Kurtis-built racing cars were shown when they won 1st, 3rd, 4th, 5th, 6th, 8th, 9th and 10th places during the 1954 Indianapolis 500 Mile Race.

KURTZ AUTOMATIC 1921–1923
Kurtz Motor Car Co, Cleveland, Ohio

The Kurtz, with its 6-cylinder Herschell-Spillman engine, was one of many assembled cars of its time, distinguished only by its preselector gear-shift on the steering column.

L

LACONIA 1914
H. H. Buffum, Laconia, N.H.

The Laconia, a cyclecar, had double, parallel cantilever springs front and rear, an aluminum body and a V-twin air-cooled engine. The manufacturer is better remembered for his earlier effort, the Buffum.

LAD'S CAR 1912–1914
Niagara Motor Corp, Niagara Falls, N.Y.

This was a juvenile car for two small passengers. It was sold in kit-form, with blueprints, for home assembly. Its power came from a single-cylinder engine with double chain drive to the rear axle.

LAFAYETTE 1920–1924
1 Lafayette Motors Co, Mars Hill, Ind. 1920–1923
2 Lafayette Motors Co, Milwaukee, Wis. 1923–1924

The Lafayette was a luxurious, lavishly equipped V-8 designed by D. McCall White, who had been responsible for the V-8 Cadillac of 1915, a car in the same class. Its L-head engine developed 100bhp at 2,750rpm. Its thermostatically-controlled radiator shutters were a pioneering feature. The price ran as high as $7,500 for the limousine. In 1923 Nash Motors acquired control of Lafayette Motors and continued to make the big eight for a short while, as a luxury line, but soon dropped it. The Lafayette name, if nothing else, was revived by Nash in 1934 for their cheapest line.

1923 LAFAYETTE Model 134 touring car. *Jacques Kupélian Collection*

LA MARNE (US/CDN) 1920
La Marne Motor Co, Cleveland, Ohio
Anglo-American Motors Ltd, Trenton, Ont.

The La Marne was a low-slung, low-priced 8-cylinder car, of which few were built. The sole model, a hard-top touring car, was listed at $1,485, the concern advertising it as 'real value, $3,000'. Its straight-8 (about 360ci) engine developed 85bhp, and was of an ohc variety similar to the Hispano-Suiza. At least one was built in Canada by Anglo-American Motors who also planned to sell a 4-cylinder car at $975.

LAMBERT 1891; 1904–1917
The Buckeye Mfg Co, Anderson, Ind.

John W. Lambert's 3-wheeler of 1891 is considered the first gasoline-engined vehicle built in the United States. The Lambert succeeded the Union (i) in 1904. All the production Lamberts used a friction drive. Up to 1910, a chassis with a small 2-cylinder engine was built with either four-passenger or five-passenger bodies; double and subsequently single chain drive was used. Shaft drive appeared on the big Lamberts in 1907. Later models used 4- and 6-cylinder engines by Continental, Buda and Rutenber. After 1917 the marque continued for two years as a commercial vehicle.

LANCAMOBILE 1899–1901
James H. Lancaster Co, New York, N.Y.

The Lancamobile was a light tiller-steered car with engine under the seat, and chain drive. It had a *vis-à-vis* body.

L. & E. 1922–1931
Lundelius & Eccleston, Los Angeles, Calif.

Although the L. & E. was announced as early as 1922, the first car may not have appeared before 1924 when a 'car without axles' was built. The prototype (or prototypes) was a touring car, weighing 2,750lb. Power was supplied by a 6-cylinder air-cooled engine. A large factory was planned in Long Beach but this never materialized. Several subsequent experimental L. & E. cars were built after 1924. The 1932 model was announced in October 1931 and proved to be a handsome wire-wheeled sedan, somewhat resembling a Franklin of the period. The car had four transverse springs at both front and rear to support the wheels, each rear wheel being driven by a short shaft with two universal joints, the shaft connecting with a bevel gear and the differential unit hung from cross members on the frame.

LANE 1899–1910
Lane Motor Vehicle Co, Poughkeepsie, N.Y.

The first Lane, Model No. 1, was a four-passenger with a 2-cylinder steam engine under the body. These cars grew larger, with boilers under front hoods, although all used 2-cylinder engines, later of compound type, up to 30hp and operating at 350psi. The last and largest model was on a 125in wheelbase. A total of 22 different models were built during the company's manufacturing life.

LANE STEAM WAGON 1900
Lane, Daley Co, Barre, Vt.

Only one Lane Steam Wagon was produced, despite plans to continue manufacture. The 6-passenger vehicle featured such safety controls as a self-closing throttle. The Lane was cumbersome at 3,200lb, however, and only able to achieve a speed of 15mph. It was a dual-purpose machine and could be used for passengers or to carry merchandise.

1909 LAMBERT 15hp touring car. *Kenneth Stauffer*
1909 LANE 30hp steam touring car. *Keith Marvin Collection*

Harley J. Earl — a very unusual practice for the period. Unlike other makers' 'cheap lines', it was manufactured to Cadillac standards throughout, though its wheelbase was 7in shorter and at $2,495 a sedan was about $700 cheaper. The engine was an L-head V-8 of 303ci displacement. Synchromesh, safety glass and chromium plating were innovations shared with Cadillac in 1929 and the car grew to 353ci in 1931. The concept was changed in 1934 — though the La Salle was the guinea-pig for the turret-top steel bodies to be used in 1935 by all G.M. divisions save Buick, the car was cheapened in other respects, having a 240ci straight-8 engine as used in the bigger Oldsmobiles. Its price was $1,595. A reversion was made to the traditional V-8 in 1937, the cars sharing body shells with Oldsmobile and the more expensive Buicks, and the price was cut again to $1,205.

The La Salle was squeezed out of the market by the lower list prices of the simpler Cadillac models. The 1940 cars were as good as their predecessors, but at $1,446 as against $1,752 for a Cadillac, there was no longer room for the La Salle.

LAUREL 1916–1920
Laurel Motors Corp, Anderson, Ind.

The Laurel was an assembled car with a G.B. & S. 4-cylinder engine, sold in two models, a four-passenger roadster and five-passenger touring car, both priced at $895. A distinguishing mark was the small script carrying the car's name on the sides of the hood above the louvres.

1930 LA SALLE all-weather touring car. *General Motors Corporation*
1940 LA SALLE Model 52 sedan. *Arthur Rippey*

LANPHER 1909–1912
Lanpher Motor Buggy Co, Carthage, Mo.

The Lanpher two-passenger car was a high-wheeler with an air-cooled 2-cylinder engine, solid rubber tires, planetary transmission and double chain drive. It sold for $550.

LANSDEN 1906–1908
Lansden Co, Newark, N.J.

This electric car, which was also known as the Electrette, had a peculiar elongated hood which housed the batteries. The two-passenger roadster was powered by a 3½hp motor and weighed 1,950lb. Instruments were limited to a clock and odometer. It had an early example of left-hand steering by wheel.

LA PETITE 1905
Detroit Automobile Mfg Co, Detroit, Ill.

This two-passenger car, designed by J. P. La Vigne (also known for the J.P.L.) had a single-cylinder air-cooled engine in front of the dash. The transmission had 2 forward speeds, and final drive was by shaft.

LA SALLE 1927–1940
Cadillac Motor Car Co, Detroit, Mich.

Launched as a smaller and less expensive running-mate for the Cadillac, the La Salle was conceived in its entirety by General Motors' stylist

LAUTH-JUERGENS 1907–1910
1 Lauth-Juergens Co, Chicago, Ill. 1907–1910
2 Lauth-Juergens Motor Car Co, Fremont, Ohio 1910

This car started as a demonstration model by J. Lauth & Co, Chicago, in 1905. Limited production of a five-passenger 'tourist' model began in 1907. It had a 4-cylinder, 40hp engine. After 1910, the make continued as a commercial vehicle.

LA VIGNE *see* JPL

LAVOIE (CDN) 1923
Lavoie Automobile Devices Ltd, Montreal, Que.

The Lavoie had a 4-cylinder engine of the firm's own design, unitary construction of chassis and body and 4-wheel brakes. It appeared in closed-car form only and was intended exclusively for sale in Canada.

LAW 1905
Law Automobile Corp, Hartford, Conn.

This auto is described as having a 20hp engine and was sold for $2,500. This was a strictly local product and further information is lacking.

LAWTER 1909
Lawter Shredder Co, Newcastle, Ind.

One model of the Lawter had solid rubber tires. Its engine was a horizontal, water-cooled 2-cylinder unit developing 20hp. Final drive was by planetary transmission and shaft. The other model was powered by a 16hp engine.

LEACH (i) 1899–1901
Leach Motor Vehicle Co, Everett, Mass.

The Leach steam car used a 6hp 2-cylinder vertical engine, single chain drive and tiller steering. With a two-passenger body it looked little different from its contemporaries, but the makers did have the honesty to say that it was 'intended only for good roads'. The price was $600.

LEACH (ii) 1920–1923
Leach Motor Car Co, Los Angeles, Calif.

The first Leach used an L-head Continental engine, but the firm was best-known for the Power Plus Six made from 1922 to 1923. This was a 347ci unit with single overhead camshaft which developed 107bhp. These cars were popular with movie stars of the day, although the make sold only in small numbers. Roadsters, touring cars and sedans were manufactured, and the make was among the first to offer the California Top, consisting of a fixed top and sliding windows which could be attached to an open touring car. A golf bag was standard equipment on the chummy roadster, and all 1922 models cost $6,500.

LEADER 1905–1912
1 Columbia Electric Co, McCordsville, Ind. 1905–1906
2 Leader Mfg Co, Knightstown, Ind. 1906–1912

Despite the original manufacturer's name, the Leader had an internal-combustion engine. Early models had 2-cylinder units with planetary transmissions and single chain drive. Later models used an F-head, 4-cylinder engine and sliding-gear transmission. The manufacturers may have moved to other Indiana sites during these years.

1916 LENOX (ii) touring car. *Keith Marvin Collection*

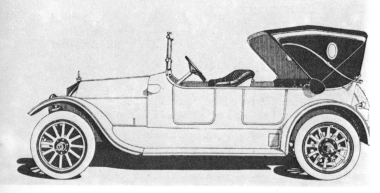

1902 LEROY runabout. *Hugh Durnford*

LENAWEE 1903–1904
Church Manufacturing Co, Adrian, Mich.

This small, rear-entrance tonneau had left-hand drive. Its single-cylinder water-cooled engine was mounted under the front seat. Final drive was by shaft, and full-elliptic springs were used. The name Murray (i) was used for earlier cars by this company.

LENDE 1908–1909
Lende Automobile Mfg Co, Minneapolis, Minn.

A five-passenger car was the single model of the Lende. It was powered by a 4-cylinder, 308ci engine and had a planetary transmission and shaft drive.

LENOX (i) 1908–1909
Maxim & Goodridge, Hartford, Conn.

Also known as the Maxim-Goodridge, this was an electrically-powered car with solid rubber tires. The batteries, weighing 800lb, were connected with a 3hp motor through a 5-speed controller. These cars, mostly open victorias, were graceful in an archaic fashion, and sold for less than $2,000.

LENOX (ii) 1911–1918
1 Lenox Motor Car Co, Jamaica Plain, Mass. 1911–1914
2 Lenox Motor Car Co, Boston, Mass. 1914–1918

The Lenox was a well-designed car of pleasing appearance which used both 4- and 6-cylinder engines. The largest model was the 1913 six with a 377ci engine. With electric starting, this five-passenger car cost $2,750. Buda engines were used latterly.

LEON RUBAY *see* RUBAY

LEROY (CDN) 1899–1902
Good Brothers, Berlin (now Kitchener), Ont.

Believed to be Canada's first production car, the Leroy was a curved-dash runabout weighing 950lb which used reverse gear as a brake and had only one forward gear. Some 32 were built.

LESCINA 1916
Lescina Automobile Co, Newark, N.J.

The Lescina, introduced in January 1916 at New York City's Grand Central Palace, failed to last out the year, although its plans were grandiose. A total of ten body styles were offered, from closed models to open cars and a panel delivery truck, on three different chassis of 125in, 112in and 106in wheelbase. The largest of these, the Model V, was presumably not produced. Prices on the other two chassis ranged from $555 to $1,288. The cars were assembled from standard components and initial plans included an auxiliary manufacturing plant in Chicago.

LEVER *see* ELCAR *and* KISSEL

LEWIS (i) 1898–1902
Lewis Cycle Co, Philadelphia, Pa.

The Lewis was a spidery-looking vehicle with large wheels, powered by a horizontal single-cylinder engine. It had friction transmission, the driven disk being made of compressed paper!

LEWIS (ii) 1913–1916
1 Lewis Motor Co, Racine, Wis. 1913
2 L.P.C. Motor Car Co, Racine, Wis. 1914–1916

The Lewis was one of the first American cars with a long-stroke engine and was sponsored by William Mitchell Lewis, formerly of the Mitchell company; designer was René Petard, who was also responsible for contemporary Mitchells. In this case the stroke was 6in, compared with a bore of 3½in. The 6-cylinder engine was used to power a five-passenger touring car. The weight of this vehicle was given as 3,250lb and the price in 1915 was $1,600.

LEWIS AIROMOBILE 1937
Lewis American Airways, Inc, Rochester, N.Y.

This was a streamlined 3-wheeled five-passenger sedan powered by a 122ci flat-4 air-cooled engine designed by the former Franklin engineers, Doman and Marks. Drive was to the front wheels. Only one prototype was built, although four other cars were under construction when the company ran out of capital.

LEXINGTON 1909 1928
1 Lexington Motor Co, Lexington, Ky. 1909–1910; Connersville, Ind. 1911–1913
2 Lexington-Howard Co, Connersville, Ind. 1914–1918
3 Lexington Motor Co, Connersville, Ind. 1918–1928

An assembled car from the beginning, the first Lexington was produced in Kentucky in 1909 but operations were moved to Indiana less than a year later. At first 4-cylinder cars were built, with sixes introduced in 1915 and remaining in production for the duration of Lexington's existence. The Lexington appeared in various models and body styles offering a wide variety of types to the potential purchaser. The peak production year was 1920 when some 6,000 were built. A year later the Ansted motor was adopted and prices ranged as high as $4,500. The concern went into receivership early in 1923, but production continued. The cars were highly regarded and had advanced lines for their day, the most famous models being the Lexington and Concord touring car and sedan of the early and mid-1920s. Also popular was the Minute Man Six, although the allusion to the Battle of Lexington-Concord in the American Revolution was odd, as the Lexington was actually named after the Kentucky city of its origin. It was eventually absorbed by the Auburn Automobile Company; extremely limited production marked the Lexington's final years and the last of them were produced in 1928.

LIBERTY (i) 1914
Belmont Auto Mfg Co, New Haven, Conn.

This make succeeded the Liberty-Brush. It was a typical cyclecar with a V-twin air-cooled engine developing 15hp. Designer Joseph A. Anglada was also responsible for the Anderson (ii) among others.

LIBERTY (ii) 1916–1924
Liberty Motor Car Co, Detroit, Mich.

This was a popular make for a short period. The Liberty discarded in 1920 the Continental 6-cylinder engine used at the beginning of its pro-

1920 LIBERTY (ii) 23hp touring car. *Autocar*

duction and the company's own six was fitted until manufacture ceased. Production reached its highest point in 1919 when 6,000 cars were sold. The Liberty was purchased late in 1923 by the Columbia Motor Car Co which planned to market the car but did not succeed. The last units sold as 1924 models were actually 1923 cars. The Liberty and the Columbia were very similar in appearance.

LIGHT 1914
Light Motor Car Co, Detroit, Mich.

The name Light must have come from the manufacturer rather than the size of the car, for it was a conventional 30hp 6-cylinder vehicle, made only in touring form, and selling for $1,250.

LINCOLN (i) 1909
Lincoln Motor Vehicle Co, Lincoln, Ill.

This car was a high-wheeler with solid rubber tires, using a 4-cycle, 2-cylinder air-cooled engine of 106ci. Three models were made, two with shaft drive and one with a single chain.

LINCOLN (ii) 1911–c 1914
Lincoln Motor Car Works, Chicago, Ill.

After the closure of the Sears venture, the Lincoln Motor Car Works made a high wheeler of similar design to the Sears for a few years. Most were commercial vehicles.

LINCOLN (iii) 1914
Lincoln Motor Car Co, Detroit, Mich.

This Lincoln was an unsuccessful light two-passenger car. Its weight was 1,050lb and it cost $595.

LINCOLN (iv) 1920 to date
Lincoln Motor Co, Detroit, Mich.

After Henry M. Leland's resignation from Cadillac in 1917, he evolved another big L-head V-8 which came on the market under the name of Lincoln in 1921. It had a capacity of 358ci and developed 81bhp. Cylinder heads were detachable and full-pressure lubrication was adopted at a time when many American makers pinned their faith to splash systems. Over 70mph was possible and it was not excessively expensive at $4,300, but the style of the bodies did not match the quality of the mechanical components, and Henry Ford acquired the company after it had encountered financial difficulties in 1922. Both Leland and his son Wilfred resigned a few months later, but Ford retained the traditions of quality, adding aluminum pistons from the time of his takeover. Lincolns were much used by both gangsters and police, the latter driving tuned versions capable of over 80mph and equipped with front-wheel brakes, a luxury not available to the general public until 1927. President Coolidge bought

1922 LINCOLN (iv) sedanca de ville. *Ford Motor Co*
1932 LINCOLN (iv) Model KB cabriolet. *Ford Motor Co*

a Lincoln in 1924, establishing a link between these cars and the White House which has lasted till this day: Franklin D. Roosevelt's Sunshine Special was one of the last 12-cylinder Ks; Harry S. Truman ordered an open Cosmopolitan in 1950; and John F. Kennedy bought a Continental in 1961.

Lincolns sold steadily in limited numbers — nearly 9,000 in 1926. Engine capacity went up to 384ci in 1928. 1931 cars had a 145in wheelbase, downdraught carburation and 120bhp engines, but in 1932 there came a new 440ci KB-type V-12 with vacuum booster brakes. This was joined the following year by a smaller 374ci KA-type 12 at $2,700, and all subsequent Lincolns made up to 1948 were to have 12-cylinder power units. In 1934 both models gave way to a 414ci K with aluminum cylinder heads, and a top speed of nearly 100mph. The Division could not, however, support itself on the dwindling prestige-car market, and for 1936 they offered a popular V-12, the 267ci, 110bhp Zephyr. Unitary construction was adopted; other characteristics were: synchromesh transmission, headlights faired into the fenders, a fastback style and an alligator-type hood. The brakes, however, were mechanical, and Ford's traditional transverse suspension was used. It cost $1,320 and its engine was used in Anglo-American hybrids of the period: the Allard, Atalanta and Brough Superior. Zephyrs of 1938 had a dashboard gear shift. Hydraulic brakes followed in 1939, and column shift in 1940. Meanwhile the Model K had at last been dropped; sales for the combined 1939 and 1940 seasons had been 120 of these cars and the black-bordered emblems on the last models were symbolic! To balance this, a new product had been launched in 1939, the Mercury. There were also some relatively inexpensive prestige cars — Edsel Ford's Zephyr-based Continental coupés and cabriolets, with 299ci engines. Options in the last pre-war seasons included overdrive, a fluid coupling, and power-operated hoods and windows. No entirely new Lincolns appeared until 1949, when a change was made to Ford's new styling and coil-spring independent front suspension, while at the same time the 12-cylinder engine was replaced by an L-head undersquare 339ci V-8. Manual transmission was dropped finally from Lincolns in 1951, and 1952 models swept the board in the touring-car class of that year's Carrera Panamericana, the winner averaging 90mph. Ohv engines of 205bhp were introduced for 1953, and the 1956 line consisted of the 368ci 285bhp Premiere and Capri as well as a revived Continental which

1936 LINCOLN (iv) Zephyr sedan. *Ford Motor Co*
1937 LINCOLN (iv) Zephyr four-door convertible. Coachwork by Le Baron. *Keith Marvin Collection.*

1941 LINCOLN (iv) Continental convertible. *Henry Ford Museum, Dearborn, Mich.*
1971 LINCOLN (iv) Continental sedan. *Ford Motor Co*

is listed as a separate make. Dual headlights were adopted for the 1957 cars, and 1958 Lincolns had unitary construction — this was the year of Lincoln-Mercury Division's disastrous Edsel. Although the Continental Mark II was dropped after 1957, the name Continental was applied to all Lincolns from 1961 onwards. These had 430ci V-8 engines, rising to 460ci in 1967. An unusual body style was a 4-door convertible. In 1968 another special Presidential limousine was built. With 160in wheelbase, bullet-proof glass and many other security features, it cost about $500,000. The Lincoln Continental was completely restyled for 1970, and 1971 models had further small styling improvements and safety features.

LINDSLEY 1907–1908
1 J. V. Lindsley, Indianapolis, Ind. 1907–1908
2 J. V. Lindsley, Dowagiac Motor Car Co, Dowagiac, Mich. 1908

This was a two-passenger car with large-diameter wheels and solid rubber tires. It was powered by a 2-cylinder air-cooled engine of 10hp under the seat, with a planetary transmission. The manufacturer moved in 1908 to Dowagiac, Mich., and commenced to build 15 cars but the company failed before these were finished. These cars were completed by the Dowagiac Motor Car Co, and for this reason the name Dowagiac is regarded as a make by some historians.

LION 1909–1912
Lion Motor Car Co, Adrian, Mich

The Lion was produced in at least three different body types, all powered by a 4-cylinder 40hp engine. The 1912 model, which cost $1,600, boasted of internal-expanding brakes with drums of 14in diameter. A fire in 1912 destroyed 150 cars in the factory and the company was unable to continue.

LIQUID AIR 1901–1902
Liquid Air Power & Automobile Co, Boston, Mass.

The Liquid Air car resembled any light steam buggy of the period, but carried a tank of liquid air under high pressure whose expansion was supposed to drive an ordinary single-cylinder steam-type engine. The efficiency of such a system has been estimated at only 4%, and it is improbable that the car could have run any distance, if at all. The scheme was probably a stock promotion project, like those of Pennington and some other companies.

LITTLE 1912–1915
Little Motor Car Co, Flint, Mich.

William H. Little was a former Buick manager whom William C. Durant employed to build cars in the Flint Wagon Works which had formerly made the Whiting. The first Little car was a 4-cylinder 20hp two-passenger roadster priced at $650. It was joined by a 6-cylinder touring car, the 220ci Little Six, in 1914. This was phased out the following year as it was too close in size and price to the Chevrolet Six, another Durant product. The Little roadster's styling influenced that of the Chevrolet Royal Mail roadster.

LITTLE DETROIT SPEEDSTER 1913–1914
Detroit Cyclecar Co, Detroit, Mich.

This was a long name for a rather small cyclecar. Despite its size, it had a 4-cylinder, water-cooled engine and 2-speed selective transmission and shaft drive. The hood front had a peculiar polyhedral design.

LITTLEMAC 1930–1931
Thompson Motor Corp, Muscatine, Iowa

Only a few Littlemac cars were built. They had short wheelbases and were equipped with the former Star Four engine. Artillery wheels were standard and 2-wheel mechanical brakes were fitted. The price was $438.

LITTLE PRINCESS 1913–1914
Princess Cyclecar Co, Detroit, Mich.

This cyclecar was made in two- and four-passenger versions, powered by 4-cylinder, 92ci air-cooled engines. Planetary transmission was used with shaft drive. The design later became the Princess (i).

LOCOMOBILE 1899–1929
1 Locomobile Co of America, Westboro, Mass. 1899–1900
2 Locomobile Co of America, Bridgeport, Conn. 1900–1929

Locomobile was one of the two companies which resulted from the purchase of the Stanley brothers' steam-car design rights in 1899 by A. L. Barber and J. B. Walker. Walker separated from Barber and formed the Mobile concern, while his former partner did good business with the little Locomobile steam runabout. This consisted of a welded 'bicycle' framework, a carriage body, a twin-cylinder simple engine and a 14in boiler under the driver's seat. It was tiller-steered and chain driven and at $600 it looked a better bargain than it was, suffering from the crudest of lubrication arrangements and an astronomical water consumption: the boiler had to be refilled every 20 miles! In spite of this in 1901 the four-story Locomobile factory was said to be the biggest of its kind in the world. The steamers survived until 1903, with bigger boilers, culminating in a 10hp wheel-steered *dos-à-dos* which sold for $1,600.

Locomobile eventually sold their steam-car rights back to the Stanleys,

1900 LOCOMOBILE 5½hp steam buggy. *The Veteran Car Club of Great Britain*

1909 LOCOMOBILE Model 30 touring car. *Antique Automobile*

but in the meantime A. L. Riker had designed a gasoline car on Panhard lines, with a 4-cylinder engine, automatic inlet valves and pressed-steel frame. Radiators were of the Mercedes honeycomb type in 1905, in which year Joe Tracy competed in the last Gordon Bennett Cup Race with a very Mercedes-like T-headed chain-driven racer. More successful was Locomobile's F-head 'Old 16', built in 1906. George Robertson drove it to victory in the 1908 Vanderbilt Cup, while another Locomobile victory was first place in the touring-car category of the 1913 Glidden Tour, this achieved with a 1909 car that had already covered 100,000 miles. In the meantime the company had settled down to a long line of expensive and beautifully-made T-headed touring cars, the early ones being chain-driven fours. In 1907 $3,800 was asked for the 199ci Model E and $4,500 for the 350ci Model H. By 1909, the bigger four had grown up to 471ci, and 1911 brought the debut of the famous T-headed 48, originally with 'square' engine dimensions of 4½in × 4½in, but later growing up to 525ci. It developed 90bhp, had dual magneto ignition (later coil) and was still being listed in 1929; its price was $4,800 in 1912, increased to $9,600

1926 LOCOMOBILE Junior Eight sedan. *Michael Sedgwick*
1908 LOGAN (i) Blue Streak 20/24hp roadster. *The Veteran Car Club of Great Britain*

towards the end of its production run. Body styles were attractive, especially the open Sportifs and Gunboat Roadsters introduced during World War 1. There was also a smaller 38 to the same specifications.

Locomobile encountered financial difficulties in 1920, and after a short spell with Crane-Simplex and Mercer in the Hare's Motors group, was acquired by W. C. Durant's last empire in 1922. Durant continued the 48 and added another luxury car, the 90 with L-head monobloc engine, but the Locomobile factories were utilized for the production of the inexpensive Flint. In 1925 came the Junior 8, a competitor for the Chrysler with a 181ci ohv engine, selling at $1,785. In 1929, the last year of production, the 48 and 90 were still available, but the staple car was a 298ci Lycoming-engined straight-8 at $2,850, a sad end for a firm which had been advertising eleven years before that 'no stock parts or ready-made units are permitted'.

LOGAN (i) 1903–1908
Logan Construction Co, Chillicothe, Ohio

The Logan was a light car using the air-cooled Carrico engine, available in either two- or five-passenger models. Model O for 1907 was a 'semi-racer' with a 4-cylinder engine, a Hassler transmission and shaft drive. The company subsequently limited itself to commercial vehicles.

LOGAN (ii) 1914
Northwestern Motorcycle Works, Chicago, Ill.

This was a minor make of cyclecar with a 2-cylinder Spacke engine, a friction transmission and V-belt drive. The side-by-side two-passenger car was priced at $375.

LONDON SIX (CDN) 1921–1924
London Motors Ltd, London, Ont.

Approximately 100 London cars were produced in a four-year period. The cars were large and well built and powered by a Herschell-Spillman 6-cylinder engine; they closely resembled the American Lincoln of the time.

LONE STAR 1920–1922
Lone Star Motor Truck and Tractor Corp, San Antonio, Texas

An assembled car, the Lone Star was available as a 4-30 or a 6-40 both using Lycoming power units. Open and closed models were listed. The cars were in fact made for the Lone Star Corporation by Piedmont Motor Car Co of Lynchburg, Va.

LOOMIS 1896–1904
1 Gilbert J. Loomis, Westfield, Mass. 1896–1897
2 Loomis Automobile Co, Westfield, Mass. 1901–1903
3 Loomis Auto Car Co, Westfield, Mass. 1903–1904

Gilbert Loomis built a pioneer steam car in 1896, but did not put it into production. His first cars built for sale used 5hp Crest air-cooled engines. About 50 of these cars were made from 1901 onwards, and Loomis also made carburetors and silencers for other firms. In 1904 a 3-cylinder 18hp car appeared with single chain drive and rear-entrance tonneau body. Loomis afterwards worked as a designer for Pope-Tribune, Payne Modern and Speedwell.

LORD BALTIMORE 1913
Lord Baltimore Motor Car Co, Baltimore, Md.

The Lord Baltimore had a 4-cylinder L-head engine of 312ci with a 4-speed selective transmission. It offered electric lights and starting by a compressed-air system. A five-passenger touring car and a two-passenger raceabout were the only models produced.

LORRAINE (i) 1907–1908
Lorraine Automobile Mfg Co, Chicago, Ill.

The Lorraine was a large car with a 392ci 4-cylinder engine. It had selective transmission and shaft drive. The range consisted of a seven-passenger limousine and a two- or four-passenger roadster.

1924 LONDON SIX sedan. *Keith Marvin Collection*
1910 LOZIER 50hp Lakewood touring car. *Autocar*

LORRAINE (ii) 1920–1922
Lorraine Motors Corp, Grand Rapids, Mich.; Detroit, Mich.

This Lorraine was an assembled car which succeeded the Hackett, and was powered by a 4-cylinder Herschell-Spillman engine. Both open and closed models were sold but total production only reached a few hundred cars.

LOS ANGELES 1913–1915
Los Angeles Cycle Car Co, Buffalo, N.Y.

Chassis for this cyclecar were shipped to Los Angeles to be fitted with bodies, which explains the Buffalo address. The Los Angeles had an underslung steel frame, friction transmission and double chain drive and was powered by a 4-cylinder, water-cooled engine or an air-cooled V-twin, both of 10hp.

LOST CAUSE 1963–1964
Lost Cause Motors, Louisville, Ky.

The Lost Cause concern was the idea of Charles Peaslee Farnsley, who founded it to offer buyers the kind of extras the motor industry did not provide. He began to supply Corvairs with 'custom' work by Enos Derham of the Derham Custom Body Works. This included such extras as racing rally timers and aircraft equipment such as altimeters and compasses. Among other items were picnic hampers, mint julep cups of vermeil, matching luggage and car rugs. The starting price of the lengthened-wheelbase Lost Cause cars was quoted at $19,600 but prices were expected to reach as high as $23,000.

LOWELL 1908
Lowell-American Automobile Co, Lowell, Mass.

This company was incorporated and announced the intention of manufacturing a car to be named the Lowell, with 4-, 6-, or 8-cylinder engines, at prices ranging from $1,250 to $2,250. Proof of actual production, however, is lacking.

LOZIER 1905–1917
1 Lozier Motor Co, Plattsburg, N.Y. 1905–1910
2 Lozier Motor Co, Detroit, Mich. 1910–1917

The Lozier was one of the highest quality American cars of its era, and was highly favored by the wealthy, conservative buyer. After three years of experimental work, which included the building of a steam car, the Lozier company launched their production car at the Madison Square Show in 1905. It had a 30/35hp 4-cylinder T-head engine, 4-speed transmission and double chain drive, and cost $5,000 for the chassis alone. After 1907 shaft drive was adopted, and two models were available, a 40hp four and a 50hp six, the latter with a displacement of 572ci. The cylinders were cast in pairs, and the T-head layout was still used. On this model third gear was direct, fourth being an overdrive. Although closed models were available, the most popular bodies were the Briarcliff sports touring car, the Lakewood torpedo and the Meadowbrook two-passenger roadster. For a short period Lozier had considerable success in racing. They won the 1910 National Stock Car Championship at Elgin, and in 1911 won the Vanderbilt Cup and came 2nd at Indianapolis. These successes were achieved with largely stock 6-cylinder cars.

In 1911 a smaller 6-cylinder, the 6-77, was introduced with an L-head engine which cost only $3,250 for the chassis. This car was designed by Frederick C. Chandler who left Lozier the same year with two other engineers, and formed the Chandler Company. This was the beginning of the end for Lozier, who brought out a 4-cylinder car in 1914 but found their sales hit by the Cadillac V-8 at the same price. They tried to interest Henry Ford in a take-over, but without success. From 1915 to 1917 prices were drastically cut, the 1916 Model 6-82 chassis costing only $2,775 as against $5,000 for the comparable 1913 6-72. The Model 84 4-cylinder cost only $1,575, but production ended the following year.

H. A. Lozier, son of the founder, and brother of co-chairman E. R. Lozier, had left the company in 1913, and afterwards manufactured the 12-cylinder H.A.L. car at Cleveland.

L.P.C. *see* LEWIS (ii)

LUCK UTILITY 1913
This car was a short-lived vehicle with an unknown manufacturer. It was a five-passenger car with a 4-cylinder 164ci engine and a 3-speed transmission. It cost $2,000.

LU-LU 1914
Kearns Motor Truck Co, Beavertown, Pa.

This oddly-named cyclecar was a side-by-side two-passenger vehicle. It used a water-cooled 14hp 4-cylinder engine, with a 3-speed transmission and shaft drive. The weight was given as 930lb and it cost $398.

LUNKENHEIMER 1902
Lunkenheimer Motor Vehicle Co, Cincinnati, Ohio

Originally a carriage-building firm, the Lunkenheimer Company broadened its scope in 1902, building two cars, each of which had a 2-cylinder opposed engine housed under the front seat. Because of difficulties encountered in production, the car range was not continued, although the company survives as manufacturers of industrial valves.

LUTZ 1917
Lutz Motor Co, Buffalo, N.Y.

This company was formed to manufacture steam cars, and was reported to be looking for a factory site in Buffalo, but there is no evidence that cars were ever made.

1914 LU-LU 12hp cycle car. *The Veteran Car Club of Great Britain*

1904 LYMAN & BURNHAM 12hp tonneau. *Keith Marvin Collection*

LUVERNE 1903–1918
Luverne Automobile Co, Luverne, Minn.

This range of cars consisted of high-wheelers at first, but by 1909 more advanced vehicles of 40hp were being built. Rutenber 6-cylinder engines of 38/40hp were used as well as some built by Beaver. Because of their uniformity of color, inside as well as outside, later cars were known as 'Big Brown Luvernes'.

L.W.C. 1916
Columbia Taxicab Co, St Louis, Mo.

This manufacturer was primarily interested in cabs, but many taxis of the period doubled as town cars. The limousine model was powered by a 4-cylinder, 27hp engine. The price of this was $3,500.

LYMAN 1903–1904
C. F. Lyman, Boston, Mass.

Although it shared the same address as the Lyman & Burnham, this make was dissimilar in lay-out as well as in appearance. It was an expensive car ($6,250) with a 30/35hp 4-cylinder engine, sliding-gear-transmission and shaft drive. The one model, a rear entrance, five-passenger tonneau, was furnished with a removable limousine top.

LYMAN & BURNHAM 1903–1904
Lyman & Burnham, Boston, Mass.

This was powered by a 12hp, 2-cylinder engine, and had sliding-gear transmission and shaft drive. The only body type was a five-passenger rear-entrance tonneau. These cars were actually manufactured in Quincy, Mass, by the Fore River Ship & Engine Co.

LYONS-ATLAS (LYONS-KNIGHT) 1912–1915
Lyons-Atlas Co, Indianapolis, Ind.

This make was an outgrowth of the Atlas Engine Co, an old builder of 2-cycle engines. The Lyons-Knight used sleeve valve Knight engines, of either 4 or 6 cylinders. The various models had generous dimensions, with wheelbases up to 130in. Five- and seven-passenger touring models were offered, as well as a closed limousine, the latter at a cost of $4,300.

M

MACDONALD 1923–1924
MacDonald Steam Automotive Corp, Garfield, Ohio
This company attempted unsuccessfully to market a steam roadster called the MacDonald Bobcat but the car failed to catch on. Closed models were also offered, but most MacDonald engines were ultimately used for those who wished to convert their gasoline cars to steam.

MACKLE-THOMPSON 1903
Mackle-Thompson Automobile Co, Elizabeth, N.J.
This two-passenger runabout was driven by a single-cylinder, air-cooled engine of 5hp. It had three forward speeds and shaft drive. Its light weight (650lb) enabled it to reach 35mph.

MACON 1915–1917
All Steel Car Co, Macon, Mo.
This light car used a 4-cylinder, 120ci Sterling engine. Wire wheels were standard equipment on this four-passenger car, which was similar in general appearance to the Scripps-Booth.

MADISON 1915–1918
Madison Motors Co, Madison, Ind.
The Madison was an assembled car built in small numbers and shown, first, as a two-passenger roadster and later as a four-passenger roadster, and also a de luxe two-passenger called the Dolly Madison model. A touring car was also made. A Rutenber 6-40 engine supplied the power with a Herschell-Spillman V-8 listed in 1916 only.

MAGNOLIA 1902
Magnolia Automobile Co, Riverside, Calif.
This company announced that a factory was being built and that 15hp touring cars would be made there, but it is not recorded that production ever started.

MAHONING 1904–1905
Mahoning Motor Car Co, Youngstown, Ohio
This car was available in single- or 4-cylinder air-cooled models. The 4-cylinder, 28hp model had three forward speeds, with final drive by single chain.

MAIBOHM 1916–1922
1 Maibohm Motors Co, Racine, Wis. 1916–1919
2 Maibohm Motors Co, Sandusky, Ohio 1919–1922
The Maibohm was an assembled car using 4-cylinder engines during the first two years of manufacture and augmenting these with a Falls six in 1918. The smaller power unit was discontinued for the 1919 season. Open and closed models were available. The Maibohm name was changed to Courier in 1922.

MAJESTIC 1917
Majestic Motor Co, New York, N.Y.
The only model of this make was an open five-passenger touring car costing $1,650. It was powered with V-8 engines of 283ci or 330 ci, with Hotchkiss drive.

MALCOLM 1914–1915
Malcolm Jones Cyclecar Co, Detroit, Mich.
The Malcolm had a single headlight inset in the hood above the radiator. It was in the cyclecar class but had a 4-cylinder *en bloc* engine of 18hp, and room for three passengers. A V-twin with friction transmission and belt drive was also made. Some lists call this the Malcolm, and the larger car the Malcolm-Jones.

MALDEN 1898
Malden Automobile Co, Malden, Mass.
The Malden was a light steam car with a two-passenger body to which two extra front seats could be fitted. It had a vertical 2-cylinder engine, and wire wheels.

MANEXALL 1921
Manufacturers' & Exporters' Alliance, New York, N.Y.
A small car, the Manexall had a 2-cylinder De Luxe air-cooled engine with a displacement of 70ci, developing 13bhp at 2,500rpm.

MANIC (CDN) 1970 to date
Les Automobiles Manic Inc, Quebec
The Manic GT is a rear-engined GT coupé using many Renault components including 1300 or 1300-Gordini engines. A model with 1600 engine is planned. A 4-speed transmission is standard, but a 5-speed box can be had to special order.

MANLIUS 1910
Manlius Motor Co, Manlius, N.Y.
The Manlius was available as a small runabout or larger roadster. The roadster was powered by a 28bhp air-cooled, 4-cylinder engine and was priced at $1,250.

1920 MAIBOHM 20hp all-weather touring car. *Autocar*

MAPLEBAY 1908
Maplebay Mfg Co, Crookston, Minn.

This was a clumsy-looking two-passenger runabout. It used a 22hp 4-cylinder, air-cooled Reeves engine with friction transmission and cost $1,400.

MARATHON 1908–1915
1 Southern Motor Works, Jackson, Tenn. 1908–1910
2 Marathon Motor Works, Nashville, Tenn. 1910–1915

The Marathon was marketed in as many as four different chassis with ten different body types. These were powered by 30/35hp 4-cylinder engines, and sixes of 50hp. These units used the flywheel as an oil pump. Wheelbases ranged from 116in to 149in. The latter was the 1913 Champion model.

MARBLE-SWIFT 1903–1905
Marble-Swift Automobile Co, Chicago, Ill.

This was a two-passenger car with a 2-cylinder, 10hp engine. It had friction transmission, double-chain drive and tubular axles. The coil radiator in front was surmounted by a magnificently large brass shell.

MARION 1904–1914
Marion Motor Car Co, Indianapolis, Ind.

Early versions of the Marion had transversely-mounted 16hp Reeves air-cooled engines, and double chain drive. Their appearance was very similar to the contemporary Premier (also an Indianapolis car). 1906 Marions had conventionally-placed 16 and 28hp 4-cylinder Reeves engines, while later models used water-cooled engines, by Continental and other firms, of up to 48hp. A prototype roadster with 577ci V-12 engine, designed by George Schebler of carburetor fame, was built in 1908. Some quite big fours and sixes were made in the 1912–1914 period. Sales for a time were under the control of John N. Willys.

MARITIME SIX (CDN) 1913–1914
Maritime Motors Ltd, Saint John, N.B.

This was based on the American Palmer-Singer and was widely advertised, although the extent of production is unknown. Expensive at $3,500, it was decidedly sporty with a Benz-style pointed radiator. Most of the models built were touring cars.

MARKETOUR 1964 to date
Marketour Electric Cars, Long Beach, Calif.

This is a small electric car for shopping and running errands.

MARLBORO 1899–1902
Marlboro Motor & Carriage Co, Marlboro, Mass.

The Marlboro was a typical New England steam car in appearance, although it used a 5hp horizontal engine in place of the more usual vertical one. Final drive was by single chain, and four-passenger bodies were available, in addition to the standard two-passenger buggy.

MARMON 1902–1933
1 Nordyke and Marmon Co, Indianapolis, Ind. 1902–1925
2 Marmon Motor Car Co, Indianapolis, Ind. 1926–1933

Howard Marmon's first cars were advanced machines, featuring air-cooled V-4 engines of oversquare dimensions, with mechanically-operated overhead valves and pressure lubrication. Something approaching independent front suspension was achieved by the use of double-three-point suspension, with a separate subframe for engine and transmission. Only the 2-speed planetary transmission conformed to American practice of the period. These cars persisted until 1908, though 1907 brought the introduction of selective sliding-type transmissions and a short-lived 60hp V-8. In 1908 buyers had the choice of air or water cooling and cylinder heads were detachable.

The following year Marmon went over to conventional T-head in-line

1910 MARION 30hp roadster. *Montagu Motor Museum*

1911 MARMON Model 32 roadster. *Kenneth Stauffer*

MARION-HANDLEY 1916–1919
Mutual Motors Co, Jackson, Mich.

The Marion-Handley was a continuation of the earlier Marion and was a fairly popular car for the few years it was produced. In appearance, the Marion-Handley resembled the typical assembled car of its time. Two models were available, a touring car and a four-passenger roadster and these were available on two wheelbases: the 6-40 on 120in and 6-60 on 125in. A Continental 6-cylinder engine was used for both. Artillery wooden wheels were standard equipment on the touring car, but wire wheels were offered as an option on the roadster.

fours rated at 40/45hp and 50/60hp, and two years later only the 318ci Model 32 with rear-axle transmission was listed. Marmons did well in contemporary competition, with 54 1st places logged between 1909 and 1912; Ray Harroun won the first Indianapolis 500 in 1911 with a specially-built 6-cylinder car, the Wasp. An enormous 572ci six rated at 48hp was available in 1914.

In 1916 the advanced ohv 6-cylinder 34 with aluminum cylinder block, body, hood and radiator shell, and double transverse rear suspension was introduced. Its engine displacement was 340ci, and its output 74bhp; developments of this model were still listed as late as 1927, acquiring

1917 MARMON Model 34 sports touring car. *Don McCray*
1931 MARMON V-16 convertible sedan. *Lucien Loreille Collection*

Delco coil ignition in 1920, and the option of front wheel brakes in 1923. They were expensive. $5,000 was asked for a touring car in 1921. A not very successful 189ci ohv straight-8 appeared in 1927, but the following season only eights were made, the cheapest L-head 68 selling for $1,395. In 1928 Marmon also entered some front-wheel-drive cars at Indianapolis, but they were in fact only revamped Millers. The company sold 22,300 cars in 1929, thanks to a cheap new straight-8 at under $1,000, the Roosevelt. This brand-name, however, did not last, for the car appeared in the 1930 program as the Marmon R, along with three other eights, the L-head 69, and two big ohv cars with 4-speed transmissions and displacements of 211ci and 303ci respectively.

Marmon's swansong was the magnificent 491ci 200bhp 16-cylinder model of 1931. It was beautifully proportioned, and had an alloy engine. The list price was $4,925; there was a companion 8-125 in 1932, but only the Sixteen was listed for 1933. At the very end Marmon was testing a 150bhp V-12 with independent front suspension, De Dion rear axle, and tubular backbone frame, but this never saw production.

MARQUETTE (i) 1912
1 Marquette Motor Co, Saginaw, Mich. 1912
2 Peninsular Motor Co, Saginaw, Mich. 1912

The Marquette succeeded both the Rainier and the Welch. It was built in four body types, using 40 and 45hp engines. These were 4-cylinder T-head units, the larger engine being used only for the seven-passenger touring model. The Marquette Motor Co was controlled by General Motors.

MARQUETTE (ii) 1929–1931
Buick Motor Co, Flint, Mich.

This Marquette, introduced for the 1929 model year, was a small Buick with prices ranging from $990 for the business coupé to $1,060 for the sedan. A total of 13,850 of these 6-cylinder cars were marketed during

1929, but by 1930, presumably because of the Depression, it was decided to withdraw the make and the name disappeared from the list of American cars early in 1931. The only Buick product to use an L-head engine, it had much in common with the contemporary Pontiac.

MARR 1903–1904
Marr Auto Car Co, Detroit, Mich.

The Marr was a two-passenger runabout powered by a single-cylinder engine of 104ci displacement. This was mounted under the seat. Steering was by wheel, and the vehicle weighed 1,000lb.

MARSH (i) 1899; 1905–1906
1 Marsh Motor Carriage Co, Brockton, Mass. 1899
2 American Motor Co, Brockton, Mass. 1905–1906

The 1899 Marsh was a steam car which was probably never produced in any numbers. From 1900 to 1905, Marsh built motor cycles which were known as Marsh-Metz from 1905 onwards, and from 1905 to 1906 a small car with a 10hp 2-cylinder air-cooled engine under the hood. In 1909 C. H. Metz bought the Waltham company and began to make the Metz car.

MARSH (ii) 1919–1921
Marsh Motors Co, Cleveland, Ohio

The Marsh was a car of which only a few were actually built. It had a 201ci 6-cylinder engine of L-head design.

MARSHALL 1919–1921
Marshall Mfg Co, Chicago, Ill.

The Marshall was a typical assembled car of its time with a 4-cylinder Lycoming engine as its power unit. A touring car was the only body style offered.

1930 MARQUETTE (ii) Six sedan. *Montagu Motor Museum*

MARTIN (i) 1920–1922
Martin Motor Co, Springfield, Mass.

Also known as the Scootmobile, the Martin was a 3-wheeler on the same lines as the Scott Sociable, except that it used a pressed steel frame instead of the Scott's tubular one. Power came from a 37.6ci air-cooled V-twin engine, and the makers claimed a speed of 40mph and fuel consumption of 75mpg.

MARTIN (ii) 1928–1932
Martin Aeroplane Co, Garden City, Long Island, N.Y.

The experimental Martin Aerodynamic car never got into production

1922 MARTIN (i) Scootmobile 3-wheeler. *Autocar*

although it was widely acclaimed in car and scientific journals. It was designed by James V. Martin and General Billy Mitchell and carried a rear-mounted engine and independent suspension on all four wheels. Its radiator was mounted at the front.

MARTIN (iii) 1929–1932
1 Martin Motors, Inc, Washington, D.C.
2 Martin Aeroplane Factory, Hagerstown, Md.; Garden City, Long Island, N.Y.

The Martin was an unsuccessful venture into the production of a midget car. The pilot models had been built as early as 1927 but despite considerable publicity to sell the $200 mail-order midget, the car failed. It used a 4-cylinder Cleveland motor-cycle engine of under 45ci, and the 60in wheelbase chassis carried a two-passenger coupé body. The price included the delivery crate, which could afterwards be used as a garage. Its 1931 catalogue referred to the car as the Dart, not the Martin. Often attributed to J. V. Martin, it was, in fact, designed by Miles H. Carpenter, creator of the Phianna.

MARTIN STATIONETTE 1954
Commonwealth Research Corp, New York, N.Y.

This was a 3-wheeled 'commuters' car' designed by James V. Martin who had been responsible for the Martin (ii) cars. The Stationette had a hoodless three-passenger body and a rear-mounted 47.3ci 4-cylinder Hercules engine. Transmission was by Martin Magnetic fluid drive, and a maximum speed of 80mph was claimed. The price was fixed at $1,000, but production never started.

MARVEL 1907
Marvel Motor Car Co, Detroit, Mich.

The single model of this make was a two-passenger runabout, with a horizontal 2-cylinder engine. It used a planetary transmission and single chain drive.

MARYLAND (i) 1900–1901
Maryland Automobile Mfg Co, Luke, Md.

The Maryland company made a wide range of steam vehicles, all with vertical 2-cylinder engines and single chain drive. Body styles included a runabout, surrey and phaeton, and prices ranged from $900 to $2,500.

MARYLAND (ii) 1907–1910
Sinclair-Scott Co, Baltimore, Md.

This was a continuation of the Ariel of Bridgeport, Conn., with no technical changes for the first models. Later, the wheelbase of the models was expanded from 100in to 116in. A four-passenger roadster and a five-passenger touring car were complemented in 1908 and 1909 by a limousine and a town car.

MASON (i) 1898–1899
William B. Mason, Milton, Mass.

This steam car was similar to the first Stanleys, and used a Stanley boiler and burner together with the Mason patent regulator in which the fire was controlled by boiler pressure. This was used in a number of other steam cars, but it is unlikely that the Mason car itself was built in any numbers.

MASON (ii) 1906–1910
1 Mason Motor Car Co, Des Moines, Iowa 1906–1908
2 Mason Automobile Co, Des Moines, Iowa 1908–1910

The Mason was launched as a five-passenger touring car powered by a 2-cylinder opposed engine of 24hp. It had planetary transmission and single chain drive. Very few changes were made in the design during the life of this make, although two- and four-passenger versions were added in 1909. The Mason was succeeded by the Maytag, these two makes being Fred S. Duesenberg's first essay in car design.

MASSILLON 1909
W. S. Reed Co, Massillon, Ohio

The Massillon had a 6-cylinder T-head engine of 477ci, with two spark plugs to each cylinder. The same chassis was used for both the roadster and the five/seven-passenger touring car. A 3-speed transmission and shaft drive were employed.

MASTER 1917–1918
Master Motor Car Co, Cleveland, Ohio

Better-known for their trucks, the Master company offered briefly a 6-cylinder automobile with 100bhp engine in roadster, phaeton, and limousine form. Prices were $5,000 and up.

MATADOR *see* AMERICAN MOTORS

1907 MATHESON 40/45hp touring car. *General Motors Corporation*

MATHESON 1903–1912

1 Matheson Motor Car Co, Grand Rapids, Mich. 1903
2 Matheson Motor Car Co, Holyoke, Mass. 1903–1905
3 Matheson Motor Car Co, Wilkes-Barre, Pa. 1906–1910
4 Matheson Automobile Co, Wilkes-Barre, Pa. 1910–1912

The first Matheson was a large chain-drive touring car powered by a 24hp 4-cylinder ohv engine. It was designed by Charles Greuter, who had previously made the Holyoke car in the factory taken over by Matheson. Not more than 100 cars were made in the first three years of production, before the firm moved to Wilkes-Barre. Here larger cars of 40/45 and 60/65hp were made, the latter costing up to $7,500. In 1908 came the first six, a 48hp car still with overhead valves. It had shaft drive, although chains were still used on some fours until 1910. The improved 'Silent Six' was made until the end of production in 1912. Approximately 800 fours and 1,000 sixes were made in all.

MATTHEWS *see* SOVEREIGN

MAXIM-GOODRIDGE *see* LENOX (i)

MAXWELL-BRISCOE; MAXWELL 1904–1925

1 Maxwell-Briscoe Motor Co, Newcastle, Ind.; Tarrytown, N.Y. 1904–1913
2 Maxwell Motor Corp, Detroit, Mich. 1913–1925

This make, the work of Jonathan Maxwell and Benjamin Briscoe, appeared in 1904 as a flat-twin runabout with square (4in × 4in) cylinder dimensions, a conventional style, mechanically-operated inlet valves, thermo-syphon cooling, and shaft drive. It sold for $750, and the make's early years were marked by distinguished performances in the Glidden Tours, with outright victories in 1911 and 1912. Inevitably, 4-cylinder versions followed, the D type being a car rated at 30/40hp, though twins were still made as late as 1912, when the Messenger runabout was listed at $625. Nine thousand Maxwells had been sold by the summer of 1909, by which time the company had become part of the short-lived United States Motor Co — other members of this group included Stoddard-Dayton and Brush.

With the collapse of the combine in 1912, Briscoe departed to form his own company, but Maxwell salvaged what was left, and continued to evolve inexpensive 4-cylinder cars from the Mascotte and Mercury which had sold for $950 and $1,150 respectively. Though a few sixes were made, Maxwell's staple during the rest of the make's career was a cheap monobloc four with 3-speed L-head which sold for $750 in 1914, and $655 in 1916, the latter price including full electrical equipment. Total production of cars and trucks in 1917 topped the 100,000 mark, and post-war Maxwells had coil ignition.

Output went up to 32hp in 1921 with the coming of the new Good Maxwell. Walter P. Chrysler took over Maxwell and its associated company Chalmers in 1923, and the Chrysler Six, introduced for 1924, outsold Maxwell's 4-cylinder cars. The 1925 Maxwells were the last; they were replaced by a 4-cylinder Chrysler which ultimately gave way to the Plymouth (ii) in 1928.

1923 MAXWELL Model 25 touring car. *Harrah's Automobile Collection*

1910 MAYTAG 30hp touring car. *Kenneth Stauffer*

MAYTAG 1910–1915

Maytag-Mason Motor Co, Waterloo, Iowa

Maytag succeeded Mason in 1910, with no change in the cars themselves. These were medium-sized cars made in six models with 2- or 4-cylinder engines of 24 to 28 and 35 to 38hp. The Model H roadster of 1911 had an early boat-tailed body. The make is most famous for its connection with Fred S. Duesenberg, who superintended the company for a short period.

McCUE 1909–1911

The McCue Co, Hartford, Conn.

The McCue had 4-cylinder L-head engines of 30 or 40hp. A runabout and a touring car were produced, with 3-speed selective transmissions, shaft drive and right-hand steering.

McCULLOUGH 1899–1900

Backbay Cycle & Motor Co, Boston, Mass.

This was a light car using a 4½hp 2-cylinder horizontal engine and chain drive. It had a two-passenger body.

McFARLAN 1910–1928

McFarlan Motor Car Co, Connersville, Ind.

A small-production prestige car, the McFarlan was made by an offshoot of the earlier McFarlan Carriage Co. The company specialized in 6-cylinder motor cars from its inception until the last vehicles were produced, except for eights which were built as a sideline in the mid and late 1920s. Several different engines were used between 1910 and 1916, when the concern adopted a larger Teetor-Hartley type and although various components were used, because of the infinite care given by the company to each of its cars the McFarlan was not considered an assembled car in the same manner as many others of the time. By 1917, an elaborate range of both open and closed body types were available to the purchaser and McFarlans became progressively larger and more expensive.

In the autumn of 1920, the enormous TV or Twin-Valve series was introduced, the engines being of McFarlan's own make and embodying triple ignition which necessitated 18 spark plugs on each car. Noteworthy among models was the ornate and over-elaborate Knickerbocker Cabriolet, a town car selling for $9,000. The McFarlan was highly regarded among American makes although no more than 235 cars were produced in any given year.

In the autumn of 1923, the company introduced a smaller version of the huge TV McFarlan, the Single Valve or SV Six. Advertised as a 'companion car' to the larger car, it used a Wisconsin engine and was

1922 McFARLAN Series TV sedan. *McFarlan Collection of Alvin J. Arnheim*
1925 McFARLAN Series SV coach-brougham. *McFarlan Collection of Alvin J. Arnheim*

able on the same chassis. Although their production did not approach that of the TV, this line, equipped with a Lycoming engine, was retained until McFarlan production ceased. Although the larger McFarlan did not change much in appearance between 1920 and 1927, the 1928 models were sleeker and lower. Only a few were built, however, and that year, the McFarlan assets were purchased by E. L. Cord.

McGILL 1922
McGill Motor Car Co, Fort Worth, Tex.

The McGill was an assembled car, mainly produced as a touring car. A 6-cylinder engine with a capacity of 210ci was standard. The touring models sold at $2,385.

McINTYRE 1909–1915
W. H. McIntyre Co, Auburn, Ind.

The McIntyre was a continuation of the Kiblinger. It appears that the principal of the original company changed his name, as the initials W.H. are identical. As many as four models of the McIntyre were available, with 4- and 6-cylinder engines and wheelbases up to 120in. Later cars were of conventional design in contrast to the Kiblinger high-wheelers. From 1913 to 1914 this company built the Imp cyclecar.

McKAY (i) 1900–1902
Stanley Mfg Co, Lawrence, Mass.

The McKay steam car was, in fact, a Stanley carefully redesigned so as not to infringe any of the patents which the Stanley twins had granted to Locomobile and Mobile. Locomobile nevertheless threatened to sue the Stanley company so they completely redesigned the car, replacing the vertical engine and chain drive by a horizontal engine and direct drive on the rear axle. This became the 1902 model of the new Stanley Motor Carriage Company.

McKAY (ii) (CDN) 1911–1914
1 Nova Scotia Carriage Co, Kentville, N.S.
2 Nova Scotia Carriage and Motor Car Co, Amherst, N.S.

Four-cylinder Buda engines were used in the 30hp torpedo (roadster) at $1,450 and the 40hp McKay touring car at $2,050. Production was rather haphazard — about 25 at Kentville and another 100 at Amherst after a major reorganization and the erection of a large factory. Based on the U.S. Penn, the McKay achieved some local racing success but lack of capital forced the firm out of business.

a quality product. Unfortunately, it was not a success and relatively few were sold. The SV was withdrawn from production by 1926. Another attempt to attract a lower-priced clientele was in the introduction of the Eight-in-Line series, these cars being priced similarly to the SV and avail-

1909 McINTYRE high-wheel surrey. *Antique Automobile*

1911 McKAY (ii) 30hp roadster. *Hugh Durnford*

McLAUGHLIN (CDN) 1908–1922; McLAUGHLIN-BUICK 1923–1942

McLaughlin Motor Car Co, Ltd, Oshawa, Ont.

The McLaughlin slogan was 'Canada's Standard Car'. In addition to being a slogan it became a statement of fact. Canada was founded in 1867, and so was the McLaughlin Carriage Company, which began by producing two hand-made sleighs. By the turn of the century McLaughlin carriages and sleighs were among the best-known and most highly regarded in the country. An attempt to build cars from the ground up failed when the chief engineer fell sick just as assembly was to start, whereupon McLaughlin agreed with W. C. Durant to put Buick engines and some other parts into their cars. The agreement was for 15 years, under terms very favorable to McLaughlin.

The first McLaughlin car was produced in 1908. Mechanically, it was like the contemporary Buick 4, but the body was all Canadian. Production the first year was between 150 and 200 units. Output climbed to 423 the next year and to 1,098 by 1914. It rose slowly to around 6,000 yearly, spurting ahead to 15,000 in the final year of 1922. McLaughlin bodies continued to be different from Buick bodies, and considerably more elaborate for as long as they were made of wood. After that they became generally similar, though hoods, dashboards and other fittings and trim continued to be more luxurious on McLaughlins. A. P. Sloan, president of General Motors, once spotted a McLaughlin outside the New York City Buick showroom and flew into a rage lest Buick buyers should see it and demand similar quality. McLaughlin cars were sold on the reputation of McLaughlin carriages. Very early in their car-building enterprise the name was changed to Buick, but sales fell so drastically that it was changed back to McLaughlin. From about 1910 until the early 1920s, McLaughlin produced a very full range of cars including a four, a light six and the standard six. These were each available in all the usual body styles, often offering a choice in trim. The light six was basically the American Oakland with a McLaughlin nameplate.

In 1915 McLaughlin also began producing Chevrolets under license, but again featuring a somewhat better-finished product than the American company. In 1918 the entire McLaughlin business was sold to General Motors and became General Motors of Canada. When the original 1907 agreement ran out in 1923 the name of the car was changed to McLaughlin Buick. Differences in the Canadian car became minute and the McLaughlin prefix was dropped entirely early in World War 2.

In 1927 the company produced a custom touring car for a visit by the Prince of Wales, and in 1939 two huge convertible limousines for the visit of the King and Queen.

1911 McLAUGHLIN 4-cylinder touring car. *Hugh Durnford*

1911 MERCER Model 35-R roadster. *William S. Jackson*

MECCA 1914–1916

1 Mecca Motor Car Co, Teaneck, N.J. 1914–1915
2 Times Square Automobile Co, Detroit, Mich. 1915–1916

The early Mecca was a cyclecar with a 95ci, 4-cylinder, water-cooled engine. In 1916 it became a light car of 1,800lb with a 188ci 4-cylinder engine, and standard track. Both five-passenger and two-passenger cars were built.

MED-BOW, MEDCRAFT *see* SPRINGFIELD (ii)

MENARD (CDN) 1908–1910

Windsor Carriage & Wagon Works, Windsor, Ont.

This 16hp 2-cylinder high-wheeler sold for $625. It featured friction drive by chains and a steel-reinforced wooden front axle. It was designed by M.B. Covert of Detroit, who had previously designed the Covert steam and gasoline cars.

MENOMINEE 1915

Menominee Electric Mfg Co, Menominee, Mich.

This company was mainly known for electric commercial vehicles, but they made an electric cabriolet to sell at $1,250. Planned production was 150 cars per year, but far fewer than that were actually made.

MERCER 1910–1925; 1931

1 Mercer Automobile Co, Trenton, N.J. 1910–1925
2 Elcar Motor Car Co, Elkhart, Ind. 1931

The Mercer was named after Mercer County, New Jersey, where it was made. The most famous Mercer of all was the Type 35 Raceabout of 1911, designed by Finlay R. Porter. The specification was ordinary enough, embracing at first a 300ci, 4-cylinder, Continental-built T-head engine that produced a little over 50bhp at a leisurely 1,700rpm. There were three forward speeds. The classic 'bodywork' consisted of a bolster tank, two bucket seats, and a monocle windshield. However, in common with other speedsters, the Mercer weighed very little and could pull a high axle ratio, which helped it to attain a guaranteed 70mph. In 1912, by contrast, a few cars were made with the Owen Magnetic's Entz transmission. A more efficient, L-head engine giving up to 89bhp at 3,000 rpm depending on tune was substituted in 1915. Also, it had a 4-speed transmission. This 22 Series was designed by E. H. Delling. However, some of the old Raceabout's character was lost, in that the body of the new version had sides and a bench-type front seat, instead of the two stark bucket seats of the first type. Indeed full touring models were offered as well. The Series 4 and 5, beginning in 1919, had yet another designer in A. C. Schultz, and even had an electric starter. Nevertheless, these cars were still European in concept in that the engines had a fixed head and a magneto, and drove through a plate clutch and, however much they had compromised with popular taste, they could still attain 75mph. A six with an ohv engine made by Rochester was introduced at the same

1939 MERCURY (iv) sedan. *Ford Motor Co*
1950 MERCURY (iv) sedan. *Ford Motor Co*

1920 MERCER Series 6 touring car. *Don McCray*

time, and sixes alone were made from 1923. The old line of Mercers finally died two years later. However magnificent they may have been, they bore too little relation to what the public wanted to survive. Production never exceeded 500 units a year. An attempt was made to revive the name in 1931, but only two cars were built. The chassis was made by the Elcar Motor Co and the engine by Continental. The latter was a straight-8 providing 140bhp and 100mph.

MERCILESS 1907
Huntington Automobile Co, Huntington, (Ill?)

The 70hp Merciless had a wheelbase of 127in. The engine was a T-head 6-cylinder unit with 610ci displacement. Drive was through a 4-speed transmission and drive shaft. The state in which this car was made is still in question.

MERCURY (i) 1904
Mercury Machine Co, Pittsburgh, Pa.

This was a two-passenger car with a 2-cylinder water-cooled engine of 7hp. A sliding-gear transmission was used and the weight of the vehicle was 1,250lb. Its price was $295 and a top cost $100 extra.

MERCURY (ii) 1914
Mercury Cyclecar Co, Detroit, Mich.

The Mercury cyclecar differed little from others of that breed, except that it had a self-supporting body which eliminated the chassis frame; in other words integral construction. The engine was a 9hp 2-cylinder air-cooled unit, and the car used friction transmission and belt final drive. Body styles were a monocar, a tandem two-passenger and a light delivery truck.

1967 MERCURY (iv) Cougar coupé. *Ford Motor Co*

MERCURY (iii) 1918–1920
Mercury Cars, Inc, Hollis, N.Y.

A small, assembled car of limited production, the Mercury used a Duesenberg or Weidely 4-cylinder engine and was equipped with a door in the floor to give the driver ready access to the service brake mechanism.

1918 MERCURY (iii) sporting touring car. *Keith Marvin Collection*

1971 MERCURY (iv) Comet sedan. *Ford Motor Co*

MERCURY (iv) 1938 to date
Ford Motor Co, Detroit, Mich.

The Mercury, a product of Ford's Lincoln Division, was intended to rival G.M.'s Oldsmobile and Buick, and widen Ford penetration of the American market. The car was in effect an enlarged Model 91 Ford V-8 with a 239ci 95bhp engine. At $957 it cost $230 more than its smaller sister, but $40 less than Buick's cheapest 4-door sedan. Hydraulic brakes were standard from the start and evolution followed established Ford lines, with no drastic changes until 1949, when the new low silhouette, hypoid rear axle, and coil-spring independent front suspension were incorporated. Displacement went up to 255.4ci and its front-end styling emphasized the association with Lincoln. Mercury, like Ford, progressed to overhead valves and oversquare cylinder dimensions and in 1955 buyers had a choice of two V-8 engines of 188 and 198bhp. An inexpensive Medalist series was added in 1956 and in 1957 the standard power unit was a 255bhp 312ci engine, with the option of a detuned Lincoln engine giving 290bhp. Mercury became bigger and more expensive in 1958 and 1959 to avoid clashing with the Edsel range from the same stable, and a 430ci, 360bhp engine was available.

In 1961 Mercury broke with tradition, and offered for the first time something other than a V-8; not only was there the option of a 223ci six in the regular range, but there was also a semi-compact, the 144ci Comet, a model with a 114in wheelbase parallel with Ford's Falcon. The Comet sold for $2,084 in 1962, when the largest of the standard V-8s was a rather modest 292ci.

In the year 1963 there was a return to bigger things, with 390ci and 436ci engines available in the top-price Monterey models, which also included a Breezeway sedan with forward-sloped rear window as already used on Ford of Britain's 1960 Anglia. Though the Comet was retained for 1966 with a 200ci engine, the bigger Mercurys looked like Lincoln's Continental on a reduced scale; the wheelbase was 123in, with 390ci, 410ci and 428ci engines available. For the more sporting motorist there was the Comet Cyclone with compact dimensions and a 390ci V-8 unit. A 1967 sports coupé version, the Cougar, heralded a return to the waterfall-type radiator grill so generally popular in the early 1950s. For 1969 the luxurious Marquis and Marauder lines borrowed styling from Lincoln's Continental and featured retractable hoods on the headlights. These were continued through 1970, together with the Cougar, and medium-sized Montego sedans.

For 1971 an all-new compact, the Comet, was introduced, with 170ci 6-cylinder engine, and options of 200ci and 250ci sixes, and a 302ci V-8. The Montego, Cougar and Marquis were continued for 1971, but the Marauder was dropped.

MERCURY SPECIAL 1946
Paul Omohundro, Los Angeles, Calif

The aluminum-bodied Mercury Special sports never got beyond the prototype stage because of material shortage. A Mercury chassis and engine were used but it was intended to supply production models with Cadillac engines and transmissions, plus bodies of fiberglass.

MERIT 1920–1923
Merit Motor Co, Cleveland Ohio

The Merit, an assembled car, used a Continental 6-cylinder engine. Production was small.

MERKEL (i) 1905–1906
Merkel Mfg Co, Milwaukee, Wis.

This car, which was built in very small numbers, was a two-passenger roadster, with left-hand steering by wheel. The final drive was by shaft.

MERKEL (ii) 1914
J. F. Merkel, Middletown, Ohio

This was a relatively heavy (1,060lb) two-passenger cyclecar, with a 4-cylinder water-cooled, 95ci engine. The drive was through a 3-speed transmission and drive shaft.

MERRY '01 1958–1962
American Air Products Corp, Fort Lauderdale, Fla.

Sometimes referred to as the Merry Olds, this was a modern plywood and steel reproduction of the curved dash Oldsmobile. It used a 4hp single-cylinder Clinton air-cooled engine providing 35mph and 60mpg.

MERZ 1914–1915
Merz Cyclecar Co, Indianapolis, Ind.

The body and hood of this cyclecar was of one-piece construction. A single headlight was inset above the false radiator. Its engine was a 70.5ci 2-cylinder De Luxe.

MESERVE 1904
W. F. Meserve, West Derry, N.H.

These were custom-built cars, using 4-cylinder 2-cycle 334ci engines built by the Lowell Motor Co of Lowell, Mass. Final drive was by chain. A speed of over 40mph was claimed.

METEOR (i) 1900
Springfield Cornice Works, Springfield, Mass.

The first of many cars to bear the name Meteor, this was a light runabout powered by a 2¾ or 3½hp De Dion engine mounted in front, and driving by a long single chain to the rear axle.

METEOR (ii) 1902–1903
Meteor Engineering Co, Reading, Pa.

The Meteor company was the successor to the Steam Vehicle Company of America, maker of the Reading steamer, and Meteor continued the Reading design for one year. The Meteor car itself was larger than the Reading, being a four-passenger tonneau powered by a 4-cylinder horizontal engine of 10hp. It had wheel steering, a De Dion-type hood and the appearance of a gasoline-engined car. The price was $2,000, compared with $800 for the smaller Reading.

METEOR (iii) 1905–1906
1 Berg Automobile Co, New York, N.Y. 1905
2 Worthington Automobile Co, New York, N.Y. 1905–1906

This Meteor had some advanced features such as aluminum engine parts, and shaft drive. The 18hp, 199ci engine weighed 314lb, and had a speed range of 200 to 1,000rpm. The car was offered as a five-passenger tonneau model.

METEOR (iv) 1907–1910
1 Meteor Motor Car Co, Bettendorf, Iowa 1907–1909
2 Meteor Motor Car Co, Davenport, Iowa 1909–1910

The Meteor differed from most Mid-Western cars, being powered by a 50hp 4-cylinder T-head engine. Circassian Walnut was used in the bodywork and prices ranged up to $4,000 for the seven-passenger touring car or limousine.

METEOR (v) 1914–1930
Meteor Motor Car Co, Shelbyville, Ind.; Piqua, Ohio

Meteor cars were produced until about 1916 as touring cars and roadsters, with Continental and Model 6-cylinder engines. A short-lived V-12 with Weidely engine was listed in 1916. The company then turned its efforts to ambulances and hearses and Meteor's passenger-car output was restricted to large sedans for funeral use and invalid cars until about 1923. Until 1930, however, passenger cars were built to special order. The company still survives.

METEOR (vi) 1919–1922
Meteor Motors, Inc, Philadelphia, Pa.

One of America's higher-priced luxury cars of the time, the Meteor, powered by a Rochester-Duesenberg 4-cylinder engine, was distinguished by careful workmanship, a variety of open and closed bodies and a radiator similar to the Austro-Daimler of the period.

1920 METEOR (v) 27hp seven-passenger sedan. *Keith Marvin Collection*

1919 METEOR (vi) 30hp touring car. *Keith Marvin Collection*

1913 METZ Model 22 roadster. *Harrah's Automobile Collection*

METEOR (vii) (CDN) 1949–1970
Ford Motor Company of Canada Ltd, Windsor, Ont.

This was identical to a Ford except for its special grill and trim and was retailed only in Canada by Mercury-Lincoln dealers in order to extend their market. This car replaced the Mercury 114, sold exclusively in Canada in 1947 and 1948, which was a standard Ford but with Mercury grill and trim. Standard 1946/48 Mercurys were also sold in Canada. From 1963 to 1970 the name Meteor was applied to Mercurys sold in Canada, but with Ford interiors and engines.

METROPOL 1913–1914
Metropol Motors Corp, Port Jefferson, Long Island, N.Y.

This sporty car, without doors, was equipped with a 448ci, 4-cylinder engine which had a cylinder bore of $4\frac{1}{4}$in with an incredible stroke of 7.9in. The resulting unit required a very high hood. Two- and four-passenger cars were produced. In 1914 the price of either body style was $1,475.

METROPOLITAN (i) 1922–1923
Metropolitan Motors, Inc, Kansas City, Mo.

This assembled car first appeared equipped with a Continental engine but this was replaced in the later months of 1922 by an 86ci 4-cylinder unit of the firm's own make, apparently because they wanted to market a smaller car.

METROPOLITAN (ii) 1954–1961
American Motors Corp, Kenosha, Wis.

The 1950 prototype of this car was called the Nash NX1, but it went into production in 1954 at the Austin Motor Company's plant in England, for sale by American Motors. The engine was a 73.2ci Austin unit, the wheelbase was 85in, and the body a three-passenger coupé or convertible. Only minor changes were made during the Metropolitan's seven year lifespan.

METZ 1908–1922
1 Waltham Mfg Co, Waltham, Mass. 1908–1909
2 The Metz Co, Waltham, Mass. 1909–1922

C. H. Metz took over the Waltham company, which was making Waltham and Orient Buckboard cars. The first car to bear his own name was a light 12hp 2-cylinder roadster with friction transmission and double chain drive. It was sold on the Metz Plan, by which purchasers bought fourteen separate packages of parts, for home assembly. This design and 'plan' was continued through 1911, but in April of that year a new car with a 22hp 4-cylinder engine was introduced, which was sold complete in the normal manner. It retained friction drive, as did all Metzes until 1917, and the two-passenger roadster body of the earlier car. In 1916 the engine was enlarged to 25hp, and in 1919 a completely new car, the Master Six, was introduced, with a 45hp 6-cylinder engine, conventional transmission and shaft drive. In 1922 this car was renamed the Waltham, thus reviving the name used by the old Waltham Mfg Company.

MEYER 1919
A. J. Meyer Corp, Chicago, Ill.

The Meyer car was a curiosity as it was available in any model, for any number of passengers and with engines ranging from 2 to 12 cylinders. The Meyer patented wheels were made of pressed steel welded to the hub shell with rubber wedges between the shell and bearing collar. The special tires were of hollow rubber construction of two hollow sections and center wall and casing for flexibility. A specially-designed automatic gearshift was also standard. Prices for the larger Meyer cars were nearly $7,000 per unit.

MICHIGAN (i) 1903–1908
Michigan Automobile Co, Kalamazoo, Mich.

Formerly called the Blood, the first Michigan was a very light two-passenger car powered by a $3\frac{1}{2}$hp air-cooled engine. Priced at $450, it was one of the cheapest cars in America at the time. Later models were larger, using two-cylinder engines with two or four-passenger bodies. Prices of these ranged up to $1,250.

MICHIGAN (ii) 1908–1914
Michigan Buggy Co, Kalamazoo, Mich.

This company began by making high-wheel buggies, but by 1911 was producing low-slung touring cars and roadsters powered by 33 or 40hp 4-cylinder engines. These were referred to in advertisements as the Mighty Michigan, but this was not an official name for the cars.

MIDDLEBY 1908–1913
Middleby Auto Co, Reading, Pa.

This make used only 4-cylinder air-cooled engines until 1911, when a 4-cylinder water-cooled engine was introduced, but without much success. Few model changes seem to have been made; for the first three seasons a standard chassis was used and all the engines were of 201ci displacement. Runabouts and five-passenger touring cars were produced, all with attractive peaked hoods.

MIDDLETOWN 1909–1911
Middletown Buggy Co, Middletown, Ohio

This was a high-wheel buggy with 2-cylinder engine, wheel steering, and double chain drive. A light delivery truck was also built, and in 1912 the firm became the Crescent Motor Company, which concentrated on cab-over-engine trucks.

MIDLAND 1908–1913
Midland Motor Co, Moline, Ill.

The Midland used 4-cylinder Milwaukee engines in all models, until 1913 when one model had a 6-cylinder unit. The 4-cylinder engines, of two sizes (25/30 and 30/35hp), powered touring cars and roadsters. Six body types were made for 1913, the T-6 roadster having the 377ci 6-cylinder engine. The roadsters were typical of the best style of the era.

MIER 1908–1909
Mier Carriage & Buggy Co, Ligonier, Ind.

This buggy-type car had wheel steering, fenders, and a 12hp, 2-cylinder engine. It had solid tires and double chain drive.

MILBURN 1914–1922
Milburn Wagon Co, Toledo, Ohio

The Milburn Wagon Company was established in 1848 as makers of horse-drawn vehicles. In 1909 the Ohio Electric was built in part of the Milburn factory, and this presumably paved the way for the production of Milburn's own electric cars, which were first made in December 1914. They were attractive to look at, having a lighter and more delicate appearance than most electrics. They were largely closed cars, although a few roadsters were made as well. In 1919 two models were made imitating the appearance of gasoline cars; they were much less successful esthetically than the undisguised electrics. Milburns were used by President Wilson's secret service men, and were among the most popular American electric cars. Over 7,000 were made.

MILLER (i) 1912–1913
Miller Car Co, Detroit, Mich.

The Miller was built on conventional lines with 30 and 40hp 4-cylinder engines. Roadsters and five-passenger touring cars were sold at prices ranging from $1,250 to $1,450.

MILLER (ii) 1915–1932
1 Harry A. Miller, Inc, Los Angeles, Calif. 1915–1929
2 Rellimah, Inc, Los Angeles, Calif. 1930–1932

Harry A. Miller, a recognized specialist in carburetors, first attracted notice in the world of motor cars when he built a replacement engine for Bob Burman's GP Peugeot in 1915, following this up by a 4-cylinder ohc

1912 MICHIGAN (ii) 40hp touring car. *Automotive History Collection, Detroit Public Library*
1910 MIDDLEBY 25hp roadster. *Automotive History Collection, Detroit Public Library*

1911 MIDLAND 40hp roadster. *Kenneth Stauffer*
1919 MILBURN Model 36L electric limousine. *Autocar*

1932 MILLER-HARTZ fwd racing car. *Indianapolis Speedway Museum*

light airplane engine which was installed in several cars, including Barney Oldfield's Golden Submarine. During World War 1 Miller was associated with the Bugatti-Duesenberg airplane engine project, and his subsequent work reflects both this influence and that of Henry of Peugeot.

By 1920 he had disposed of his wartime interests to Leach-Biltwell and in conjunction with Fred Offenhauser and Leo Goossen was working on the first of his advanced racing power units, a 182ci double ohc hemispherical-head straight-8 commissioned by Tommy Milton. This was not ready in time for the 1921 Indianapolis 500 Mile Race and though a complete Miller did compete in 1922, ironically enough victory went to Milton's great rival, Jimmy Murphy, at the wheel of a GP-type Duesenberg with Miller engine.

With the coming of the 122ci Formula, Miller cars began to make themselves felt. Throughout its career the company concentrated on track-racing machines which dominated late-1920s 500 Mile Races (apart from 1924, 1925, and 1927, when Duesenberg won), but lacked

1938 MILLER Gulf Oil Special 4-wheel drive racing car. *Indianapolis Speedway Museum*

the handling and brakes to compete on equal terms with European Grand Prix cars on their home ground. In spite of this, a Miller finished 3rd in the 1923 European G.P., but subsequent attempts by Leon Duray and Peter de Paolo to race them in Europe proved abortive. The basic Miller was still a straight-8 on the established lines, with dry-sump lubrication, eight carburetors, and Delco coil ignition: output was 120bhp. In 1924 appeared the first of the fwd cars with engine reversed in the frame and De Dion *front* axle. Jimmy Murphy, who had commissioned it, was killed before he could take delivery, but the car finished 2nd at Indianapolis in 1925.

Millers were doing well in 1926, when America followed Europe in adopting the 91ci displacement limit, and the new Miller 91 sold at $15,000 with front-wheel drive or $10,000 with conventional transmission. The engine was the old 121ci unit with short-stroke crankshaft and magneto ignition: a centrifugal supercharger (as pioneered by Duesenberg) running at five times engine speed boosted power to 154bhp at 7,000rpm, and the 3-speed transmission had ball shift. All but one of the first ten finishers in that year's Indianapolis were Millers, while in 1927 Frank Lockhart took the International Class Flying-Mile record at 164mph in an unstreamlined single-passenger Miller 91 tuned to give 252bhp. Lou Meyer (later of Meyer-Drake, the firm that took over the development of the Miller racing engine from Fred Offenhauser) won the 1928 '500', and Ray Keech won in 1929. Experiments were also made with Miller engines and cars in Europe. A Miller-powered Lea-Francis was prepared for record work in 1927. Ettore Bugatti purchased the two fwd racers that Leon Duray brought to Europe in 1928 (it may be significant that *Le Patron* produced a 4 × 4 sprint car, the Type 53, in 1932). Douglas Hawkes of Derby used a similar fwd machine as the basis for the successful Derby-Miller sprint and record cars of the early 1930s.

Though Millers won again at Indianapolis in 1930 and 1931, the advent of the 'junk formula' caused Harry Miller to sell out; but he was soon in partnership again with Goossen and Offenhauser as Rellimah, Inc. ('H. A. Miller' spelled backwards). New designs included an abortive plan for a World Land Speed Record machine for Barney Oldfield, and a fearsome 311ci 4-wheel-drive 4-ohc V-16. More significant historically, however, was the 183ci 4-cylinder double ohc Miller with integral head which Shorty Cantlon drove into 2nd place at Indianapolis in 1930. This power unit was developed from a 1926 marine engine and formed the basis for the legendary Offenhauser (later Meyer-Drake) units which in 274ci unsupercharged form with fuel injection dominated the Indianapolis scene until the 1960s.

Miller went bankrupt in 1932, but not before he had built one sports car: a speedster in the classic American idiom using the V-16 engine (said to develop 400bhp) and 4-wheel drive. Its price was $35,000 and the client had to have it finished elsewhere after Miller closed down.

Miller went on designing until his death in 1943. He ran three reworked 221ci Ford V-8s in the 1935 Indianapolis Race: they had all-round independent suspension and front-wheel drive, but suffered from sheer lack of horse-power. Complexity killed the last of the Millers, the 1938 'Gulf Special' which resembled the Auto Unions and had rear-mounted 300bhp double ohc 180ci 6-cylinder engines, and all four wheels independently sprung and driven. In 1938 there was also a more conventional car with exposed lateral oil and water radiators and disk brakes.

MILWAUKEE (i) 1900–1902
Milwaukee Automobile Co, Milwaukee, Wis.

The Milwaukee steam car used a 5hp vertical 2-cylinder engine, and single chain drive. Various body styles were available, including a four-passenger surrey steered from the rear seat.

MILWAUKEE (ii) 1906
Eagle Automobile Co, Milwaukee, Wis.

This was made only as a small two-passenger car on a wheelbase of 98in and powered by a 2-cylinder engine of 13–15hp. The transmission was the friction type. This may have been no more than a prototype model.

1910 MITCHELL 35hp touring car. *Kenneth Stauffer*

MINO 1914

Mino Cyclecar Co, New Orleans, La.

The Mino was a single-passenger cyclecar, using a 4-cylinder, water-cooled engine of 74.8ci. Connected with this was a 2-speed transmission, with shaft drive. The car sold for $350.

MITCHELL 1903–1923

1 Mitchell Motor Car Co, Racine, Wis. 1903–1910
2 Mitchell-Lewis Motor Co, Racine, Wis. 1910–1916
3 Mitchell Motors Co, Inc., Racine, Wis. 1916–1923

Mitchell and Lewis had been wagon builders since 1834, and their first car was a light two-passenger powered by a 7hp air-cooled 2-cylinder engine, using single chain drive, and priced at $1,200. In 1905 a 9hp

1923 MITCHELL Model F50 29hp sedan. *Automotive History Collection, Detroit Public Library*

engine was used, and air or water cooling was available. 4-cylinder engines of 18 and 30hp appeared in the 1906 range, and in 1907 shaft drive was employed on all models. Until 1910, 20 and 35hp fours were made, having pair-cast cylinders in 1910 when they were joined by a 50hp 6-cylinder car. In 1913 a new range of T-head engines was introduced in a car designed by René Petard and known as the 'American-built French car'. A 40hp four and 50 and 60hp sixes were made in this range, which had high-cowled torpedo-style bodies and electric starters. Piston strokes were very long at 7in. At this time it was said that the Mitchell company made 96% of all components. In 1916 a short-lived 48hp V-8 was made, and the following year the company settled down to making a range of conventional sixes of no great distinction. In 1920 a sloping radiator gave rise to the epithet, 'the drunken Mitchell' and this was hastily replaced by a vertical radiator for 1921. However, the company had lost a lot of money on their 1920 models, and few of the redesigned cars were sold, as they lacked any distinctive qualities. After production ceased in 1923, the factory was bought by Nash.

MOBILE 1899–1903

Mobile Company of America, Tarrytown, N.Y.

The Mobile Company was founded by J. B. Walker who, together with A. Lorenzo Barber, had acquired the Stanley patents. After a disagreement Barber left to make the Locomobile at Bridgeport, Conn., while Walker retained the former Stanley works at Tarrytown where he made the Mobile. At first this was almost identical with the Locomobile, and differences were restricted to body styles. Mobile offered as many as 20 different models in 1902, and 15 in 1903, by which time about 6,000 vehicles had been made. They ranged from a $550 Runabout, which was one of the cheapest American steamers, to a $3,000 enclosed limousine, which was one of the most expensive.

MOBILETTE 1965 to date

Mobilette Electric Cars, Long Beach, Calif.

This is an electric runabout of a type quite popular in southern California for shopping.

MODEL 1903–1909

1 Model Gas Engine Co, Auburn, Ind. 1903–1904
2 Model Gas Engine Works, Auburn, Ind. 1904–1906
3 Model Automobile Co, Peru, Ind. 1906–1909

Early versions of the Model used 2-cylinder opposed engines with a long 7in stroke. Engines of 12 and 16hp were available. An unusual transmission gave three forward and two reverse gears. Final drive was by single chain. Later models had engines up to 50hp. This manufacturer also built the Star (ii). The Model Gas Engine Works were building engines as late as 1912, which would indicate that the Model Automobile Co was an offshoot of this company.

MODERN *see* PAYNE-MODERN

MODOC 1913

The Modoc was a conventional 30/40 hp 4-cylinder car sold by the mail order firm of Montgomery-Ward. The price was $1,250. It is not known where the car was actually made.

MOHAWK (i) 1903–1904

Mohawk Auto & Cycle Co, Indianapolis, Ind.

This was a small car, made as a two- or five-passenger car, with single- and 2-cylinder engines, giving 7hp and 18hp respectively. The smaller car was steered by tiller, while the larger used a steering wheel. Both had wire wheels and pneumatic tires.

MOHAWK (ii) 1914–1915

Mohawk Motor Co, Boston, Mass.

The Mohawk was available in either two- or five-passenger models. It was powered by a 4-cylinder Farmer engine with overhead valves.

MOHLER 1901
Mohler & Degress, Astoria, Long Island, N.Y.

This was a light two-passenger car powered by a single-cylinder vertical engine mounted at the front. It had shaft drive.

MOHS 1968 to date
Mohs Seaplane Corp, Madison, Wis.

Bruce Baldwin Mohs' Ostentatienne Opera Sedan was one of the most unusual and expensive cars made in America. Powered by either a 304 or 549ci V-8 engine, it was a four-passenger sedan with rear entry for safety. Other safety features included cantilever seats that swung laterally on turns and pivoted to horizontal in the event of a head-on collision, and an extra wide tread of 74in. All cars were equipped with refrigerator and two-way all-transistor radio with two base stations for home and office. Prices were from $19,600 for the 304ci model, and $25,600 for the larger car. Four were built. For 1971 Mohs introduced a new series, the Model C and D KamperKars; these were metal-top convertibles to sleep three people, with hingeless doors that moved out from the side on linear bushings. Model C had a 392ci International engine, Model D a 530ci V-12 F.W.D. unit normally used in Seagrave fire apparatus. Mohs also plans a Model E two-passenger GT car.

MOLINE; MOLINE-KNIGHT 1904–1913; 1914–1919
Moline Automobile Co, E. Moline, Ill.

The Moline was launched as a modest five-passenger car with flat-twin or 4-cylinder engines. The twin was chain-driven, with a 2-speed planetary transmission. In 1912, Moline was among the first manufacturers to make a feature of a long-stroke engine (6in), of 35hp. In 1914 the sleeve-valve Knight engine was used; it was standardized a year later, when a 4-speed transmission was adopted. Body types included a limousine and a closed sedan. In 1916, the wheelbase was shortened and smaller engines were used. The last models offered 4-cylinder power units of 221 and 302ci. In 1919, the Moline-Knight became the R. & V. Knight.

MOLLER 1920–1921
Moller Motor Car Co, Lewistown, Pa.

The Moller was an 850lb car, constructed on European lines and designed with right-hand drive, intended primarily for export. It was powered by a 4-cylinder 94ci engine. Few were manufactured.

MONARCH (i) 1903
This was a very light two-passenger runabout with a 5hp single-cylinder engine and tiller steering. It was sold by the P. J. Dasey Company of Chicago, who also sold the Buffalo-built Morlock, but it is not certain if the Monarch was also built by Morlock.

MONARCH (ii) 1905–1909
Monarch Motor Car Co, Chicago Heights, Ill.

The Monarch was a motor buggy with large diameter wheels. Two- or 4-cylinder air-cooled engines were mounted beneath the seat. A planetary transmission with shaft drive was used. Both two- and four-passenger bodies were made.

1906 MOLINE Model C touring car. *Automotive History Collection, Detroit Public Library*

MONARCH (iii) 1908
Monarch Machine Co, Des Moines, Iowa

This high-wheeled motor buggy was a four-passenger car with a 4-cylinder, 127ci, water-cooled engine. The drive was by planetary transmission and double chains. The weight was 1,500lb and the price was $750.

MONARCH (iv) 1914–1917
Monarch Motor Car Co, Detroit, Mich.

This Monarch was advertised as 'The Car with the Silver Wheels'. Originally it had a Continental Six engine, but at least as early as 1916, the makers used a V-8 engine of 282ci. The five-passenger open model weighed 3,000lb and was priced at $1,500.

MONARCH (v) (CDN) 1946–1961
Ford Motor Co of Canada Ltd, Windsor, Ont.

Identical to the American Mercury except for special grill and trim, the Monarch was sold only in Canada by Ford dealers to widen their market coverage. For the 1958 model year there were no Monarchs as the make was replaced by the Edsel.

MONCRIEFF 1901–1902
The J. A. Moncrieff Co, Pawtucket, R.I.

Although it was called a Steam Wagon, the Moncrieff was a two-passenger car of slightly more solid appearance than many of its contemporaries. It used a 7hp 2-cylinder engine, tiller steering and solid tires on its wooden wheels.

MONDEX-MAGIC 1914
Aristos Co, New York, N.Y.

This rare car had a Fischer slide-valve engine, in which the sleeves oscillated as well as having a reciprocating motion. Two sizes of 6-cylinder engines were used, of 255 and 424ci. The prices of these large cars ranged from $4,500 for a four-passenger car to $6,500 for a closed limousine.

MONITOR (i) 1909
Monitor Automobile Works, Janesville, Wis.

This was a solid-tired vehicle with a 2-cylinder engine. Mainly commercial models were made, but a few two-passenger runabouts and four-passenger surreys also appeared.

MONITOR (ii) 1915–1922
1 Cummins Monitor Co, Columbus, Ohio
2 Monitor Motor Car Co, Columbus, Ohio

1968 MOHS Ostentatienne Opera Sedan. *Bruce Baldwin Mohs*

An assembled car which offered the buyer 4-, 6- or 8-cylinder models between 1915 and 1917 and fours and sixes only from 1918 on. The bulk of production came in the years after 1918 when the 4-cylinder G. B. & S. or 6-cylinder Continental engine was used to power the cars. Closed and open models were offered.

MONROE 1914–1924
1 Monroe Motor Co, Flint, Mich. 1914–1916
2 Monroe Motor Co, Pontiac, Mich. 1916–1918
3 William Small Co, Flint, Mich. 1918–1922
4 Premier Motor Corp, Indianapolis, Ind. 1923–1924

The Monroe was a fairly popular low-priced car which was powered by 4-cylinder engines by Mason or Sterling, and from 1918 of the company's own make. Open models constituted the factory's output for the first three years of manufacture, but a sedan was added in 1917 and closed cars were subsequently listed as well as open models. In 1923, it was rumored that Monroe would be taken over by Premier and appear as a smaller model of that make, but instead Stratton Motors obtained Monroe and continued production. Shortly thereafter, Premier obtained control of both Monroe and Stratton and marketed the Monroe briefly in a redesigned model which included a flat, squared radiator in place of the earlier rounded type. Few were built and the final cars were marketed as the Model B Premier.

MOON 1905–1930
Moon Motor Car Co, St Louis, Mo.

Like so many American car manufacturers, Moon started life making buggies; buggies were to the American industry what bicycles were to Europe. The first Moon cars were designed by Louis P. Mooers, who had been responsible for the Peerless. The Model A of 1906 was a conventional, expensive 30/35hp 4-cylinder with a Rutenber engine and shaft drive. In 1912, 318 and 353ci fours with dual ignition were sold. A six was introduced in 1913, and three years later the four had vanished, in favor of 175 and 303ci Continental-powered cars. The 1919 Moon was a good-looking, well-made, though assembled, machine powered by a 219ci engine by Continental. The radiator was by now a copy of that of the Rolls-Royce, showing the class of market at which the Moon was aimed. There was an ohv engine in 1921, and a smaller, L-head unit, also by Continental, was listed as well. Moon refinements included four main bearings (a rarity in American 6-cylinder engines of the time), demountable rims on detachable wheels and, from 1924, Lockheed hydraulic 4-wheel brakes. Two years later there arrived the Diana (named after the moon goddess) which had an L-head straight-8 engine of 240ci, and imitated the radiator shape of the luxurious Minerva from Belgium; the 1927 215ci Moon Six also appeared with this radiator. The first Moon to use an 8-cylinder engine was the Aerotype of 1928, a 287ci L-head machine. A new six, the 6-72, accompanied it and was continued to 1929. That year brought one of the best-looking of the company's products, the Prince of Windsor, named after the Prince of Wales. The specification was a 268ci straight-8 engine and a 4-speed transmission — an unusual refinement, this — in a dropped frame with hydraulic brakes and automatic chassis lubrication. Unfortunately, this attempt to produce a European-type high-quality car ended after Moon acquired control of New Era Motors Inc, the firm which brought out the front-wheel-drive Ruxton. The new venture promptly collapsed, killing two famous names, Moon and Kissel.

MOORE (i) 1906
Moore Automobile Co, Walla Walla, Wash.

This was an assembled car with 4-cylinder engine and 60in tread. Most roads in the U.S. were built for wagons with a 56in tread, but the State of Washington's roads were built for 60in treads. The Moore Automobile Co was organized in order to compel Eastern manufacturers to supply Washington State with 60in-tread cars. When Franklin and several other companies began to do this, Moore promptly ceased manufacture.

1915 MONROE 15hp roadster. *Kenneth Stauffer*

MOORE (ii) (AUBURN-MOORE) 1906
H. S. Moore, Cleveland, Ohio

This five-passenger car had a 2-cylinder, water-cooled engine which was mounted amidships. It used a planetary transmission and single-chain drive.

MOORE (iii) 1906–1908
Moore Automobile Co, New York, N.Y.

One chassis was offered by this manufacturer, at a price of $5,000. It was equipped with a 4-cylinder water-cooled engine, a 4-speed selective transmission and shaft drive. Continental racing tires were standard equipment on this car.

1924 MOON 20hp touring car. *Autocar*
1929 MOON 8-80 White Prince of Windsor roadster. *Autocar*

137

MOORE (iv) 1916–1921
1 Moore Motor Vehicle Co, Minneapolis, Minn. 1916–1917
2 Moore Motor Vehicle Co, Danville, Ill. 1917–1921

The Moore was a very conventional 4-cylinder tourer with a 22hp Golden, Belknap & Schwartz engine. Originally priced at a modest $350, It had risen to $895 by 1919 as a result of war-time inflation, but the design changed little.

MOORE (v) 1917
Indianapolis, Ind.

This 2-wheeled two-passenger machine was a curious hybrid which combined the features of a car and a motor cycle. It was powered by a 22hp air-cooled engine and was complete with 3-speed transmission and shaft drive, but it had handlebar steering and was without bodywork. The name of its manufacturer is not known.

MOOSE JAW STANDARD (CDN) 1916–1918
Canadian Standard Auto & Tractor Co, Moose Jaw, Sask.

This firm was formed by five local shareholders who hired an American engineer and bought enough parts for 25 cars as a start. Production problems caused so much delay that the first five cars were outdated by the time they were built. The cars went to the shareholders, everything else went to the engineer and the firm was wound up. These were large, handsome touring cars with wire wheels, Continental 6-cylinder engines and Packard-style radiators. They are often referred to as Continentals or Canadian Standards.

MORA 1906–1910
Mora Motor Car Co, Newark, N.Y.

The Mora was produced in a variety of models with 25, 45 and 60hp engines, the last two being 6-cylinder units. The most memorable Mora was the 45hp two-passenger Racytype given an aura of exclusiveness by limiting production to 100 a year. The last Mora was a small car with a sloping hood and a 4-cylinder engine.

MORLOCK 1903
Morlock Automobile Co, Buffalo, N.Y.

This vehicle was a somewhat crude four-passenger car with *dos-à-dos* seating. Its single-cylinder 5hp engine was mounted beneath the seat, with a single chain driving the rear axle.

MORRIS & SALOM 1895–1897
Morris & Salom, Philadelphia, Pa.

The first car by this firm was known as the Electrobat. It had front-wheel-drive by two Lundell electric motors, with larger wheels at front than at rear. One was entered in the 1895 Chicago Times-Herald Race but did not finish. Later, some cars with equal wheels were also made.

MORRISON 1890–c.1896
William Morrison, Des Moines, Iowa

This was the second electric car to be built in America, and the first to be sold commercially. Sturgis cars were Morrisons used by Harold Sturgis for publicity purposes in 1895–96.

MORRISS-LONDON 1919–1925
1 Crow-Elkhart Motor Car Co, Elkhart, Ind.
2 Century Motor Co, Elkhart, Ind.

The Morriss-London was an assembled car built for export to England only, under an agreement with the manufacturer and F. E. Morriss of 64 Piccadilly, London. The cars were nearly identical with the Crow-Elkharts which were built until 1924 by the parent company, and were distinguished by a slightly pointed radiator. They were available as touring cars or landaulets, the latter designed for use as taxicabs. Artillery, wire or disk wheels were optional and although some Morriss-Londons were completely built in the United States, most of the coachwork was added in England, a number of bodies being made by Morgan.

1910 MORA Light Four 24/28hp touring car. *Automotive History Collection, Detroit Public Library*
1910 MOTORETTE 7hp 3-wheeler. *Henry Ford Museum, Dearborn, Mich.*

MORSE (i) 1904–1909
Morse Motor Vehicle Co, Springfield, Mass.

Launched at the end of 1904, the Morse steamer had a 3-cylinder horizontal single-acting 20hp engine, with direct drive to the rear axle. It had a five-passenger tonneau body, and a hood like that of a gasoline car. Made from 1904 to 1906, it was joined by a conventional 4-cylinder gasoline car, which lasted until 1909. The company was then reorganized as the Easton Machine Company, and made the Morse (ii).

MORSE (ii) 1909–1916
Easton Machine Co, South Easton, Mass.

The Morse used 4-cylinder, ohv engines of 24 and 34hp and 4-speed transmissions with direct drive in third. Prices for four open models ranged from $3,900 to $4,200 over the years 1911 to 1914.

MORSE (iii) 1914–1917
Morse Cyclecar Co, East Pittsburgh, Pa.

This cyclecar had an unusual drive system to the front wheels by chain. It was powered by a 67ci V-twin engine. The body was steel, but an aluminum body, lighter by 50lb, could also be had.

MOTORETTE 1910–1912
C. W. Kelsey Mfg Co, Hartford, Conn.

The famous 3-wheeled Kelsey Motorette was produced in limited numbers for little over two years. Designed and manufactured by the automobile pioneer C. W. Kelsey, the car had a single wheel at the rear. The first models were air-cooled and power was supplied by a 2-cycle 2-cylinder engine. Steering was by tiller. As the first cars showed a tendency to roll on turns, Kelsey developed the stabilizer or anti-sway bar which counteracted this. By 1911, Motorettes were water-cooled and to promote advertising the manufacturer sent two men from Hartford across the continent to California. The factory price of the Motorette was $385. A delivery car was priced somewhat higher. A third model, a rickshaw, was added and exported to Japan. Several hundred units were built before the company failed and these were marketed throughout the U.S. as well as Japan, Denmark, Mexico and Canada.

MOYEA 1902–1904
1 Moyea Automobile Co, New York, N.Y. 1902–1904
2 Consolidated Motor Co, New York, N.Y. 1904

This car which was built under Rochet-Schneider license, was powered by a 4-cylinder, 25hp engine and had a 4-speed transmission and shaft drive. The bodies were built by Springfield Metal Body Co, Springfield, Mass. The 1903 chassis were built by the Alden Sampson Manufacturing Co, Pittsfield, Mass., who subsequently purchased Consolidated Motor Co in order to obtain the license from the French manufacturer.

MOYER 1911–1915
H. A. Moyer, Syracuse, N.Y.

The early offerings by this manufacturer were three models with 4- and 6-cylinder engines. This line was later reduced to a single chassis in which was fitted a 308ci 4-cylinder engine. Both two- and five-passenger models were made at prices ranging from $2,200 to $3,000.

M.P.M. 1914–1915
Mount Pleasant Motor Co, Mount Pleasant, Mich.

The M.P.M. was a conventional medium-sized car made in 4- and 8-cylinder versions. The company planned to move to Alma or Saginaw at the end of 1915, but apparently never did so.

MUELLER 1895–1900
Mueller & Co, Decatur, Ill.

Hieronymus A. Mueller imported a Benz in 1892 or 1893, to which he made various modifications such as replacing the two forward speeds by three and adding a reverse, making a new cooling system, and using his own spark plug and carburetor. This car was driven in the 1895 Chicago Times-Herald Race by his son Oscar B. Mueller, and finished 2nd. Mueller senior built five more cars and planned to become a manufacturer, but was killed in a workshop explosion in 1900. The parent company concentrated on the making of brass forgings.

MULTIPLEX (i) 1912–1913
Multiplex Mfg Co, Berwick, Pa.

The Multiplex was built in three versions on a standard wheelbase: a two-passenger roadster, a two-passenger raceabout and a five-passenger touring car, powered by Waukesha 4-cylinder engines. A 4-speed transmission was used with direct drive in third gear. Under 20 were made.

MULTIPLEX (ii) 1954
Multiplex Mfg Corp, Berwick, Pa.

The Multiplex 186 was a short-lived sports car powered by a 121ci 4-cylinder or 161ci Willys F-head 6-cylinder engine. The chassis had independent front suspension. Only 3 were made.

1913 MOYER 30hp roadster. *Montagu Motor Museum*
1951 MUNTZ JET convertible. *Autosport*

MUNSON 1899–1902
Munson Electric Motor Co, La Porte, Ind.

The Munson was probably the first gasoline-electric car to be made and sold in America. Two- and 4-cylinder engines were used, and only chassis were provided. They could be fitted with any kind of body, either passenger or commercial.

MUNTZ JET 1950–1955
1 Muntz Car Co, Inc, Evansville, Ind. 1950–1951
2 Muntz Car Co, Inc, Chicago, Ill. 1951–1955

Taken over from designer-producer Frank Kurtis, who sold it as the Kurtis Sports, this 2-door convertible was built by Earl Muntz, a prominent American businessman. The Evansville works turned out a model with a 331ci 133hp Cadillac V-8 power unit, but this was replaced by a 317ci Lincoln V-8 of 205hp when the firm moved to Chicago. The wheelbase was lengthened to 113in to accommodate four passengers. The Jet enjoyed good sales during its lifetime.

1918 MURRAY Model 70-T town car. *Keith Marvin Collection*

1926 MURRAY-MAC sedan. *Keith Marvin Collection*

MURDAUGH 1901
Murdaugh Automobile Co, Oxford, Pa.

This two-passenger small car had a 'reach' frame and was driven by a 3¼hp engine. It was steered by a tiller. Drive was by a single chain from a friction transmission.

MURENA 1969 to date
Murena Motors, Inc, New York, N.Y.

The Murena 429GT is a luxury station wagon with a body by Intermeccanica of Turin, Italy, powered by a 429ci Ford V-8 engine. Annual production is restricted to 100 cars, and the price at New York port of entry is $14,750.

MURRAY (i) 1902–1903
Church Mfg Co, Adrian, Mich.

The Murray was a light runabout on similar lines to the Curved Dash Oldsmobile, built by a former Olds engineer. It had a 6hp single-cylinder water-cooled engine, planetary transmission and single chain drive. About 1,000 Murrays were produced before the makers turned to a larger car, the Lenawee.

MURRAY (ii) 1916–1918
Murray Motor Car Co, Pittsburgh, Pa.

The Murray Eight, with its V-8 motor and Rolls-Royce style of radiator, was a prestige car of the World War 1 period which sold at a reasonable price and had an enviable clientele of owners and enthusiasts. The cars featured an electric clock and a slanted windshield as early as 1917.

MURRAY-MAC 1921–1928
Murray Motor Car Co, Atlantic, Mass.

The Murray-Mac was the earlier Murray Eight after it had been taken over by John J. McCarthy. Few Murray-Macs were produced and these appeared throughout the 1920s, one or two at a time. The Murray Eight designs were retained and standard engines of 6-cylinder type as well as other standard components were used.

MUSTANG 1948
Mustang Engineering Corp, Seattle, Wash.

This was a prototype six-passenger sedan with a door in the center of each side. The rear-mounted 59hp, 4-cylinder Hercules engine was in unit with the transmission and axle for ease of removal and repair.

N

NANCE *see* TOURAINE

NAPOLEON 1916–1917
Napoleon Auto Mfg Co, Napoleon, Ohio
This was a light, assembled car with five-passenger or seven-passenger touring bodies on a standard chassis. It was powered by a 4-cylinder engine of 166ci.

NASH 1917–1957
1 Nash Motor Co, Kenosha, Wis. 1917–1954
2 American Motors Corp, Kenosha, Wis. 1954–1957
Charles W. Nash, the former President of General Motors, acquired the Thos. B. Jeffrey Co in July 1916, and from the 1918 season onward the cars were marketed under his name. The first Nash was a 249ci six with push-rod-operated overhead valves, followed in 1922 by a 4-cylinder car which also had overhead valves at a time when most American manufacturers adhered to the L-head. Rubber-mounted engines appeared in the same year, when Nash sold 41,000 medium-priced cars (the four cost $985, the six about $500 more). In 1924 Nash acquired the defunct Mitchell concern at Racine and the ailing Lafayette Co of Milwaukee, producers of a luxury V-8 (when the latter name was revived in 1934 it was used for an uninspired L-head 6-cylinder machine selling for under $600). They also produced, in 1925–1926, the 6-cylinder Ajax, an L-head machine that they developed into a cheap line. During the latter part of the Vintage era the company concentrated on L-head 6-cylinder cars, in the cheaper models and overhead valves in the higher-priced range, though 1930 brought a 299ci straight-8 with dual coil ignition and overhead valves, a type that was progressively developed until 1942. Engines of this type were used in the British Jensen of 1939.
The company successfully rode out the Depression though sales fell to below 15,000 cars in 1933, when Nash were constructing a really big eight with a 142in wheelbase and a displacement of 322ci as well as two sixes and a smaller straight-8. Synchromesh had been adopted in 1932, and overdrive became an option in 1935, when the bigger Nashes had the fashionable fastbacks and enclosed rear wheels. Other options widely publicized in the later 1930s were seats convertible into a bed and the firm's 'Weather Eye' system of air conditioning. Coil-spring independent front suspension and steering-column gear-shift followed in 1939, in which year a version of the Ambassador Six was available in England with the option of a Perkins 287ci diesel engine in place of the usual push-rod ohv gasoline unit. Unitary construction appeared for the first time on the inexpensive L-head 6-cylinder 600 sedan, introduced for 1941 at $785. This was the ancestor of the famous Rambler series and reappeared in 1945. Only 6-cylinder cars were made from 1945 until 1954, and with the advent of the Airflyte range in 1949 unitary construction was standardized. They also had all four wheels enclosed, and a one-piece wrap-around windshield.
In 1950 there came the experimental NX.1 convertible with an Austin A40 engine, later made for Nash by Austin of Birmingham as the Metropolitan, and in 1951 there appeared the 235ci Nash-Healey roadster, a British Healey with an ohv 6-cylinder Nash engine. From 1950 onward the Rambler accounted for most of Nash's production, but the original name survived the amalgamation with Hudson and the creation of American Motors in 1954.

1926 NASH Model 21 Light Six sedan. *American Motors Corporation*
1936 NASH Lafayette coupé. *American Motors Corporation*

1951 NASH Ambassador Six sedan. *American Motors Corporation*

In 1955 the big Nashes were fitted with an ohv 319ci V-8 engine, this and its Ultramatic transmission being made by Packard. A 352ci A.M.C.-built eight was adopted in 1957, but sales were negligible and the 1958 models were known as Rambler Ambassadors.

1913 NATIONAL Model 40 roadster. *Kenneth Stauffer*

1917 NELSON 4-cylinder touring car. *Automotive History Collection, Detroit Public Library*

NATIONAL 1900–1924
1 National Automobile & Electric Vehicle Co, Indianapolis, Ind. 1900
2 National Motor Vehicle Co, Indianapolis, Ind. 1900–1916
3 National Motor Car & Vehicle Corp, Indianapolis, Ind. 1916–1924

The first National vehicles were light electric runabouts, which were supplemented in 1903 by a gasoline-engined car with a 4-cylinder Rutenber engine, 3-speed transmission and shaft drive. In 1905 electric cars were dropped and the round radiator which was to characterize Nationals for several years was introduced. In 1906 came the 6-cylinder model, one of the first sixes in America; as on the four, cylinders were separately cast, but in 1908 there appeared a range of cars with pair-cast cylinders, and in the same year the round radiator was replaced by a shield-shaped design. From 1909 to 1915, 4- and 6-cylinder cars up to 60hp and $5,000 were made, and in the years 1909 to 1912 many competition successes were achieved, including victory in the Elgin National Trophy and Illinois Trophy in 1911, and the Indianapolis 500 Mile Race in 1912. The driver was Joe Dawson, who won at an average speed of 78.7mph.

In 1915 a new range of models was announced with 6- or 12-cylinder engines in the same chassis. The six was a Continental Red Seal, and the twelve was National's own make, but curiously the most expensive of the range was the old six, known as the Newport Six. The twelve was dropped in 1920 and for the last four years Nationals were undistinguished cars, although of good quality. A merger in 1922 between National, Dixie

Flyer and Jackson led to a range of three cars for 1923–1924, of which only the largest, the '6-71' was a genuine National. Although bearing the National name, the '6-31' was a Dixie Flyer and the '6-51' a Jackson.

NAVAJO 1953–1955
Navajo Motor Car Co, New York, N.Y.

This was a two-passenger sports car powered by a 130bhp Mercury V-8 engine. The fiberglass body had an appearance similar to that of the Jaguar XK-120, and maximum speed was 125mph.

NAVARRE 1921
A. C. Schulz, Springfield, Mass.

Designed by the engineer A. C. Schulz, for many years assistant chief with both Locomobile and Marmon, the 6-cylinder Navarre was to have been priced at $5,000 and $6,000 for open and closed models respectively. Although production was planned, only one closed model was shown and the Navarre name never appeared on the price lists.

NELSON 1917–1921
E. A. Nelson Motor Car Co, Detroit, Mich.

Emil A. Nelson, who had formerly served with Oldsmobile, Packard and Hupmobile, designed the Nelson car along European lines and powered it with a 224ci 4-cylinder airplane-type engine with overhead camshaft. A few roadsters were built in 1917 and 1918 as well as a handful of closed models, but the bulk of production was of touring cars. Approximately 350 cars were built up to the end of 1920 and although the cars may have been sold as late as 1921, production had probably ceased by then.

NEUSTADT-PERRY 1902–1907
Neustadt Motor Car Co, St Louis, Mo.

This company made a variety of cars with gasoline and steam engines. The steamers were made from 1902 to 1903 only, and were powered by 10hp 2-cylinder vertical engines mounted under the rear seat and driven by single chain. Gasoline cars used single- and 2-cylinder engines in the light runabouts, and 4-cylinder engines in the larger touring cars. High wheel buggies were made from 1904 to 1907, using air or water-cooling, planetary or friction-disk transmission, and final drive by single or double chains.

NEW ENGLAND (i) 1898–1900
New England Motor Carriage Co, Waltham, Mass.

This was a typical light steam buggy with a vertical 2-cylinder engine, chain drive and tiller steering. It had little to distinguish it from its contemporaries, including two other makes (Waltham and American Waltham) made in the same town at the same time.

NEW ENGLAND (ii) 1899–1901
New England Electric Vehicle Co, Boston, Mass.

This company was formed to manufacture electric cars under the patents of the Barrows Vehicle Co of Willimantic, Conn. The design was a 3-wheeler with the single front wheel driving.

NEW ERA (i) 1902
The Automobile and Marine Power Co, Camden, N.J.

This was a tiller-steered two-passenger buggy, with a 7hp single-cylinder engine under the seat. Drive was by double chain. Its weight was 950lb and its price $850.

NEW ERA (ii) 1916–1917
1 New Era Engineering Co, Joliet, Ill. 1916
2 New Era Motors, Inc, Joliet, Ill. 1917

This light car was made only as a five-passenger touring car. It had a 4-cylinder L-head engine, and was priced at $660.

NEW PARRY *see* PARRY

1921 NOMA Six 27hp speedster. *Montagu Motor Museum*

NEW YORK SIX 1928–1929
1 Automotive Corp of America, Moline, Ill.
2 New York Motors Corp, Moline, Ill.
   The New York Six was a subsidiary car to the Davis (i). Both makes were taken over by the Automotive Corp of America in order to extend the Davis range. Few of these cars were built. They had a radiator and hood louvres similar to the Reo Wolverine car of the same era. New York Six cars were equipped with 'Parkmobile' attachments.

NIAGARA (i) 1903–1907
Wilson Auto Mfg Co, Wilson, N.Y.
   The two-passenger Niagara could be converted into a four-passenger car by opening the front to provide an extra seat. It was a tiller-steered car with a single-cylinder, 5hp engine under the seat. With wooden wheels and pneumatic tires, its appearance was rather primitive.

NIAGARA (ii) 1915–1916
Mutual Motor Car Co, Buffalo, N.Y.
   This was a lightweight five-passenger touring car powered by a 36hp 4-cylinder engine. It was of thoroughly conventional design, and cost $740.

NIELSON 1907
Nielson Motor Car Co, Detroit, Mich.
   The only model of the Nielson was a two-passenger runabout with a single-cylinder 12hp air-cooled engine located behind the seat. With friction transmission and double chain drive, it was priced at $800.

NOBLE 1902
Noble Automobile Mfg Co, Cleveland, Ohio
   Two models of the Noble were made, a 6hp single-cylinder runabout, and a 10hp 2-cylinder touring car. Both had two forward speeds and chain drive.

NOMA 1919–1923
Noma Motors Corp, New York, N.Y.
   Although the Noma was an assembled car, with a choice of Continental or Beaver 6-cylinder engines available, it was attractively low-slung and sporty with a distinctive oval radiator and wire wheels. Open and closed models were produced, all of them equipped with individual step-plates in place of running-boards. Several hundred cars were built by Noma during five years of production.

NORCROSS c.1907
United Electrical Mfg Co, Norcross, Ga.
   This car is somewhat of a mystery as it was offered for sale only through local advertisements. The 1907 versions were four- and five-passenger touring cars, and a roadster with a price range of $800 to $850.

NORTHERN 1902–1909
1 Northern Mfg Co, Detroit, Mich. 1902–1905
2 Northern Motor Car Co, Detroit, Mich. 1906–1909
   The Northern company was founded by two ex-Oldsmobile engineers, J. D. Maxwell and C. B. King. Their first and most popular car was the Silent Northern, a single-cylinder two-passenger runabout not unlike the Oldsmobile, but with a straight dash. These cars were made under license in Sweden as the Norden. Flat-twins with hoods were sold from 1904 and in 1906 King designed a 4-cylinder 18hp car with air-operated brakes and clutch. In 1908 he left the company — later to make the King car — and in 1909 Northern merged with E.M.F.

NORTHWAY 1921
Northway Motor Sales Co, Natick, Mass.
   The Northway was built for a few months only by the parent truck concern of the same name. Resembling the Roamer or Kenworthy, the car carried a Rolls-Royce-type radiator and used a Northway 6-cylinder engine. A roadster, a touring car and a sedan priced from $4,200 to $5,200 constituted the range. Individual fenders with step-plates were substituted for running-boards. Several were made and marketed before production was discontinued.

NORTHWESTERN *see* HAASE

NORWALK 1910–1922
1 Norwalk Motor Car Co, Norwalk, Ohio 1910–1911
2 Norwalk Motor Car Co, Martinsburg, W.Va. 1911–1922
   The Norwalk's most distinguishing feature (up to 1916) was its underslung frame. The first model used a 4-cylinder 251 engine. This grew to a long, low and formidable car with a 4-speed transmission and direct drive in third gear, powered by a 6-cylinder engine of 525ci. With a six-passenger touring body its cost was $3,750. Smaller models with 35hp to 45hp engines were also built up to 1916. The Norwalk cars manufactured after 1918 were of standard size with 191ci 6-cylinder engines. A five-passenger touring car was priced at $975.

NOVARA 1917
Herreshoff Mfg Co, Bristol, R.I.
   The Novara was a magnificent two-passenger runabout with a body of mahogany. The influence of yacht design, the main business of Herreshoff Mfg Co, is evident in the appearance of the Novara. Its 4-cylinder engine with overhead valves was rated at 37hp and was built by the American & British Mfg Co, Bridgeport, Conn., which later made the Porter (ii). There was no connection with the Herreshoff car.

NYBERG 1912–1914
1 Nyberg Automobile Works, Anderson, Ind. 1912
2 Nyberg Automobile Works, Indianapolis, Ind. 1913–1914
   The Nyberg was made in as many as four different models, ranging up to the Model 6-45. This was a seven-passenger car which used a 6-cylinder 332ci engine and cost $2,100.

OAKLAND 1907–1931

Oakland Motor Car Co, Pontiac, Mich.

The original Oakland was the work of A. P. Brush, designer both of the original single-cylinder Cadillac and of the Brush Runabout. It was a 152ci vertical-twin with planetary transmission, selling for $1,300. The power unit rotated counter-clockwise. In 1909, when General Motors took over, the company was also marketing a conventional 4-cylinder car with sliding-type transmission at $1,600. For the next few years fours were the staple product, 202, 302 and 334ci engines being used in 1912. In 1913 Oaklands had rounded-V radiators reminiscent of the Belgian

1911 OAKLAND 25hp touring car. *Don McCray*
1924 OAKLAND 6-54 sedan. *General Motors Corporation*

Métallurgique, and were made in 4- and 6-cylinder forms with electric lighting and starting. Left-hand drive was adopted in 1915, when the bigger '6-49' model used a Northway engine. Four models — a 346ci V-8, two sixes, and a four — were offered in 1916, in which year the firm's own small ohv 6-cylinder unit appeared. This was in a car modestly priced at $795, of which Oakland sold over 35,000 in 1917. From 1919 to 1923, this ohv car was the only model listed, but in 1924 the firm brought out a new and inexpensive L-head six which offered both front-wheel brakes and Duco cellulose finish for $995. The companion make, Pontiac, was introduced in 1926, but unlike other makers' cheap lines this rapidly overshadowed the Oakland, sales of which dropped from some 58,000 in 1926 to 30,826 in 1929.

An inexpensive L-head V-8 on the lines of Oldsmobile's Viking was introduced as a replacement for the six in 1930, but demand continued to fall and after 1931 only Pontiacs were made.

O'CONNOR 1916

O'Connor Corp, Chicago, Ill.

The O'Connor was offered in six different models. The larger models used 25hp 6-cylinder engines. The prices ranged from $755 to $985.

ODELOT 1915

Lawrence Stamping Co, Toledo, Ohio

The Odelot (Toledo in reverse) was a two-passenger runabout, with a 4-cylinder 20hp engine. It was equipped with bucket seats and wire wheels. This car sold for $450 with a black hood and fenders, and a choice of green, red or yellow cowl and seats.

OFELDT 1899–c.1902

F. W. Ofeldt & Sons, Nyack-on-the-Hudson, N.Y.

Made by a company well-known for their steam launches, the Ofeldt steamer had a V-twin engine and tiller steering. Later the company built a 4-cylinder steam engine and fitted it to a delivery wagon, but it is not certain how many passenger cars were actually built.

OGREN 1915–1923

1 Ogren Motor Car Co, Chicago, Ill. 1915
2 Ogren Motor Works, Chicago, Ill.; Waukegan, Ill. 1916–1918
3 Ogren Motor Car Co, Milwaukee, Wis. 1919–1923

Designed by Hugo W. Ogren, this was a high-quality car powered by a 6-cylinder Continental engine of 325ci displacement. Priced at $4,375 for the touring car, it had attractive lines with individual step plates. In 1922 a new company, Commander Motors Corp, was formed to build a new car called the Commander, also designed by Hugo Ogren, but none appeared.

OHIO (i) 1909–1913

1 Jewel Carriage Co, Cincinnati, Ohio 1909–1912
2 Ohio Motor Car Co, Cincinnati, Ohio 1912
3 Crescent Motor Co, Cincinnati, Ohio 1913

The Ohio used a 40hp 4-cylinder engine for most of its models. Seven body styles were offered in one year on a chassis using shaft drive and with a wheelbase of 115in.

1912 OHIO (ii) electric brougham. *William S. Jackson*

OHIO (ii) 1910–1918
Ohio Electric Car Co, Toledo, Ohio

The Ohio electric car used Crocker-Wheeler motors, with 4-speed controllers. Steering in all models was by tiller and pneumatic tires were fitted. As many as four closed models were offered in a year.

OKEY 1907–1908
Okey Motor Car Co, Columbus, Ohio

The Okey runabout was powered by a 2-cycle 3-cylinder engine of 140ci. This was claimed to produce 22hp at 1,300rpm. The car used a planetary transmission and shaft drive.

OLDSMOBILE 1896 to date
1 Olds Motor Works, Lansing, Mich. 1896–1943
2 Oldsmobile Division of General Motors Corp, Lansing, Mich. 1943 to date

Ransom Eli Olds built an experimental 3-wheeled steam car in 1891, following this six years later with a single-cylinder gasoline-engined vehicle of dogcart type. He then made a small number of electric cars, before producing his famous Curved Dash Runabout, the world's first mass-production automobile. This consisted of a very short and simple buggy-type chassis with two long springs serving as auxiliary side-members, on which was mounted a single-cylinder moiv engine of 95.4ci displacement, with vibrating coil ignition, a 2-speed planetary transmission, and central chain drive. The engine possessed an immense muffler and turned at 500rpm — 'one chug per telegraph pole'. Despite a fire at the factory in March 1901, which destroyed everything except a single prototype, the little Olds was an instant success, 2,100 being sold in 1902 and 5,000 in 1904. Though at its best as a town runabout, it made a number of epic runs, notably Whitman's and Hammond's drive from San Francisco to New York in 1903. This type of car was made under license in Germany as the Polymobil, and Ultramobil.

By 1904 Ransom Olds had left to found the Reo company and the Oldsmobile started to grow up. Dummy-hooded versions were available in 1905. These were followed by a twin-cylinder 2-cycle car with front engine and a conventional transmission selling for $1,250, and by the Palace touring car, a four of square cylinder dimensions which combined pressure lubrication and automatic inlet valves. Oldsmobiles grew bigger and bigger; by 1908 the smallest was a 302ci four and the largest a six of over 454ci displacement, and this trend was not reversed when General Motors took over in 1909. Compressed-air starters were available in 1911 and the 1912 line was obviously designed for the carriage trade, being headed by the immense Limited, with a 6-cylinder 706ci engine, a wheelbase of 138in, wooden wheels of 43in diameter and a top speed of over 70mph, all for $5,000. Even the baby of the family, the 4-cylinder Defender had a displacement of 301ci and cost $3,000, while all the range boasted 4-speed transmissions. Oldsmobiles were a little smaller at 427ci in 1914 and had acquired Delco electric lighting and starting, though right hand drive was retained.

The company did not return to prosperity until the following year,

when a modestly-priced L-head 4-cylinder 42 with streamlined dash was marketed and over 7,500 were sold. This was followed in 1916 by an L-head V-8 with a Fiat-like radiator selling at about $1,500, which Oldsmobile continued to offer until 1923. They also listed both a 169ci six and an ohv Northway-engined four in the early 1920s. In 1924 only the six was available, and a wide range of sport equipment (such as trunk racks and step plates) was advertised. Over 44,000 were sold, and touring cars were listed at $785. Mechanical pump feed and front-wheel brakes followed in 1927 and bodies were restyled in 1928.

Sales climbed to over 100,000 in 1929, in which year Oldsmobile launched the abortive 8-cylinder Viking. Synchromesh was available in 1931, and a 240ci straight-8 closely resembling the Buick in outward appearance joined the range in 1932. The cars had independent front suspension in 1934, and turret top styling characterized the 1935 models. In 1938, when a 6-cylinder sedan could be bought for $967, Oldsmobile became the first of the G.M. group to offer the option of automatic transmission, evolved by 1940 into the famous Hydramatic. 273,000 cars were sold in 1941.

Oldsmobile became G.M.'s technical leader after World War 2; Hydramatic was optional on all models in 1946 and in 1948 the company's offi-

1903 OLDSMOBILE 5hp curved-dash runabout. *The Veteran Car Club of Great Britain*

1916 OLDSMOBILE 6-cylinder sedan. (This was the one millionth General Motors car). *General Motors Corporation*

1937 OLDSMOBILE L-37 sedan. *Harley J. Usill*
1971 OLDSMOBILE Toronado coupé. *Chrysler Corporation*

cial half-centenary was made the occasion to give the cars 'Futuramic' styling, a preview of what G.M.'s other cars were to look like in 1949. Oldsmobile's 1949 303ci ohv oversquare Rocket V-8 was the first of its kind to appear, and by 1951 the old sixes had been dropped altogether. The Rocket was giving 202bhp in 1955 and 305bhp from 371ci in 1958. In this year G.M.'s X-frame was standardized, air suspension was optional, the cars came in two wheelbase lengths and manual transmission was available only on the cheaper models.

Oldsmobile's compact, the F-85 of 1961, was an interesting car with unitary construction, coil springing all round, a 112in wheelbase and an aluminum V-8 of only 215ci displacement, developing 155bhp. Fastest of the full-size V-8s was the Starfire convertible with 330bhp, while a sporting version of the F-85 came out the following year in the shape of the Cutlass. In 1963 there was a companion Jetfire model, capable of 110mph, and listed at $3,633 with a turbo-supercharger. The aluminum V-8 was replaced on 1964 model F-85s by Buick's V-6, and a Jetstar line of economy cars was evolved by fitting a modestly-rated 8-cylinder engine in the regular chassis. 1966 Oldsmobiles covered a wide range from the small six up to V-8s of 383bhp, but the Division achieved a real technical breakthrough once more with the big Toronado coupé. This had front wheel drive and Hydramatic transmission, and was powered by the most potent version of Oldsmobile's 425ci engine. Displacement of the largest V-8 engine went up to 455ci in 1968. The 1971 models ranged from the intermediate F-85 and Cutlass to the full-size luxury 88 and 98, and the Tornado coupé.

OLIVER 1905

This is a make whose manufacture is unknown. The car was a five-passenger, with side-entrance. The power came from a 415ci 2-cylinder engine under the hood, driving the rear axle by chain. Its cost was $1,500, with a weight given as 1,750 lb.

OLYMPIAN 1917–1921
Olympian Motors Co, Pontiac, Mich.

The Olympian was an assembled car with a 4-cylinder engine. Two models were available, a touring car and a four-passenger roadster,

designated as the Tourist and the Gypsy respectively, both of which sold at $965.

OMAHA 1912–1913
Omaha Motor Car Co, Omaha, Neb.

The only unusual feature of this make was its underslung frame. It used an L-head 4-cylinder engine of 233ci, with shaft drive. Both roadster and seven-passenger bodies were mounted on a chassis with a wheelbase of 118in.

OMEGA 1968 to date
Suspensions International Corp, Charlotte, N.C.

Steve Wilder took over the former Griffith project and renamed the car the Omega. In its current form it has a 302ci Ford V-8 engine and all-steel body by Intermeccanica of Turin, Italy. Maximum speed is 150mph.

ONLY 1909–1915
Only Motor Car Co, Port Jefferson, N.Y.

The name for this make came from the original single-cylinder engine of massive displacement. This 206ci cylinder had a ball-bearing mounted crankshaft, with a flywheel at each end. The car was built as a two-passenger 'racytype', and was claimed to achieve 60mph. A four-passenger version was made for 1911. After 1912 a 4-cylinder engine with 7⅞in stroke was used, and only a five-passenger model was offered.

1910 ONLY 12hp single-cylinder roadster. *Automotive History Collection, Detroit Public Library*

OPHIR 1901

The Ophir was in most respects a typical light steam runabout of the period, with a 2-cylinder engine and tiller steering. However, in place of the usual single chain drive, it had shaft drive in which the propeller shaft was an extension of the crankshaft running at quite a sharp angle from just below the floor to the rear axle.

ORIENT BUCKBOARD *see* WALTHAM (ii)

ORLO 1904
Jackson Automobile Co, Jackson, Mich.

The Orlo was a side-entrance five-passenger car costing $1,125. Its 16/17hp 2-cylinder engine was mounted under the front seat and drive was through a single chain. The radiator for the water-cooled engine was a finned coil mounted beneath the front of the hood. The firm was also responsible for the better-known Jackson.

ORMOND 1904–1905
United Motor & Vehicle Co, Boston, Mass.

The Ormond was an expensive steam car made in very limited numbers. It had a 4-cylinder opposed engine of 15hp, and carried elaborate seven-passenger bodywork. The price was $3,000.

ORSON 1908–1909
Brightwood Mfg Co, Springfield, Mass.

The Orson was probably the only example of a car built by a cooperative of wealthy businessmen for their own use. Named after Orson Kilbourn, son of the designer, it was a large conventional 4-cylinder car whose chassis was made by the Brightwood Mfg Co, and bodies by the Springfield Metal Body Co. There were a hundred subscribers whose total wealth was said to be $250 million, and each paid what the car cost (average $4,000), no profit being made. The 100 cars were completed in about a year, after which the sponsors decided that the American market was almost saturated, and so did not put the car on general sale. It was called by the press 'the bankers' car', and the showrooms were appropriately at 52 Wall Street.

OTTO; OTTOMOBILE 1909–1912
1 Otto Gas Engine Works, Philadelphia, Pa. 1909–1911
2 Ottomobile Co, Mt Holly, N.J. 1912
3 Ottomobile Co, Philadelphia, Pa. 1912

The initial models of the Otto were roadsters; later touring and limousine models were added. These cars looked long and low, this effect being enhanced by a wheelbase of 123in. The later models used a 241ci 4-cylinder engine. The bodies had no overhang, being bracketed front and rear by the wheels. The last models were known as Ottomobiles and used engines of 286 or 318ci displacement.

OTTOCAR (OTTOKAR) 1903–1904
Otto Konigslow, Cleveland, Ohio

The single model of the Ottocar was a light two-passenger roadster. It was driven by a single-cylinder water-cooled engine of 6hp. Also used were a planetary transmission and single-chain drive. Painted Brewster green, it was priced at $750.

OTTOMOBILE see OTTO

OVENDEN 1899
W. C. Ovenden, West Boylston, Mass.

Ovenden made a light steam buggy with which he intended to go into production, but he only sold one car.

OVERHOLT 1909; 1912
The Overholt Co, Galesburg, Ill.

The four-passenger Overholt used solid rubber tires and a 2-cylinder, air-cooled engine of 12/14hp. The drive was by friction transmission and single chain to the rear axle.

OVERLAND see WILLYS

1910 OTTO 35hp roadster. *Kenneth Stauffer*

1910 OWEN 50hp touring car. *Automobile Manufacturers' Association*

OVERMAN 1899–1904
1 Overman Wheel Co, Chicopee Falls, Mass. 1899–1900
2 Overman Automobile Co, Chicopee, Mass. 1901–1904

The Overman Wheel Co were manufacturers of Victor bicycles and began development work on autos in 1896 when H. A. Knox was hired to design a gasoline engine. This was never put on the market and Knox left, later to manufacture Knox, and Atlas cars. A steam car, the Victor, appeared in 1899. It was typical of the many New England steamers of the period, with 4hp vertical 2-cylinder engine and single chain drive. In 1900 the Victor bicycle business was sold to the Stevens Arms & Tool Co, and for a few months Overman leased the top floor of the building to assemble Victor cars. In January 1901 a new company was formed, and they took over space in a factory at Chicopee, where Victor steamers continued to be built. In 1902 A. L. Riker joined the firm, and they became associated with Locomobile. The first Locomobile gasoline cars were developed at Chicopee as well as new Overman gasoline cars and the steamer. By 1904 the firm was wholly absorbed by Locomobile. Meanwhile the Chicopee Falls plant was used for the manufacture of Stevens-Duryea cars.

OWATONNA 1903
Virtue & Pound Mfg Co, Owatonna, Minn.

Virtually nothing is known about this vehicle other than that it was powered by a 9hp gasoline engine and was placed on the market early in 1903.

O-WE-GO 1914–1915
O-We-Go Car Co, Owego, N.Y.

This was a tandem two-passenger cyclecar with a V-twin air-cooled engine rated at 10/12hp. It had a friction transmission and belt drive. The only distinguishing feature was that the headlights were mounted on the front fenders, later a feature of the Pierce-Arrow.

OWEN 1910–1914
Owen Motor Car Co, Detroit, Mich.

The Owen used a 50hp 425ci 4-cylinder engine. It had a central gear shift and was one of the first cars with this improvement. The single model was a seven-passenger touring car for $4,000. Its 42in tires gave a ground clearance of 12in.

OWEN MAGNETIC; CROWN MAGNETIC 1914–1922
1 Baker, Rauch & Lang Co, Cleveland, Ohio; Wilkes-Barre, Pa. 1914–1919
2 Owen Magnetic Motor Car Corp, Wilkes-Barre, Pa. 1919–1922

1918 OWEN MAGNETIC 33hp roadster. *Kenneth Stauffer*

1914 OXFORD (ii) 6-cylinder touring car. *Hugh Durnford*

The American battleship *New Mexico* was provided with gearless Entz magnetic transmission across an air gap. Ray M. Owen, of Baker, Rauch & Lang, the manufacturers of electric cars (Baker, Raulang), adapted it for automotive use in the Owen Magnetic, a luxury car introduced in 1914. A normal 6-cylinder gasoline engine generated the electric power which operated the transmission. The Owen Magnetic disappeared in 1921, but J. L. Owen took over the system and offered it in a car called the Crown Magnetic: a push-rod ohv six of nearly 427ci displacement. With British engines, he also sold it in the United Kingdom (British Ensign). Electrical transmission, with its smoothness and flexibility, obviated the need for gear-shifting, but was expensive and unconventional.

OWEN-SCHOENECK 1915–1916
The Owen-Schoeneck Co, Chicago, Ill.

The Owen-Schoeneck was a conventional touring car powered by a 289ci 4-cylinder Herschell-Spillman engine.

OWEN-THOMAS 1909
Owen-Thomas Motor Car Co, Janesville, Wis.

This unusual vehicle was powered by a 6-cylinder engine of 429ci, with a crankshaft which ran in four ball-bearings 9in in diameter, and rotary valves in the cylinder heads. Ball-bearings were also used in the valve-train, in the transmission and in the fan-shaft. The steering was on the left-hand side with center controls. The five-passenger car, with a wheelbase of 132in, was priced at $3,000. A two-passenger version had a wheelbase of 108in. In November 1909 the Wisconsin Engine Co purchased the rights of Owen-Thomas and planned to make the car at Corliss, Wisconsin.

OXFORD (i) *see* DETROIT-OXFORD

OXFORD (ii) (CDN) 1913–1915
Oxford Motor Cars & Foundries Ltd, Montreal, Que.

The Oxford was the handsome, well-made product of a family of French Canadian industrialists. Four- and 6-cylinder models were offered but production was limited to a handful of sixes: touring cars and one roadster. Almost all components were imported from the U.S. When these became hard to get during World War 1 and sales failed to match expectations, the car-manufacturing section of the family business was liquidated.

P & Q

PACIFIC 1914
Portland Cyclecar Co, Portland, Ore.

The Pacific was a two-passenger cyclecar with tandem seating, which used an air-cooled, 2-cylinder engine of 70ci. It is claimed that this model was succeeded by a full-sized car named the Portland.

PACIFIC SPECIAL 1914
Cole California Car Co, Oakland, Calif.

This company listed a 33hp 4-cylinder roadster and touring car for one year only, at a price of $1,950. There was apparently no connection with the better-known Cole Motor Car Co of Indianapolis.

PACKARD 1899–1958
1 New York & Ohio Co, Warren, Ohio 1899–1901
2 Ohio Automobile Co, Warren, Ohio 1901–1902
3 Packard Motor Car Co, Warren, Ohio 1902–1903
4 Packard Motor Car Co, Detroit, Mich. 1903–1955
5 Studebaker-Packard Corp, Detroit, Mich. 1955–1958

The brothers J. W. and W. D. Packard bought a Winton in 1898 and determined to improve upon it. The result was the first 12hp Packard of 1899. This followed traditional early-American lines with a single horizontal cylinder, central chain drive, buggy styling and wire wheels, but was more advanced than its competitors in having a 3-speed and reverse transmission and automatic spark advance. This gave way to the wheel-steered Model C, which proved capable of 40mph. An even more powerful single sold for $3,000 in 1903 and on one of these Fetch and Krarup successfully drove from San Francisco to New York in 61 days. In the same year a very big four of over 730ci displacement was designed on European lines by Charles Schmidt, late of Mors. This sold for $7,500 and led to the famous Model L, the first car to bear the classic Packard radiator. It had an L-head engine and the transmission was mounted in unit with the back axle; a similar engine was used in the racing car Gray Wolf, a streamlined lightweight capable of 75mph. Packards for 1906 had T-head engines and magneto ignition in place of coil; engine displacement was 350ci, increasing to 432ci in 1907 with the introduction of the famous '30', from which 60bhp was claimed. For the next few years these high-quality fours engaged all Packard's attentions, the '30' at $4,200 being joined by a short-wheelbase '18' intended for use as a town car. Dry-plate clutches were adopted in 1910 and in 1911 a third model joined the range: Packard's first six, the 352ci '48'.

Sixes only were offered in 1913, when electric lighting and starting were standardized. Spiral bevel final drive followed in 1914. Revolutionary was the world's first series-production 12-cylinder, the Twin-Six, which was announced in 1915 for 1916; it was also the first American touring car to use aluminum pistons and was quite modestly priced at $2,600. First series cars had the unusual combination of left-hand drive and left-hand gear-shift, abandoned on later series, which also had detachable cylinder heads. A special racing car version, the 905 with a much bigger engine, recorded 149.9mph in the hands of Ralph de Palma at Daytona in 1919. From 1916 to 1920 only the Twin-Six was made, but it was then joined by a straightforward L-head Single-Six selling from $2,350 up. This car was given front-wheel brakes in 1924 and remained in production until 1928, accounting for most of Packard's sales while it was current. A 358ci

1915 PACKARD Twin Six touring car. *Henry Ford Museum, Dearborn, Mich.*
1925 PACKARD sedan. Coachwork by Freestone & Webb. *Monty Bowers*

1934 PACKARD Super Eight cabriolet. Coachwork by Graber. *G. N. Georgano Collection*

1937 PACKARD 120 convertible coupé. *G. N. Georgano Collection*
1939 PACKARD Eight touring car. Coachwork by Derham. *Keith Marvin Collection*

4-speed transmissions was introduced. 1932 Packards had V-radiators. An inexpensive Light 8 at $1,750, using the 326ci engine, proved uneconomic to make, but there was also an excellent 445ci V-12 and all cars had synchromesh transmission; vacuum-servo brakes came in for 1933. The company's styling with its traditional radiator shape continued up to 1939.

In 1935 Packard made a bid for the low-priced market with the 224ci straight-8 '120' with hydraulic brakes and independent front suspension, priced from $980, as against $2,475 for the Standard-eight, $2,990 for the Super-eight and $3,820 for the Twelve. The new model accounted for 24,995 of the 31,889 cars sold by Packard that year and was joined two seasons later by a very similar 211ci six, the '115' at $860; this and the '120', now enlarged to 282ci, were made in a separate factory. In 1938, 50 per cent of the company's labor force was engaged in making the senior Packards which accounted for no more than 8 per cent of total production!

In 1937 hydraulic brakes and independent front suspension were standardized throughout the range. The last year of the true senior Packards was 1939; column gear-shift was introduced and overdrive was available on all models except the Twelve. Air conditioning was a 1940 option and 1941 brought the first of the handsome Clipper line, made in 245ci 6-cylinder and 282ci straight-8 versions. Expensive cars were still made, with custom bodywork by Rollson, Le Baron and Darrin available on the 356ci chassis. During World War 2, body dies for the bigger, conventionally-bodied Packards were sold to the Soviet Government, the result being the 1945 Z.I.S.

Production was resumed with the Clipper 6 and 8 in 1946, but Packard never regained their former pre-eminence. Styling was unfortunate and

84bhp straight-8 with front-wheel brakes as standard replaced the Twin-Six during 1923; it came in two wheelbase lengths. A touring car cost $3,750 and it was the ancestor of the whole line of 'Senior' Packards up to 1939. The 1925 cars had centralized chassis lubrication and over 40,000 sixes were sold, as against less than 5,700 eights. Innovations for 1927 were a hypoid rear axle, and a bigger 8-cylinder engine of 384ci displacement, developing 106bhp. Only eights were made in 1929, in which year a 326ci Standard model was catalogued at $2,435, while in 1930 a limited series of '734' sports models with high axle ratio, 145bhp engines and

1955 PACKARD Clipper sedan. *Autosport*

1946 PACKARD Clipper sedan. *Montagu Motor Museum*

the company retained the old straight-8 until 1954, though they evolved their own 'Ultramatic' automatic transmission in 1949 and had power brakes, steering and power window lifts in 1954. Super-luxury cars included the eight-passenger Executive limousine at $6,900 in 1953 and the big Caribbean convertible.

The 1954 merger with Studebaker brought about a new 260bhp ohv V-8 with an ingenious inter-linked torsion level suspension, while engines were sold to American Motors for their Nash and Hudson lines. Sales fell to a depressing 13,000 in 1956 and though the Packard lingered on until 1958, the last two seasons' cars were nothing more than disguised Studebakers.

PACKET 1916–1917
Packet Motor Car Mfg Co, Minneapolis, Minn.
    Formerly known as the Brasie, the Packet was a two-passenger cyclecar, selling for $325. It had a 95ci 4-cylinder engine.

PACO 1908
Pietsch Auto & Marine Co, Chicago, Ill.
    This make was a two-passenger high-wheeler, which used a 10/12hp engine, a 4-cycle, 2-cylinder unit mounted under the seat. With a false hood and wheel steering the price was $400.

PAGE 1906–1907
Page Motor Vehicle Co, Providence, R.I.

This car was a two-passenger runabout with a 2-cylinder, air-cooled engine of 10hp. It had a 2-speed transmission and shaft drive. It sold for $750.

PAGÉ 1921–1924
Victor W. Pagé Motors Corp, East Stamford, Conn.

The Aero-type Four designed by Victor W. Pagé, an inventor, designer and engineer, had an aircraft-type 4-cylinder engine. This rare make was available as a four-passenger roadster with disk wheels as standard equipment at $1,250, and as a coupé at a slightly higher price.

1921 PAIGE Daytona roadster. *Kenneth Stauffer*

PAIGE-DETROIT; PAIGE 1908–1927
Paige-Detroit Motor Car Co, Detroit, Mich.

The first model of the Paige-Detroit was a two-passenger roadster powered by a 2-cycle, 3-cylinder engine of 133ci. In 1910, the power unit was changed to a 4-cycle, 4-cylinder engine, and the following year the car's name was changed to Paige. For 1914, a 6-cylinder model with a rating of 36hp was added. In 1916 two sixes were built with displacements of 230 and 303ci (1915 was the last year in which 4-cylinder engines were used). The larger model, the Six-46 was made as a seven-passenger touring car and in three closed types. The smaller six was offered only as a five-passenger touring car.

The 1919 models were known as Paige-Linwood (Duesenberg engine) and Paige-Larchmont (Continental engine).

The most notable Paige model was the Daytona roadster, first produced in 1922. This was a sporty three-passenger car with a 6-cylinder, 332ci engine. The third seat was a drawer-like affair on the right side which pulled out over the running-board. This car had wire wheels and was named to commemorate the 1921 record of 102mph by a stripped version of this model. The Daytona was continued until 1926.

From 1921 on, the radiator shell was remarkably similar to that of the more familiar and later Bentleys. For the last model year of 1927, the Paige was offered with three chassis using 6-cylinder engines, and one with a straight-8 engine.

A cheaper car built by Paige from 1923 to 1926 was the Jewett. In 1928, the Paige became the Graham-Paige.

PALM 1918–1919
Distributed by E. W. Brown Motors Pty, Ltd, Melbourne, Victoria

The Palm car was nothing more than a pirated Model T Ford. It was basically a Canadian Ford with the steering wheel changed to the right-hand position and a Palm emblem replacing the obliterated Ford insignia. In 1920, the Renown emblem replaced the Palm and the cars were known by the former name. Although the car was simply a rechristened Ford, it is important to list it under the Palm and Renown names to avoid possible confusion.

PALMER 1906
Palmer Automobile Mfg Co, Ashtabula, Ohio

This was a two-passenger car of the buggy type with a single-cylinder engine rated at 8hp. The drive was through a planetary transmission and cables, rather than chains. The car weighed 800lb.

PALMER-SINGER 1907–1914
Palmer & Singer Mfg Co, Long Island City, N.Y.

The Palmer & Singer company had been agents for Matheson and Simplex cars, and the first P & S cars were built in the Matheson factory. Four- and 6-cylinder models were made, the largest six being a 610ci 60hp and, unusually for such a large car at that time, it had shaft drive. A 28/30hp 4-cylinder roadster was called the Skimabout; other 4-cylinder models were town cars with dashboard radiators and Renault-style hoods. Victory in the Long Island Derby at Brighton Beach led to the 1913 models being called Brightons; these were very handsome cars with pointed radiators and streamlined torpedo bodies. In an effort to avert bankruptcy the company announced their 1915 line in late 1913. This included one car with a 378ci 6-cylinder L-head Magic engine, made under Fischer patents. However, the company failed, and was replaced by the Singer Motor Co, Inc, makers of the Singer car from 1915 to 1920.

PAN 1918–1922
Pan Motor Co, St Cloud, Minn.

The Pan was the tangible result of what became one of the biggest stock swindles in the history of the American car industry. Samuel Conner Pandolfo conceived the idea of a practical car built in a single plant by workers who lived in company housing. He built his own village around a large factory, and started production of touring cars and roadsters with a Pan 4-cylinder engine. An adjustable lever allowed the seats of Pan cars to be made into a double bed. Pandolfo also planned to build a tractor but was arrested, convicted of using the mails to defraud, and imprisoned. The company went out of business in 1922 after building 737 cars.

PAN AMERICAN (i) 1902
The Pan American Motor Co, Mamaroneck, N.Y.

This company announced a 16hp 4-cylinder car with tonneau body, designed by W. M. Power.

PAN AMERICAN (ii) 1917–1922
Pan-American Motor Corp, Chicago, Ill.; Decatur, Ill.

The Pan-American was a 6-cylinder assembled car which used a Continental engine, one of many of its kind. Approximately 4,000 cars were turned out in Pan American's six years of production, including the American Beauty model, built in 1920 and 1921, which is sometimes misrepresented as a make in its own right.

1911 PALMER-SINGER 50hp touring car. *Kenneth Stauffer*

1921 PARENTI 35hp V-8 touring car. *Automobile Manufacturers' Association*

PANDA 1955–1956
Small Cars, Inc, Kansas City, Mo.

The Panda was a light two-passenger car with alternative power units of a flat-twin 67.1ci Kohler, or a minute 4-cylinder 35.6ci Aerojet. The wheelbase was only 70in, and the price was $1,000.

PANTHER 1962–1963
Panther Automobile Co, Bedford Hills, N.Y.

This was a fiberglass sports car powered by a 157ci V-8 engine developing 190bhp. Claimed maximum speed was 150mph, and the price $4,995.

PARAGON (i) 1905–1907
Detroit Automobile Mfg Co, Detroit, Mich.

This car with its diminutive 42.4ci 2-cylinder 5hp engine was not aptly named. The total weight of this very small two-passenger car was 650lb.

PARAGON (ii) 1921–1922
Paragon Motor Car Co, Connellsville, Pa.

This 6-cylinder phaeton was to have been made at Cumberland, Md., but the few cars produced were built elsewhere. The Paragon had an engine of the company's own design and disk wheels were standard.

PARENTI 1920–1922
Parenti Motors Corp, Buffalo, N.Y.

This car was designed without axles, transverse springing being used as a substitute: two springs were located in the front and one in the rear. Plywood was extensively used in the construction of both frame and body. The Parenti was powered by a V-8 air-cooled engine of the firm's own design but for 1922 a water-cooled Falls Six was substituted. To attract the public, Parenti salesmen exhibited some of the first models in bright orange, yellow and purple.

Whether it was the design of the Parenti or its price ($5,000 for the town car and formal limousine) which defeated the car is not now known. Relatively few cars were sold, however, before the company failed.

PARKER (CDN) 1921–1923
Parker Motor Car Co Ltd, Montreal, Que.

The Parker looked identical to the American Birmingham, but while it used the same Haskelite bodies it had a traditional suspension system instead of the Birmingham's Wright-Fisher independent front suspension. Parkers were built in the former Forster plant, but only a handful of them. A Continental 6-cylinder engine was used.

PARKIN 1908
Parkin & Son, Philadelphia, Pa.

The Parkin was a 6-cylinder, 60hp auto which cost more than $3,000. Its manufacturer tried unsuccessfully to make a name in local races in 1908. One source claims that the Parkin was produced as early as 1903.

PARRY; NEW PARRY 1910–1912
1 Parry Auto Co, Indianapolis, Ind. 1910–1911
2 Motor Car Mfg Co, Indianapolis, Ind. 1912

The Parry was built as a two- or five-passenger open car with 20 or 30hp 4-cylinder ohv engines. After reorganization in 1911, the name was changed to New Parry. The last models, with 4-cylinder engines developing 35hp, were priced at $1,750.

PARSONS 1905–1906
Parsons Electric Motor Carriage Co, Cleveland, Ohio

The Parsons was a diminutive two-passenger electric car with a 66in wheelbase and 46in tread. Its 8hp motor was connected to the drive axle by double chains. It weighed 900lb and cost $1,600.

PARTIN; PARTIN-PALMER 1913–1917
1 Partin Mfg Co, Chicago, Ill. 1913–1915
2 Commonwealth Motors Co, Chicago, Ill.; Rochelle, Ill. 1915–1917

The Partin was a six-passenger car, powered by a 6-cylinder Rutenber engine. After combining with Palmer Motor Car Co, late in 1913 (with no change in the company name), this became the Partin-Palmer. The latter was made in two versions. The smaller model, with a 22hp 4-cylinder engine, with full electrical equipment, was a two-passenger car selling for $495. The larger model, with a 6-cylinder Mason engine, designated the 38, seated five on a longer wheelbase. It was replaced by the 32, a Lycoming powered four, which, with alterations, became the Commonwealth.

PATERSON 1908–1923
W. A. Paterson Co, Flint, Mich.

The Paterson started as a typical Mid-Western motor buggy. The Model 14 had solid rubber tires and an air-cooled 2-cylinder engine, with planetary transmission and double chain-drive. By 1910 this had evolved into a car with a 30hp 4-cylinder engine, sliding-gear transmission and shaft drive, in three body styles. The use of 4-cylinder engines was continued into 1915 when the line was complemented by a car with a 6-cylinder, 289ci engine and a longer wheelbase. After 1915, only sixes were made. It is likely that all the sixes were built by Continental; at all events from 1919 until 1923 this was the engine make. The body styles were conservative and there were no outstanding types. The distinguishing feature of the later models was a radiator and hood cross-section with sharp shoulders, probably in imitation of the Packard.

PATHFINDER 1911–1918
1 Motor Car Mfg Co, Indianapolis, Ind. 1911–1915
2 The Pathfinder Co, Indianapolis, Ind. 1916–1918

The Pathfinder succeeded the New Parry and was noted for several advanced body innovations, such as the disappearing top, the boat-tailed roadster and spare wheels under cover. The various models were large with 120 to 132in wheelbases. Early Pathfinders had 4-cylinder engines; V-radiatored sixes followed, and in 1916 a model with a 390ci 12-cylinder Weidely power unit was launched.

PATTERSON-GREENFIELD 1916–1918
C. R. Patterson & Sons, Greenfield, Ohio

This was a conventional-looking car, powered by a 4-cylinder engine, made in touring and roadster form. About 30 were built.

PAWTUCKET 1900–1901
Pawtucket Steam Boat Co, Providence, R.I.

This company made a small number of an unusual vehicle, a one-passenger steam car. It had a 7hp 2-cylinder engine and solid tires.

PAYNE-MODERN (MODERN) 1907–1909
Modern Tool Co, Erie, Pa.

The Payne-Modern used ohv air-cooled 4- or 6-cylinder engines of V configuration, with 60° between the cylinder banks. The gearshift lever was mounted on the steering column, and the final drive was by shaft.

1910 PARRY 30hp touring car. *Automotive History Collection, Detroit Public Library*
1916 PATERSON 25hp touring car. *Kenneth Stauffer*

1915 PATHFINDER 40hp touring car. *Don McCray*

The semi-elliptic springs were inclined so that the outboard ends were above the frame, while the inside ends were beneath the level of the frame. Both touring and roadster models were made, with 4-speed transmissions.

PECK (CDN) 1913
Peck Electric Ltd, Toronto, Ont.

The very elegant Peck coupé cost $4,000 but offered a choice of chain or shaft drive and wheel or tiller steering. The factory serviced Toronto buyers' cars, though its slogan insisted that the car 'Keeps Pecking'. It was also available as a roadster, with chain drive and wheel steering standard.

PEDERSEN 1922

The Pedersen was a shaft-driven light car with a 9hp 2-cylinder air-cooled engine. It was intended for mail-order distribution, and the factory address is uncertain.

PEERLESS 1900–1931
Peerless Motor Car Co, Cleveland, Ohio

The Peerless was known in its heyday as 'One of the Three P's' (Packard, Peerless and Pierce-Arrow), the great trio of American motoring. It first appeared in 1900, the product of a concern which had built clothes wringers and bicycles since 1869. Its début was not auspicious, the 1900 prototype being a typical horseless carriage with bicycle wheels and a single-cylinder De Dion-Bouton engine. This was followed in 1901 by the Type C Motorette, with a 3½hp single-cylinder water-cooled engine, priced at $1,300. This was augmented later in the year by the Type B, similar but smaller and cheaper.

Louis P. Mooers came to Peerless as chief engineer in 1901 and it was he who shaped the policy of the company during its first formative years. He designed the 1902 range of cars. These were shaft-driven and the engine was mounted vertically at the front of the car in what was to be the conventional arrangement in most cars, but was an innovation at the time. Selective sliding-gear transmission was used and side-entrance tonneaus were included in the range, possibly the first cars of this type. The prototypes of the 1902 lines were equipped with a single-cylinder Mooers-designed engine, although the production cars had 2-cylinder power plants. The 1903 series were based on 1902 Peerless racing cars (also designed by Mooers). Two models were available, a 24 and a 35hp, both with 4-cylinder T-head engines of Mooers design.

The year 1903 was notable for the appearance of the Peerless limousine, probably America's first closed car that was not custom-built.

In 1904, Mooers designed the famous Peerless Green Dragon racing

1904 PEERLESS 24hp touring car. *Burton H. Upjohn*

153

1923 PEERLESS coupé. *Keith Marvin Collection*
1929 PEERLESS Six-81 sedan. *Keith Marvin Collection*

car, a behemoth with a 6in × 6in bore and stroke. Driven from track to track by Barney Oldfield, 'The Boy in Green' test driver for the company's racing cars, the Green Dragon brought Peerless an enviable reputation as Oldfield continued to break records — frequently his own! He crashed the Green Dragon in 1905, but a new car was built and continued the record set by its earlier namesake.

By this time, the company was rapidly expanding and production was increased. The Peerless was regarded as one of the prestige cars of America and was priced accordingly. In 1907, the first 6-cylinder model was introduced although the fours continued for many years. Changes were largely limited to perfection of details. In 1912, prices ranged from $4,200 to $7,200. By 1913, Peerless cars were equipped with self-starters of the firm's own design.

An important development in Peerless design was the introduction of a V-8, a year after the rival Cadillac concern. This Peerless V-8 appeared late in 1915 and was reasonably priced in comparison with the expensive sixes which were discontinued at this time. With 80bhp at 2,700rpm, low speeds as well as high were possible in top gear. In appearance the V-8 closely resembled the Cadillac. The 1915 model continued without basic change until 1922, by which time its appearance had become outmoded. For 1923, bodies were lowered and rounded and the rear platform spring given up. Strangely enough, the newer design also closely resembled the contemporary Cadillac, although the latter had changed gradually through the years since 1915.

By 1923, business was good with some 5,000 cars being sold. A year later, a six was introduced as a companion car to the larger eight, now termed the 'Equipoised Eight'. In 1925, for the first time, an outside engine was utilized in a six by Peerless. This was a Continental and was used on the 6-80 chassis. Prices ranged from $1,400 for the cheapest six to more than $4,100 for the most expensive eight. Between 1926 and 1929, Peerless continued to market two lines of sixes and one of eights at prices from $1,895 to $3,795. But despite a wide price range, sales were falling steadily, possibly because of generally uninspired and rather unattractive

bodies. In 1929, the Peerless range was redesigned, the new models resembling the Marmon or Stutz to a considerable degree. A Continental straight-8 replaced the old V-8 engine. The two sixes were continued and toward the end of 1929, with sales increasing, the outlook seemed brighter. Count Alexis de Sakhnoffsky was hired to design the 1930 line. These cars were the sleekest and best-looking Peerless had ever produced. Three sixes and one eight were offered with prices ranging from $995 to $2,195. The eight was dropped shortly after its introduction.

Then came the Depression and this finished the Peerless. The make had slipped from 25th to 28th place among American car manufacturers from 1928 to 1929 and to 30th place in 1930.

It was early in 1931 that the company decided to attempt to recapture its former position by introducing a new prestige car which would compare with the Cadillac V-16 and the Marmon Sixteen. This was the Peerless V-16; only one prototype was built and this still survives today. Built in 1931, it was to have been produced as a 1933 or possibly even a 1932 model.

This car was almost entirely built of aluminum. With a 42lb frame, an aluminum engine of 464ci and 173bhp at 3,300rpm it was one of the handsomest cars ever made in the U.S. then or at any other time. Its custom sedan body was built by Murphy.

Actual production of Peerless cars ended on 30th June 1931. The plant remained idle for more than two years; then, Prohibition having been repealed, the Peerless Motor Car Co became the Peerless Corp, brewers of Carling's Ale, and as such, it survives to this day.

PENDLETON 1905
Trumbull Mfg Co, Warren, Ohio

The Pendleton was a five-seater tonneau. Its 284ci 4-cylinder engine was rated at 28/30hp.

PENN 1911–1913
Penn Motor Car Co, Pittsburgh, Pa.

The Penn Thirty had a 4-cylinder engine of 226ci. It was built in two-passenger and five-passenger versions, both with 105in wheelbases. A 45hp model was also listed.

PENNINGTON 1894–1902
1 E. J. Pennington, Cleveland, Ohio 1894–1895
2 Great Horseless Carriage Co Ltd, Coventry, England 1896–1897
3 Pennington and Baines, London, England 1898–1899
4 Pennington Motor Co Ltd, London, England 1899
5 Anglo-American Rapid Vehicle Co, New York, N.Y.; Philadelphia, Pa. 1899–1902

This complicated list of companies must be regarded as principal *claimants* to manufacture, since Edward Joel Pennington was the company promoter and charlatan *par excellence* of the horseless-carriage era; total production during its heyday probably amounted to no more than 15 vehicles, of which not one went to a private buyer. Pennington himself claimed to have built an electric 3-wheeler in 1887, an airship in 1890, and the first of his internal-combustion devices in 1893, but it was not until 1894 that he devoted himself seriously to the motor car. His ideas included a fuel-metering device in place of a carburetor, the much-discussed 'long-mingling spark', (which was not found on any Penningtons made after 1896), steel-tube cylinders without water-jacketing, large-section 'unpuncturable' pneumatic tires, and the ability to run on ordinary kerosene —a claim which does not seem to have been put to practical test. The first Pennington was a motorcycle, which was said to have sailed through the air for 65 feet, and to have attained 57mph. From this evolved the first 'Victoria', a primitive quadricycle made up of two ladies' bicycles joined together by a central platform which housed the working parts. Before he left America he had persuaded the Hitchcock cycle firm in Cortland, N.Y., and Thomas Kane and Co of Racine, Wisconsin, to finance his astonishing projects — hence the name Kane-Pennington applied to the engines on his earlier English press releases. It was announced that six Kane-Pennington 'motorcycles' were to be entered for the Chicago

1896 PENNINGTON Autocar 2hp 3-wheeler. *Montagu Motor Museum*

Times-Herald race of 1895, but none materialized. By the end of the year Pennington and his prototypes were in London.

Thereafter a stream of wild claims, challenges and projects poured from Pennington's fertile brain: fire-engines, 'war-motors', and even a propeller-driven motor cycle which was actually exhibited at the London Cycle Show in December 1896. The presence of water jacketing on the Victoria's cylinders was an initial disappointment; nonetheless, Pennington was able to sell his patent rights to H. J. Lawson's British Motor Syndicate for a reported $480,000 and by the summer of 1896 it was announced that Coulthard's of Preston were going into production with a commercial vehicle powered by a 16hp V-4 Kane-Pennington engine. Pennington himself was assigned a floor of the Lawson-owned Motor Mills at Coventry, from where emerged the best-known of his cars, the 3-wheeled Torpedo. This had a parallel-twin engine of immensely long cycle (2.46in × 12in, or 154ci); though the long-mingling spark was not used in practice, the fuel-metering nozzle was, and the only other engine control was an ignition switch. The tubular frame was made by Humber, the vehicle was intended to be steerable either by driver (at the rear on a saddle) or front passenger, and four transverse saddles were mounted on top of the frame for additional passengers. Pennington asserted that it could carry nine people. It certainly managed 40mph on occasion and defeated a Bollée in a much-publicized tug of war, but its retirement from the London-Brighton Emancipation Run was occasioned by the bursting of one of the 'unpuncturable' tires. Five were probably made at Coventry, and in March 1897 the Irish Motor and Cycle Co was floated in Dublin. This concern collapsed five months later without doing anything, and even the Great Horseless Carriage Co gave up advertising early delivery of Penningtons.

In 1898 the inventor was back, publicizing (from a new London address) the Raft-Victoria, a 3½hp device with front-wheel drive, rear-wheel steering, vibrating-coil ignition and a horizontal under-floor engine with horizontal rope (later belt) drive, all for less than £100 ($480) — later increased to £115 10s ($554) on the strength of over 400 orders booked! Hubert Egerton attempted to drive one of these from Manchester to London, but gave up at Nuneaton after 72 spark plugs had been consumed. An illusion of series-production (which deceived S. F. Edge, among others) was created by commissioning two Lancashire firms (later to make the Rothwell and Bijou cars respectively) to build components for the Raft-Victoria, but not more than three were completed, one of these having bodywork by Stirling of Granton (the Stirling-Pennington of 1899). When frustrated customers pressed for the return of their deposits, a new company was hurriedly formed, but this was short-lived, and in October 1899, Pennington returned to his native land, where he managed to sell his rights for $750,000 to the Anglo-American Rapid Vehicle Co; this concern offered either to refund the outstanding deposits or supply would-be clients with American made 'Pennington or Daimler' cars.

The self-styled 'largest motor vehicle company in the world', however, made nothing more than a handful of 4-wheeler, wheel-steered derivatives of the old Torpedo, said to do 72mph and to be the subject of an order of 1,000 vehicles for use by the British Government in the South African War. Pennington was back in England in the winter of 1900–1901 with his latest 'war motor', a reworked tricar with cylinders of 12in cycle and a light shield over the forecarriage, which careered around Richmond Park for a while. Nothing was heard of Anglo-American after 1902, but Pennington was involved in the Tractobile steam-driven fwd attachment for buggies (1901), the Continental spark plug with self-contained combustion chamber (1905), a scheme to market a 16hp car for only $288 (1907) and with yet another supposititious airship (1910). He died in 1911.

PENNSY 1916–1919
Pennsy Motors Co of Pittsburgh, Pittsburgh, Pa.

This medium-sized car sold for $855 in 1917, either in two- or five-passenger form. It used a 4-cylinder engine of 193ci, rated at 30/35hp. A six was added in 1918.

PENNSYLVANIA 1907–1911
Pennsylvania Auto-Motor Co, Bryn Mawr, Pa.

The earliest Pennsylvania was a four-passenger car with a 32hp 4-cylinder engine, on a 112in wheelbase. The models grew rapidly larger, culminating in the Model H for 1910–1911 which had a 557ci 6-cylinder engine. The large seven-passenger version was on a 137in wheelbase.

PEOPLE'S 1900–1902
People's Automobile Co, Cleveland, Ohio

As a result of a prolonged strike by employees of the Cleveland trolley company, a concern was formed to build and operate motorbuses in opposition to the trolley. This People's Automobile Co also built a few cars with single-cylinder engines. One of the founders of the company was Paul Gaeth who later built the Gaeth car.

PERFECTION 1906–1908
Perfection Automobile Works, South Bend, Ind.

The Perfection was made in both 4- and 6-cylinder versions. The latter was rated at 70hp, with a 477ci displacement. This five-passenger car sold for $2,500.

PERFEX 1912–1914
Perfex Co, Los Angeles, Calif.

The Perfex was a sturdy-looking two-passenger roadster with a 22.5hp G.B. and S. 4-cylinder engine of 198ci displacement and 3-speed transmission. It cost $1,050.

P.E.T. 1914
P. E. Teats, Detroit, Mich.

The P.E.T. was a cyclecar with a 4-cylinder engine on a chassis of 42in tread and 104in wheelbase. Price was given as $350.

1909 PENNSYLVANIA Type D 29hp touring car. *The Veteran Car Club of Great Britain*

PETER PAN 1914–1915
Randall Co, Quincy, Mass.

This cyclecar had a 4-cylinder water-cooled engine with overhead valves which produced 24hp at 3,200rpm. Both two- and four-passenger models were made. They had a V-shaped radiator, 3-speed transmission and shaft drive, and were priced at $400 to $450.

PETERS 1921–1922
Peters Autocar Co, Trenton, N.J.

The Peters was a short-lived air-cooled car powered by a 2-cylinder engine of 70ci displacement, developing 14bhp. The types offered were a roadster, a two-passenger speedster and a light station wagon, all priced at $345 and all with wire wheels.

PETERS-WALTON-LUDLOW 1915
Peters-Walton-Ludlow Auto Engineering Co, Philadelphia, Pa.

This was a cyclecar with a 9hp 2-cylinder engine, but, unusually for such vehicles, a five-passenger tourer body was offered. The price of this car was $390.

PETREL 1908–1912
1 Petrel Motor Car Co, Kenosha, Wis. 1908–1909
2 Petrel Motor Car Co, Milwaukee, Wis. 1910–1912

1909 PETREL 30hp roadster. *Montagu Motor Museum*
1910 PICKARD Model H touring car. *Harrah's Automobile Collection*

This make is said to have succeeded the Earl (i). The Petrel was made in two-passenger roadster and in five-passenger touring versions, with L-head 286ci engines. The early models used friction transmissions and double chain drive. By 1910 this self-proclaimed 'Aristocrat of Medium Priced Cars' had reduced its wheelbase to 108in and had adopted shaft drive. The 30hp 4-cylinder two-passenger model cost $1,350. For 1912, the name of the make was changed to F-S, after the parent company Filer and Stowell.

PHELPS 1903–1905
Phelps Motor Co, Stoneham, Mass.

The Phelps, in its original version, was a five-passenger car with rear entrance and a 3-cylinder water-cooled engine. Its radiator was a finned coil mounted beneath the front of the car. The body was hinged at the rear and could be raised to expose the entire running gear. Later models used 3- and 4-cylinder engines and honeycomb radiators. It was succeeded by the Shawmut.

PHIANNA 1916–1922
1 Phianna Motors Co, Newark, N.J. 1916–1918
2 M. H. Carpenter, Long Island City, N.Y. 1919–1922

One of America's finest prestige motor cars, the Phianna, successor to the S.G.V., was built in limited numbers for its six years of existence. The earlier cars had oval radiators and laminated walnut and ash fans mounted co-axially with the flywheel. In 1919, the radiator was changed to a square type and hood louvres were eliminated. The 4-cylinder Phianna engine was continued. Although the Phianna wheelbase was not as large as many contemporary cars of similar price, comfort was achieved by the use of 60in rear springs. The Phianna was a favorite with several heads of government as well as with a number of U.S. officials in Washington. Plans for a larger and longer 6-cylinder Phianna were outlined, and pilot cars were constructed, but the make failed in 1921. Cars were assembled from stock and marketed until 1922.

PHIPPS-GRINNELL 1901–1912
Phipps-Grinnell Automobile Co, Detroit, Mich.

The Phipps-Grinnell electric car was made in very small quantities of not more than 15 to 20 per year, at least until 1911, when the firm announced that expansion would take place. This make was succeeded by the Grinnell.

PICKARD 1908–1912
Pickard Bros, Brockton, Mass.

The Pickard used 4-cylinder air-cooled engines of 202 and 298ci with sliding-gear transmissions and shaft drive. The brake-bands were lined with camel hair, and the hoods were oval in cross-section.

PIEDMONT 1917–1922
Piedmont Motor Car Co, Inc, Lynchburg, Va.

This assembled car was produced in a variety of open and closed body styles powered by 4- and 6-cylinder Lycoming and Continental engines. The concern also made cars for other firms, notably Alsace, Bush, and Lone Star.

PIERCE; PIERCE-ARROW 1901–1938
1 The George N. Pierce Co, Buffalo, N.Y.
2 Pierce-Arrow Motor Car Co, Buffalo, N.Y.

Of the many prestige cars built in the U.S., probably none enjoyed more favor for a longer period than the Pierce-Arrow. This car began humbly enough. The first model, the Pierce Motorette, appeared in 1901. It was produced by George N. Pierce, a builder of bicycles and birdcages and was powered by a 2¾hp De Dion engine. This initial venture proved successful and was followed in 1902 by a similar car but with the output increased to 3½hp. For 1903, the Arrow name appeared and the company introduced a 15hp 2-cylinder car, with a 6½hp machine as a sideline.

In 1904 the name was changed to Great Arrow and the cars had power

1904 PIERCE Arrow 15hp roadster. *Henry Ford Museum, Dearborn, Mich.*
1911 PIERCE-ARROW 66 touring car. *Henry Austin Clark*

1933 PIERCE-ARROW V-12 convertible sedan. Coachwork by Le Baron. *Kenneth Stauffer*
1938 PIERCE-ARROW 1801 convertible. *Bernard Weis*

units capable of 28hp. It was such a car which won the Glidden Tour, a reliability test, and from this point onward, the name was one to be reckoned with. Power was gradually increased as was the size of the car through the immediate years and by 1908, the Pierce Great-Arrow boasted 60bhp at 1,000rpm. Up to 1909, steering-column shift was used. This was the last year in which the word Great appeared in the Pierce nomenclature.

The Pierce-Arrow was introduced in 1909 and such was the firm's reputation that production was limited and the supply seldom met the demand of the public. An interesting option on the enclosed-drive limousine for 1911 and later was a bulge in the roof to allow ladies to enter through the rear doors without crushing the elaborate hats then in fashion, against the roof.

In 1913, the first Pierce-Arrows appeared with the headlights attached to the tops of the front fenders, although this innovation was optional. The greater percentage of Pierce-Arrow cars were to appear with this type of headlight fitting, but the earlier arrangement was available until the early 1930s.

By 1914, Pierce-Arrow cars were available in three sizes. The 66 (reputedly the largest stock car built in the U.S.) was powered by a 6-cylinder engine with a 5in × 7in bore and stroke, giving a displacement of 825ci. The wheelbase was 147½in and the tires were 37in. A complete line of bodies was offered with prices ranging from $5,850 to $7,300. The 524ci 48 was built on a wheelbase of either 134½in or 142in with a price range of $4,850 to $6,300 and the 38, with a wheelbase and prices of 127in or 132in and $4,300 to $5,400, constituted the smallest line. Transmission was 4-speed with direct drive in fourth gear.

By 1915, with somewhere between 12,000 and 13,000 cars having been built and of these a good percentage still on the road, the Pierce-Arrow was considered as a top prestige car compared with anything in its price class, or even above it. Except for 1928, the name never appeared on the radiator, as it was felt the cars were easily recognizable without it. In frequent cases, Pierce-Arrows of this period were sold with a single chassis and two bodies, one open and one closed, which could be alternated with the seasons. Tires were reduced to 35in in size and the plant was expanded about 1916 to accommodate the increased orders, not only for passenger cars, but for the commercial vehicles which the company had been building since 1911. The enormous 66 was discontinued during 1917 and the 38 and 48 were continued at prices ranging from $4,800 for the cheapest 38 to $7,000 for the most expensive 48, exclusive of custom bodies. In 1920, the two cooling vents located above the hood were eliminated and the cowl parking lights were removed, all lighting being replaced in the headlights. The last right-hand-drive Pierce-Arrows were built late this year, Pierce-Arrow being one of the very last American cars to change over to left-hand steering.

A new series was introduced for 1921, the line being split in size between the 38 and 48 models. These retained the 6-cylinder engine. For the first time, hood louvres were used.

By 1923, sales were dropping and less than two years later, the company introduced a smaller companion car, the Model 80. This was the first Pierce-Arrow to be equipped with 4-wheel brakes. Its L-head 6-cylinder engine developed about 70bhp. Prices ranged from $2,895 to about $4,000. They sold reasonably well in comparison with the larger 36 but the company was showing an annual deficit and production was diminishing. In 1928, the stockholders voted to place the company under the control of the successful Studebaker Corp because of prevailing business conditions.

A new model was introduced for 1929, the company adopting a straight-8 engine of 366ci in place of the old six. The car was offered on two wheelbases at prices beginning at $2,775, and this was Pierce's best year, with 9,700 cars delivered. For 1930, three different 8-cylinder engines were offered the prospective purchaser. Because of the relationship between Pierce-Arrow and Studebaker, a number of the Pierce-Arrow cars bore a striking resemblance to the Studebaker President Eight, largest of the Studebaker line.

Demand continued to fall, and production with it, in 1931, and for

1932 the company introduced two 12-cylinder lines in addition to its eight, but even then, only 2,692 units were built during the year. These twelves came in 140bhp, 398ci, and 150bhp 429ci forms, priced from $3,900 up.

For 1933, Pierce introduced a special show car, the Silver Arrow, of which only five were made but which served as an intimation of the shape of cars to come. Priced at $10,000, the Silver Arrow had a 12-cylinder 175bhp engine and no running-boards. A tapered back, split rear window and spare wheels concealed in compartments behind the front wheels made this one of the most talked about cars of the year. It was displayed at the 1933 Chicago World's Fair.

In 1933, a group of Buffalo businessmen made the Pierce-Arrow an entity of its own once more. Ab Jenkins was breaking racing records with Pierce-Arrows but although the publicity was excellent, business was not. After 1934, the basic changes in design were slight. The company turned out both eights and twelves but by 1935, with less than 1,000 cars produced, it was apparent that the end of the make was in sight. Retaining its classic radiator, the Pierce-Arrow limped through the years 1936 and 1937 and with a handful produced in 1938 the company went out of business.

PIERCE-RACINE 1904–1909
Pierce Engine Co, Racine, Wis.

This company made its first car in 1894, and the second in 1899, but public sale did not begin until 1904. The 1904 model was a two-passenger car with a water-cooled 8hp engine, selling for $750. Four models were made in 1906. The Model D lasted from 1907 to the end of production in 1909. This was a 40hp car with shaft drive, claimed to be capable of 60mph. The company was bought in 1910 by the J. I. Case Threshing Machine Co, makers of the Case.

PIGGINS 1909
Piggins Brothers, Racine, Wis.

The Piggins was a very large car with wheelbases up to 133in. T-head, 6-cylinder engines of 36hp and 50hp were used. The latter unit was of 477ci displacement and drove a seven-passenger car weighing 3,700lb which cost $4,500.

PILGRIM 1914–1918
Pilgrim Motor Car Co, Detroit, Mich.

This was termed a light car, weighing only 1,450lb. The five-passenger model was powered by a 4-cylinder, water-cooled engine of 141ci.

PILLIOD 1915–1918
Pilliod Motor Co, Toledo, Ohio

This car had an advanced single-sleeve-valve engine and was one of the earliest examples of the extensive use of aluminum. This allowed the 257ci engine to produce 27hp with a weight of 390lb. The Pilliod was available in two-, four- and five-passenger forms.

PILOT 1909–1924
Pilot Motor Car Co, Richmond, Ind.

Throughout its life, the Pilot was an assembled car, with little evidence of imagination in either engineering or style. It started as a two-passenger roadster which was soon joined by five-passenger touring versions. These early models used a 4-cylinder, 35hp engine. In 1913, a 6-cylinder model was added and this was also the last year of the 4-cylinder cars. The 6-cylinder engine of 298ci was built by Teetor and developed 90hp. For 1916, a 298ci V-8 was added to the range. In this year the purchaser had an odd choice of either right- or left-hand steering position, with center controls. Model 6-45 originated in 1916, with a Teetor six of 230ci. With variations only in the wheelbase, this model was built until the end in 1924. In 1922, a 6-cylinder Herschell-Spillman engine of 50hp was added as the Model 6-50 and was continued into 1924.

In the last year of production, three chassis were offered. Two had H-S engines and the smallest, the 6-45, had a Teetor unit.

1947 PLAYBOY convertible. *Autocar*

PIONEER (i) 1909–1911
Pioneer Car Co, El Reno, Okla.

This was a lightweight car driven by a 4-cylinder, 30hp engine through a planetary transmission. The Model B Surrey cost $1,050.

PIONEER (ii) 1914
American Mfg Co, Chicago, Ill.

The Pioneer Cyclecar used a 9hp 2-cylinder air-cooled engine and semi-tandem or staggered seating for two. Transmission was by friction disks, and final drive by belts.

PIONEER (iii) 1959
Nic-L-Silver Battery Co, Santa Ana, Calif.

The Pioneer, or Lippencott Pioneer as this little electric was also known, had a fiberglass body and motors linked to the rear wheels. Suspension was by torsion bars and there was a toggle switch for forward or reverse.

PITTSBURGH (i) *see* AUTOCAR

PITTSBURGH (ii) 1909–1911
Fort Pitt Motor Mfg Co, New Kensington, Pa.

Pittsburgh cars were driven by T-head 6-cylinder 558ci engines. Aluminum bodies were furnished for the runabout and two touring models. These cars had an advanced exhaust system for the period, and the manufacturer claimed an added 300rpm engine speed by proper exhaust design. The single 1911 model was a seven-passenger touring car.

PLAYBOY 1946–1951
Playboy Motor Car Corp, Buffalo, N.Y.

Playboy nearly outlasted the flood of short-lived post-war American makes. The company struggled valiantly and managed to manufacture 97 examples of this compact three-passenger convertible before bankruptcy. It was driven by a 40bhp 4-cylinder Continental (originally Hercules) L-head engine, had an automatic transmission and a 90in wheelbase. Price was $985.

PLYMOUTH (i) 1910
Plymouth Motor Truck Co, Plymouth, Ohio

Although this was offered to the public as a five-passenger touring car with 40hp engine, only one was actually built.

PLYMOUTH (ii) 1928 to date
Chrysler Corp, Detroit, Mich.

The 4-cylinder 21hp Plymouth appeared in 1928 at a list price of $725 for a sedan. It replaced the earlier 4-cylinder Chryslers and represented a serious challenge for Ford and Chevrolet in their lowest price class. Its L-head engine, internal-expanding hydraulic brakes and ribbon-type radiator gave it a close resemblance to the 1928 Chryslers and De Sotos, and it sold over 100,000 in its first year, even improving its sales position in the bleak economic climate of 1932. Plymouth adhered to four cylinders until 1933, when the PD-series 6-cylinder was listed at less than $600. The 1934 de luxe models had independent front suspension, but this was dropped after a year and did not reappear for some time. The standard engine in the later 1930s had a displacement of 201ci, rather smaller than that used in comparable Chevrolets and Fords: a small-bore 170ci version was made for export up to 1939, but the name Plymouth was not usually found on cars sold in England, which were nominally Chrysler Kew and Wimbledon sixes. After World War 2 evolution followed that of other Chrysler Corp cars closely, the old-fashioned styling losing the division its long-held third place in American sales to Buick. Further, Plymouth retained the L-head six as its staple power unit right up to 1955, when 'flight sweep' versions were introduced with over-square ohv V-8 engines on accepted American lines in a variety of powers from 157 to 177bhp. The displacement of these was 260ci, while the six, now of 230ci, remained available. These 1955 cars were lower and longer than their predecessors and could be obtained with synchromesh, overdrive or automatic transmissions.

The Fury models of the ensuing decade represented a breakaway from the traditional stolid Plymouth family car. The Division was also responsible for Chrysler's contribution to the compacts, the Valiant, launched for 1960. This had rather more European styling than its competitors, with a dummy spare-wheel molding on the tail; interesting items of specification were its unitary construction, alternator ignition, and inclined in-line 170ci ohv 6-cylinder engine. The influence of the GT car on America resulted in the Barracuda of 1964, a fastback coupé using the Valiant's 106in wheelbase and a 273ci V-8 power unit. Plymouth, like Ford and Chevrolet, was aiming at comprehensive coverage of the low and medium price market in 1966, with the compact Valiant, the sports-compact Barracuda, the medium-sized Belvedere, the full-size Fury, and the luxurious 'V.I.P.' 4-door hardtop, offered only with a 318ci V-8 engine and selling for $2,930. This comprehensive coverage continued through 1971, with sporting models increasingly in evidence. These included the Duster coupé in the Valiant range and the Road Runner coupé and convertible in the intermediate Satellite (previously Belvedere) range. A new 360ci V-8 engine was available in the 1971 Fury, while Chrysler's largest engine, the 440ci, was used in the GTX and Sport Fury GT.

Late in 1970 the Chrysler Corporation's sub-compact car was announced. Known as the Plymouth Cricket, it was a 4-door sedan on a 98in wheelbase, powered by a 91.4ci 4-cylinder engine. Similar to the British Hillman Avenger, it was built in England by Chrysler United Kingdom Ltd.

P.M.C. 1908

C. S. Peets Mfg Co, New York, N.Y.

The P.M.C. was a two-passenger runabout with solid rubber tires. It was powered by a 2-cylinder opposed engine of 12hp. Its cost was $550, with a top for $30 extra.

PNEUMOBILE 1915

Cowles-McDowell Pneumobile Co, Chicago, Ill.

The Pneumobile appears to have been the first American car to use air-springs in place of mechanical springing. The cylindrical springs also acted as shock absorbers. It was built as a seven-passenger on a wheelbase of 132in. It had a 6-cylinder, 298ci Buda engine. In appearance this was quite an advanced car, with a radiator of compound curvature.

POKORNEY *see* TRICOLET

POMEROY (i) 1902

Pomeroy Motor Vehicle Co, Brooklyn, N.Y.

Sometimes mistakenly listed as Pomroy, this was a small electric runabout made for less than one year.

1931 PLYMOUTH (ii) Model PA sedan. *Montagu Motor Museum*
1936 PLYMOUTH (ii) convertible. Coachwork by Carlton. *Montagu Motor Museum*

1960 PLYMOUTH (ii) Valiant sedan. *Chrysler Corporation*
1971 PLYMOUTH (ii) Satellite Sebring coupé. *Chrysler Corporation*

1923 POMEROY (ii) sedan. *Aluminum Co of America*

1931 PONTIAC (iii) Model 401 coupé. *Arthur Ingram*
1939 PONTIAC (iii) Quality Six sedan. *G. Marshall Naul*

POMEROY (ii) 1920–1924

1 Aluminum Co of America, Cleveland, Ohio 1920–1922
2 Pierce-Arrow Motor Car Co, Buffalo, N.Y. 1923–1924

The Pomeroy was not, as is sometimes claimed, an 'all-aluminum car', but it did contain about 85 per cent of aluminum parts, notable exceptions being the semi-elliptic springs and the gears. It was designed by L. H. Pomeroy, who was also responsible for the Prince Henry Vauxhall and Double-Six Daimler, and was made in two models. The first was made by Alcoa and used a 4-cylinder engine of about 244ci (six of these were made), while the second was made in the Pierce-Arrow factory and used a 6-cylinder engine similar to the Pierce-Arrow 80, except for a smaller bore. These cars were never sold to the public, and large-scale manufacturers were unwilling to commit themselves to a material of which one company had a near monopoly of supplies.

PONDER 1923

Ponder Motor Mfg Co, Shreveport, La.

The Ponder was the continuation of the earlier Bour-Davis car after that make had been taken over by J. M. Ponder. A Continental 6-cylinder engine was used in this short-lived assembled car.

PONTIAC (i) 1907–1908

Pontiac Spring and Wagon Works, Pontiac, Mich.

This was a two-passenger high-wheeler with right-hand steering by wheel. It was powered by a 2-cylinder, water-cooled engine mounted under the body. The drive was through a friction transmission and double chains to the rear wheels. The cost was $600.

PONTIAC (ii) 1915

Pontiac Chassis Co, Pontiac, Mich.

A chassis without body was all that this company marketed. It was furnished with a 4-cylinder engine, by Perkins, rated at 25hp, driving through a 3-speed transmission.

PONTIAC (iii) 1926 to date

1 Oakland Motor Car Co, Pontiac, Mich. 1926–1932
2 Pontiac Motor Co, Pontiac, Mich. 1933 to date

Oakland's Pontiac Six was intended as a lower-priced running mate, and prices of this conventional 187ci L-head six started at $825. Only closed bodies were offered initially, but a sale of over 140,000 cars was an indication of acceptance, especially when followed by an increase to 210,890 in 1928. The 1930 Pontiacs closely resembled Buick's Marquette, and had 200ci engines, the six being joined in 1932 by a V-8 which was really a revamped 1931 Oakland.

In 1933 Pontiac scored an important success with a 223ci, 77bhp straight-8 selling for less than $600 with General Motor's new no-draft ventilation, the 6-cylinder models being dropped for the time being. The

1934 cars had Dubonnet-type independent front suspension, and 'turret-top' all-steel bodies. Fencer's mask radiator grills were found on the 1935 Silver Streak line. Displacements of the six and the eight were 222ci and 251ci respectively in 1937. In 1939 Pontiac's cheaper cars had body shells very similar to those of the Chevrolet, as befitted a make which ranked next in the G.M. hierarchy — though in fact only $20 separated the cheapest Pontiac 4-door sedan from the corresponding Oldsmobile model.

1961 PONTIAC (iii) Tempest coupé. *General Motors Corporation*
1971 PONTIAC (iii) Catalina 2-door hardtop. *General Motors Corporation*

Pontiac's Torpedo Streamliners brought back the fastback style in 1941, and the immediate pre-war models were continued with little alteration until 1949, when the whole group's products were restyled, and Pontiacs emerged with lower bodies, redesigned X-frames, and the option of Hydramatic transmission. Though maintaining high sales — they beat Plymouth into 4th place overall in 1954 — Pontiac remained conservative in engine design, and the well-tried 127bhp L-head straight-8 was not supplanted until 1955, when all U.S.-produced Pontiacs received a 287ci ohv V-8. The L-head six was retained for some models made for the Canadian market.

Along with some of the other more staid American makes, such as Plymouth and Mercury, Pontiac strove to build their reputation on performance in the later 1950s; the 1958 Super Tempest attained 330bhp, and in 1959 Pontiac came out with a wide-tread chassis and concentrated on a 390ci V-8 available in a variety of powers from 245 to 345bhp.

The Division's compact, the Tempest, arrived in 1961, and was an unusual ohv oversquare four of 194ci displacement, mounted in a unitary-construction hull, with its 3-speed synchromesh transmission in the rear axle. Floor shift was standard: it was listed at $2,240. A small V-8 was available as an option in 1963. The big Pontiacs went over to G.M.'s perimeter-type frame in 1963, when the V-8 engine was available in a variety of guises from a 'cooking' 215bhp version burning regular-grade gasoline at $2,725 up to the sporting Grand Prix coupé with 303bhp and a tachometer as standard equipment, at $3,489. The Tempest's 4-cylinder engine was dropped in 1965 in favor of a 140bhp six or 327ci eight. Sporting qualities were emphasized in 1966, by which time the Tempest had grown from a 112in wheelbase to 116in, and the range included the G.T.O. Grand Prix and 2 plus 2 models, all disposing of more than 330bhp from engines of 390 and 421ci displacement. In 1967, 230ci ohc 6-cylinder engines were introduced: in the sporting Firebird Sprint this unit developed 215bhp. These had grown to 250ci by 1971 when they were used in the smaller Firebird models; larger Firebirds used the 455ci V-8 developing 335bhp also found in the full-sized Catalina, Bonneville, and Grand Ville models, as well as the sporting Grand Prix SJ.

POPE-HARTFORD 1903–1914
Pope Mfg Co, Hartford, Conn.

This is one of the best-remembered cars of the period; Pope-Hartfords were apparently reliable vehicles although the design was very conservative. A single-cylinder model was included in the 1905 range, and 2-cylinder models were made as late as 1906. Double chain drive was retained in some models for 1908.

In price and size the Pope-Hartford came between the larger Pope-Toledo and the inexpensive Pope-Tribune.

In 1912, 4- and 6-cylinder models, of 50hp (389ci) and 60hp (444ci) respectively, were part of a large range of 17 different models. This type

of marketing led to the collapse of the Pope group of companies, which at one period encompassed five makes of cars as well as motor cycles and bicycles. Pope-Hartford also offered, in 1911, the FIAT-Portola, a chain-driven FIAT chassis fitted with their own engine: later sporting models used their own chassis as well.

POPE-ROBINSON *see* ROBINSON

POPE-TOLEDO 1903–1909
Pope Motor Car Co, Toledo, Ohio

Of the several makes produced by the Pope companies, this was the elite car. It grew out of the Toledo steamer, although none of the Pope-Toledos had steam engines. All models were distinguished by peaked hoods and were powered by 4-cylinder, water-cooled engines; 1904 models retained automatic inlet valves. Early Pope-Toledos were rear-entrance tonneaus, but by 1907 limousines and seven-passenger touring cars were being built. The company was taken over in 1909 by the Apperson-Toledo Motor Co, who discontinued this make.

POPE-TRIBUNE 1904–1907
Pope Mfg Co, Hagerstown, Md.

This was the smallest and least expensive of the several Pope-owned makes. Two- and four-passenger models, using single- and 2-cylinder engines, were built, both with shaft-drive. In 1907, a 4-cylinder car was brought out. The prices of the several models ranged from $500 to $900. After financial difficulties in 1907, the Pope-Tribune was dropped.

1906 POPE-TOLEDO Type 12 35/40hp touring car. *Burton H. Upjohn*
1904 POPE-TRIBUNE 7hp runabout. *The Veteran Car Club of Great Britain*

1914 POPE-HARTFORD 35hp roadster. *Western Reserve Museum, Cleveland, Ohio*

POPE-WAVERLEY *see* WAVERLEY

POPPY CAR 1917
Eisenhuth Motor Co, Los Angeles, Calif.

This company announced a 5-cylinder car with 'self-starting motor, conventional transmission done away with, and a secret reverse system'. The car was to sell at the low price of $650, but there is no evidence that it was made.

PORTER (i) 1900–1901
Porter Automobile Co, Boston, Mass.

The Porter steam car used a 2-cylinder engine and had a maximum speed of about 25mph. Steering was by tiller which was usual on such cars, but the aluminum body had less angular lines than most of the Porter's contemporaries.

1921 PORTER (ii) town car. *Keith Marvin Collection*

PORTER (ii) 1919–1922
American & British Mfg Corp, Bridgeport, Conn.

The Porter was a high-priced luxury car designed by Finlay Robertson Porter, formerly designer of the T-head Mercer and the F.R.P.; it was the logical successor to the F.R.P. from an engineering standpoint. Using a 4-cylinder engine of the firm's design, the Porter car, which somewhat resembled the Rolls-Royce, was equipped with a right-hand steering position, an anomaly on American roads. A variety of custom body builders, including Brewster, Holbrook and Demarest, supplied open and closed coachwork to the Porter chassis at prices from $10,000. A total of 34 cars constituted the complete Porter output.

PORTLAND *see* PACIFIC

POSTAL 1907–1908
Postal Auto & Engine Co, Bedford, Ind.

The Postal was an unsophisticated tiller-steered high-wheeler, with rear fenders only. Its 2-cylinder engine was placed under the seat for two passengers. Its weight was 900lb and its price was $475.

POWELL SPORT WAGON 1954–1956
Powell Sport Wagons, Compton, Calif.

The Powell utility had the rare distinction of being a 'used' new car as all were built of reclaimed Plymouth parts. A 1941 Plymouth chassis was the basis of this machine and added to it were rebuilt 90bhp Plymouth 6-cylinder engines, dating from 1940 to 1950. The metal and fiberglass pickup body was a boxy design with provision for a camping unit on the back and fishing rods in the rear fenders. A station wagon was added to the range in 1955.

POWERCAR 1909–1912
Powercar Auto Co, Cincinnati, Ohio

Although this car had sliding-gear transmission and shaft drive, its 4-cylinder engine, rated at 30hp, hardly justified the make's name. In its final year of manufacture both a touring model and a torpedo roadster were offered.

POWERCAR SPECIAL 1953–1954
Mystic River Sales Co, Mystic, Conn.

This was a vehicle for a single child and was electrically powered. Its overall length was 62in and width 33in. The body was fiberglass.

PRADO 1920–1922
Prado Motors Corp, New York, N.Y.

Built in extremely restricted numbers, the Prado was an 8-cylinder car using as its motive power a converted Curtiss OX-5 aircraft engine. Bore and stroke were 4in × 5in (giving a displacement of 503ci). Disk wheels and individual cycle-type fenders were standard.

PRATT 1907
Pratt Chuck Works, Frankfort, N.Y.

The Pratt was one of the few 6-wheeler cars produced in the U.S. Four wheels were mounted at the rear and two at the front. Both the front and the intermediate set were steerable, the intermediate pair turning in a lesser angle than the leading pair. Power was supplied by a 75hp engine to the rear pair of wheels only, through the medium of an ordinary transmission gear and a 2-part rear-axle shaft. The touring-car, the only model listed, was 168in long.

PRATT-ELKHART; PRATT 1911–1917
1 Elkhart Carriage & Harness Mfg Co, Elkhart, Ind. 1911–1915
2 Pratt Motor Car Co, Elkhart, Ind. 1916–1917

This make started as a medium-sized car with a 4-cylinder engine of 270ci. The last models had longer wheelbases (132in) and were powered by a 6-cylinder, 348ci engine rated at 50hp.

PREMIER 1903–1925
1 Premier Motor Mfg Co, Indianapolis, Ind.
2 Premier Motor Corp, Indianapolis, Ind.

The Premier started life as a conventional machine made on modern lines, with a pressed-steel frame, mechanically-operated inlet valves, and shaft drive. A four-cylinder air-cooled car was made in 1905. Its designer was G. A. Weidely, who made his name with proprietary engines. A line of conventional water-cooled big fours and sixes followed, starting with a 24/28hp model in 1907. From 1913, sixes alone were built, the 6-60 at

1907 PREMIER 24hp roadster. *Automotive History Collection, Detroit Public Library*

$3,250 having a displacement of 501ci. The special racing Premiers of 1916 had a twin ohc, 4-cylinder, 16-valve engine reminiscent of the Peugeot. The touring Premier of 1919–1920 was notable mainly for its use of the Cutler-Hammer Magnetic Gear Shift, an electric transmission system controlled by a lever mounted on the steering wheel. The ohv 295ci engine was an unusually advanced six, with aluminum block, crankcase and pistons, and iron sleeves.

PREMOCAR 1921–1923
Preston Motor Corp, Birmingham, Ala.

The first Premocars offered to the American public were available in two distinct types, a low-priced 6-cylinder model which had a Falls ohv engine, and a 4-cylinder model with a Rochester-Duesenberg unit which sold for a considerably higher figure. The four was almost immediately dropped, however, and most of the Premocars built were sixes.

1902 PRESCOTT 7½hp steam surrey. *Montagu Motor Museum*

PRESCOTT 1901–1905
Prescott Automobile Mfg Co, New York, N.Y.

This was a tiller-operated steamer with a 2-cylinder Mason engine rated at 7½hp. The body was an open four-passenger, with a fold-down seat in front of the driver, or a standard four-passenger surrey. Specifications for the Prescott included brass brake-shoes and a steam-operated air pump for inflating the tires.

PRIDEMORE 1914–1915
Pridemore Machine Works, Northfield, Minn.

This was a tandem two-passenger cyclecar with a 2-cylinder, air-cooled engine rated at 12/18hp. The transmission was of the friction type and final drive was by chains. The frame was underslung.

PRIMO 1910–1912
Primo Motor Co, Atlanta, Ga.

The Primo company used small 25hp 4-cylinder engines, with Schebler carburetors, to power their various models. Prices ranged from $1,250 for a two-passenger roadster to $1,750 for the five-passenger touring car. The optional wheel treads of 56in or 61in were the Primo's only unusual feature.

PRINCESS 1914–1918
Princess Motor Car Co, Detroit, Mich.

The original Princess was a light two-seater, costing $475, powered by a 97.6ci 4-cylinder Farmer engine. It had a Renault-style hood, although the radiator was mounted in front of the engine. For 1916 this model was supplemented by a conventional-looking five-passenger touring car powered by a 187ci G.B. & S. engine. This model was continued to 1918.

PRINCETON 1923–1924
Durant Motors, Inc, Muncie, Ind.

The Princeton was William C. Durant's attempt to produce a prestige car for a market between that covered by the largest Flint and the smaller Locomobile, both Durant subsidiaries. Produced in the former Sheridan plant, the Princeton used an Ansted 6-cylinder ohv engine. Few were marketed.

PUBLIX (US/CDN) 1947–1948
Publix Motor Car Co, Buffalo, N.Y.; Fort Erie, Ont.

This 3-wheeled convertible coupé was 72in in length, with an aluminum body and chassis. It was powered by an air-cooled 1.75hp Caufflel engine mounted in a special shock-absorbing rig connected to the drive mechanism and the rear wheels. The steering wheel could be shifted from the left-hand side to the right at will.

PULLMAN (i) 1903–1917
1 Broomell, Schmidt & Steacy, York, Pa. 1903–1905
2 York Motor Car Co, York, Pa. 1905–1909
3 Pullman Motor Car Co, York, Pa. 1909–1917

A. P. Broomell's first Pullman car was a 6-wheeler named after the Pullman railroad cars. This model proved impractical, and in 1905 Broomell introduced a 4-wheeled car under the name York. By 1907 the cars were again known as Pullmans, and had 20 or 40hp engines and shaft drive, priced at $1,850 to $3,500. By 1912 the largest model was the 60hp 6-cylinder Model 6-60, a 525ci car with compressed air starter, although smaller fours were also made. In 1915 the Cutler-Hammer push-button magnetic gearshift was introduced, on the 6-46A with Continental engine. Later in 1915 a new management took over, and introduced a much cheaper line of cars, powered by 187ci 4-cylinder G. B. & S. engines and selling at prices from $740 to $990. As late as 1925 cars with similar specification to these were being advertised in England under the name London-Pullman, although American production ceased in 1917. The London-Pullmans were presumably dead stock, possibly fitted with English bodies.

1903 PULLMAN 6-wheel touring car. *Hardinge Co*

1910 PULLMAN (i) 35hp touring car. *Kenneth Stauffer*

1902 PURITAN (i) 6hp steam car. *Keith Marvin Collection*

PULLMAN (ii) 1907–1908
Pullman Motor Vehicle Co, Chicago, Ill.

This car had a 4-cylinder water-cooled engine of 432ci. A 3-speed sliding-gear transmission and shaft drive were used. The only model, a seven-passenger touring car, was priced at $3,600. There is no known connection with the better-known Pullman (i) of York, Pa.

PUNGS-FINCH 1904–1910
Pungs-Finch Auto & Gas Engine Co, Detroit, Mich.

The Pungs-Finch started as an advanced vehicle, with shaft drive and a sliding-gear transmission but few improvements were made during its life. In 1905 there appeared the even more advanced Finch Limited, with inclined overhead valves operated by a gear-driven overhead camshaft, and displacement of more than 610ci. Only one was built. The last Pungs-Finch, for 1910, was the Model H which had a 4-cylinder, 40hp T-head engine of 354ci. Both a two-passenger and a five-passenger model was available.

PUP 1947
Pup Motor Car Co, Spencer, Wis.

With an automatic clutch, the 600lb Pup was a small two-passenger car offering either a 7½hp single-cylinder or a 10hp 2-cylinder engine in the rear.

PURITAN (i) 1902–1903
Locke Regulator Co, Salem, Mass.

The Puritan steam car used a 6hp 2-cylinder vertical engine and single chain drive, but among its more modern features were wheel steering (the column folded for easy access to the seats), and a foot throttle.

PURITAN (ii) 1913–1914
Puritan Motor Co, Chicago, Ill.

This cyclecar used a 10hp De Luxe engine and V-belt drive. The body was a side-by-side two-passenger. Semi-elliptic springs were used in front, and three-quarter elliptics at the rear.

QUEEN (i) (CDN) 1901–1903
Queen City Cycle & Motor Works, Toronto, Ont.

Not related to the later U.S. Queen, this single-cylinder runabout was steered by wheel and featured a forward-opening folding seat for two extra passengers. Its performance was considered poor even by the standards of the day and production ceased when the company president bought a Cadillac.

QUEEN (ii) 1904–1907
C. H. Blomstrom Motor Co, Detroit, Mich.

The Queen started as a single-cylinder car with single chain drive. Later models used 2- and 4-cylinder engines, but all of them were relatively small. These cars had very graceful lines. The manufacturer also marketed Blomstrom and Gyroscope cars.

QUICK 1899–1900
1 H. M. Quick, Paterson, N.J. 1899
2 Quick Mfg Co, Newark, N.J. 1900

The Quick was a light two-passenger buggy with a 2-cylinder 4hp horizontal engine, single chain drive and tiller steering.

QUINSLER 1904
Quinsler & Co, Boston, Mass.

This was an attractive two-passenger car with a removable rumble seat for a third person. It used a De Dion engine under the front hood. Steering was by wheel and the price was $950.

1905 QUEEN (ii) 4-cylinder touring car. *Senator N. Larsen*

R

R.A.C. *see* DIAMOND (i)

RAILSBACH 1914
L. M. Railsbach, Saginaw, Mich.
 The manufacturer classed this make as a light car, although its 36in track would place it in the cyclecar category. It had a water-cooled 4-cylinder, 73ci engine. The two-passenger car with staggered seating sold for $350.

RAINIER 1905–1911
1 Rainier Co, Elyria, Ohio; Saginaw, Mich. 1905–1907
2 Rainier Motor Car Co, Saginaw, Mich. 1907–1911
 The first Rainier was a 22/28hp touring car. In 1906 it had progressed to a 30/35hp 4-cylinder engine. By 1908 the range had increased to three, with a landaulet priced at $5,800, and this 'Pullman of Motor Cars' was guaranteed to be free of repairs for one year. In 1911, four body types were built on a chassis with a 120in wheelbase. The engine was a 45/50hp 4-cylinder unit with a 4-speed transmission. In 1912, the Rainier was succeeded by the Marquette (i).

RALEIGH 1920–1922
Raleigh Motors, Inc, Reading, Pa.; Bridgeton, N.J.
 Probably less than 25 Raleigh motor cars ever got into the hands of customers. These were assembled cars with 6-cylinder Herschell-Spillman engines. The price of the touring car was $2,750.

RAMAPAUGH *see* BALL

RAMBLER (i) 1900–1903
1 Rockaway Bicycle Works, Rockaway, N.Y.
2 Rockaway Automobile Co, Rockaway, N.Y.
 This company made a light two-passenger runabout powered by a water-cooled single-cylinder engine. Final drive was by single chain. The price was $650.

RAMBLER (ii); (iii) 1902–1913; 1950–1970
1 Thos. B. Jeffery Co, Kenosha, Wis. 1902–1913
2 Nash Motors Co, Kenosha, Wis. 1950–1954
3 American Motors Corp, Kenosha, Wis. 1954–1970
 Despite the interval of 37 years, these two makes are directly connected. The original Rambler derived its name from the bicycle built by Gormully and Jeffery, who had a branch factory in Coventry in the 1890s. In 1902 form it was a light runabout in the American idiom with a single horizontal cylinder, chain drive, cycle-type wire wheels and tiller steering, selling for $750. In the first season 1,500 cars were sold, a figure which places the makers in the same category as Oldsmobile, among the world's first mass producers.
 By 1905 the Rambler had grown into a sizable twin-cylinder machine with front hood, and with the introduction of a 4-cylinder model in 1907 the make had moved up into the semi-luxury class; another parallel with Oldsmobile, but one which had less unfortunate financial consequences, for Rambler sold over 3,000 cars in 1911 and 4,435 in 1913, the last year of production. The bigger of two fours offered in 1912 had a 432ci engine

1908 RAINIER 30/35hp touring car. *Automotive History Collection, Detroit Public Library*
1911 RAMBLER (ii) Model 64 touring car. *American Motors Corporation*

with separate cylinders. The 1914 models went under the name of Jeffery. Advanced features of these late Ramblers were sidelights faired into the dashboard, and detachable wooden wheels.
 Nash Motors, successors to the Jeffery company, revived the name in 1950 for the first of the modern generation of American 'compacts'. This was a 172ci L-head six with a wheelbase of 100in and an overall length of under 180in, priced at $1,800. It featured unitary construction of chassis

and body, and weighed only 2,576lb at a time when a regular Chevrolet sedan turned the scales at around 3,360lb. Nash sales went up by 50,000 as a result of the Rambler, which was offered as a Nash until 1957, acquiring styling by Pininfarina in 1952, the option of an automatic transmission in 1953, and an alternative V-8 engine in 1957. Some cars were also sold under the Hudson name after the merger which brought American Motors into being in 1954.

From 1958 on, all A.M.C. cars were known as Ramblers, the former full-sized Nashes continued as Rambler's Ambassador model. The Rambler was the first of the contemporary compacts, and set a fashion imitated later by the Big Three. In the recession year, 1958, George Romney's criticisms of large cars were widely quoted. In 1958 the low-priced American model reverted to the 100in wheelbase, and in 1961 a die-cast aluminum ohv push-rod six was introduced which eventually supplanted the old L-head unit. The last vestiges of the 1949 Nash Airflyte styling vanished in 1963, and disk brakes were offered as an option in 1965, in which year a sporting fastback coupé, the Marlin, was introduced. The 1967 models were made on three wheelbase lengths — 106, 112 and 116in — and with a choice of ohv 232ci 6-cylinder or 290 and 343ci V-8 engines. From 1968 the name Rambler became less prominent in the range, new models such as the Javelin being known under their own names. For the 1970 season the name Rambler was dropped altogether in the U.S. and Canada, although the Hornet was sold as a Rambler in export markets. For the 1971 season, the name Rambler was no longer used at all.

RANDALL 1904
J. V. & C. Randall, Newtown, Pa.

The Randall was a 3-wheeled vehicle, with a fringed top. It was steered by a tiller acting directly on the front wheel, and powered at the rear by an air-cooled 12hp 2-cylinder engine with chain drive. It seated four passengers, and 20mph was claimed for it.

RAND & HARVEY 1899–1900
Rand & Harvey, Lewiston, Me.

This was a light steam buggy which probably never passed the prototype stage.

R. & V. KNIGHT 1920–1924
R. & V. Division of the Root & Vandervoort Engineering Co, East Moline, Ill.

Although the R. & V. Knight was never a popular car, with production never exceeding 760 per year, it was of outstanding quality. Known as the Moline-Knight between 1914 and 1919, it was sold with a complete line of body styles in the $2,500 to $4,000 price range. Its 260ci sleeve-valve Knight engine developed 57bhp at 2,400rpm. The radiator was distinctive and slightly pointed and all cars were sold with unusually full equipment including tire chains, windshield wipers, etc. The cars had a steel and pressed-lead seal around the entire engine and the two years' guarantee which came with the car depended on this remaining unbroken, although

1924 R. & V. KNIGHT sedan. *Automobile Manufacturers' Association*

authorized service stations could reseal this if work on the car became necessary.

RANGER (i) 1908–1910
1 Ranger Motor Works, Chicago, Ill.
2 Ranger Automobile Co, Chicago, Ill.

The Ranger was a small two-passenger runabout, of the buggy type, with a 2-cylinder, air-cooled engine, planetary transmission and tiller steering. It cost $395.

RANGER (ii) 1920–1922
Southern Motor Mfg Association, Houston, Tex.

Ranger cars for 1920 and 1921 were powered by a 4-cylinder engine of the firm's own make, and a touring car, sport roadster and a conventional roadster were offered. The 4-cylinder car with artillery wheels was continued in 1922, the five-passenger touring model selling at $1,485. A 6-cylinder line was introduced this year, the larger cars having wire wheels as standard equipment. Cycle fenders and aluminum step plates were also featured on the Pal o'Mine, Blue Bonnet, Commodore and Newport sport types. The 6-cylinder touring car cost $3,550. Few of the sixes were built.

RAUCH & LANG ; RAULANG 1905–1928
1 Rauch & Lang Carriage Co, Cleveland, Ohio 1905–1916
2 Baker, Rauch & Lang Co, Cleveland, Ohio 1916–1922
3 Rauch & Lang Electric Car Mfg Co, Chicopee Falls, Mass. 1922–1928

Rauch & Lang were an old-established carriage building firm (founded 1853) when they began to make electric cars in 1905. These followed the usual pattern of such vehicles, being mainly closed town cars, although a few open phaetons were also made. The biggest Rauch & Langs were heavier vehicles and included a six-passenger limousine with separate outside seat for the chauffeur. Some cars had 4 doors, a very unusual feature in electric cars. In 1916 they became parts of the Baker, Rauch & Lang group and production declined. From 1919 onward they were sometimes listed as Raulangs, and from 1922 this became the official name of the cars.

By this time production had been transferred to the Stevens-Duryea factory at Chicopee Falls where the number of passenger cars made was very small. The factory, which was still turning out a few Stevens-Duryeas, also made gasoline and electric taxi-cabs under the name R. & L., and bodies for Stanley Steamers.

RAYFIELD 1911–1915
Rayfield Motor Car Co, Springfield, Ill.

The Rayfield's distinguishing feature was its radiator mounted behind the engine in Renault style, with sloping hood. The 4- and 6-cylinder engines developed 18 and 22/25hp respectively. The 4-cylinder engine used for the first three years was a diminutive 88.5ci unit.

RAYMOND 1912–1913
Raymond Engineering Co, Hudson, Mass.

The Raymond was a 4-cylinder light roadster, which sold for $445.

R.C.H. 1912–1916
Hupp Corp, Detroit, Mich.

This was a small car with a wheelbase of 86in. The first models had left-hand drive, and central gear-shift. Both two- and four-passenger models were produced, powered by 25hp 4-cylinder engines with a 3-speed selective transmission. R. C. Hupp resigned from Hupmobile in 1911 to form this company.

READ 1913–1914
Read Motor Co, Detroit, Mich.

The Read car was an undistinguished, inexpensive ($850) five-passenger touring car with gray body and black striping, powered by a 4-cylinder 199ci engine.

1909 RAUCH & LANG electric stanhope. *The Veteran Car Club of Great Britain*

1914 R.C.H. 16hp touring car. *Automotive History Collection, Detroit Public Library*

1904 RED JACKET 2-cylinder tonneau. *Keith Marvin Collection*

READING (i) 1900–1903
1 Steam Vehicle Co of America, Reading, Pa. 1900–1902
2 Meteor Engineering Co, Reading, Pa. 1902–1903

The Reading was a typical light steam carriage, although 4-cylinder engines were available as well as the more usual twins. The company was absorbed by the Meteor Engineering Co in 1902, who introduced a larger car under their own name, although the light Reading design was continued to the end of 1903.

READING (ii) 1910–1913
Middleby Auto Co, Reading, Pa.

This car was a companion make to the Middleby but larger, on a 120in wheelbase. A two-passenger speedster, selling for $1,350, had a 4-cylinder 304ci engine with a massive exhaust system.

REAL 1914–1915
H. Paul Prigg Co, Anderson, Ind.

The Real cyclecar had a spruce frame. The rear-mounted engine was an air-cooled 2-cylinder Wizard and drive to the rear wheels was by belts. This three-passenger car was priced at $290.

REBEL *see* AMERICAN MOTORS

REBER 1902–1903
1 Reber Mfg Co, Reading, Pa. 1902–1903
2 Acme Motor Car Co, Reading, Pa. 1903

The Reber was a five-passenger car, with rear entrance, driven by a vertical 2-cylinder engine. This unit was water-cooled, and the coil radiator was mounted beneath the frame in front of the sloping hood. Drive was by double chain. This make became the Acme (i).

RED ARROW 1915
Red Arrow Automobile Co, Orange, Mass.

The Red Arrow was made by the successors to the Grout Brothers Automobile Co. As a change from the steamers and large gasoline cars made by Grout, the new company made a cyclecar with a 12hp 2-cylinder engine. It cost $350 and lasted less than a year.

RED BUG 1923–1928
1 Automotive Electrical Service Co, Newark, N.J.
2 Standard Automobile Corp, North Bergen, N.J.

Sometimes listed as the Auto Red Bug, this vehicle was the Briggs & Stratton Buckboard redesigned with an electric motor powered by a 12-volt battery driving the nearside rear wheel. A brake acted on the opposite rear wheel. Otherwise the Red Bug offered no more amenities than the Briggs & Stratton, but at least it was quieter.

RED JACKET 1904
O.K. Machine Works, Buffalo, N.Y.

This five-passenger, rear-entrance car used a water-cooled, 2-cylinder engine. Its transmission was a 3-speed selective type, and final drive was by double chain. Lighting was by a single headlight. With much brass, including upholstery binding strips, it cost $1,500.

REDPATH (CDN) 1903
Berlin (later Kitchener), Ont.; Toronto, Ont.

A typical single-cylinder runabout known as the Redpath Messenger was the only model produced. It featured a $4\frac{1}{2}$in × $4\frac{1}{2}$in engine mounted under a rounded, slightly streamlined hood, and shaft drive. Three of these cars were built.

REEVES 1896–1898, 1905–1912
1 The Reeves Pulley Co, Columbus, Ind. 1896–1898; 1905–1910
2 Milton O. Reeves, The Reeves Sexto-Octo Co, Columbus, Ind. 1911–1912

The first five Reeves vehicles were known as Motocycles. Designed by

1911 REEVES Octoauto 8-wheeled touring car. *Automotive History Collection, Detroit Public Library*
1911 REGAL (i) 18/20hp roadster. *Autocar*

Milton O. Reeves, they had 6 or 12hp Sintz 2-cylinder 2-cycle marine engines, variable belt transmission, and double chain final drive. Size varied from a three-passenger car to a twenty-passenger bus.

In 1905 a new series of cars appeared powered by 12 or 18/20hp 4-cylinder air-cooled engines of Reeves design and manufacture, joined by water-cooled fours and sixes, and an air-cooled Big Six in 1906. Chain drive was used on the Big Six, the other cars having shaft drive. Smaller 2-cylinder cars with solid tires and chain drive followed, and the last production Reeves was a 2-cylinder high-wheeler known as the Buggymobile or Go-Buggy. Production ceased in 1910, and Milton Reeves then began experimenting on his own account with multi-wheeled cars. The 1911 OctoAuto was based on an Overland, and had a 180in wheelbase with overall length of 248in. The first SextoAuto was the OctoAuto with a normal front axle, the second SextoAuto was based on a Stutz. A price of $5,000 was quoted for this car, but only one was made.

Reeves engines were supplied to many firms, including Aerocar, Auburn, Autobug, Chatham, Maplebay, Moon, and Sears.

REGAL (i) 1907–1920
Regal Motor Car Co, Detroit, Mich.

In 1907 Regal made 50 of their 20hp 4-cylinder cars, but the following year they took them all back, and gave the owners a new 1908 model free. Apparently this generosity was not repeated in following years, and they settled down to making a range of conventional 4-cylinder cars. The best-

known was the 201ci 18/20hp 'underslung' model, which, like the American Underslung, had frame members which passed underneath the axles. It was made in open two-passenger, and closed coupé form. Other models were the 20/30hp and 40hp which had normal chassis design. Regals were imported into England by Seabrook of Great Eastern Street, and from 1911 to 1915 the models sold in England were known as R.M.C.s or Seabrook-R.M.C.s. In 1915 a 10/15hp four of 128ci with unit construction of engine and transmission was introduced, together with a short-lived V-8. At the 1919 London Show Seabrooks showed a large R.M.C. touring car powered by a 232ci 6-cylinder engine, but shortly afterwards American production ceased, and Seabrooks began to make their own light cars.

REGAL (ii) (CDN) 1910
Having no connection with the better-known Berlin-built Regal (iii), this was a 30hp car made as a touring car or runabout at Walkerville, Ont.

REGAL (iii) (CDN) 1914–1917
Canadian Regal Motor Car Co, Berlin (later Kitchener), Ont.

The Regal was a lightweight touring car which resembled the Detroit model bearing the same name. Available with a Lycoming 4-cylinder engine at $875 or a V-8 at $1,350, it had a radiator filler concealed under the hood. The company was under the direction of Henry Nyberg, who had built the U.S. Nyberg car before going to Canada. In 1917 the company moved to a new plant and started producing Dominion trucks. About 200 Regal cars were built.

REGAS 1903–1905
Regas Automobile Co, Rochester, N.Y.

The Regas was powered by 2- or 4-cylinder engines, both of V configuration. These were of 127 and 252ci respectively. These cars used a Marble-Swift friction transmission.

REID *see* WOLVERINE (i)

REINERTSEN *see* REX BUCKBOARD

RELAY 1904
Relay Motor Car Co, Reading, Pa.

The Relay used a 24hp 3-cylinder engine with overhead valves. Final drive was by propeller shaft and a five-passenger tonneau body was standard.

RELIABLE DAYTON 1906–1909
Dayton & Mashey Automobile Works, Chicago, Ill.

The Reliable Dayton cars were two- and four-passenger high-wheelers. Their 2-cylinder air-cooled engines were located under the body, with rope drive to the rear wheels, and solid rubber tires. The dummy hood in front was complete with dummy radiator.

RELIANCE 1903–1907
Reliance Automobile Mfg Co, Detroit, Mich.

This car was produced as a five-passenger side-entrance tonneau, with a fixed top. It was powered by a 2-cylinder water-cooled engine of 212ci and cost $1,250.

REMINGTON (i) 1900–1901
Remington Auto & Motor Co, Kingston, N.Y.

This car used a 4-cylinder engine of unusual design, burning a mixture of hydrogen and acetylene gas. The 1901 model was called the Remington Standard, the name of the famous typewriter made by the same firm.

REMINGTON (ii) 1900–1904
Remington Motor Vehicle Co, Utica, N.Y.

This car was built as a five-passenger tonneau at $1,350 and as a two-passenger runabout at $850. Each was driven by a 2-cylinder 2-cycle engine of 10hp. This was water-cooled, and drive to the rear axle was by belt.

REMINGTON (iii) 1914–1915
Remington Motor Co, Rahway, N.J.

The Remington began as a sophisticated cyclecar with a 107ci 4-cylinder engine and shaft drive. The Hollister automatic transmission was preselective and actuated by the clutch, a system employed successfully 20 years later by Hudson. In 1915, a V-8 engine was used in a car with standard tread on a 116in wheelbase. The cars were designed by Philo E. Remington, grandson of the founder of the famous arms company.

REO 1904–1936
1 R. E. Olds Co, Lansing, Mich. 1904
2 Reo Car Co, Lansing, Mich. 1904
3 Reo Motor Car Co, Lansing, Mich. 1904–1936

The name derives from the initials of Ransom E. Olds, who left Oldsmobile to form a new company. The first Reos were single-cylinder 8hp runabouts with under-floor engines, dummy hoods, planetary transmissions, and chain drive; they sold for $685, reduced to $500 by 1909. A companion 16hp twin at $1,250 had a displacement of 212ci and a carburetor for each cylinder. These represented the company's main effort up to 1909, though a short-lived four had been marketed in 1906. The Reo The Fifth came in 1911/1912, another 4-cylinder car with 219ci F-head engine, which offered central shift and left-hand drive for $1,055.

Reo cars were steady sellers right up to the Depression of 1929–1931, and the company did very well with their subsequent F-head fours and sixes, which were made with V-radiators during the World War 1 period. In 1918, 4-cylinder cars sold for $1,225, $1,550 being asked for the 295ci 6-cylinder version. Only a four was made in 1919, but for 1920 Reo standardized a six, their famous F-head Model-T with 'back-to-front' gear shift, and two foot-operated brakes with no hand lever; 2-wheel brakes were deemed sufficient right up to the end of production in 1926. In 1927 there was a switch to L-heads and hydraulic 4-wheel brakes, and in 1928 the company offered the Wolverine, a cheaper car with a Continental engine which sold for $1,195, as against the $1,685 asked for the Flying Cloud with Reo's own engine. This was the company's best year, with 29,000 cars sold. The Wolverine was dropped in 1929, and produc-

1928 REO 25/65hp coupé. *Automobile Manufacturers' Association*
1931 REO Custom Royale Eight sports sedan. *Autocar*

1909 REO 16hp touring car. *Kenneth Stauffer*

tion centered on two versions of the Flying Cloud with 213 and 268ci engines.

An 8-cylinder Flying Cloud followed in 1931, along with a bid for the luxury market with the 358ci straight-8 Custom Royale, styled by Alexis de Sakhnoffsky. It had automatic chassis lubrication, and could be obtained in three wheelbase lengths, the longest being 152in.

The Reo 4-speed automatic transmission was available on all models from 1933 onward, as an alternative to synchromesh, but though the 268ci Flying Cloud with Graham-like sedan bodywork could still be bought for $845 in 1936, that was the end of Reo's passenger cars. The company still builds trucks as a division of the White Motor Co.

REPUBLIC 1911–1916
1 Republic Motor Car Co, Hamilton, Ohio 1911–1912
2 Republic Motor Car Co, Tarrytown, N.Y. 1913–1916

This car, called 'the classiest of all', used a T-head, 4-cylinder engine rated at 35/40hp. The crankshaft was off-set, and each cylinder had two sparking plugs. Five-passenger touring cars and roadsters were priced at $2,250.

REVERE 1917–1926
1 ReVere Motor Car Corp, Logansport, Ind. 1917–1922
2 ReVere Motor Co, Logansport, Ind. 1922–1926

The ReVere was a short-lived luxury car that was best known in speedster form. In its fiercest guise, it was powered by a horizontal-valve 360ci Rochester-Duesenberg racing engine providing 103bhp at 2,600rpm and 85mph. Alternatively, there was a smaller, 81bhp unit. A 4-speed transmission was supplied. Formal bodies, such as that for King Alfonso XIII of Spain, were also worn. As happened so often with cars of this exotic type, the ReVere lost appeal in its later years. Continental 6-cylinder engines were fitted in 1924. When balloon tires arrived the ReVere was furnished with two superimposed steering wheels, one with a lower ratio for parking.

REX 1914
Rex Motor Co, Detroit, Mich.

The two-passenger Rex cyclecar had a 4-cylinder, water-cooled engine of 15/18hp. A friction transmission and shaft final drive were used.

REX BUCKBOARD 1902
Pennsylvania Electrical & Railway Supply Co, Pittsburgh, Pa.

This was a very simple car on the lines of the Orient Buckboard, powered by a 4½hp engine. It was designed by Rex Reinertsen, an employee of the Pennsylvania Supply Co, and built in their workshops.

RICHARD 1914–1917
Richard Automobile Mfg Co, Cleveland, Ohio

This car had a 4-cylinder engine with a piston stroke of nearly 9in, giving a displacement of 352ci. The resulting hood was considerably higher than the rest of the body. Initially, a seven-passenger touring body was made. Later, the wheelbase was extended to 137in to accommodate a nine-passenger body with a boat-tail. This model was listed with a 596ci V-8 engine.

RICHELIEU 1922–1923
Richelieu Motor Car Corp, Asbury Park, N.J.

The Richelieu was designed by Newton Van Zandt, formerly with ReVere: this accounts for the general similarity between the two makes. (It has been said that the Richelieu prototype was built in the ReVere factory.)

It was a luxury car powered by a 4-cylinder Rochester-Duesenberg engine. The 4-door models cost $6,000, the open cars slightly less. These handsome cars with high, rounded radiators were discontinued in 1923 after fewer than 50 had been delivered. The company was acquired by Advanced Motors.

RICHMOND (i) 1902–1903
Richmond Automobile & Cycle Co, Richmond, Ind.

The Richmond Steam Runabout differed little from its contemporaries with its 6hp vertical engine and chain drive. The body style was a four-passenger with *dos-à-dos* arrangement.

RICHMOND (ii) 1908–1917
Wayne Works, Richmond, Ind.

Until 1911, the Richmond used air-cooled engines, all 4-cylinder units of 22 to 30hp. By 1913, larger models, on wheelbases of up to 121in, were using water-cooled engines of 318ci. Five-passenger touring cars and two-passenger runabouts were the only body types offered.

RICKENBACKER 1922–1927
Rickenbacker Motor Co, Detroit, Mich.

Captain Eddie Rickenbacker was already famous, as a racing driver and a World War 1 aviator, when he began to offer a remarkable car bearing his name. It bore his personal symbol of a hat in a ring, and was powered by a small L-head 6-cylinder engine, which was very smooth thanks to its two flywheels. This unit developed 58bhp at 2,800rpm. The chassis frame was boxed and rigid, and there were internal expanding brakes on all four wheels. The 1923 Rickenbacker was the first cheap car to have front-wheel brakes. The last Rickenbackers were 268ci and 315ci

1920 ReVERE Model C roadster. *Keith Marvin Collection*

1922 RICHELIEU touring car. *Automobile Manufacturers' Association*
1927 RICKENBACKER coach sedan. *Automotive History Collection, Detroit Public Library*

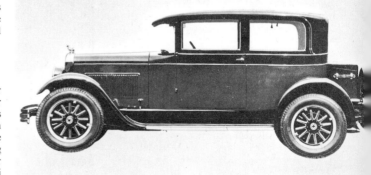

straight-8s of the same design. This engine gave 107bhp at 3,000rpm in sports form, and was said to propel the Rickenbacker at 90mph.

The whole machine was exceedingly well made, as well as original, but high quality, low price and unconventionality killed it. The design was bought by J. S. Rasmussen in Germany and used in two models of the Audi.

RICKETTS 1908–1909
Ricketts Auto Works, South Bend, Ind.

The Ricketts used Brownell 4- and 6-cylinder engines of 35 and 50hp respectively. A baby tonneau and a five-passenger touring car were available on a 116in wheelbase; the Model D was a seven-passenger touring model on a longer wheelbase, priced at $2,250. These cars all had 3-speed selective transmissions and shaft drive.

RIDDLE 1916–1926
Riddle Mfg Co, Ravenna, Ohio

The Riddle firm which existed from 1831 until 1926, was one of the earlier manufacturers of motor ambulances and hearses. In the 1920s and probably as far back as 1916, a handful of invalid sedans were built to special order. These cars had bodies without pillars on the right-hand side to facilitate entrance and egress for wheel chairs or beds. A few were bought as passenger cars for bearers' use at funerals. They closely resembled the contemporary Cadillacs and were powered by a Continental 6-cylinder engine developing 50bhp.

RIDER-LEWIS 1908–1910
Rider-Lewis Motor Car Co, Muncie, Ind.

This make was advertised as 'The Excellent Six', which referred to its 40/50hp engine with overhead camshaft and valves. Four-cylinder cars of 26hp were also built. Body types available included a five-passenger touring car, a two-passenger roadster, a limousine, landaulet and 'tonneauette'.

RIKER 1896–1902
1 Riker Electric Motor Co, Brooklyn, N.Y. 1896–1899
2 Riker Electric Vehicle Co, Elizabethport, N.J. 1899–1900
3 Riker Motor Vehicle Co, Elizabethport, N.J. 1901 1902

One of A. L. Riker's first electric vehicles, a two-passenger phaeton, won a race at Providence, R.I., running against several gasoline-engined cars. This sporting tradition was continued in 1900 when a special low-slung torpedo racer established a number of records for electric cars, including the mile in 1 minute 46 seconds.

Production Rikers included two-passenger runabouts, four-passenger dos-à-dos, an enclosed coach driven from a hansom cab position, and heavy trucks. In December 1900 Riker merged with the Electric Vehicle Co, makers of the Columbia, and only the trucks were continued under the Riker name. After A. L. Riker sold his company to the Electric Vehicle Co, he offered them his designs for a gasoline car. They were not interested, so he formed the Riker Motor Vehicle Co. The first car from this company was an 8hp 2-cylinder machine with chain drive, followed later in 1901 by a 16hp 4-cylinder car. This design was the basis of the first Locomobile gasoline-engined car. Riker was also concerned with the Overman Automobile Co, which made a few cars before the works were taken over by Stevens-Duryea.

RITZ 1914–1915
1 Ritz Cyclecar Co, New York, N.Y. 1914
2 Driggs-Seabury Ordnance Corp, Sharon, Pa. 1915

This cyclecar was claimed to be 'The Miniature Car for Everyone' although it carried only two passengers side-by-side. It had a V-twin engine of 10/12hp, tubular front axle, and quarter elliptic springs. Drive was by shaft, with planetary transmission. By 1915 a 10hp four with L-head monobloc engine and detachable head was available.

RIVIERA see SCHNADER

1896 RIKER electric 3-wheeler. *Henry Ford Museum, Dearborn, Mich.*
1915 RITZ 10hp cyclecar. *David Filsell Collection*

R.M.C. see REGAL (i)

RITTER 1912
Ritter Automobile Co, Madison, Wis.

This was listed for the year 1912 only, as a torpedo roadster using a 4-cylinder engine of 112ci displacement. The wheelbase was 90in and the price $685.

ROACH 1899
W. E. Roach (formerly Roach & Barnes), Philadelphia, Pa.

The Roach light car used a 2-cylinder engine mounted under the seat, wire wheels and tiller steering. Probably only prototypes were made.

ROADER 1911–1913
Roader Car Co, Brockton, Mass.

The Roader was a small two-passenger roadster with a 4-cylinder 130ci engine. With its wheelbase of about 96in, and a price of $650, this appears to have been a forerunner of the light car which appeared after the cyclecar craze. Roader was a New England term for a spirited horse.

1921 ROAMER touring car. *Montagu Motor Museum*
1904 POPE-ROBINSON 24hp tonneau. *Dr Alfred Lewerenz Collection*

1932 ROCKNE coupé. *Studebaker-Packard Corporation*

ROAMER 1916–1930
Barley Motor Car Co, Kalamazoo, Mich.

Albert C. Barley, who earlier made the Halladay from Streator, Ill., sold his Roamer frankly as a cheap Rolls-Royce — which it was in radiator shape if not in any other significant respect. It was an assembled car.

By 1920, it was produced with four sizes of proprietary engine. The best-known was a 303ci 6-cylinder unit by Continental. The powerful 4-cylinder, horizontal-valve Rochester-Duesenberg engine and a Rutenber unit were also used in the period up to 1920. The rear suspension was by double cantilever springs — an unconventional touch. Touring and sport models were offered. From 1922 to 1925 a rather smaller six was sold, on its own: by this time, production of the Rochester-Duesenberg engine had stopped. By 1927, all Roamers were straight-8s of 226 and 299ci, and remained so to the end.

ROBE 1914
W. R. Robe Co, Portsmouth, Ohio

The Robe cyclecar used a 4-cylinder, water-cooled engine and shaft drive. Further details are unknown.

ROBERTS SIX (CDN) 1921
Canadian Automobile Corp. Lachine, Que.

Several body styles of the Roberts Six announced, to sell between $4,500 and $5,800. Possibly only a prototype was built.

ROBIE 1914
Robie Motor Car Co, Detroit, Mich.

The Robie cyclecar used a 4-cylinder Perkins engine of 98ci and was produced as a side-by-side two-passenger car. The only distinguishing feature was a rounded radiator, similar to that of the contemporary Delage Grand Prix car.

ROBINSON; POPE-ROBINSON 1900–1904
1 John T. Robinson & Co, Hyde Park, Mass. 1900–1902
2 Robinson Motor Vehicle Co, Hyde Park, Mass. 1902
3 Pope-Robinson Co, Hyde Park, Mass. 1902–1904

The Robinson superseded the Bramwell-Robinson. The early models were two-passenger cars with water-cooled 151ci 2-cylinder engines behind the seat. The 1900 model had left-hand steering with an aluminum steering wheel. Later models were five-passenger rear-entrance tonneaus, powered by 4-cylinder T-head engines of up to 302ci. The final drive was by double chain. They were expensive, high-quality cars, among the best made in New England at that time.

ROBSON 1908–1909
Robson Mfg Co, Galesburg, Ill.

The Robson was offered in four basic chassis with either single-, 2- or 4-cylinder engines. In the largest chassis was a 40/45hp 4-cylinder engine, 3-speed selective transmission and shaft drive. Four body types were available in this chassis, including a two-passenger 'beetle-backed' roadster.

ROCHESTER 1901–1902
Rochester Cycle Mfg Co, Rochester, N.Y.

The Rochester was one of the many light steam buggies of the period. It had a vertical 2-cylinder engine, single chain drive and tiller steering. Like most of its contemporaries, it had full elliptic springing at the rear, and a single transverse elliptic at the front, but an 'unusually flexible frame' was said to allow 15in of vertical movement by either front wheel without appreciable disturbance of body level.

ROCKEFELLER YANKEE 1949–1950
Rockefeller Sports Car Corp, Rockville Center, L.I.

This was a fiberglass four-passenger sports car using the standard Ford V-8 engine together with many other Ford components such as axles, suspension and steering. The car could be supplied without engine and transmission for those buyers who wanted to fit a more powerful engine. Price of the car complete was $2,495.

ROCKET (i) *see* SCRIPPS-BOOTH

ROCKET (ii) 1948
Hewson Pacific Corp, Los Angeles, Calif.

The choice of a 4- or 6-cylinder rear engine was offered on this proto-type, which was rather 'teardrop' in shape, and fitted with an early example of the padded instrument panel.

ROCKFALLS 1919–1925
Rock Falls Mfg Co, Sterling, Ill.

Powered by a Continental 6-cylinder engine, these cars were mainly used as funeral cars. Less than 50 per year were manufactured.

ROCK HILL 1910
Rock Hill Buggy Co, Rock Hill, S.C.

This five-passenger car, of toy tonneau design, was equipped with a 471ci 4-cylinder engine. It had 3-speed selective transmission and shaft drive. A peculiar option was the tread: either the standard 56in, or 60in. This car was an unsuccessful venture by this manufacturer who later, through a subsidiary, made the more successful Anderson (ii).

ROCKNE 1931–1933
Rockne Motors Corp, Detroit, Mich.

The Rockne was in effect a small Studebaker. Apparently it was thought that a hero's name would sell the car: Knute Rockne, the great American football coach, held this position at Notre Dame University in South Bend, Ind., where the Studebaker Corp was also based. In 1931 it announced that Rockne had been appointed to the Studebaker staff as sales manager, but shortly afterwards he was killed in a plane crash and the Rockne Corp was set up in Detroit. The cars had 189ci 6-cylinder engines and a complete range of body styles at prices from $585 to $675. The 1933 models had fender skirts. The Rockne was withdrawn from the Studebaker list for 1934 after a total of 30,293 had been sold.

ROCKAWAY see RAMBLER (i)

RODGERS see IMPERIAL (i)

ROEBLING-PLANCHE 1906–1909
Walter Automobile Co, Trenton, N.J.

This car was an ancestor of the famous Mercer. The name Roebling came from the famous wire-rope family, and Planche from the French designer. Although this make used 4-cylinder engines exclusively, Roebling-Planches ranged from a 20hp, five-passenger landaulet for $3,500 to a two-passenger racing model with a massive engine rated at 120hp. This latter model cost $12,000.

ROGERS 1911–1912
Rogers Motor Car Co, Omaha, Neb.

The Rogers was a two-passenger, high-wheeler with an 18hp, air-cooled 2-cylinder engine. This was placed under the single seat and the drive was through friction transmission and double chains. With a surrey top, it cost $750.

ROLLIN 1923–1925
Rollin Motor Co, Cleveland, Ohio

Rollin White had been chief engineer of the White company before he made his own cars. These were of European rather than American type, with an efficient 4-cylinder, 4-bearing, 149ci engine, low fuel consumption, 4-wheel brakes and low-pressure tires. The quality in general was extremely high, and the price low ($975 in 1923), but the Rollin's 'foreign-ness' told against it. A big, American six could be had for the same money, and a small 6-cylinder Rollin introduced in 1925 was too late.

ROLLS-ROYCE 1921–1931
Rolls-Royce of America Inc, Springfield, Mass.

The American Rolls-Royce company was formed in November 1919 to build the famous British cars in an American factory and so avoid high import duties. The plant was bought from the American Wire Wheel Co, and the Silver Ghost went into production there in 1921. It had a 6-cylinder 453ci L-head engine developing 80bhp, and came in two wheelbases, 144in and 150½in. Right-hand drive was used until 1923. Unlike the British company, Rolls-Royce of America always advertised coachwork and supplied complete cars if customers wished. Most bodies were by Brewster, and in 1926 this firm was taken over by Rolls-Royce. In 1926 came the New Phantom, or Phantom I as it was later called. This had a 6-cylinder 468ci engine with overhead valves, and again came in two wheelbases, 143½in and 146½in. The Depression badly hit sales of the American Rolls-Royce, and production at Springfield came to an end in 1931, although a few British cars were assembled there later. A total of 2,944 American Rolls-Royces were made, of which 1,703 were Silver Ghosts and 1,241 were Phantom I's.

1924 ROLLIN 16/45hp sedan. *Autocar*
1928 ROLLS-ROYCE Phantom I speedster phaeton. Coachwork by Brewster. *Montagu Motor Museum*

ROLLSMOBILE 1958 to date
1 Starts Mfg Co, Fort Lauderdale, Fla. 1958–c.1960
2 Horseless Carriage Corp, Fort Lauderdale, Fla. c.1960 to date

Using 3hp Continental air-cooled engines, Rollsmobiles are built as 3/4 scale replicas of the 1901 Oldsmobile and the 1901 Ford. Equipped with automatic transmissions and sealed beam headlights, the cars may be licensed for highway travel. Bodies with mahogany overlay and 20in chrome plated sulky wheels add a touch of authenticity to this modern 'antique'. Cruising speed is reported to be 30mph and fuel consumption 100mpg.

ROMANELLI (CDN) 1970 to date
Romanelli Motors Ltd, Montreal, Que.

Designed and built by Francesco Romanelli, an Italian immigrant to Montreal, this is an ambitious sports car using its own design of 366ci V-12 engine of cast aluminum alloy which develops 520bhp. A 5-speed Romanelli-designed transaxle gives a maximum speed of 203mph on top gear. The car has a fiberglass two-passenger coupé body, and sells for $9,000.

ROMER 1921

Romer Motors Corp, Danvers, Mass.

The Romer was an assembled car with a Continental 6-cylinder engine and other components, sold at prices ranging from $1,975 to $2,700. The car was discontinued late in 1921 although the company went on to make a few 1¼ ton trucks.

ROOSEVELT 1929–1931

Marmon Motor Co, Indianapolis, Ind.

The Roosevelt, named after President Theodore Roosevelt, was in fact the smallest of the Marmon line, and was introduced on New Year's Day, 1929. With its trim lines and horizontal hood louvres, it closely resembled the smaller Peerless or Stutz of the time and was the only straight-8 priced at under $1,000. The 1930 Roosevelt was renamed the Marmon-Roosevelt and the radiator emblem embodying the late President's likeness was dropped. The line was discontinued early in 1931.

ROSS (i) 1905–1909

Louis S. Ross, Newtonville, Mass.

The Ross steamer used a single-acting 2-cylinder engine of 126ci, rated at 25hp at an operating pressure of 375psi. The main model was a wooden-bodied five-passenger touring car. It weighed 2,800lb and was priced at $2,800. In 1908 a two-passenger runabout was also built, for $2,250.

ROSS (ii) 1915–1918

1 Ross & Young Machine Co, Detroit, Mich. 1915
2 Ross Automobile Co, Detroit, Mich. 1915–1918

The original Ross was a five-passenger car, with a Herschell-Spillman V-8 engine of 254ci, rated at 45hp, which sold for $1,350. Later models used a Continental 6-cylinder 317ci engine. The Ross was an assembled car, although six body styles were offered, both open and closed.

ROTARY (i) 1904–1905

Rotary Motor Vehicle Co, Boston, Mass.

Despite its name, the Rotary did not use a revolving engine in the manner of the Adams-Farwell, but its design was unorthodox enough. It had an 8hp single-cylinder vertical engine with two connecting rods and two crankshafts. The latter were geared to a central shaft, which drove a conventional transmission and live axle. The design was supposed to eliminate vibration. An alternative, and perhaps appropriate, name for the car was Intrepid.

ROTARY (ii) 1922–1923

Bournonville Motors Co, Hoboken, N.J.

The Rotary touring car, powered by a 303ci 6-cylinder, rotary-valve engine of the company's own manufacture, cost $6,000 when introduced, but was available at $3,800 in 1923. The rotary-valve principle as used in the car was invented by Eugene Bournonville, president of the company, as early as 1914. The solid sleeve, which was the rule in the heads of most L-head engines, was changed to an adjustable sleeve and shoe which acted as a seal. Few of these rakish looking cars, designed by Bournonville himself, were built.

ROYAL and **ROYAL PRINCESS** 1905

Royal Automobile Co, Chicago, Ill.

The Royal was a tiller-steered electric runabout with a piano-box body guaranteed to go 75 miles on one charge. Four models were available; another model named the Royal Princess was a 2-cylinder, gasoline-engined five-passenger car with planetary transmission and single chain drive which sold for $1,500.

ROYAL TOURIST 1904–1911

1 Royal Motor Car Co, Cleveland, Ohio 1904–1908
2 Royal Tourist Car Co, Cleveland, Ohio 1908–1911
3 Consolidated Motor Car Co, Cleveland, Ohio 1911

The Royal Tourist was the successor to the Hoffman (i). The first model

1904 ROYAL TOURIST 18/20hp tonneau. *Antique Automobile*

was a rear-entrance tonneau with a 2-cylinder engine of 18/20hp. All subsequent models used 4-cylinder engines of up to 48hp. In 1908, this car was the first to have the horn bulb at the hub of the steering wheel, with the horn under the hood. During the last three seasons the same chassis was used. In 1911 the company combined with the Croxton-Keeton Motor Car Co to form the Consolidated Motor Car Co.

RUBAY 1922–1924

The Rubay Co, Cleveland, Ohio

Leon Rubay was a bodybuilder who, like Brewster, went over to car manufacture. His machine was of European type, an advanced and efficient light car featuring front-wheel brakes and a 97.5ci 4-cylinder ohc engine, producing 36bhp at 3,000rpm. Such a vehicle had no appeal in America, where bigger cars with more cylinders and costing less were the fashion. In 1924, the company was acquired by Baker, Rauch & Lang, formerly makers of electric cars.

RUGBY *see* STAR (iii)

RUGER 1969 to date

Sturm, Ruger & Co, Inc, Southport, Conn.

The Ruger is a replica vintage car with the lines of a 4½-litre Bentley, powered by a 427ci Ford V-8 engine developing 425bhp. Suspension is non-independent, by semi-elliptic springs all round.

RULER 1917

Ruler Motor Car Co, Aurora, Ill.

The Ruler was a 4-cylinder 166ci car built on the 'frameless' principle, i.e. the chassis was entirely eliminated. Instead of the usual chassis or frame, the Ruler had a patented 3-point cradle with two wheels as two points and a ball and socket in the center of the front transverse member, carrying the front wheels, as the third point. In the cradle were the clutch, transmission and differential. The body could be removed by unfastening the ball on the forward end of the cradle and disconnecting the brakes and rear springs. The engine had a roller-type camshaft with lubrication by means of the flywheel rim, and was equipped with overhead valves.

RUSSELL (i) 1902–1904

Russell Motor Vehicle Co, Cleveland, Ohio

This make of motor buggy, with small diameter wire wheels, used a diminutive 4-cylinder engine of 6hp, placed under the body. The engine was claimed to be self-starting and was available with either hot-tube or magneto ignition. The steering was by tiller.

1914 RUSSELL (ii) touring car. *Hugh Durnford*

1929 RUXTON roadster. *Kenneth Stauffer*

RUSSELL (ii) (CDN) 1905–1915
Canada Cycle and Motor Co, Toronto, Ont.

The Russell Motor Car Co Ltd was a subsidiary of CCM, a very old Canadian concern which had earlier produced the Ivanhoe electric and the Queen cars. The Russell itself was introduced as a rather ordinary 4-cylinder car of modest dimensions, but in 1909 the company obtained the exclusive Canadian rights for the Knight sleeve-valve engine. A series of more elaborate 4- and 6-cylinder cars was introduced, ranging in price from $2,500 to $5,000.

The Russell was the pre-eminent Canadian car before World War 1, and the company occupied several large plants, first in central Toronto, then in a new plant built specially for car and engine production. Complete manufacturing facilities were available in the new plant, which was very large for its time. In addition to cars the firm also produced a line of trucks in capacities of up to 5 tons. These were of the cab-over-engine pattern and chain-driven. Several formed the basis of armored cars early in World War 1, and Russell cars were used by the Canadian troops overseas. Car production ceased in 1915 to make way for expanded military output, and the plant was soon acquired by Willys-Overland for Canadian production of its cars.

RUXTON 1929–1931
New Era Motors, Inc, New York, N.Y.; Moon Motor Corp, St Louis, Mo.; Kissel Motor Car Co, Hartford, Wis.

The Ruxton was a front-drive car which, like its rival, the Cord L-29, was built in limited numbers during roughly the same period. The Ruxton was the idea of Archie M. Andrews, a promoter and financier who was also a director of the Hupp Motor Corp. An experimental car embodying the front-drive principle was built late in 1928 and named after William V. C. Ruxton, one of Andrews' acquaintances who showed an interest in the production of this type of car. A long, low prototype was built in the spring of 1929. This car was powered by a 268ci Continental Straight-8 engine which produced a maximum of about 100bhp at 3,400rpm. All Ruxton cars followed this initial pilot model both in engine and overall design.

Actual production began in June 1930 in both the Moon and Kissel factories; Ruxtons of either origin had to struggle in an increasingly competitive market. Sedan bodies were built by Budd on dies and tooling used by some models of the English Wolseley. Open models were built by Raulang. The cars were low, rakish, and carried no running-boards. The price of the sedan, at $3,195, was approximately that of its rival, Cord. Because of the collapse of Moon and Kissel and a flagging Depression market, Ruxton failed late in 1930 or early 1931 after between 300 and 500 cars had been built, some of which were not actually sold until 1932. Of these, two were phaetons, one a town car and the remainder almost equally divided between roadsters and sedans.

S

SAFETY 1901

Safety Steam Automobile Co, Boston, Mass.

This simple two-passenger steam buggy had a single-cylinder engine of 2.5in bore and 4in stroke. It had a 'reach' frame with elliptical springs and tiller steering.

SAGER (CDN) 1910

United Motors Ltd, Welland, Ont.

This 4-cylinder touring car of 30hp was priced at $1,650. It was named after Frederick Sager, a company official who had worked with the American Olds Motor Works.

SAGINAW (i) 1914–1915

Valley Boat & Engine Co, Saginaw, Mich.

The Saginaw was a two-passenger cyclecar with belt drive. Its only distinguishing feature was that the headlights were inset into the front fenders in Pierce-Arrow fashion. It is said that this manufacturer built the Valley Dispatch truck at Elkhart, Indiana in 1927.

SAGINAW (ii) 1916

Lehr Motor Co, Saginaw, Mich.

In the latter part of 1916 a few 1917 model Saginaws were built. They were equipped with Massnick-Phipps V-8 engines. Before the end of the year, the name had been changed to Yale (ii).

ST JOHN 1903

S. H. St John & Son, Canon City, Colo.

The St John car had a single-cylinder engine mounted under the rear seat, and single chain drive. It was started by spinning the flywheels which were loose from the engine, so that there was no problem of overcoming compression. The makers wanted to sell the patent, so they probably did not make the car in any numbers.

ST LOUIS 1898–1907

1 St Louis Motor Carriage Co, St Louis, Mo. 1898–1906
2 St Louis Motor Car Co, Peoria, Ill. 1906–1907

The early models of this manufacture were *dos à dos* four-passenger cars with single- and 2-cylinder engines. These were tiller-steered, and the engines were beneath the seat. 1902 cars were wheel steered, and in that year came George P. Dorris' first four, a chain-driven experimental machine. Dorris was responsible for subsequent designs. In 1904 this make was still using a single wooden brake-shoe operating on the transmission. The last models, Types XV and XVI, used water-cooled 4-cylinder engines, sliding-gear transmissions, and shaft drive.

SALTER 1909–1912

Salter Motor Co, Kansas City, Mo.

The Salter was built in five-passenger touring models and two-passenger roadsters, both types costing $1,750. Both used an F-head 4-cylinder, 390ci engine and a planetary transmission.

SALVADOR 1914

Salvador Motor Co, Boston, Mass.

The Salvador cyclecar was powered by a water-cooled 4-cylinder Farmer engine. It had a 3-speed selective transmission, shaft drive and what was termed a 'gearless differential'. It was a two-passenger car and sold for $485.

SAMPSON 1904; 1911

1 Alden Sampson Mfg Co, Pittsfield, Mass. 1904
2 United States Motor Corp. Alden Sampson Division, Detroit, Mich. 1911

The 1904 Sampson was a copy of the Moyea, for which Sampson had built chassis in 1903. It had a 4-cylinder engine which produced 18hp at 810rpm, and a 4-speed sliding-gear transmission with final drive by

1906 ST LOUIS 32/36hp touring car. *Keith Marvin Collection*

1904 SAMPSON 40hp Gordon Bennett racing car. *G. Marshall Naul*

double chains. The Sampson missed a minor opportunity for fame by failing to have a car ready for the Gordon Bennett Cup trial in 1904. The later model, called the Sampson 35, had a 4-cylinder, 35hp engine. The five-passenger 4-door model, with a claimed 17 coats of paint, sold for $1,250.

SAMSON 1922
Samson Tractor Co, Janesville, Wis.

Although only one Samson car was built, the make is unique in being the only car ever advertised by General Motors which never went into production. Built by the Samson Division of General Motors, the Samson was a nine-passenger touring car powered by a Chevrolet FB engine and had auxiliary seats which could readily be removed, with the rear seat, to convert the car into a truck. The truck was built until 1923.

S & M 1913–1914
S & M Motors Co, Detroit, Mich.

The S & M (Strobel & Martin) Six-43 model was an assembled car using a 6-cylinder Continental engine. The only model was a distinguished looking five-passenger touring. This was on a wheelbase of 130in and had early side-mounted spare wheels. For $2,485, standard equipment included two dash compartments, electric cigar lighter, two vacuum bottles fitted into the rear compartment and Houk wire wheels. In 1914, this became the Benham.

S & M SIMPLEX 1904–1907
Smith & Mabley Mfg Co, New York, N.Y.

The original version of the S & M Simplex, Model AA, was a two-passenger car with an 18hp 4-cylinder engine and double chain drive. For 1905 and 1906, the engine was increased to 30hp and had a capacity of 350ci. This was on a chassis of 106in wheelbase, priced at $5,000. Bodies were to order only. There was a special two-passenger racing version with a 70hp engine. In 1907, a longer chassis was made and in it there was a 519ci, 4-cylinder T-head engine with a 4-speed transmission. Smith & Mabley became defunct in 1907 and were succeeded by the Simplex Auto Co. The S & M Simplex was, therefore, the ancestor of the great Simplex and the Crane-Simplex.

S. & S. 1924–1930
Sayers & Scovill Co, Cincinnati, Ohio

The S. & S. cars were successors to the earlier Sayers and a sideline to the Sayers and Scovill hearses. They were large, expensive 6- and 8-cylinder cars produced as sedans and limousines for funeral use, invalid cars and, in a few instances, as cars for customers wanting something different from the standard cars of other makes. The S. & S. catalogue of 1929 listed an eight-passenger Lakewood sedan with 323ci straight-8 engine at $4,295 as its only private car. After 1929 or 1930, S. & S. passenger cars were only available to special order.

SANDUSKY 1902–1903
Sandusky Automobile Co, Sandusky, Ohio

The Sandusky was a typical light runabout with a single-cylinder engine under the seat, single chain drive and tiller steering.

SANTOS DUMONT 1902–1904
Columbus Motor Vehicle Co, Columbus, Ohio

Named after the famous balloonist, the Santos Dumont car was first made with a 2-cylinder engine mounted under the front seat, chain drive, and a four-passenger tonneau body. The 1904 model had a 20hp 4-cylinder engine mounted vertically under a hood, and was priced at $2,000. From February 1904 the car was usually advertised under the name Dumont.

SAVIANO SCAT 1960
Saviano Vehicles, Inc, Warren, Mich.

The Scat (Saviano Cargo And Touring) was a utility vehicle powered

1904 S. & M. SIMPLEX 18hp touring car. Coachwork by Quimby. *Automotive History Collection, Detroit Public Library*
1924 S. & S. 27hp Brighton limousine. *Keith Marvin Collection*

1913 SAXON roadster. *Don McCray*

177

by a 25hp Kohler aircooled engine. The 2-door, four-passenger, body used 16 gauge sheet steel; fuel consumption was 25–30mpg and top speed 52mph.

SAXON 1913–1923
Saxon Motor Car Co, Detroit, Mich.; Ypsilanti, Mich.

The Saxon appeared in the winter of 1913–14 as a small two-passenger roadster with a 86.7ci 4-cylinder engine, and 2-speed transaxle, soon replaced by a 3-speed unit. Electric lights were available at extra cost. At $395, these wire-wheeled cars caught the public fancy and although they looked more like cyclecars than conventional small automobiles, sales were high from the first. Peak year was 1916, with 27,800 delivered. Continental and Ferro engines were used and after several thousand Saxons had been sold, wooden artillery spoke wheels were available as an option. Various improvements were noted through 1915 and a small number of delivery cars were produced to augment the roadster in the Saxon range. By 1915, electric lighting was standard equipment. A 176ci 6-cylinder touring car still with transaxle appeared in 1915 as a companion to the 4-cylinder roadsters which were retained until 1917, when Saxon reached tenth place in sales among American manufacturers. In 1920, a 4-cylinder ohv car reappeared and by 1921, sixes were discontinued. In the years following this reappearance the Saxon models were known as Saxon-Duplex. Production dropped rapidly, the last cars being sold early in 1923.

SAYERS 1917–1924
Sayers & Scovill Co, Cincinnati, Ohio

The firm of Sayers & Scovill had been building chassis as well as bodies for hearses and ambulances since 1907 and entered the passenger-car market in 1917 with a touring car to sell for $1,295. A Continental 6-cylinder engine was used and artillery wheels were standard. The Sayers was an especially fine car from the standpoint of body workmanship. A roadster was added to the line for 1918 and a sedan, limousine and coupé shortly after. In 1923, the production of the Sayers was suspended in favor of a larger car to be called the S. & S.

SCARAB 1934–1939
Stout Engineering Co, Detroit, Mich.

Developed from the experimental Sterkenberg car designed by John Tjaarda, the Scarab was designed by William B. Stout. It had a streamlined sedan body with no hood, a rear-mounted Ford V-8 engine and integral construction. Apart from the driver's, the seats could be moved to any position, and a card table set up if desired. A price of $5,000 was quoted, and a few cars were made to special order, several orders coming from Hollywood stars. In 1946 Stout built another version of his streamlined car, but this did not go into production.

1919 SAYERS Model BP 27hp touring car. *Keith Marvin Collection*

SCHACHT 1905–1913
1 Schacht Mfg Co, Cincinnati, Ohio 1905–1909
2 Schacht Motor Car Co, Cincinnati, Ohio 1909–1913

Up to 1909 the Schacht models were high-wheelers with 12hp 2-cylinder engines under the seat and chain drive. Steering was by wheel. After 1909, the make became more conventional with 40hp 4-cylinder engines. Some of the later cars were sold with combination truck/touring bodies. As Le Blond-Schacht, the company made trucks up to 1938.

SCHARF GEARLESS 1914
Scharf Gearless Cycle Car Co, Westerville, Ohio

This cyclecar used a friction transmission, hence the name. Drive to the rear wheels was by chain. The car had a 4-cylinder, 60ci engine. Wheelbase was 100in.

SCHAUM 1901
Schaum Automobile Co, Baltimore, Md.

The Schaum used full elliptical springs, double chain drive and tiller steering. This two-passenger car was driven by a gasoline engine rated at 4hp.

SCHLOSSER 1912–1913
A make of car whose manufacturer is not known, the Schlosser had a 4-cylinder, 471ci engine. The five-passenger touring was priced at $2,370.

SCHNADER 1907
Milton H. Schnader, Reading, Pa.

This car was previously called the Riviera. It was made only as a five-passenger open model, powered by a flat 2-cylinder engine of 196ci. Its transmission was of a planetary type and final drive was by shaft.

SCHRAM 1913
Schram Motor Car Co, Seattle, Wash.

This was a large car with a 6-cylinder engine of 377ci capacity, developing 38hp. The five-passenger was priced at $2,300.

SCIOTO *see* ARBENZ

SCOOTMOBILE (i) *see* MARTIN (i)

SCOOT-MOBILE (ii) c.1946
Norman Anderson, Corunna, Mich.

Built mostly from aircraft parts, the Scoot-Mobile was a prototype 3-wheeler with automatic gear shift, 3-wheel brakes, and a speed of 40mph.

SCOTT 1899–1901
1 St Louis Electric Automobile Co, St Louis, Mo. 1899–1900
2 Scott Automobile Co, St Louis, Mo. 1900–1901

The Scott was a light two-passenger electric car of very simple appearance and limited range. The St Louis Electric Automobile Company was organized by A. L. Dyke, who later made cars under his own name.

SCOTT-NEWCOMB *see* STANDARD (vii)

SCRIPPS-BOOTH 1913–1922
The Scripps-Booth Co, Detroit, Mich.

James Scripps-Booth planned to make a tandem two-passenger cyclecar steered from the rear, but the production model had front-seat steering. It was powered by a Spacke air-cooled V-twin engine, had a 2-speed planetary transmission, and final drive by two leather V-belts. About 400 were sold at $385 each, up to the end of 1914. These cyclecars were sometimes known as Rockets. From 1914 to 1916 a staggered-seat roadster, the Model C, was made, powered by a 25hp Sterling 4-cylinder ohv engine, and using shaft drive. This was replaced in 1916 by the Model D, with a Ferro V-8 engine, made in roadster, touring and town car

1909 SCHACHT 12hp motor buggy. *Henry Ford Museum, Dearborn, Mich.*

1916 SCRIPPS-BOOTH Model D town car. *Don McCray*
1902 SEARCHMONT 10hp tonneau. *Kenneth Stauffer*

models. Both Models C and D had pointed radiators, some of the Model D town cars being very similar to the Mercedes in this respect.

In July 1918 Scripps-Booth was acquired by General Motors, and the cars rapidly lost their individuality. The 1918 Model G had a Mason-built Chevrolet 490 engine, transmission and rear axle, and so was really a Chevrolet in Scripps-Booth clothing, but at a much higher price than the Chevrolet. 1919 to 1923 models had Oakland chassis and Northway engines, with Scripps-Booth bodies and radiators. In 1921 even the V-radiator was abandoned.

SEAGRAVE 1960
Seagrave Fire Apparatus Co, Columbus, Ohio

After examining several independently designed prototype compact cars from a Detroit firm, the Seagrave Co, long known for its fire engines, decided against producing them. One of these cars was 156in long, stood 48in high and used a 4-cylinder Continental engine of 65bhp.

SEARCHMONT 1900–1903
1 Searchmont Motor Co, Philadelphia, Pa. 1900–1902
2 Fournier-Searchmont Co, Chester, Pa. 1902–1903

In November 1900 the Searchmont company acquired the rights to manufacture the light car developed by the Keystone Motor Company. Known as the Wagonette, this car had a 5 or 10hp rear-mounted engine, two-passenger body and tiller steering. It was made until 1902 when, under the direction of the French racing driver Charles Fournier, a new range of front-engined cars with 8 or 10hp 2-cylinder engines and double chain drive was made. Very expensive at $2,500 for the 10hp, they were nevertheless the first American-built cars to have forced-feed lubrication. They were designed by L. S. Chadwick who later made the famous Chadwick car. In 1903 a 32hp 4-cylinder car was made.

SEARS 1906–1911
Sears Motor Car Works, Chicago, Ill.

The Sears was a high-wheeler built in both passenger and utility versions, for marketing by the Sears, Roebuck mail-order company. All models had solid-rubber tires and 2-cylinder horizontally-opposed air-cooled engines, and were steered by tiller. The most advanced model was the 1911 closed coupé selling for $485. Some 3,500 Sears cars were sold. The firm made a brief return to the mail-order car business in 1952 (see Allstate).

1909 SEARS 12hp motor buggy. *Henry Ford Museum, Dearborn, Mich.*

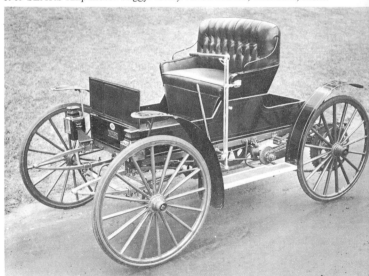

SEBRING 1910–1911
1 Sebring Motor Car Co, Sebring, Ohio 1910
2 Sebring Automobile Co, Sebring, Ohio 1911
   The Sebring used 6-cylinder engines exclusively. These were of 239ci, and 35hp. Three body types were offered on a 122in wheelbase. Some models had monocle-type windshields.

SEKINE 1923
I. Sekine & Co, New York, N.Y.
   I. Sekine was an importer who built, or had built, a car for sale in the Japanese market for a short time. The Sekine had no differential, the drive being taken from a 4-cylinder engine of 120ci displacement, angled at 17° from the longitudinal axis of the car to the left rear wheel, thence through fabric universals to the right wheel by way of a shaft. There were no conventional axles, their place being taken by double transverse springs. The sole brake was connected to the right rear wheel. Only a touring car model was made.

SELDEN 1906–1914
Selden Motor Vehicle Co, Rochester, N.Y.
   This manufacturing company was founded by George B. Selden of patents fame. The early models of the car used 4-cylinder Continental engines, under a peculiarly shaped hood. By 1912 the Selden had grown to a vehicle with a 125in wheelbase with a 4-cylinder 47hp engine. It is ironic that this make succumbed just as Selden's rival at law, Henry Ford, was booming with his Model T. Commercial vehicles were, however, manufactured until 1932.

SELLERS 1909–1912
Sellers Motor Car Co, Hutchinson, Kan.
   This was a conventional 4-cylinder touring car built largely for local consumption.

SENATOR 1906–1910
Victor Auto Co, Ridgeville, Ind.
   The Senator used air-cooled engines of up to 4-cylinders and 201ci with 3-speed selective transmission. Three body types were available at $2,000.

SENECA 1917–1924
Seneca Motor Car Co, Fostoria, Ohio
   The Seneca was a typical assembled car with touring cars and roadsters the only body types available. All Senecas were 4-cylinder cars, a Le Roi engine being used before 1922 and a Lycoming being substituted afterwards. Only a few hundred Senecas were built during any year and about half of the output was exported, most of the other half being sold in and around Fostoria.

SERPENTINA 1915
Claudius Mezzacasa, New York, N.Y.
   This was an experimental car using a diamond-formation wheel layout, used earlier on the British Sunbeam-Mabley.

SERVITOR 1907
Barnes Mfg Co, Sandusky, Ohio
   The 12/14hp Servitor had an air-cooled, 4-cylinder engine and a patented 2-speed transmission with final drive by shaft. The only model was a two-passenger roadster.

SEVERIN 1920–1922
Severin Motor Car Co, Kansas City, Mo.
   Using a Continental 6-cylinder engine, the Severin was a typical assembled car of the early 1920s.

S.G.V. 1911–1915
1 Acme Motor Car Co, Reading, Pa. 1911–1912
2 S.G.V. Co, Reading, Pa. 1913–1915
   The S.G.V. succeeded the Acme (i), and was inspired by the Lancia.

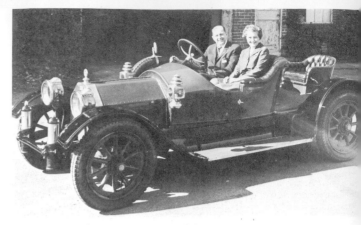

1912 S.G.V. roadster. *Antique Automobile*

These were high quality cars with luxury features such as Circassian walnut dashes. All models had 4-cylinder engines, of up to 264ci. As many as six body types were available, with limousines selling for $3,850. In 1913, the S.G.V. introduced the Vulcan electric shift with four forward speeds. This transmission was actuated by push-buttons mounted in a steering-wheel spoke.

SHAD-WYCK 1917–1923
Shadburne Brothers, Chicago, Ill.; Frankfort, Ind.
   Few Shad-Wycks were sold. The first cars were sixes but starting in 1920 and continuing through 1923, they were available with Rochester-Duesenberg 4-cylinder engines with closed and open models listed at $5,000 and $4,000 respectively.

SHARON 1915
Driggs-Seabury Ordnance Corp, Sharon, Pa.
   The Sharon was a short-lived tandem cyclecar with an underslung chassis. Its 4-cylinder engine was rated at 12/15hp and power was transmitted through friction drive. This prolific manufacturer also produced the Twombly (iii), Driggs-Seabury and Ritz.

SHARP 1914–1915
Sharp Engineering & Mfg Co, Detroit, Mich.
   At $295 the Sharp was one of the cheapest of the cyclecars. It was a two-passenger roadster with a 49ci, 2-cylinder, air-cooled engine. It had a 2-speed transmission, and shaft drive.

SHARP-ARROW 1908–1910
1 William H. Sharp, Trenton, N.J. 1908
2 Sharp-Arrow Automobile Co, Trenton, N.J. 1908–1910

1909 SHARP-ARROW roadster. *Kenneth Stauffer*

The Sharp-Arrow was a high-performance car claimed to be 'The King of American Stock Cars'. The runabout, powered by a 4-cylinder 390ci engine with two spark plugs per cylinder was said to exceed 70mph. Touring and toy tonneau models were available at $3,050.

SHATSWELL 1901–c.1903
H. K. Shatswell & Co, Dedham, Mass.

Shatswell sold accessories and components, especially for steam cars. They advertised a complete set of components, including a Mason engine, for home assembly of a light steam runabout.

SHAW (i) 1920–1921
Waldron W. Shaw Livery Co, Chicago, Ill.

For many years builders and operators of taxicabs, the Shaw Company introduced its passenger car line in 1920 with a phaeton powered by a 4-cylinder Rochester-Duesenberg engine and selling for $5,000. This was augmented by a roadster, sports-phaeton, coupé, sedan and limousine, and the cars were sold in limited numbers. For a brief time, the Shaw name was temporarily dropped in favor of Colonial. In 1921, the Duesenberg four was replaced by a Weidely 12-cylinder power unit, but few were marketed. Shaw was taken over later in 1921 by the Yellow Cab Company which sold the remaining cars with a Continental engine under the Ambassador name.

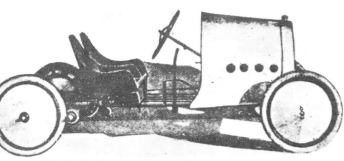

1924 SHAW (ii) 2½hp speedster. *Dr Alfred Lewerenz Collection*
1968 SHELBY (ii) GT-500 coupé. *Shelby Automotive*

SHAW (ii) 1924–1930
Shaw Mfg Co, Galesburg, Kan.

The Shaw Sport Speedster was an ultra-light two-passenger car, designed mainly for children. It was powered by a 2½hp engine of either Shaw or Briggs & Stratton manufacture, and had only one speed. Early models had belt or chain drive, but shaft was available from 1926. Prices varied from $120 to $151.

SHAWMUT 1905–1909
Shawmut Motor Co, Stoneham, Mass.

The Shawmut — the name is of Indian origin — succeeded the Phelps. Its 4-cylinder, 390ci engine was rated at 35/40hp and powered touring cars and roadsters. A 4-speed transmission and shaft drive was used.

SHELBY (i) 1902–1903
Shelby Motor Car Co, Shelby, Ohio

The Shelby used a horizontal single-cylinder double piston engine on Gobron-Brillié lines. In other respects it was a conventional light car with a De Dion-type hood and low-mounted radiator, shaft drive and a four-passenger tonneau body.

SHELBY (ii) 1962–1970
1 Shelby-American, Inc, Santa Fe Springs, Calif. 1962
2 Shelby-American, Inc, Venice, Calif. 1962–1967
3 Shelby Automotive, Ionia, Mich. 1967–1968
4 Ford Motor Co, Detroit, Mich. 1968–1970

The first of race driver Carroll Shelby's Cobras used a 221ci Ford V-8 engine in a modified British-built AC chassis. Early production versions used a 260ci engine, but the majority of the 1,140 Shelby Cobras had 289 or 427ci units. In 1965 Shelby began building the 289ci GT–350 coupé, a tuned and lightened version of Ford's Mustang, and this was joined in 1967 by the GT–500 which used the 427ci engine. The Cobra was discontinued in 1968, and the name applied to the Mustang-based cars. At about the same time, manufacture of this car was taken over by Ford, and continued until early 1970 when the Shelby line was dropped. Total production of Shelby GT's was 14,810.

SHERIDAN 1920–1921
Sheridan Motor Car Co, Muncie, Ind.

The Sheridan was a short-lived General Motors product which was to have been produced both in 4- and 8-cylinder types, although the latter failed to appear on the market. The car was equipped with a Northway engine and sold for less then $2,000. Production was in the old Interstate car factory and the Sheridan was presumably made to fill the gap between the Chevrolet and Oakland cars in the G.M. empire. The 8-cylinder model was to have appeared just below the Cadillac size and price range. In 1922, the factory was acquired by William C. Durant and was henceforth used for the manufacture of Durant Six and Princeton cars.

SHOEMAKER 1907–1909
Shoemaker Automobile Co, Freeport, Ill.

The Shoemaker was a five- to seven-passenger car with a 35/40hp 4-cylinder engine. It had a 3-speed selective transmission and shaft drive. Among the features of this car were a tubular front axle, and camel-hair brake shoes.

SIBLEY 1910–1911
Sibley Motor Car Co, Detroit, Mich.

The Sibley was a two-passenger roadster with a 4-cylinder 221ci engine rated at 30hp, driving through a 3-speed selective transmission. Eugene Sibley, one of the founders of this company, was later to form the Sibley-Curtis Motor Co of Simsbury, Conn. The firm made only one car.

SIGNET 1913–1914
Fenton Engineering Co, Fenton, Mich.

The Signet was sometimes called the Fenton. It was a two-passenger, side-by-side cyclecar. The power was furnished by a 2-cylinder, air-cooled De Luxe engine of 9/13hp. The transmission was of the friction type, and final drive was through belts.

SILENT KNIGHT 1906–1909
Knight & Kilbourne Co, Chicago, Ill.

This car was built to advertise Charles Y. Knight's 4-cylinder, 40hp sleeve-valve engine. The drive was through a selective transmission and drive shaft. As a five-passenger touring car, it was priced at $3,500. The Silent Knight was not a success, and the Knight engine did not gain popularity in America until after it had been adopted by Daimler and other European makes.

SILENT SIOUX 1909–1912
1 Sioux Auto Mfg Co, Sioux Falls, S. Dak. 1909–1910
2 Sioux Auto Mfg Co, Milwaukee, Wis. 1910–1912

The Silent Sioux was a large touring car with a 40hp 4-cylinder engine. It was designed by T. L. Fawick, who was listed as making a car under his own name in Sioux Falls in 1912.

SIMMS 1920–1921
Simms Motor Car Corp. Atlanta, Ga.

The Simms was only available as a five-passenger tourer with its own design of 4-cylinder engine. Few were sold and no price was announced.

SIMPLEX 1907–1917
Simplex Automobile Co, Inc, New Brunswick, N.J.

After the 1907 bankruptcy of Smith & Mabley, the firm was taken over by Herman Broesel, who formed the Simplex Automobile Company. The best-known model of the new company was the 50hp, a massive chain-driven car of high quality whose 4-cylinder T-head had a capacity of 676ci. The chassis price was $4,500 and bodies were made for Simplex under contract by such firms as Quimby, Demarest, Holbrook and Brewster. In 1908 a stripped version won the 24-hour race at Brighton Beach, and famous drivers who drove for Simplex included George Robertson, Al Poole and Joe Tracy. The cars were designed by Edward Franquist, who introduced a 38hp 485ci shaft-drive model in 1911, and a 75hp 597ci chain drive roadster in 1912. By 1914 this was the only chain-driven model in the range, and was said to be the last chain-driven American car. Some of these cars had a sharply-pointed V-radiator,

1913 SIMPLEX 75hp roadster. *Don McCray*

although most Simplexes used a flat radiator of the Mercedes-type.

The 1914 range consisted of the 38hp, 50hp and 75hp fours, and a 50hp six, but towards the end of that year a new model appeared which heralded a complete change in the Simplex company. This was the 46hp L-head Simplex Crane Model 5, designed by Henry M. Crane who had replaced Franquist as chief designer after a company reorganization. The new car was a very high quality machine and carried beautiful coachwork, mainly by Brewster, but it lacked the sporting qualities of its predecessor. It was made until 1917, and bodies were still being fitted to Crane chassis in 1921. By this time the company had been bought by Hare's Motors, and a reorganized company, The Crane-Simplex Company of New York, made a few cars in 1923 and 1924.

SIMPLICITIES 1905
Simplicities Automobile Co, Middletown, Conn.

The only model of this make was a five-passenger car with rear entrance which used a water-cooled 4-cylinder engine of 24hp with a 3-speed transmission. The manufacturer claimed that a number of these cars were exported to Great Britain before 1905.

SIMPLICITY 1906–1911
Evansville Automobile Co, Evansville, Ind.

This company offered touring cars, roadsters and limousines, with friction transmission. The latter feature presumably determined the name of this make. The engines used were all 4-cycle, 4-cylinder, water-cooled units. The Simplicity may have used double chain drive as late as 1911.

SIMPLO 1908–1909
Cook Motor Vehicle Co, St Louis, Mo.

This small four-passenger runabout had solid rubber tires and a 4-cycle, 2-cylinder engine, with friction transmission and double chain drive. The car sold for $650, or for $700 with pneumatic tires.

SINGER 1915–1920
Singer Motor Co, Inc, Mount Vernon, N.Y.

The Singer was the successor to the Palmer-Singer, which had been produced since 1906, and was one of the finest and most expensive luxury cars manufactured in America in its few years of existence. Distinguished by a sharply pointed radiator and a wide choice of custom bodies from leading coachbuilders, the cars produced between 1915 and 1919 were powered by a Herschell-Spillman 6-cylinder engine. In 1920, the series HEH20 line was introduced. This series, which proved to be the last, had a 12-cylinder Weidely engine. Prices on the last Singer cars were as high as $9,000. Wire wheels were standard.

SINGLE-CENTER 1906–1908
Single-Center Buggy Co, Evansville, Ind.

This motor buggy had a 4-cycle 2-cylinder water-cooled engine of 157ci. The drive was by double chains, and the wheelbase was only 84in. It was available with either solid rubber or pneumatic tires. The significance of the name Single-Center is not clear, but it may have referred to a swiveling front axle.

S.J.R. 1915–1916
S.J.R. Motor Co, Boston, Mass.

The S.J.R. was a small car which offered only a single model, a four-passenger roadster, at $945. The car was low hung and equipped with wire wheels. The windshield was slanted and the appearance was that of a foreign car. Powered by a 4-cylinder Wisconsin engine, few were marketed before the company failed.

SKELTON 1920–1922
Skelton Motor Car Co, St Louis, Mo.

The Skelton was an assembled car with a 4-cylinder Lycoming engine. Touring cars and roadsters were available at $1,295 each.

1908 GREAT SMITH 50hp touring car. *Keith Marvin Collection*

SKENE 1900–1901
J. W. Skene Cycle & Automobile Co, Lewiston, Me.

The Skene company boasted that every part of their light steam buggy was made at their works, which, if true, distinguished it from many assembled machines. In design, however, it was conventional, using a vertical 2-cylinder engine of 5hp, single chain drive and tiller steering. An unusual feature was that a single-passenger body could be fitted, as well as the typical two-passenger stanhope.

SMITH; GREAT SMITH 1898–1911
Smith Automobile Co, Topeka, Kan.

From 1898 to 1905 the Smith company made a number of light buggy-type cars sometimes known under the name Veracity. They then turned to the manufacture of larger 4- and 6-cylinder shaft-drive cars called Great Smith. It was claimed that a Great Smith was the first car to climb Pike's Peak entirely under its own power, but they were too expensive, and did not sell well. In 1911 H. Anton Smith, the builder, decided to abandon car manufacture, and made a large bonfire in which he destroyed all the files and records of the Smith Automobile Company.

SMITH FLYER 1917–1920
A. O. Smith, Milwaukee, Wis.

The single model of the Smith Flyer was a 5-wheeled buckboard. In addition to the four main wheels of bicycle type there was a smaller wheel at the rear driven by the single-cylinder engine. This design was later made by Briggs and Stratton.

SNYDER (i) 1906–1908
D. D. Snyder & Co, Danville, Ill.

The Snyder was called a motor buggy by the manufacturer, and had large diameter wheels and solid rubber tires. The original tiller steering was changed to a steering wheel in the 1908 models. The power unit was a 4-cycle, 2-cylinder opposed engine of 10/12hp. A planetary transmission and double chain drive were used.

SNYDER (ii) 1914
Snyder Motor & Mfg Co, Cleveland, Ohio

This cyclecar was built in three models. The smallest had a 2-cylinder, air-cooled 9hp engine, the largest a water-cooled, 4-cylinder, 95ci unit with a 2-speed transmission. All models were two-passenger roadsters.

SOMMER 1904–1907
Sommer Motor Co, Detroit, Mich.

This company was an offshoot of the Hammer-Sommer Auto Carriage Company which was dissolved in 1904. The first Sommer car was similar to the Hammer-Sommer, with 12hp 2-cylinder engine mounted under the seat. It had a De Dion-type hood, but by 1906 this had been replaced by a conventional hood with front radiator. Mechanically the 1907 models were unchanged, as was the price of $1,250.

SOUTH BEND 1914
South Bend Motor Car Works, South Bend, Ind.

This company made a two-passenger roadster with a 4-cylinder 50hp engine, priced at $1,800.

SOUTHERN (i) 1906
Southern Automobile Mfg Co, Jacksonville, Fla.

The Southern was a high-wheeler reported as being built in 1906. This was, undoubtedly, the first attempt at auto production in the citrus belt.

SOUTHERN (ii) 1909
Southern Motor Works, Jackson, Tenn.

The Southern was more advanced than its manufacturer's address might suggest. It used a 4-cycle water-cooled engine of 30hp, a 3-speed selective transmission and shaft drive. Either a five-passenger touring body or two-passenger roadster were available, both of these models being priced at $1,500.

SOUTHERN (iii) 1921–1922
Southern Automobile Manufacturing Co, Memphis, Tenn.

The Southern Six was a rarely-seen assembled car, produced in strictly limited numbers. With 6-cylinder Herschell-Spillman engines, the few Southern Six cars which did appear were well built and sold in the $3,000 price range.

SOVEREIGN 1906–1907
Matthews Motor Co, Camden, N.J.

Sometimes known, after the makers, as the Matthews, this car had a large 4-cylinder engine of 48hp, dual ignition, and double chain-drive. It was claimed that the aluminum touring car could seat eight, and the car was advertised as being 'especially adapted for protracted touring.' Maximum speed was 70mph.

SPACKE *see* BROOK-SPACKE

SPARTAN 1911
C. W. Kelsey Mfg Co, Hartford, Conn.

Although the Spartan was introduced as a companion product to the Motorette 3-wheeled cars being built by the Kelsey Manufacturing Company at the time, it never went into production. The only model built was a conventional five-passenger touring car.

SPAULDING (i) 1902–1903
Spaulding Motor & Auto Co, Buffalo, N.Y.

This company made a number of light runabouts powered by single-cylinder engines. They were said to be preparing a touring car for 1903, but it is uncertain if it was made.

SPAULDING (ii) 1910–1916
Spaulding Mfg Co, Grinnell, Iowa

This Spaulding used 4-cylinder water-cooled engines with either planetary or sliding-gear transmissions. As many as thirteen models were offered in one year. Apparently all models were on a standard chassis of 112in wheelbase.

SPEEDWAY 1904–1905
Gas Engine & Power Co, Morris Heights, N.Y.

This was a five-passenger side-entrance tonneau with a 28hp, 4-cylinder engine. The car had a pleasant appearance, a 4-speed transmission and shaft-drive at prices ranging from $4,700 to $5,350. The Gas Engine & Power Co later combined with the manufacturer of the Howard (ii).

SPEEDWELL 1907–1914
Speedwell Motor Car Co, Dayton, Ohio

Early models of the Speedwell used a 40hp, 4-cylinder engine with shaft drive. Six different body styles were offered in 1909. Later models

1923 SPERLING sedan. *Keith Marvin Collection*

1909 SPEEDWELL 50hp touring car. *Automotive History Collection, Detroit Public Library*
1910 SPEEDWELL 50hp touring car. *Kenneth Stauffer*

were very large, with 421ci 6-cylinder engines. In 1913 the buyer had a choice of a Mead rotary valve engine, or one with standard poppet valves.

SPENCER 1921–1922
Research Engineering Co, Dayton, Ohio

Few Spencers were ever produced. The car used a 4-cylinder engine of the company's own make and was equipped with artillery wheels. The price of the five-passenger touring model was $850.

SPENNY 1914–1915
Spenny Motor Car Co, Chicago, Ill.

This company made a 4-cylinder 30hp roadster and touring car to sell at $1,075, and a 6-cylinder 60hp touring car priced at $3,750.

SPERLING 1921–1923
Associated Motors Corp, Elkhart, Ind.

The Sperling was built with right-hand drive for the export market.

The cars were distinguished by a slightly V-shaped radiator. Both open and closed models appeared in the company's catalogs.

SPERRY *see* CLEVELAND (i)

SPHINX 1914–1915
Sphinx Motor Car Co, York, Pa.

This was a light, five-passenger tourer with a 4-cylinder Lycoming engine of 166ci. The only unusual feature of this car was the use of cantilever springs all round. This manufacturer was apparently succeeded by the du Pont Motor Car Co, the maker of the du Pont (i).

SPOERER 1907–1914
Carl Spoerer's Sons Co, Baltimore, Md.

Original models of the Spoerer had 30hp and 50/60hp 4-cylinder engines. For 1910 this was reduced to one engine of 40hp in four different body types, including a seven-passenger touring car. Later, as many as eleven models were offered, with engines of 25 and 40hp. Prices for these cars ranged up to $4,150.

SPRINGER 1904–1906
1 John H. Springer, New York, N.Y. 1904
2 Springer Motor Vehicle Co, New York, N.Y. 1904–1906

The original Springer was a two-passenger car with a 2-cylinder water-cooled engine of 12hp for which 12mph was claimed. A larger five-passenger model was soon offered, with an air-cooled 4-cylinder engine of 40hp.

SPRINGFIELD (i) 1904
Springfield Automobile Co, Springfield, Ohio

The Springfield had a single-cylinder, 2-cycle, water-cooled engine of 98ci, rated at 8hp. The drive was through a planetary transmission and single chain.

SPRINGFIELD (ii) 1907
Med-Bow Automobile Co, Springfield, Mass.

This car was made only in five-passenger form. It had a 4-cylinder, 318ci Rutenber engine with special high-lift valve cams. Painted either Brewster green or maroon, this vehicle cost $2,500.

SPRINGFIELD (iii) 1908–1911
Springfield Motor Car Co, Springfield, Ill.

This car, it was announced, was made to order. Available were both a torpedo and a touring model for $2,500 on a wheelbase of 128 in. These had F-head 4-cylinder, water-cooled engines of 373ci. Three-speed selective transmissions were used.

SPRITE 1914
W. S. Frasier & Co, Aurora, Ill.
This two-passenger, side-by-side cyclecar was driven by a 2-cylinder air-cooled engine. Its weight was 700lb and its cost was $425.

S.S.E. 1916–1917
S.S.E. Co, Philadelphia, Pa.
The S.S.E. was made in nine body styles, on a standard chassis in which was a 6-cylinder, 288ci engine. This was an expensive car with prices from $5,000 for the five-passenger touring car, to $8,000 for the closed berline.

STAFFORD 1910–1915
Stafford Motor Car Co, Topeka, Kan.; Kansas City, Mo.
The Stafford used a 4-cylinder water-cooled engine of 247ci which had an early example of overhead camshaft driven by a chain. The final drive was through selective transmission and drive shaft, and the weight of this five-passenger model was 2,250lb.

STANDARD (i) **(STANDARD TOURIST)** 1903–1907
Standard Motor Construction, Jersey City, N.J.
This make succeeded the U.S. Long Distance. The only model was a five-passenger in wood at at $3,250, or in aluminum for $3,500. The engine was a 4-cycle, 4-cylinder one of 25hp.

STANDARD (ii) 1909–1910
1 St Louis Motor Car Co, St Louis, Mo. 1909
2 St Louis Car Co, St Louis, Mo. 1910
From 1906 to 1909 this company made three models of the Mors under the name American Mors, but in 1909 they introduced a car of their own design. This had an ohv 50hp 6-cylinder engine of 425ci capacity. Five body styles were listed, including a limousine at $4,000. The rear springs were of the platform type.

STANDARD (iii) 1910
Standard Gas Electric Power Co, Philadelphia, Pa.
This car had a 4-cylinder, 226ci engine with a 3-speed sliding-gear transmission and shaft drive. The only feature of interest was electric starting. The single model for 1910 was a four-passenger torpedo which weighed 2,000lb.

STANDARD (iv) 1912–1915
Standard Electric Car Co, Jackson, Mich.
This electric car used Westinghouse motors and was claimed to have a range of 110 miles on a charge. It was operated from a tiller on the left-hand side. The controller gave six forward speeds, the maximum speed being 20mph. The Model M, a four-passenger closed model, cost $1,885.

1917 STANDARD (v) 34hp V-8 touring car. *Kenneth Stauffer*

STANDARD (v) 1912–1923
1 Standard Steel Car Co, Butler, Pa. 1912–1923
2 Standard Auto Vehicle Co, Butler, Pa. 1923
For most of its life the Standard was built by a firm whose main product was steel and composite railway passenger and freight cars. Up to 1916 it was a conventional 38hp 6-cylinder car built in touring and closed models, at prices up to $3,600. In 1916 an 8-cylinder model was introduced which was to become the staple product of the company. Smaller than the six, it was rated at 29hp (50bhp) and cost only $1,950 for the most expensive model. For 1917 it was increased to 34hp (80bhp) and by 1921 prices were up to $5,000. In 1923 a new company acquired the design from the Standard Steel Car Co. They assembled a few of the V-8s, but did not introduce any new models, and were out of business the same year.

STANDARD (vi) 1914
Standard Engineering Co, Chicago, Ill.
This was a cyclecar powered by an air-cooled 2-cylinder Spacke engine. Transmission was by friction disks, and final drive by single chain.

STANDARD (vii) 1920–1921
Standard Engineering Co, St Louis, Mo.
The Standard Steam Car was equipped with a Scott-Newcomb 2-cylinder, horizontal kerosene-burning steam engine and was advertised as being able to raise a head of steam in less than 60 seconds. The car carried a Rolls-Royce-type condenser-radiator and closely resembled the then well-known Roamer. A touring model was the only body style available. It was sometimes known as the Scott-Newcomb.

STANDISH 1924 1925
Luxor Cab Mfg Co, Framingham, Mass.
The Standish, of which only a few were ever completed, was produced by the Luxor taxicab company, itself a subsidiary of the Crawford/Dagmar empire. The Standish cars were designed with a pointed radiator and powered by a Continental six engine. The radiator was later used on the Elysée truck, also a subsidiary division of M. P. Möller's Dagmar and taxicab enterprise. Like the Dagmar, most Standish cars were seen with brass rather than nickel trim. They were made in the taxicab factory formerly occupied by the R. H. Long Co, makers of the Bay State car.

STANLEY (i) 1897–1927
1 Stanley Dry Plate Co, Newton, Mass. 1897–1899
2 Stanley Mfg Co, Lawrence, Mass. 1899–1901
3 Stanley Motor Carriage Co, Newton, Mass. 1901–1924
4 Steam Vehicle Corp of America, Newton, Mass. 1924–1927
The Stanley twins, F. E. and F. O., were partners in a photographic dry plate business in Newton, where they produced their first light steam car in 1897. This proved a great success, over 200 being sold in the first year of production. In 1898 a Stanley was timed over a mile at Charles River Park at 27.40mph. Among the customers were A. L. Barber and J. B. Walker, who purchased the manufacturing rights of the vehicle, and produced it as the Locomobile and Mobile respectively. In 1899 some Stanleys were advertised by the Locomobile Co of America under the name Stanley-Locomobile. The Stanleys proceeded to evolve an entirely new design, which appeared in 1902 with a simple non-condensing engine, driving directly on the rear axle. The boiler was mounted at the front, frames were of wood, and steering was by tiller. Locomobile went over to gasoline cars at the end of 1903, but the Stanleys prospered, listing an 8hp model at $750, and selling their cars to police and fire departments. More powerful versions rated at 10 and 20hp were available by 1904, and by 1906 the Stanley had assumed its characteristic appearance, with coffin-like hood concealing the boiler, and wheel steering. It could out-accelerate gasoline cars, and that year Frank Marriott was timed at 127.66mph on Daytona Beach with the streamlined Woggle-Bug. Marriott tried again the following year, but a spectacular crash at about

1904 STANLEY (i) 8hp runabout. *Rea Publicity (Western) Ltd*
1910 STANLEY (i) Model 71 20hp touring car. *Keith Marvin Collection*

c. 1920 STANLEY (i) Model 735 sedan. *Keith Marvin Collection*

150mph destroyed the car. Stanley's 1908 Gentleman's Speedy Roadster was capable of 60mph, and could run over 50 miles on a filling of water. The 1913 cars were electrically-lighted, and 1915 brought the introduction of steel framed and V-shaped front condensers on a 130in wheelbase chassis which lent itself to seven-passenger coachwork. However, the advent of Cadillac's electric self-starter in 1912 had signalled the end of the steamer, with its need for a long warm-up from dead cold. The 1920 Model 735 Stanley resembled a conventional gasoline car in outward appearance with a flat radiator of typically American aspect, but the boiler was still under the hood, and the double-acting 2-cylinder engine still drove direct on the back axle. Acceleration was well above par for the standards of the day, and the car would cruise at 45mph, with more available. But at around the $2,600 mark sales were low (about 600 a year), and the Stanleys had retired from the company during World War 1. The firm was reorganized in 1925, and the last Stanleys had hydraulic front-wheel brakes and balloon tires. An attempt was made to revive the name in 1935, but nothing came of this.

STANLEY (ii) 1907–1910
1 Stanley Automobile Mfg Co, Mooreland, Ind. 1907
2 Troy Automobile & Buggy Co, Troy, Ohio 1908–1910
This Stanley was a five-passenger touring car weighing 1,550lb. It was powered by a 2-cylinder, water-cooled engine of 216ci. A friction transmission was used, with a single chain to drive the rear axle.

STANLEY-WHITNEY *see* WHITNEY (i)

STANWOOD 1920–1922
Stanwood Motor Car Co, St Louis, Mo.
The Stanwood was a typical assembled car of its day, offering both open and closed body styles. The engine was a Continental six and other standard components were employed.

STAR (i) 1903–1904
1 Star Automobile Co, Cleveland, Ohio
2 H. S. Moore, Cleveland, Ohio
This car was driven by a single-cylinder, water-cooled engine of 118ci, mounted beneath the front seat, with false hood and coil radiator in front. A Champion planetary transmission and double chain drive was used. Both two- and five-passenger models were made, the latter with rear entrance.

STAR (ii) 1908
Model Automobile Co, Peru, Ind.
The short-lived Star from Peru was offered in conventional 2- and 4-cylinder forms. The twin was chain-driven, while the big, expensive four ($4,000) had shaft drive.

1926 STAR (iii) touring car. *William S. Jackson*

STAR (iii) 1922–1928
Durant Motor Co of New Jersey, Elizabeth, N.J.; Lansing, Mich.; Oakland, Calif.

William Crapo Durant's Star Four was one of the more serious attempts to take away some of the Model T Ford's market, for the cheapest practical car. Unlike the Ford, the Star was an assembled machine. It had a 130ci, 4-cylinder engine by Continental, and was conventional in design in every way except the transmission, which was separate; a feature common to all the vehicles in Durant's empire, but very unusual in American mass-produced cars by the early 1920s. The touring car cost only $443 in 1923, which helped Star to be the seventh biggest seller in America that year. It was sold outside the United States under the name Rugby. In 1926, a 169ci six was introduced. Fwb appeared in 1927 but a year later the make disappeared in the collapse of the Durant interests. By this time, 250 cars a day were being turned out. Only the Four was still called the Star for the 1928 model year, as the Six was now known as the Durant Model 55.

STARIN 1903–1904
The Starin Co, North Tonawanda, N.Y.

The Starin was a typical light runabout powered by a 6hp horizontal single-cylinder engine, mounted under the seat. Drive was via a 2-speed planetary transmission and single chain to the rear axle.

STATES 1915–1919
1 States Cyclecar Co, Detroit, Mich. 1915–1916
2 States Motor Car Co, Kalamazoo, Mich. 1917–1919

The States succeeded the Greyhound cyclecar, and initially used a 74ci 4-cylinder engine. When the cyclecar went out of fashion the company turned to a larger car with 22hp G.B. & S. 4-cylinder engine, or their own 6-cylinder engine. These came with roadster, phaeton, and sedan bodies, at prices from $895 for the four, and $995 for the six.

STATIC 1923
Static Motor Co, Philadelphia, Pa.

This company was listed as the maker of the Static Super-Cooled Six, but no details are available.

STAVER 1907–1914
1 Staver Carriage Co, Auburn Park, Ill. 1907–1910
2 Staver Carriage Co, Chicago, Ill. 1910–1914

For its first two seasons, the Staver was a typical high-wheeler with a 2-cylinder engine and double chain drive. Later models used 4-cylinder monobloc engines of 30, 35, and 45hp. Capacities ranged up to 318ci in 1912. Body types were limited to four- and five-passengers, with wheelbases up to 120in. In 1914 a 6-cylinder car was made.

STEAMOBILE 1900–1902
1 Keene Automobile Co, Keene, N.H. 1900–1902
2 Steamobile Co of America, Keene, N.H. 1902

This was a typical tiller-steered steam buggy, powered by a 7/9hp 2-cylinder vertical engine, and having single chain drive. A dos-à-dos four-passenger body was available in addition to the two-passenger. The Steamobile had a curved dash like that of the Oldsmobile, although it was higher-built.

STEARNS (i); STEARNS-KNIGHT 1899–1930
F. B. Stearns Co, Cleveland Ohio

This company's first product was a typical gas buggy in the American idiom with horizontal underfloor engine, planetary transmission, chain drive, and bicycle-type wheels. In its 1901 form it had one enormous cylinder (6¼in bore and 7in stroke) and wheel steering. By 1902 the Stearns had grown into a 325ci 25hp twin retailing for $3,000. The 1905 cars were altogether more European, with their mechanically-operated L head, paired cylinders, and Mercedes-style radiators. A 40hp four sold for $4,000, and led to even greater things, such as a chain-driven 45/90hp

six, with the rear pair of cylinders vanishing into the dash. Displacement was 800ci, and it could achieve nearly 90mph. The smaller 431ci 4-cylinder 30/60 was a 60mph car available with shaft or chain drive at $4,600. In 1909 there was a modest 15/30hp town carriage with a monobloc engine. The trademark of these cars was the white line running round the inside of the radiator shell. Sporting machines subsequently gave way to more staid cars with the Knight double-sleeve valve engine, 1914 versions being a 312ci four and a 489ci six, both with electric lighting and starting. By 1917 Stearns were cashing in on the V-8 fashion with a 332ci car, but fours and sixes engaged the company's attention during the early and middle 1920s, the former disappearing in 1926, one year after the firm had been acquired by Willys-Overland. This change of ownership did not affect the quality of the Stearns, which were kept on as a prestige line. During the make's last two seasons — 1929 and 1930 — there was a 27.3hp six retailing at $2,095, and a big 384ci straight-8 with a 9-bearing crankshaft and 145in wheelbase, for which prices started at $5,500.

1904 STEARNS (i) 24hp tonneau. *Keith Marvin Collection*
1907 STEARNS (i) 30/60hp touring car. *Burton H. Upjohn*

1929 STEARNS-KNIGHT convertible. *Keith Marvin Collection*

STEARNS (ii) 1900–1904

Stearns Steam Carriage Co, Syracuse, N.Y.

Designed by E. C. Stearns, this car had no connection with the better-known Cleveland-built Stearns. It was a steam car of conventional design using a 2-cylinder slide-valve engine of 8hp, chain drive and steering by side tiller. A wide variety of body styles was offered, including a six-passenger with three rows of seats and roll-down canvas sides. The latter model was introduced in 1902, and has been called, probably correctly, the world's first production station wagon.

STECO 1914

Stephens Co, Chicago, Ill.

This cyclecar had an ash frame and used a 2-cylinder, air-cooled engine of 10hp. Final drive was by belt. The body was designed for two passengers in tandem, and the price was $450.

STEELE 1915

The William Steele Co, Worcester, Mass.

This company made trucks but are reported to have built a small number of 2-cylinder cyclecars during the boom period for such vehicles.

STEEL SWALLOW 1907–1908

Steel Swallow Auto Co, Jackson, Mich.

This two-passenger runabout was probably not as swift nor as silent as its name implied. It had an air-cooled 2-cylinder engine under the hood. With a friction transmission and a 84in wheelbase, its cost was $700.

STEPHENS 1916–1924

1 Moline Plow Co, Moline, Ill. 1916–1921
2 Stephens Motor Car Co, Freeport, Ill. 1922–1924

The Stephens was a highly regarded car which used a 225ci 6-cylinder L-head Continental engine up to 1918, and thereafter a similar sized ohv unit of its own manufacture. It was unofficially considered as a rival to the Buick in price and general appearance. Nearly 25,000 were sold during the years of production and a variety of open and closed models constituted its catalog. Until 1922, Stephens were prosaic in appearance, if good dependable cars. That year, the Salient Six Model 10 appeared as the 1923 line and the moderately-rounded radiator was replaced by a high rounded type similar to that used by Kissel or ReVere. Among its more aesthetically appealing types, the new line featured a four-passenger, close-coupled sports phaeton with cycle fenders and side-mounted spare wheels. Wire wheels were used for this model, which was sold in French gray with apple-green wheels and trim.

STERLING (i) 1909–1911

Elkhart Carriage and Motor Car Co, Elkhart, Ind.

The Sterling succeeded the Elkhart and preceded the Elcar, while the company also made a 4-cylinder assembled car, the Komet, in 1911. The Sterling was built in five open body styles, ranging in price from $1,500 to $1,850. They used a T-head, 4-cylinder engine of approximately 255ci capacity. The rear springs were of the old-fashioned platform design.

STERLING (ii) 1914–1916

Sterling Motor Car Co, Brockton, Mass.

This Sterling was a small five-passenger touring car weighing 1,250lb. It had a 4-cylinder engine and was priced at $650, with electric lighting.

STERLING (iii); AMS-STERLING 1915–1923

1 Sterling Automobile Mfg Co, Paterson, N.J.: Amston, Conn. 1915–1917
2 Amston Motor Car Co, Amston, Conn. 1917
3 Consolidated Car Co, Middlefield, Conn. 1917–1923

This was an assembled car powered by a 4-cylinder, 127ci Le Roi engine with overhead valves. The two-passenger roadster was listed at $590. One source gives the name of the second make as Royal Amston, but this cannot be confirmed. Later models, made by the Consolidated Car Company, used 4-cylinder Le Roi or 6-cylinder Herschell-Spillman engines.

STERLING-KNIGHT 1923–1925

Sterling-Knight Motors Co, Cleveland and Warren, Ohio

Introduced in October 1923, the Sterling-Knight was one of the lesser-known Knight-engined cars. The 6-cylinder car failed in early 1925 after a total production of about 425.

STEVENS-DURYEA 1902–1927

1 J. Stevens Arms & Tool Co, Chicopee Falls, Mass. 1902–1906
2 The Stevens-Duryea Co, Chicopee Falls, Mass. 1906–1923
3 Stevens-Duryea Motors Inc, Chicopee Falls, Mass. 1923–1927

In 1900 J. Frank Duryea, one of the famous Duryea brothers, organized the Hampden Automobile & Launch Co at Springfield, Mass., to build a car called the Hampden. It is unlikely that it was ever built under this name, but late in 1901 he joined the Stevens company, a well-known armaments firm, and the car was built by them in the former Overman plant at Chicopee Falls. It had a 6hp 2-cylinder horizontal engine, tubular frame and two-passenger stanhope body. Starting was from the driver's seat, and the price was $1,200. A 4-cylinder car was introduced

1922 STEPHENS Salient Six 25hp sedan. *Kenneth Stauffer*

1908 STEVENS-DURYEA limousine. *Henry Ford Museum, Dearborn, Mich.*

in 1905, and the company's first six in 1906. This was an enormous machine, with displacement of 559ci. It had shaft drive and 3-point engine support, and cost $5,000. From 1907 only 6-cylinder cars were made; large, high quality conservative machines whose design change little over the years. They were mostly touring and town cars, although a few two-passenger roadsters were made around 1914. The last basically new model was the Model D of 1915, a 47.2hp six of 472ci which developed 80bhp at 1,800rpm. This was continued as the Model E in 1920, by which time inflation had brought the price as high as $9,500 for a limousine. Production continued until 1924 at about 100 cars per year, and a few cars were still being sold off as late as 1926 or 1927. In its final years the company was also manufacturing Raulang electric cars and taxicabs.

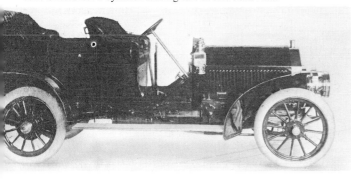

1915 STEWART 29hp touring car. *Keith Marvin Collection*
1907 STILSON 6-cylinder touring car. *G. Marshall Naul*

STEWART 1915–1916
Stewart Motor Corp, Buffalo, N.Y.

This was a large car, with a 6-cylinder 288ci Continental engine. The radiator was mounted to the rear of the engine, which allowed a sloping hood. Three- or seven-passenger models were available at $1,950. The manufacturer was better-known for commercial vehicles.

STICKNEY 1914
Charles A. Stickney Co, St Paul, Minn.

This was a tandem two-passenger cyclecar, with driver's controls in the rear seat. The engine was a 119ci, T-head 4-cylinder unit, with water cooling. A friction transmission was used with double chain drive. The wheelbase of 120in gave a low profile and the hood had a distinct slope, with a V-shaped radiator.

STILL (CDN) 1899–1903
Canadian Motor Syndicate, Toronto, Ont.

The first car was a 5hp *dos-à-dos* weighing 750lb, with an air-cooled

engine and wheel-steering. Later, 4 and 5hp electric cars were made, and a twenty-five-passenger bus was also planned, with power to each wheel.

STILSON 1907–1910
1 Pittsfield Motor Carriage Co, Pittsfield, Mass. 1907
2 Stilson Motor Car Co, Pittsfield, Mass. 1907–1910

Five models of the Stilson were produced, all powered by 6-cylinder Herschell-Spillman engines. The transmission used was a patented unit with early hydraulically-controlled clutch. These were large cars with wheelbases from 120 to 141in, and weighing up to 3,300lb.

STODDARD-DAYTON 1904–1913
1 Stoddard Mfg Co, Dayton, Ohio 1904–1905
2 Dayton Motor Car Co, Dayton, Ohio 1905–1912
3 U.S. Motor Co, Stoddard-Dayton Division, Dayton, Ohio 1912–1913

This was one of the great American cars of the era. The first models used 4-cylinder Rutenber engines of 201ci and were designed by a young English engineer, H. S. Edwards. These had the gear shift on the steering column. Pearl gray was the standard color. In 1907, both 4- and 6-cylinder engines were used, the fours having overhead valves. For 1910,

1908 STODDARD-DAYTON 45hp touring car. *Kenneth Stauffer*

a total of twelve models was offered, on three different chassis; these included a 50hp engine on a wheelbase of 128in. For 1911, a 6-cylinder, 525ci Knight engine was introduced. This model was sometimes referred to as the Stoddard-Knight. Three other models, with 4-cylinder, poppet-valve engines, were continued through 1913. The Stoddard-Dayton had an illustrious racing career, including victory in the inaugural Indianapolis race meeting of 1909. The Stoddard-Dayton ceased to exist with the collapse of the U.S. Motor Co.

STORCK 1901–1903
Frank C. Storck, Red Bank, N.J.

Frank Storck was a cycle repairer who assembled a small number of light steam cars of the Whitney type, and sold them for $750 each.

STORK KAR 1919–1921
Stork Kar Sales Co, Martinsburg, W. Va.

The Stork Kar was a conventional touring car powered by a 4-cylinder Lycoming engine. Specifications were identical to those of the later

Norwalks, also made in Martinsburg, and to the Piedmont, from Lynch-burg, W. Va. As Piedmont sold their cars under a number of different names, it is possible that both the Stork Kar and the Norwalk were in fact made by Piedmont.

STORM 1954
Sports Car Development Corp, Detroit, Mich.

The Storm Z-250 sports car used a 250bhp Dodge V-8 engine and a two-passenger Bertone body.

STORMS 1915
William E. Storms, Detroit, Mich.

The Storms was apparently the only American-built electric cyclecar, produced with either three-passenger or two-passenger (side-by-side) bodies. Prices ranged from $750 to $950.

STRATHMORE 1899–1902
Strathmore Automobile Co, Boston, Mass.

This company advertized two-passenger cars and delivery cars, but no details are available. Steam as well as gasoline-driven vehicles were listed.

STRATTON (i) 1909
C. H. Stratton Carriage Co, Muncie, Ind.

This make was a high-wheeler with solid rubber tires and right-hand steering by wheel. It was built in two- and five-passenger versions. Its 2-cylinder horizontally opposed air-cooled engine was under the hood in front, and drive was by double chain.

STRATTON (ii) 1923
Stratton Motors Corp, Indianapolis, Ind.

This car with a 4-cylinder engine of Stratton design was an attempt by Frank S. Stratton, formerly sales manager of the Grant Company, to market his own car. For a short time, the concern obtained control of Monroe and built the latter, but shortly after both Monroe and Stratton were absorbed by Premier.

STRINGER 1901
Stringer Automobile Co, Marion, Ohio

This company made a steam carriage with a 4-cylinder engine, and 'enclosed chainless drive'. It never went into production.

STRONG & ROGERS 1900–1901
Strong & Rogers, Cleveland, Ohio

This company made a light two-passenger electric powered by a 2½hp motor. On one model the seat and tiller bar were covered with goatskin, the handle of pearl with sterling silver ferrules. The wooden body had hand-carved decorations. For all this the price of $2,000 was perhaps not excessive, although cheaper models were also available.

STROUSE 1915–1916
Strouse, Ranney & Knight Co, Detroit, Mich.

The Strouse two-passenger roadster was priced at $300 with 42in tread or $325 with standard tread. It was powered by a water-cooled, 4-cylinder engine, with friction transmission and single chain drive.

STRUSS 1897
Henry Struss, New York, N.Y.

The Struss was a two-passenger car with a straight dash and rear-mounted 4hp 4-cylinder engine built by Richard Burr. Final drive was by side chains. Struss was specially commissioned to build this car, and apparently made no others.

STUART 1961
Stuart Motors, Kalamazoo, Mich.

This was a proposed electric car, seating two adults and several children, with a 4hp motor driven by eight 6-volt batteries. The enclosed

body was of fiberglass and the range was about 40 miles per charge at 35mph.

STUDEBAKER (US/CDN) 1902–1964; 1964–1966
1 Studebaker Corp, South Bend, Ind. 1902–1954
2 Studebaker-Packard Corp, South Bend, Ind. 1954–1964
3 Studebaker Corp of Canada Ltd, Hamilton, Ont. 1964–1966

The brothers Henry and Clem Studebaker opened a blacksmith's and wagon-building shop in South Bend in 1852, horse-drawn vehicles of their construction serving in both the American Civil War and World War 1, and production continuing until 1919. Their first cars were electrics, made in modest numbers from 1902 to 1912: these were joined in 1904 by the Model-C gasoline car, a typically American 16hp flat-twin with amidships engine, 2-speed transmission, and chain drive. This was followed a year later by a vertical 4 on more European lines, selling for $3,000. For the next few seasons, however, Studebaker elected to act as selling agents for cars built to their order, and their more expensive offerings were built by Garford of Elyria. The cheaper machines were the E.M.F. and Flanders built by the Everitt-Metzger-Flanders Co, and these two makes accounted for 9,700 cars in 1910. In 1913 a pair of Studebaker models were made at South Bend, both with L-head mono-bloc engines, dual ignition, and electric lighting and starting: the 3-speed transmissions were mounted in unit with the back axles, and the 6-cylinder version was claimed to be the first such car to retail in the U.S.A. for less than $2,000. In 1914 there was a smaller, 15/20hp 192ci 4 with coil ignition only. Studebaker sold over 45,000 cars in 1915, and their sixth position in 1916 U.S. sales was matched by a seventh place in 1920. 1919 was the last year for 4-cylinder cars, and the 1920 models, while retaining separate transmissions, abandoned the transaxle layout. Models available were sixes of 289 and 354ci, the latter establishing a line of really large 6-cylinder cars which survived until 1928. An in-

1913 STUDEBAKER Model AA 27.2hp touring car. *M. A. Harrison*
1923 STUDEBAKER Big Six touring car. *Keith Marvin Collection*

1929 STUDEBAKER President 8 sedan. *Studebaker-Packard Corporation*
1939 STUDEBAKER Commander sedan. *Autocar*

expensive 207ci Light 6 joined the range in 1921, and 1923 Studebaker models had all-metal bodies with welded steel pressings. Balloon tires were standardized in 1925, in which year contracting-type hydraulic fwb were an option; open cars were made with permanent tops of the 'California' type and roll-up side-curtains. Fwb were standard in 1926, but the company reverted to mechanical actuation in 1927, in which year a 'compact', the Erskine, was marketed. Studebaker went after stock-car records in a big way in the later 1920s, an outstanding performance being 25,000 miles in 25,000 minutes. The 1929 range consisted of two sixes, the 'Dictator' and 'Commander' (at $1,265 and $1,495 respectively), and a pair of straight-8s of 254 and 339ci displacement. Pierce-Arrow was acquired in 1928, but regained its independence five years later. In 1930 Studebaker, with Plymouth, pioneered free-wheeling, offered initially on 8-cylinder cars alone, but available throughout the range by the latter part of the year.

Another compact appeared under the Rockne nameplate in 1932. Special versions of the 'President 8' distinguished themselves in the Indianapolis 500-Mile Race, Cliff Bergere's Studebaker Special finishing 3rd, while in 1933 6th to 12th places were filled by similar cars. Studebaker

1956 STUDEBAKER Golden Hawk coupé. *Studebaker-Packard Corporation*

went into receivership in 1933, but came back strongly in 1934 with an unattractively-styled three-model range — the 205ci 'Dictator 6', the 221ci 'Commander 8', and the 250ci 'President 8', all with synchromesh, free wheeling, and X-braced frames. Subsequent evolution followed accepted American lines: transverse ifs, automatic overdrive, and hydraulic brakes once more in 1935; a hill-holder (modernized version of the sprag) in 1936; headlights half-faired into the fenders in 1938; and column shift in 1939, when Raymond Loewy became responsible for the Corporation's styling. 1939 was also the first year for one of America's longest-lived modern economy cars, the 164ci 6-cylinder L-head 'Champion' selling at $765. Fluid drive was available on the 1942 range, which included Studebaker's last straight-8s. The revolutionary post-war 'coming or going' style with wrap-around rear window was launched by Loewy on the 1946/47 models with 170 and 226ci 6-cylinder engines. Sales climbed to 239,000 in 1949, and the inevitable ohv V-8—a relatively small one of 233ci — replaced the bigger 6 in 1951. Studebaker's answer to the big battalions was the low and elegant line of the 1953 cars, which unfortunately became more cluttered down the years, and finances were not improved by the merger with Packard in 1954. An interesting departure was the sporting 'Hawk' coupé powered by Packard's V-8 engine and Ultramatic transmission in 1956; 1957 versions had supercharged Studebaker engines. The company managed to get their 'Lark' compact sedan tooled and into production in ten months in 1959, and this descendant of the old 'Champion' was the only model now offered with the exception of the 'Hawk'. The small 6 achieved ohv at long last in 1961, and 1962 brought the exciting fiberglass-bodied 'Avanti' coupé with disk brakes on the front wheels, a 4-speed transmission, and optional supercharger. It established 29 stock-car records, including a flying mile at 168.15mph, but neither this nor the continuing 'Lark' range could save Studebaker. A wide choice of models — two sixes and three eights — was listed for 1964, but early in the season South Bend stopped making cars, and production was transferred entirely to the Canadian plant which had been assembling cars since 1915. Even as an 'import', the Studebaker did not sell well: the last examples of the make had 194ci 6-cylinder and 283ci 8-cylinder Chevrolet engines, but even these were abandoned in the spring of 1966. Production of the 'Avanti' was continued on a small scale by an independent factory in South Bend.

STURGIS *see* MORRISON

STURTEVANT 1904–1908
Sturtevant Mill Co, Boston, Mass.
Sturtevants were large cars with 120in wheelbases and powered by 4- or 6-cylinder engines. The 4-cylinder engine was of 476ci displacement. An automatic transmission was standard on Sturtevants from 1905 on. The Flying Roadster, a three-passenger weighing 2,200lb, was priced at $4,000.

STUTZ (i) 1911–1935
1 Ideal Motor Car Co, Indianapolis, Ind. 1911–1913
2 The Stutz Motor Car Co of America, Indianapolis, Ind. 1913–1935
The Ideal Motor Car Company was the name of the firm which made the first Stutz racing cars, but it was changed to the Stutz Motor Car Company in 1913. Harry C. Stutz' most famous passenger car was the Bearcat speedster of 1914 — probably the best known of all American sports cars. It followed the usual recipe of a low-hung chassis, a big, slow-turning proprietary engine (in this case, a T-head, 4-cylinder Wisconsin unit, producing 60bhp at 1,500rpm), and very little else, just a hood, fenders, raked steering column, two bucket seats, and a fuel tank behind them. A Stutz-made 3-speed transmission was integral with the rear axle; an uncommon feature. This component had been sold by Stutz before he made complete cars. A 376ci 6-cylinder engine was available, but seldom seen. The Stutz Bearcat was the most popular of its breed, in spite of its high price, and its appeal was boosted by Stutz successes with ohc, 16-valve racing cars. It was the Mercers' greatest rival. Touring Stutzes were made as well, but were comparatively little known. Total production

1906 STURTEVANT Automatic 40/50hp touring car. *M. A. Harrison*
1914 STUTZ (i) coupé. *John Newman Collection*

Hispano-Suiza, and Frank Lockhart was killed at Daytona Beach while trying to take the World Land Speed Record with a Miller-engined car built by the company, both setbacks taking place in 1928.

Sales fell, and a range of cheaper models with, it was hoped, wider appeal was introduced for the next year, alongside the existing models. These cars had little in common with the classic models, so were called Black Hawks, not Stutzes. One used a 6-cylinder, ohc engine of 242ci displacement made by Stutz, and the other a straight-8 L-head unit by Continental. At the other end of the scale, there appeared in 1931 the superb DV (dual valve) 32, to compete with the new multi-cylinder cars being brought out by Lincoln, Cadillac, Marmon, and others. The design was basically similar to that of the SV16, still current, but there were two overhead camshafts and four valves per cylinder, 32 in all. The DV32 was listed in speedster form, as the Bearcat, and, on a shorter chassis, as the Super Bearcat. These stubby, formidable cars were guaranteed to exceed 100mph. The expensive, high-quality, specialist Stutz went the way of most of its kind in the Depression years. Instead, the company sold, and later made a light delivery car, called the Pak-Age Car. This had a rear engine and all-independent suspension, and was current from 1928 to 1938, after which manufacture was taken over by Diamond T.

STUTZ (ii) 1970 to date
Stutz Motor Car of America, New York, N.Y.

Unlike replica cars such as the Auburn and Cord, the makers of the Stutz Blackhawk coupé have merely borrowed the name of the pre-war car for their machine. It is powered by a 400ci Pontiac V-8 engine stripped and modified so that the original power of 365bhp is raised to 425bhp. This is mounted in a modified Pontiac chassis, and the Virgil Exner-

1929 STUTZ (i) Black Hawk Six sedan. *G. N. Georgano Collection*
1933 STUTZ (i) DV32 convertible. Coachwork by Rollston. *Keith Marvin Collection*

grew from 759 cars in 1913 to 2207 in 1917. Two years later, Stutz left to make another car, the H.C.S., although the cheaper Stutzes of the 1915 period were also known as H.C.S. The transmission was moved back to the normal position in 1921, and shortly after this Stutz began making their own engines: an L-head four giving 88bhp and a 75bhp ohv six. The latter was developed to give 80bhp in the 289ci Speedway Six of 1924, the last of the old line.

In 1926, there was a change of management, and Frederick E. Moskovics, the new president, initiated a radically new policy. Paul Bastien, who had designed the splendid 2-liter Métallurgique from Belgium, was responsible for the Stutz AA, or Vertical Eight. It was a beautifully-made fast tourer, more typical of Europe than America. Its specification embraced a straight-8 289ci engine with a single overhead camshaft, and dual ignition, including two spark plugs per cylinder. Power output was 92bhp at 3,200rpm. This was a modern, reasonably efficient engine by any standards, and distinctly advanced in these respects by American standards. There were, however, only three forward speeds. The hydraulic brakes were very good indeed, and the underslung worm final drive allowed the fitting of low-built, good-looking bodies. Centralized chassis lubrication and safety glass were provided. Glamorous though the AA was, it was sold on the slogan of 'The Safety Stutz', and a year's free passenger insurance was given with each car. In 1927, the engine was enlarged to 298ci, now giving 95bhp, and a speedster option, the Black Hawk, was added. In the following year, Weymann fabric body construction was adopted; another European touch. The engine was enlarged again in 1929 and this made 113bhp available. Better still, there were 4 forward speeds. Special Black Hawk speedsters were 2nd at Le Mans in 1928, but they came no higher than 5th in 1929. These cars had Roots superchargers and vacuum servo brakes. The type was put on sale as the Bearcat, reviving a famous name. Stutzes also competed at Le Mans in 1930, 1931 and 1932. Unfortunately, a Stutz lost a well-publicized challenge match at Indianapolis with a

1971 STUTZ (ii) Blackhawk coupé. *Stutz Motor Car Co of America*

designed body is hand-built by Carrozzeria Padana of Modena, Italy, where the final assembly of the cars is done. The first model, the 2-door hardtop, is priced at $22,500; other models in the Stutz range include a convertible at $25,000, the Indy, an Indianapolis 500 style racer modified for street use, at $25,000, a limousine at $29,000, and an automobile for parade and ceremonial use at $75,000.

STUYVESANT 1911–1912
Stuyvesant Motor Car Co, Sandusky, Ohio

The 6-cylinder Stuyvesant was a large and expensive car for the period, with a 128in wheelbase. The 4-door five-passenger touring car was listed at $4,200. The engine was of 620ci, and had a 4-speed transmission. This, originally, was the Gaeth.

SUBURBAN LIMITED 1912
1 Suburban Motor Co, Detroit, Mich.
2 De Schaum Motor Car Co, Detroit, Mich.

This was built in runabout, torpedo and touring models. All were on a chassis with 110in wheelbase. The common engine was a six with 260ci displacement. As with other De Schaum promotions, this make may never have progressed beyond the prototype stage.

SUCCESS 1906–1909
Success Auto-Buggy Mfg Co, St Louis, Mo.

This high-wheeled motor buggy started with an air-cooled, single-cylinder engine and ended as a line of four models with either 2- or 4-cylinder engines. The late versions came with a choice of water or air cooling. They all used a planetary transmission with chain drive.

SULTAN 1909–1912
Sultan Motor Co, Springfield, Mass.

The Sultan company specialized in taxicabs, but also manufactured similar passenger cars. These had closed four-passenger landaulet bodies. Power was supplied by 4-cylinder, 4-cycle engines of 128ci or 6-cylinder 226ci units. A 3-speed transmission was used with shaft drive. A predecessor, the Elektron Manufacturing Co of Springfield, Mass., had obtained rights to manufacture the French-made Sultan.

SUMMIT 1907
Summit Carriage-Mobile Co, Waterloo, Iowa

Also known as the Carriage-Mobile, this was a high-wheel motor buggy powered by a 10hp single-cylinder engine.

SUN (i) 1915–1918
1 Sun Motor Car Co, Buffalo, N.Y. 1915
2 Sun Motor Car Co, Elkhart, Ind. 1916–1918

The Sun from Elkhart was a small, low-priced, conventional six, rated at 22hp. The men behind it, R. Crawford and R. C. Hoff, were former Haynes personnel. Touring, roadster, and sedan models were listed.

SUN (ii) 1921–1924
The Automotive Corp, Toledo, Ohio

The Sun Runabout from Toledo was an ephemeral light car, a breed killed by the Ford and others. It was powered by a 4-cylinder, air-cooled, ohv engine of Cameron manufacture, and had three forward speeds. Suspension was by quarter-elliptic springs at both ends.

SUNSET 1901–1904
Sunset Automobile Co, San Francisco, Calif.

The Sunset steamer, although made on the West Coast, was very similar to its many contemporaries from New England. It had a vertical 2-cylinder engine, chain drive and tiller steering. The price was $900.

SUPERIOR (i) (CDN) 1910
William English, a wagon maker of Petrolia, Ont., built about 60 touring cars with 4-cylinder Atlas engines and planetary transmissions. The bodies could be converted to light trucks.

SUPERIOR (ii) 1914
Crescent Motor Car Co, St Louis, Mo.

For a few months, this car was called Crescent. It was a five-passenger car with a 4-cylinder, 198ci engine and right-hand drive.

SUPER KAR 1946
Louis R. Elrad, Cleveland, Ohio

The Super Kar was a prototype 3-wheeled midget with a 15hp air-cooled engine in a streamlined body.

SURREY '03 1958–1959
E. W. Bliss Co, Canton, Ohio

Looking like a 1903 Curved Dash Olds, the Surrey had an 8hp Cushman air-cooled engine with chain drive and modern refinements such as Sealbeam headlights and improved brakes. It could be purchased in kit form or fully assembled and had a maximum speed of 35mph.

SWEANY 1895
The Charles S. Caffrey Co, Camden, N.J.

The Sweany was a most original steam car driven by four small 3hp single-cylinder engines acting directly on each wheel. Steam at 150psi was provided by a single water-tube magnesia-lined boiler mounted at the front of the car. Hardly surprisingly, it never went into production.

SWIFT 1959
1 Swift Mfg Co, El Cajon, Calif.
2 WM Mfg Co, San Diego, Calif.

Three models were built: the Swift-T, Swift-Cat, and Swifter, rather like 5/8 scale versions of the 1910 Ford, Stutz Bearcat and 1903 Cadillac, propelled by single-cylinder Clinton air-cooled engines with governors to limit engine strain. Drive was by belts and the two-passenger bodies were the same basic unit, with different trim and accessories.

SYNNESTVEDT 1904–1908
Synnestvedt Machine Co, Pittsburgh, Pa.

So far as can be determined, this make consisted only of electric-powered cars, although some writers claim that gasoline models were also built. The Synnestvedt two-passenger car had 40 battery cells connected with a 4-speed controller and an 8hp motor. The rear axle was chain-driven. The wheelbase was 123in.

SYRACUSE 1899–1903
Syracuse Automobile Co, Syracuse, N.Y.

This was a light two-passenger electric with tiller steering. Designed by William Van Wagoner, it was originally known as the Van Wagoner.

T

TARKINGTON 1922–1923
Tarkington Motor Car Co, Rockford, Ill.

The Tarkington was a short-lived car using a 6-cylinder engine of the company's own manufacture. Only one model was produced, a five-passenger touring car. Wire wheels were standard on all cars built.

TASCO 1948
American Sports Car Co, Hartford, Conn.

Designed by Gordon Buehrig, former Cord engineer, the Tasco sports had a Derham body on a Mercury chassis. The unorthodox machine featured a radiator-cowl bumper, fenders that turned with the front wheels and a removable acrylic roof. Only one car was constructed.

TATE (CDN) 1912–1913
Tate Electrics Ltd, Windsor, Ont.

This ambitious firm offered the usual coupé, as well as a roadster, delivery cars of 500 and 1,000lb capacity, and trucks of 2,000 and 4,000lb capacity. Seating arrangements in the coupé put the driver in front, facing forward, as in gasoline cars. The coupé cost $3,600 and the roadster $2,700. All vehicles had wheel steering.

TAUNTON 1901–1904
Taunton Motor Carriage Co, Taunton, Mass.

This was a small tiller-steered runabout with a single-cylinder engine under the seat. Normally a two-passenger, two additional seats could be provided by dropping the front dash. The Taunton was available with tubular spoked or wire wheels for $850.

TEMPLAR 1917–1924
Templar Motors Corp, Cleveland, Ohio

The Templar was the best-known of several American attempts to make a high-grade small car just after World War 1, but was just as surely doomed by the development of American tastes in automobiles. It was a well-proportioned machine, with radiator and body well within the wheelbase. Materials and finish were superb, the aluminum bodies being given 27 coats of paint. The 197ci (later 212ci) 'Top-Valve' (i.e. overhead-valve) engine was smooth in spite of having only four cylinders, and very clean in appearance. It was also more efficient than most American power units. Much aluminum was found beneath the hood, too. Standard equipment in the roadster included a compass and a Kodak camera. A 213ci six was also listed for 1917 only, while a 259ci 6-cylinder engine was listed at the end of the Templar's career. Power was transmitted through open Hotchkiss drive, not through a torque tube as on most American cars.

TEMPLE-WESTCOTT 1921–1922
This was a 6-cylinder assembled car, whose chassis were made at Amesbury, Mass., and bodies by the Bela Body Co, Framingham, Mass. Only about 20 were made. There is no connection with the better-known Westcott from Springfield, Ohio.

TENNANT 1914–1915
Tennant Motors Co, Chicago, Ill.

This firm made a conventional 30/35hp 4-cylinder roadster and also a five-passenger tourer.

TERRAPLANE 1932–1937
Hudson Motor Car Co, Detroit, Mich.

The Terraplane replaced the original compact Essex Six late in 1932. It was a conventional 156ci L-head 6-cylinder car with a 3-speed transmission selling for $475 in the U.S.A. and £295 in England; though it failed to make much impression at home, its 70mph top speed and low running costs brought it many admirers in Europe. A companion 254ci straight-8 for 1933 had a 94bhp engine and offered 85mph; it formed the

1922 TEMPLAR touring car. *Kenneth Stauffer*

1934 TERRAPLANE roadster. *American Motors Corporation*

194

basis for the first Railtons. The 1934 line was restyled with a striking V-grill and independent front suspension, and used Hudson's 211ci 6-cylinder engine, though 166ci versions were made for export. The cars were again restyled, along with the Hudsons in 1936, when hydraulic brakes were added. After 1937, the name was dropped and its place taken by Hudson's new small six, the 112.

TEXAN 1918–1922
Texas Motor Car Association, Fort Worth, Tex.

An assembled car, the Texan had a Lycoming 4-cylinder engine and other standard components together with outsize tires, presumably suited for service in the oil-fields of Texas. About 2,000 cars and 1,000 trucks were made.

TEXMOBILE 1921–1922
Little Motors Kar Co, Dallas, Tex.

This was a small car powered by a 22½hp 4-cylinder L-head engine of the company's own make.

1910 THOMAS Flyer 72hp touring car. *Kenneth Stauffer*

THOMAS 1902–1919
1 E. R. Thomas Motor Co, Buffalo, N.Y. 1902–1911
2 E. R. Thomas Motor Car Co, Buffalo, N.Y. 1911–1919

The first Thomas-built car was the Autotwo of 1899, but from 1900 to 1902 Thomas built engines only, having granted a license to the Buffalo Automobile & Auto-Bi Company to build light cars and motorcycles (see Buffalo (i)). In 1902 Thomas took over Buffalo's operations and in July 1903 introduced a touring car powered by a 24hp 3-cylinder in-line engine. A De Dion-type hood was used with a finned-tube radiator slung low in front, but by November 1903 this had been replaced by a conventional hood and honeycomb radiator. These cars used double chain drive. For 1905 the model was called a 24/30hp, and this year saw the introduction of larger 40 and 50hp 4-cylinder cars, together with a 60hp six. The name Thomas Flyer was applied to the cars from 1905 onwards, and a wide range of bodies was offered, from two-passenger racer to limousine. The most famous model was the K-6-70, with a 72hp 6-cylinder engine; it was one of these which won the 1908 New York to Paris Race. This car, which was sold at auction in 1913 for $200, is now a priceless part of Harrah's Automobile Collection at Reno.

One chain-driven model was continued into 1909, but later Thomases tended to be more sedate, with emphasis on town cars and landaus. In 1911 and 1912 only 6-cylinder models were made. The Model 6-70 was continued to the end, its massive 783ci engine being the largest in the range. Cars were listed up to 1919, available to special order only.

THOMAS-DETROIT 1906–1908
E. R. Thomas-Detroit Co, Detroit, Mich.

This car differed very little from the parent Thomas. For 1908, it was powered by a 354ci 4-cylinder engine with two spark plugs per cylinder. A 3-speed transmission with shaft drive was used. This firm then became the Chalmers Motor Co.

THOMPSON (i) 1901–1902
Andrew C. Thompson, Plainfield, N.J.

This was a light electric runabout powered by a 1¼hp motor geared directly to the rear axle. A speed of 12mph, and a range of 25–30 miles were modest even for 1901, but with a special battery, the range could be extended to 60 miles.

THOMPSON (ii) 1906
Thompson Automobile Co, Providence, R.I.

This was a heavy steam brake which could carry six passengers on bench seats facing each other, and two forward facing passengers at the front. It is possible that only one was made.

THOMSON 1900–1902
Thomson Automobile Co, Philadelphia, Pa.

This was a light two-passenger powered by a 5hp single-cylinder engine, priced at $500. An unusual feature in so small a car was double chain drive.

THRIF-T 1955
Tri-Wheel Motor Corp, Springfield, Mass.

A 3-wheeled utility car, the Thrif-T had an 85in wheelbase, weighed 900lb and possessed a flat-twin Onan engine of 10hp. Body combinations included a canvas topped five-passenger model, a pickup and a delivery.

TIFFANY 1913–1914
Tiffany Electric Car Co, Flint, Mich.

The Tiffany succeeded the Flanders (ii) electric car. The sole model, an open two-passenger, had very sweeping body lines fore and aft, with wire wheels and cycle fenders. It was powered by a Wagner electric motor, was lever-steered, and cost $750. The name Tiffany only applied to the car from October 1913 to March 1914, after which the Flanders name was revived.

TIGER 1914
Automobile Cyclecar Co, Detroit, Mich.

This cyclecar was made in two-passenger and four-passenger models. These were powered by a 4-cylinder Farmer engine with overhead valves and had shaft drive.

TILEY 1904–1906; 1908–1913
Tiley Pratt Co, Essex, Conn.

The Tiley used 4-cylinder Rutenber engines of 32/36hp. These were water-cooled, and had sliding-gear transmission and shaft drive. A very few cars with 6-cylinder engines were also built. Less than 25 Tileys were constructed.

TILICUM 1914
Yukon Auto Shop, Seattle, Wash.

The Tilicum cyclecar used a 2-cylinder 14hp engine. Its transmission was a crude system with V-belts and split pulleys on the rear axle. Torque variation was accomplished by moving the entire rear axle forward or backward, the maximum movement being 3in.

TINCHER 1904–c.1907
1 Chicago Coach & Carriage Co, Chicago, Ill.
2 Tincher Motor Car Co, South Bend, Ind.

This company made large, heavy cars powered originally by 4-cylinder engines of 20 or 45hp, with massive hoods and finned tube radiators, and twin chain drive. Brakes on rear wheels were operated by compressed air. Later models were as large as 50 or 80hp. The 1906 '50' cost $5,000.

TIN-LIZZIE T-10 1960 to date
1 McDonough Power Equipment Co, McDonough, Ga. 1960–1965
2 Crue Cut Mfg Co, Sugar Creek, Mo. 1965 to date

This is a half-scale replica of the 1910 Model T Ford coupé, propelled by a 3hp, 4-cycle air-cooled engine giving it a normal driving speed of 12mph. The vehicle is not recommended for general road travel but is frequently used for publicity purposes.

TISCHER 1914
Linton G. Tischer Tri-Car Co, Peoria, Ill.

The Tischer was a 3-wheeled car, with the single, powered wheel in the rear. This was driven by a belt from a 9hp, 2-cylinder, air-cooled engine, through a friction transmission.

TMF 1909
Termatt, Monahan & Farney, Oshkosh, Wis.

This was a high-wheeler with a 2-cycle, 4-cylinder engine. Not more than three were built.

TOLEDO (i) 1900–1903
1 American Bicycle Co, Toledo, Ohio 1900–1902
2 International Motor Car Co, Toledo, Ohio 1902–1903

The first Toledo cars were steamers, powered by vertical 2-cylinder double-acting engines of 6¼hp. Steering was by tiller, and several different body styles were made, prices varying from $800 to $1,600. In 1902 a gasoline car with a 18hp vertical 3-cylinder engine was introduced. The steamers were dropped at the end of 1902, and the gasoline cars were known as Pope-Toledo from 1903 on.

TOLEDO (ii) 1913
Toledo Autocycle Car Co, Toledo, Ohio

Also known as the Autocycle, this was a 2-cylinder cyclecar with shaft drive.

TOQUET 1905
Toquet Motor Car & Construction Co, New York, N.Y.

This rare car was furnished with a T-head, 4-cylinder 455ci engine rated at 45hp, fitted with a flyball governor, and connected so that the clutch and brake operated the throttle. The transmission was of two speeds, and progressive, and the final drive was by shaft. The weight of the five-passenger model was 3,200lb.

TOURAINE 1912–1915
1 Nance Motor Car Co, Philadelphia, Pa. 1912–1913
2 Touraine Co, Philadelphia, Pa. 1913–1915

The Touraine was a larger car than average, with wheelbases up to 134in. It was driven by a 4-cylinder, T-head engine of 265ci. Two-, five- and seven-passenger open models were offered at prices from $2,200 to $3,200. After 1915, this company became the Vim Motor Truck Co, building only commercial vehicles.

TOURIST 1902–1909
Auto Vehicle Co, Los Angeles, Calif.

The Tourist was the best-known West Coast make of the era. These cars used 2- and 4-cylinder water-cooled engines, and were mainly five-passenger touring models. The smaller engines had a friction transmission while a sliding-gear type was employed with the 4-cylinder engine.

TOWANDA 1904
Towanda Motor Vehicle Co, Towanda, Pa.

This car was one of several of the period which were built without an engine, this being supplied by the customer. Steering was by wheel, and the rear axle was fitted for single chain drive.

TOWNE SHOPPER 1948
International Motor Car Co, San Diego, Calif.

The aluminum-bodied Towne Shopper was a prototype two-passenger car for running errands. It had a 2-cylinder, 10.6hp rear engine and weighed 600lb.

TRACTOBILE 1900–1902
Pennsylvanian Steam Vehicle Co, Inc, Carlisle, Pa.

The Tractobile was an *avant train* attachment for horse-drawn vehicles, but was unique in that it was steam powered. The boiler was made up of five separate units, each with 40 small tubes, and one or more units could be removed for cleaning. Two vertical cylinders acted on each front wheel direct, although it is difficult to see this in surviving photographs. As the Tractobile was an enterprise of E. J. Pennington, it may be wondered whether any ever ran at all, or if they were merely a stock-promotion scheme.

TRASK-DETROIT *see* DETROIT STEAM CAR

TRAVELER (i) 1906–1913
1 Traveler Motor Car Co, Evansville, Ind. 1906–1910
2 Traveler Auto Co, Evansville, Ind. 1911–1913

Models of the Traveler were of moderate size, with 30 to 36hp 4-cylinder, L-head engines. Both two-passenger runabouts and five-passenger touring cars were made. All models had selective, 3-speed transmissions and shaft drive.

TRAVELER (ii) 1914–1915
Traveler Motor Car Co, Detroit, Mich.

Model 36 of the Traveler (1914) used a 4-cylinder L-head engine of 221ci. It had a 3-speed transmission and a wheelbase of 120in. A two-passenger roadster was priced at $1,275, with a five-passenger version at $20 more. Model 48 had a 6-cylinder engine of 346ci, with a wheelbase of 130in. This model was also made in two- and five-passenger versions, the latter selling for $2,000.

TRIBUNE 1913–1914
Tribune Motor Co, Detroit, Mich.

This company was formed by L. G. Hupp, who had been with Hup-mobile. The Tribune was a light car with a 243ci 4-cylinder Buda engine. The only body type, a five-passenger touring car, cost $1,250.

1915 TRUMBULL 13hp roadster. *Neubauer Collection*

TRI-CAR 1955
The Tri-Car Co, Wheatland, Pa.

Known as the Suburbanette, the Tri-Car was a 3-wheeled coupé with a three-passenger fiberglass body. A Lycoming vertical twin engine drove the single rear wheel through a Westinghouse-Schneider torque converter, and the car had Goodrich rubber suspension. A maximum speed of 65mph was claimed, and the price was fixed at $995.

TRICOLET 1905
H. Pokorney Automobile & Gas Engine Co, Indianapolis, Ind.

This 3-wheeler, wrongly referred to as the Pokorney, had an air-cooled, 2-cylinder engine in the rear. Its two-passenger body was mounted on a 66in wheelbase. The planetary transmission had no reverse. A tiller steered the single front wheel. A 4-wheeled model was available for an extra $25.

TRI-MOTO 1900–1901
Western Wheel Works, Chicago, Ill.

Also known as the Crescent Tri-Moto, this was a very light front-wheel-drive 3-wheeler on the lines of the Lawson Motor Wheel made in England. Steering was by tiller. It was sold by the American Bicycle Company, which was an enterprise of Colonel Pope.

TRIUMPH (i) 1900–1901
Triumph Motor Vehicle Co, Chicago, Ill.

This company made an electric stanhope known as the Ellis, and announced that they would accept orders for gasoline or steam cars, for delivery in 90 days. Whether such vehicles were actually built is not certain.

TRIUMPH (ii) 1906–1909
Triumph Motor Car Co, Chicago, Ill.

These were open cars in four- and five-passenger models. Their engines were 4-cylinder units of 30hp and 45hp. In 1907 this car used 'the *only* self-contained, automatic, self-starting in the world'. This starting method stored exhaust gases in a tank under the seat, at a pressure of 125psi. This gas could be bled back into the cylinders for starting.

TRUE 1914
Badger Brass Mfg Co, Kenosha, Wis.

The True cyclecar carried two persons in tandem with the driver in the rear. It had a 2-cylinder, 10hp engine; the wheelbase was 104in. Very few were built and they sold for $400.

TRUMBULL 1913–1915
1 American Cyclecar Co, Bridgeport, Conn. 1913–1914
2 Trumbull Motor Car Co, Bridgeport, Conn. 1915

This make succeeded the American (iii) made by the American Cyclecar Co. of Detroit. The Trumbull was apparently superior to the typical cyclecar, having a water-cooled 4-cylinder engine of 104ci. This was connected with a friction transmission and double chain drive.

TUCK 1904–1905
Tuck Petroleum Motor Co, Brooklyn, N.Y.

This car was designed to run on kerosene, and used a 4-cylinder water-cooled engine, of 59ci displacement. No transmission was used, as drive was direct, by shaft. The starting system operated by stored exhaust-gas pressure. No reverse gear was used, as it was claimed that the engine was reversible, although the means of controlling direction of rotation was not explained.

TUCKER (i) 1900–1903
William Tucker, San Jose, Calif.

The Tucker was a crude-looking car with a 2-cylinder air-cooled engine and artillery wheels. About 16 were made.

1947 TUCKER (ii) 6-cylinder sedan. *Henry Ford Museum, Dearborn, Mich.*

TUCKER (ii) 1946–1948
The Tucker Corp, Chicago, Ill.

Designed by the engineer Preston T. Tucker of Ypsilanti, Mich., this car progressed through a number of stages, beginning with the projected Tucker Torpedo sports and ending with the actual Tucker '48 sedan. Innovations were chiefly the work of Tucker and the former Auburn-Cord-Duesenberg stylist Alex Tremulis. Safety was stressed with disk brakes, padded dash, front passenger crash compartment and pop-out windshield. The 3,600lb car was 60½in high, had independent suspension and a 128in wheelbase.

Plans for a central steering wheel and front fenders that turned with the wheels were shelved, but the three headlights were retained from the original Torpedo design. A flat opposed 589ci engine and a rear wheel double torque direct drive system were also abandoned. The flat opposed 6-cylinder engine ultimately used was developed from a Franklin air-cooled model used on Bell helicopters. It was redesigned as a rear-mounted liquid-cooled sealed-system unit with a compression ratio of 7:1, hydraulic valve lifters and a separate exhaust leading from each cylinder. Advertised as a 150hp machine, the actual output proved to be somewhat greater.

Of the finished vehicles not all were exactly alike. Most contained a 4-speed manual Y-1 (Ypsilanti) transmission with a preselector or electric shift. A few were left with rebuilt Cord transmission, attached during the waiting period for the Y-1 to be finished, and some were built with the R-1 (Rice) Tuckermatic automatic transmission which had less than 30 basic parts. Forty-nine examples were assembled in a former Dodge aircraft engine plant in Chicago before the company's demise. All too few Tuckers exist to prove exactly what kind of performance could have been expected from the Model '48, but some rare units in the hands of private collectors are reported to be running well after many thousands of miles, with good fuel consumption figures and a maximum speed of 120mph.

Argument continues between those who claim the Tucker to be a greatly over-rated engineering error, and those who defend it as superior to any production car then on the American roads. Some features of the car have in fact since been incorporated into present-day cars, features unique in 1948.

After a costly court battle with the Securities Exchange Commission, in which he was charged with fraud and violations of its regulations, Tucker was vindicated in 1950. With much of his holdings wiped out, Tucker abandoned further plans until 1952, when he planned to build a small car in Brazil. Negotiations were still pending when Preston Tucker died in 1956.

TUDHOPE (CDN) 1906–1913
Tudhope Motor Car Co Ltd, Orillia, Ont.

Several thousand automobiles were turned out by this firm, which had been making horse-drawn vehicles since 1865. From 1906 to 1909 the company built the Tudhope-McIntyre, a highwheeler using the U.S. McIntyre engine and available as a roadster, touring or pickup truck. A flash fire destroyed the factory in 1909, and when the new one was

1906 TUDHOPE-McINTYRE motor buggy. *Hugh Durnford*
1910 TWOMBLY (ii) 40hp limousine. *Autocar*

finished it turned to production of a more conventional 4-cylinder car based on the U.S. EMF. Regular EMF cars were also built for the Canadian market, but this arrangement did not work so a new Tudhope was created, based on the U.S. Everitt. Like earlier Tudhopes, it found many buyers across Canada.

In 1912, the company produced yet another Tudhope, this one a conventional model of entirely Canadian design, available as a four or a six, though mechanically similar to its predecessor. Bodies were streamlined and electric lighting and starting fitted in 1913, but lagging sales forced the company into bankruptcy. The firm was reorganized as the Fisher Motor Car Co, producing the Fisher car, which was almost identical to the last Tudhope. It sold fairly well, but in 1914 the company turned to war work and never built cars again. After World War 1 the plant did turn out some bodies for Essex and Brooks.

TULSA 1917–1923
Tulsa Automobile Corp, Tulsa, Okla.

The Tulsa was one of the few cars built in Oklahoma. It used Herschell-Spillman 4- and 6-cylinder engines. Production was limited and ceased in 1922, cars remaining in stock being designated 1923 models.

TURNER 1900–1901
Turner Automobile Co

This company made very light voiturettes with bicycle-type tubular frames and rear-mounted engines. 1¼ and 3hp engines were used in the 3-wheelers, called Lilliputian and Gadabout, and a 3hp engine in the Runabout 4-wheeler.

TWIN CITY 1914
Twin City Cyclecar Co, Minneapolis, Minn.

This cyclecar used an unusual 4-cylinder air-cooled engine with piston valves, producing 20hp at 2,000rpm. A friction transmission was used and suspension was by coil springs all round.

TWOMBLY (i) 1903
Twombly Motor Carriage Co, New York, N.Y.

The Twombly steamer used a 250psi boiler, at which pressure, it was claimed, the car could achieve 50mph. The 4-cylinder engine could be changed from single acting to compound. As a compound, engine output was 12hp, or 28hp as single-acting. An aluminum body was fitted, and touring or limousine styles were available at up to $3,000.

TWOMBLY (ii) c.1910–1911
Twombly Motors Co, New York, N.Y.

Apparently no connection with other makes of this name, this Twombly had a 40hp 392ci flat-4 engine, and dashboard radiator. The engine was designed for easy removal for servicing, and the aluminum body was transformable from limousine to tourer.

TWOMBLY (iii) 1913–1915
Twombly Car Corp, Nutley, N.J.

This make began as a cyclecar, and was actually manufactured by Driggs-Seabury. The last model was a light car for two passengers with a 4-cylinder L-head engine. With wire wheels and 3-speed transmission, the price was $660.

TWYFORD 1902–1908
Twyford Motor Car Co, Brookville, Pa.

The Twyford was a crudely engineered car with 4-wheel drive. It used 2-cylinder engines with a choice of 10 or 18hp. The drive was by shaft, with open bevel gears, and no differential. This five-passenger car with side-entrance was priced at $2,700.

1905 TWYFORD 10hp touring car. *Keith Marvin Collection*

U & V

UNION (i) 1902–1905
Union Automobile Co, Union City, Ind.

This make was a small 2-cylinder car, with a single headlight. The engine was either air- or water-cooled, with friction transmission and double chain drive. Models included both two- and five-passenger cars.

1905 UPTON (ii) 4-cylinder touring car. *Dr Alfred Lewerenz Collection*

1901 U.S. LONG DISTANCE 7hp runabout. *Kenneth Stauffer*

UNION (ii) 1911–1914
Union Sales Co, Columbus, Ohio

The Union from Columbus was a conventional car with a 25hp 4-cylinder pair-cast engine, and 3-speed transmission. Touring car and roadster models were available, at a price of $650.

UNITED 1914
National United Service Co, Detroit, Mich.

The United cyclecar was a side-by-side two-passenger car. Its 4-cylinder, 89ci engine was water-cooled, and friction transmission with double chain drive were used. Its weight was 850lb and its price $395.

UNIVERSAL 1914
Universal Motor Co, Washington, Pa.

The Universal was a two-passenger roadster with an 18hp 4-cylinder engine. It was classed as a light car and had a 3-speed transmission. Its price was $475.

UNIVERSITY see CONTINENTAL (ii)

UPTON (i) 1900–1907
1 Upton Machine Co, Beverly, Mass. 1900–1905
2 Beverly Mfg Co, Beverly, Mass. 1905–1907

The first Upton was a light runabout powered by a 3½hp De Dion engine. It had chain drive to a 2-speed transmission and single chain drive to the rear axle. The most interesting model was the Beverly of 1904 which had a large 4-cylinder engine, chain drive, and the unusual feature of headlights which turned with the steering. The price was $4,000. This model was also made in Lebanon, Pa. as the Upton (ii).

UPTON (ii) 1904–1907
Upton Motor Co, Lebanon, Pa.

The 4-cylinder Upton was initially furnished with double chain drive, shaft drive being introduced in 1905. A five-passenger tonneau was the only model offered. The bullet-shaped headlights were connected to turn with the steering. Later models with 268ci engines were priced at $2,500.

U.S. 1908
U.S. Motor Car Co, Upper Sandusky, Ohio

This was a small two-passenger car on a wheelbase of 96in. Its 4-cylinder, 108ci, air-cooled engine was mounted beneath the seat. The drive was through a 3-speed transmission and propeller shaft. The cost was $900.

U.S. ELECTRIC 1899–1901
U.S. Automobile Co, Attleboro, Mass.

This company made a small number of electric cars, mainly open two- and four-passenger machines.

U.S. LONG DISTANCE 1901–1903
United States Long Distance Automobile Co, Jersey City, N.J.

This marque started life as a light runabout powered by a single-cylinder horizontal 7hp engine mounted under the seat, a 2-speed planetary gear and single chain final drive. In 1903 a 2-cylinder four-passenger tonneau model appeared, and in the same year the name of company and car was changed to Standard (i).

UTILITY 1921–1922
Victor W. Pagé Motors Corp, Stamford, Conn.

Built by Major Victor W. Pagé, whose Aero-Type Four car carrying his name had already been produced, the Utility was an attempt to produce a car the size of the contemporary Ford or Chevrolet. The cars were equipped with disk or artillery wheels and hood louvres were confined to the rear of each side, as on the Ford. Models known to have been produced were a roadster, a touring car, a station or estate wagon and a small truck.

VALIANT see PLYMOUTH (ii)

VALKYRIE 1967 to date
Fiberfab, Division of Velocidad, Inc, Santa Clara, Calif.

Driven by a rear mounted V-8 of 450bhp, the Valkyrie GT sports car is a sleek two-passenger coupé of advanced design, priced at $12,000. A 5-speed Z-F transaxle enables the machine to attain speeds in excess of 180mph. The chassis is of steel tubing, suspension is independent and the brakes are 11.75in disks. A Simpson Drag parachute is used for primary braking at speeds over 140mph. Acceleration in fifth gear is 0–60mph in 3.9 seconds. The Valkyrie may be had in kit form with provision for use of Corvair parts if desired. Fiberfab also make fiberglass bodies for mounting on Volkswagen chassis.

VAN 1910–1911
Van Motor Car Co, Grand Haven, Mich.

The Van 22 was 'the car for you', with an ohv 4-cylinder engine. It was a two-passenger roadster with full elliptical springs for $850.

VAN WAGONER see SYRACUSE

V.E. (V.E.C.) 1903–1905
Vehicle Equipment Co, Long Island City, N.Y.

The V.E. electric was a three-passenger car with shaft drive. Its wheelbase was 94in and the tread an unusual 54in. This manufacturer was a large producer of electric commercial vehicles.

VEERAC 1913
Veerac Motor Co, Anoka, Minn.

The name Veerac was a mnemonic for 'valveless, explosion every revolution, air-cooled'. This car with its 2-cycle engine, and air-cooling, was first proposed by Frank Merrill of New Jersey in 1905. Later he was chief engineer for the Veerac Motor Co. The original two-passenger car had a 2-cylinder engine of 101ci, planetary transmission and shaft drive.

VELIE 1909–1928
1 The Velie Motor Vehicle Co, Moline, Ill. 1909–1916
2 The Velie Motor Corp, Moline, Ill. 1916–1928

Velie were already well-known carriage builders when they launched their first car in May 1909. It was a conventional machine with a 30/35hp 4-cylinder engine made by the American & British Manufacturing Company of Bridgeport, Conn., who later made the luxurious Porter (ii) car. The Velie Corporation was backed by the John Deere Plow Company, and the cars were distributed through Deere dealers until 1915. By 1914 a range of two fours and a six was made, with power ratings from 25 to 34hp. From 1917 onwards Velie made sixes only, standardizing on Continental engines. One of the most striking Velies was the Sport Car of 1918, a four-passenger touring car with wire wheels and outside exhaust pipes. This was the only model with the 29hp engine, but the 25hp was supplied with a wide range of open and closed bodywork. In 1922 Velie began to make their own 6-cylinder engines, joined in 1927 by a straight-8 Lycoming. In 1928, the last year of production, there

1926 VELIE Model 60 coupé. *Harrah's Automobile Collection*
1929 VIKING (ii) V-8 sedan. *General Motors Corporation*

were three sixes, the Standard 50, the 6-66, and the 6-77, in addition to the 8-88 Lycoming developing 90bhp. 1929 models were announced but not built. However, the name survived in the town of Velie, Louisiana, a suburb of Shreveport. This obtained its name in 1916 because of the local popularity of Velie cars.

VERA 1912
Vera Motor Car Co, Providence, R.I.

This was an imposing car with pleasing lines, in five-passenger and seven-passenger models. The engine was a 6-cylinder, T-head of 477ci.

VERNON 1915–1920
Vernon Automobile Corp, Mount Vernon, N.Y.

The Vernon's production was never large and was confined primarily to touring cars. It had an 8-cylinder engine of Vernon make, with a displacement of 168ci. Artillery wheels were standard, with wire wheels available as an option. An alternative name was Able Eight.

VETTA VENTURA see APOLLO (ii)

VICTOR (i) 1907–1911
Victor Automobile Mfg Co, St Louis, Mo.

The Victor was a high-wheeler powered by a 2-cycle single-cylinder water-cooled engine, rated at 12hp and driving through friction transmission. Seven different styles were offered with either solid rubber or pneumatic tires.

VICTOR (ii) 1913–1914
Victor Motor Car Co, Philadelphia, Pa.

The Victor cyclecar had a more substantial appearance than most cars of its class. The 134ci, 4-cylinder engine was water-cooled and drove through a 3-speed transmission and a shaft to the differential. Semi-elliptic springs were used.

VICTOR (iii) 1914–1915
Richmond Cycle Car Mfg Co, Richmond, Va.

This two-passenger cyclecar used a 2-cylinder, 13hp air-cooled De Luxe engine. The manufacturer was forced to get rid of the last of these cars at $245 each after the cyclecar boom ended.

VIKING (i) 1908
Viking Co, Boston, Mass.

The only known information about this make is that it was a five-passenger touring car with a 126in wheelbase and a 40hp Rutenber engine. This car may have been manufactured in Maine but sold by the Boston company.

VIKING (ii) 1929–1930
Olds Motor Works, Lansing, Mich.

By 1929, General Motors were making a remarkably complex range of cars, including ranges within ranges. Alongside the reliable Oldsmobile six, Lansing introduced a quite new model for a more expensive market, the Viking. In general, it bore a close resemblance to its more luxurious relative, the La Salle, of which it was intended to be a cheaper version, but its 259ci, V-eight engine was unusual in that the chain-driven camshaft operated horizontal valves between the banks of cylinders. It developed 81bhp. The rationalization forced on American car manufacturers by the Depression killed the Viking after two seasons.

VIQUEOT 1905
Viqueot Co, Long Island City, N.Y.

This car used a chassis built at Puteaux, France, with bodies fitted in America. Two 4-cylinder engines were available, of 28/32hp and 40/45hp. These had 3-speed transmission and double chain drive. The Viqueot Co was controlled by the Vehicle Equipment Co, of the same city, whose main business was commercial vehicles.

VIRGINIAN 1911–1912
Richmond Iron Works, Richmond, Va.

The Virginian was a large car driven by a 50hp 4-cylinder engine of 393ci. A four-passenger roadster and a seven-passenger touring car were available at $3,000.

VIXEN 1914
Davis Mfg Co, Milwaukee, Wis.

This cyclecar used a water-cooled 4-cylinder engine with a friction transmission. The drive to the rear wheels was by chains. The front suspension was by double cantilever springs.

VOGUE 1917–1923
Vogue Motor Car Co, Tiffin, Ohio

A typical assembled car, the Vogue was built for its first two years in the same factory as the Economy and the differentiation between the two makes and the two companies remains a mystery. The cars had a 119in wheelbase and, except for an 8-cylinder type, which was discontinued late in 1918, sixes with Continental and Herschell-Spillman engines were standard. Slanted louvres gave the cars a rakish appearance and wire wheels were available at extra cost. Prices ranged from $1,995 upwards. Several hundred were built in seven years of production.

VULCAN 1913–1914
1 Vulcan Motor Car Co, Painesville, Ohio 1913
2 Vulcan Mfg Co, Painesville, Ohio 1913–1914

This was a cleanly-designed light car with a 27hp 4-cylinder engine. A two-passenger speedster on a 105in wheelbase with electric lights sold for $750. A five-passenger version with the same engine, but on a longer wheelbase, cost $850.

WACO 1915–1917

Western Automobile Co, Seattle, Wash.

The Waco was a very conventional 4-cylinder car made mainly in five-passenger tourer form, and selling for $950.

WAGENHALS 1913–1915

Wagenhals Motor Co, Detroit, Mich.

The Wagenhals was one of the few American 3-wheelers, and used an exceptionally large engine for such a type, of four cylinders and 24hp, carried under a hood which projected well in front of the front axle as in some commercial vehicles. Final drive was by chain to the single rear wheel. Wagenhals delivery vans were used by the U.S. Post Office; probably more of these were made than passenger cars.

WAHL 1913–1914

Wahl Motor Car Co, Detroit, Mich.

Wahl is the German word for 'choice' and it was with this idea that the manufacturer offered the customer a standard assembled car with a 4-cylinder 199ci engine, 4-speed transmission and other components, at a reasonable price. The buyer then might attach his own nameplate to the car and, in effect, become an automobile 'manufacturer'. Five-passenger touring and two-passenger roadster models were available. The make was out of business within about a year.

WALDRON 1909–1910

Waldron Runabout Mfg Co, Kankakee, Ill.

The Waldron was mechanically a simple car, with an opposed 2-cylinder engine under the body, a friction transmission and double chain drive. Three body types were offered.

WALKER 1905–1906

Walker Motor Car Co, Detroit, Mich.

This car used 2-cylinder, 4-cycle engines of 101ci, with a claimed output of 10hp. They had planetary transmissions and shaft drive. The two-passenger runabout cost $600.

WALL 1901–1904

R. C. Wall Mfg Co, Philadelphia, Pa.

The Wall used a 3-cylinder engine rated at 9hp. Final drive was by double chains to the rear wheels. The five-passenger tonneau was $1,500.

WALTER 1904–1909

1 American Chocolate Machinery Co, New York, N.Y. 1904
2 Walter Automobile Co, Trenton, N.J. 1905–1909

The Walter was an expensive and well-designed car. It was available with 30, 40 or 50hp 4-cylinder engines with overhead inlet valves. Open touring models and limousines were produced, ranging in price up to $5,700. These had sliding-gear transmissions with three forward speeds and shaft drive.

WALTHAM (i) 1898–1900

Waltham Automobile Co, Waltham, Mass.

The Waltham steamer was a typical New England runabout with a

1906 WALKER 10hp roadster. *Floyd Clymer Publications*

1904 WALTHAM (ii) Orient Buckboard 4hp runabout. *G. N. Georgano Collection*

2-cylinder engine, single chain drive and tiller steering. It was designed by John Piper and George Tinker, who built the prototype in the bicycle factory of the Waltham Manufacturing Company (see Waltham (ii)), although there was no financial connection between the two companies. Another steamer made in Waltham at the same time was the American Waltham.

WALTHAM (ii) 1902–1908

Waltham Mfg Co, Waltham, Mass.

This company made an experimental electric runabout in 1898, but did not put it into production. Their first gasoline-engined vehicles were motor cycles, tricycles and light runabouts powered by De Dion engines. In 1902 they introduced the Orient Buckboard, a very simple car consisting of two seats on a wooden platform, with a 4hp air-cooled engine geared to the rear axle, and, originally, only one speed. There were no springs, as the wooden platform was said to have enough resilience. The weight was 350lb and the price $375.

Although the simple Buckboard was continued, more sophisticated cars were gradually introduced, including a four-passenger version which in turn became a side-entrance tonneau. Wheel steering and small hoods to cover the driver's feet appeared in 1904, although the engine was still at the back, and the Buckboard ancestry remained obvious.

In 1905 a completely new car appeared, known as the Waltham Orient. This had a 4-cylinder air-cooled 18/20hp engine mounted in front in the conventional manner, friction transmission and shaft drive. A slightly smaller 16hp model was also made. In 1908 Waltham merged with the C. H. Metz Company, and for the following years the cars were known as Metz.

WALTHAM (iii) 1922
Waltham Motor Manufacturers, Inc, Waltham, Mass.

Formerly makers of the Metz, the Waltham Motor Manufacturers, Inc, produced a car under their own name, but only during 1922. A Rutenber 6-cylinder engine was used and prices began with the touring car at $2,450. Few Walthams were produced.

WALWORTH 1905–1906
A. O. Walworth & Co, Chicago, Ill.

This car was powered by a 14hp 2-cylinder opposed engine. A five-passenger tonneau with rear entrance had a wheelbase of 80in. A planetary transmission and shaft drive were used.

WARD (i) 1914–1916
Ward Motor Vehicle Co, New York, N.Y.

The Ward electric was made as a closed four-passenger car with two doors. The drive was by shaft and the manufacturer claimed 100 miles per charge. The body had an awkward and boxy appearance. It was priced at $2,100.

WARD (ii) 1914
Ward Cyclecar Co, Milwaukee, Wis.

This cyclecar was made in two models, both for two passengers, on a wheelbase of 100in. One had an air-cooled, 2 cylinder engine of 70ci, the other a water-cooled, 4-cylinder, 95ci unit. Both models used friction transmission.

WARD LEONARD *see* KNICKERBOCKER

WARREN (WARREN-DETROIT) 1909–1914
Warren Motor Car Co, Detroit, Mich.

This make was available in models with imaginative designations such as Pilgrim, Resolute and Wolverine. These were furnished with 4- and 6-cylinder engines. Larger models, with a 377ci 6-cylinder engine, were priced at $2,500.

WARWICK 1903–1904
Warwick Cycle & Automobile Co, Springfield, Mass.

This four-passenger car with its engine under the body, was built with either 1-, 2- or 3-cylinder power units. The cars had a reach frame, with a non-standard tread (54in) and the body was hinged at the rear for complete access to the mechanism. They were steered by tiller.

WASHINGTON (i) 1909–1911
1 Carter Motor Car Corp, Washington, D.C. 1909–1910
2 Carter Motor Car Corp, Hyattsville, Md. 1910–1911

The Washington had up to five body types, most using 4-cylinder engines. This power unit was water-cooled and had a capacity of 255ci.

A later model with a 286ci engine was a $3,350 limousine. In 1909 a six, the 6-60, was introduced, at $2,750. The company had previously made the Carter Twin Engine car.

WASHINGTON (ii) 1921–1924
Washington Motor Co, Middletown, Ohio; Eaton, Ohio.

The Washington was a conventional assembled car made in touring and sedan versions. Prototypes of 1921 used 196ci Falls engines, but production cars were powered by the 224ci Continental Red Seal 7-R in 1922, and the 241ci Continental Red Seal 8-R in 1923. A steam car was planned for 1924, but only one was completed. Not more than 35 Washingtons were made in all.

1912 WARREN 4-cylinder touring car. *J. Price*
1924 WASP 31hp rickshaw touring car. *Keith Marvin Collection*

WASP 1919–1925
Martin-Wasp Corp, Bennington, Vt.

Karl H. Martin, designer of the Wasp, had been a successful coach-builder and was the designer of the Deering-Magnetic and the Kenworthy cars. Between 1919 and 1925, a total of 18 Wasps were constructed, with sharply pointed fenders and custom-built rickshaw-type bodies, and costing between $5,500 and $10,000. Earlier models were 4-cylinder types with Wisconsin T-head engines; the later cars used a Continental 6 unit. The Wasp was the only car ever built in the United States, and perhaps in the world, which carried a St Christopher medal on its dashboard as standard equipment. This bronze medallion was also fabricated and cast by Martin.

1905 WATROUS 12hp touring car. *Dr Alfred Lewerenz Collection*
1907 POPE-WAVERLEY electric runabout. *Museo dell' Automobile, Turin*

WATT 1910
Watt Motor Co, Detroit, Mich.

The only model of this make was a five-passenger touring car, powered by a 339ci 6-cylinder engine with overhead valves. The price of this car was $1,850.

WAVERLEY 1896–1903; 1908–1916
POPE-WAVERLEY 1903–1907
1 Waverley Co, Indianapolis, Ind. 1896–1901
2 International Motor Car Co, Indianapolis, Ind. 1901–1903
3 Waverley Dept, Pope Motor Car Co, Indianapolis, Ind. 1903–1907
4 Waverley Co, Indianapolis, Ind. 1908–1916

The original Waverley electric was a two-passenger car with tiller steering and a single headlight which sold for $850. During the Pope régime the line of models was expanded to include closed bodies, including a miniature limousine with a wheelbase of only 90in. After the failure of Pope, a large range of cars was marketed, with four different shaft drive models in 1914, and similar in appearance to gasoline cars.

WAYNE (i) 1904–1908
Wayne Automobile Co, Detroit, Mich.

The Wayne line included as many as five models in a single year. These ranged from two-passenger runabouts with 2-cylinder engines, to 50hp cars of 4-cylinders. The smaller cars used planetary transmissions, and the larger models had 3-speed, selective transmissions. This company was absorbed by the E.M.F. Co in 1908.

WAYNE (ii) 1905–1910
Wayne Works, Richmond, Ind.

The earliest model of this make was a 2-cylinder, water-cooled runabout of 16hp. The later models were all powered by 4-cylinder, L-head engines. As late as 1910 one model had a progressive transmission and an air-cooled 4-cylinder engine. The manufacturer also made the Richmond (ii).

WEBB JAY 1908
Webb Jay Motor Co, Chicago, Ill.

This steamer was built as a single model, a five-passenger touring car. Its 2-cylinder engine was a compound type with 3in and 6in diameter cylinders for high and low pressure steam. The stroke was 4in and the boiler operating pressure was 500psi. The car weighed 2,900lb and its price was $4,000.

1909 WELCH Model 4-0 touring car. *Harrah's Automobile Collection*

WATERLOO-DURYEA 1904–1905
Waterloo Motor Works, Waterloo, Iowa

This was nearly identical with the original Duryea and was built under license. Two-passenger phaetons had graceful Empire-inspired lines, peculiar to the Duryea of this period. The Duryea's folding front seat was not used in this car.

WATROUS 1905–1907
Watrous Automobile Co, Elmira, N.Y.

The Watrous was made as either a five-passenger touring, or as a two-passenger runabout. Both were powered by a 12hp 2-cylinder engine, which drove through a planetary transmission. These were small cars, the runabout being on a 89in wheelbase, and priced at only $400. Later this firm confined their efforts to fire engines, Elmira now being the center of this manufacture.

WELCH 1903–1911
1 Chelsea Mfg Co, Chelsea, Mich. 1903–1904
2 Welch Motor Car Co, Pontiac, Mich. 1904–1911
3 Welch Motor Car Co, Detroit, Mich. 1909–1911

The Chelsea Manufacturing Company was a bicycle shop in which the Welch brothers experimented with cars from 1901 to 1903. They showed their Welch Tourist for the first time at the 1903 Chicago Show. It had a 20hp 2-cylinder engine with the advanced features of overhead valves and hemispherical combustion chambers. A few were made at Chelsea before the Welch brothers set up their own factory at Pontiac. Here larger cars were made with 36hp 4-cylinder engines, and later, 6-cylinder engines of up to 75hp. With wheelbases of up to 138in they were among the largest cars of their time, and carried spacious limousine or touring car bodies. The hemispherical combustion chambers and overhead valves were retained, now operated by a single overhead camshaft.

In 1909 a new factory was set up at Detroit to make a smaller 4-cylinder car, known as the Welch-Detroit. A. B. C. Hardy, who had designed the Flint (i), was general manager at the Detroit plant, and in 1911, acting on instructions from General Motors, he removed the machinery from Detroit and Pontiac, and combined with the Rainier plant at Saginaw, Michigan to make the Marquette (i).

WEL-DOER (CDN) 1914
Welker-Doerr Co, Berlin, Ont.

This was one of the few Canadian cyclecars. It had side-by-side seating for two persons. The 2-cylinder, air-cooled engine, was quoted at 9–13hp. Drive was by friction transmission with belts to the rear wheels. Three-quarter elliptical springs were used all around.

WEST & BURGETT 1899
William S. West- C. E. Burgett, Middleburg, N.Y

Although its builders intended to start car production, the West & Burgett 2-cylinder steamer only appeared as a prototype. This wire-wheeled car resembled others of its type.

WESTCOTT 1912–1925
Westcott Motor Car Co, Richmond, Ind.; Springfield, Ohio

The Westcott Motor Co marketed a highly-regarded, assembled car, briefly at Richmond, Ind., and then at Springfield, Ohio. Continental 6-cylinder engines were used exclusively in Westcotts and several thousand units were produced through its years of production, although a peak of 1,850 in 1920 indicates that the cars were never common. Unlike many assembled cars of the period, Westcotts did not necessarily sell only in the area of manufacture, and the care with which they were made commanded a relatively high price through the years. A complete line of body styles was available.

After about 1920, Westcott concentrated on two models of different size (241 and 303ci), but the reputation of the make depended on the larger car. In an unsuccessful attempt to remain active in a market dominated by larger corporations, Westcott introduced 4-wheel brakes and balloon tires as standard equipment for its 1925 line, but that year proved to be the company's last.

WESTFIELD 1902–1903
The C. G. Moore Mfg Co, Westfield, Mass.

This company made running gear and bodies ready to be fitted with engines, and also a few light steam- and gasoline engined complete cars. The steamer had a 6hp 2-cylinder engine, single chain drive and tiller steering, while the gasoline car had a single-cylinder engine.

W.F.S. 1911–1913
W.F.S. Motor Car Co, Philadelphia, Pa.

This obscure make offered at least five body styles, from a runabout to a five-passenger limousine, on a standard chassis. The 280ci, 4-cylinder engine had a drilled crankshaft for positive lubrication. Final drive was by shaft, and the transmission was at the rear axle.

WHARTON 1921–1922
Wharton Motors Co, Dallas, Texas

The Wharton was an ambitious attempt by a Texas firm to market an 8-, a 6- and a 4-cylinder series of private cars in addition to a 4-wheel-drive truck and a tractor. Of its private cars, only a handful of the eights actually got on the road. These were imposing vehicles, using a Curtiss O.X.5 aero engine and with a price range from $3,450 for the tourer to $4,975 for the 'suburban' car. The four was planned to start at $1,450 and the six at $1,750.

WHEELER 1900–1902
Wheeler Automobile Mfg Co, Marlboro, Mass.

The Wheeler light car had a single-cylinder De Dion engine, planetary transmission and shaft drive. Only three were made.

WHIPPET *see* WILLYS

WHITE (i) 1900–1918
1 White Sewing Machine Co, Cleveland, Ohio 1900–1906
2 The White Co, Cleveland, Ohio 1906–1918

Rollin H. White of the Cleveland sewing-machine concern produced his first steamer in 1900. This was a light chain-drive stanhope with tiller steering and a simple 2-cylinder under-floor engine. It had an underslung frontal condenser, and 193 were sold in 1901, the first year of full production. This gave way in 1903 to a model with a front-mounted compound engine under a hood, condenser in the normal 'radiator' position, wheel steering, and shaft drive.

These and subsequent Whites used a semi-flash type of boiler, and could run a hundred miles between fillings of water. Frames were of armored wood, and a tonneau cost $2,000.

The cars did well in early Glidden Tours, and racing versions, such as Webb Jay's Whistling Billy with an underslung frame, were also successful; this car covered a mile at 74.07mph. Theodore Roosevelt used a White during his tenure of the White House. 1905 Whites had a 2-speed back axle, and also a 'free engine' enabling the pumps to work without manual assistance when the car was stationary in traffic. 1906 was the best sales year, with 1,534 cars delivered, but steam-car production was held at over 1,000 a year to the end. By 1908, the company was offering two models, a 20hp Model L at $2,500, and the big seven-passenger Model K with a 122in wheelbase at $3,700. Joy valve motion replaced the Stephenson link type on 1909 cars, which had both sets of brakes working on the rear wheels.

1901 WHITE (i) steam surrey. *Montagu Motor Museum*

1909 WHITE (i) Model O 15hp steam touring car. *G. N. Georgano Collection*
1913 WHITE (i) 30hp gasoline touring car. *Don McCray*

Steamers continued to be listed into 1911, though the 1910 MM and OO were the last new models. For the 1910 season the company offered a 225ci L-head gasoline car with a monobloc engine inspired by the Delahaye; the 4-speed transmission had direct drive in third gear. This was joined in 1912 by a really big six rated at 60hp, and selling for $5,000, still with four forward speeds. Electric lighting and starting were added during the year, and these 4- and 6-cylinder Whites were continued until 1916.

The 1917 models were 16-valve fours of over 326ci displacement, with magneto ignition, selling at $5,000 upwards. By this time the company was firmly established in the truck field, and after 1918 passenger cars were made to special order only, and in very small numbers. The last of these 'specials' was made in 1936.

Rollin White was subsequently responsible for the Rollin car in 1923, while the firm also absorbed two truck-makers who had previously built passenger cars, Autocar and Reo.

WHITE (ii) 1909
George White Buggy Co, Rock Island, Ill.
This was a high-wheel buggy, but the mounting of the engine at the front under a hood gave it more the appearance of an ordinary car than many of its kind. The engine was a 2-cylinder 12/14hp unit which drove via a 2-speed planetary transmission and propeller shaft. Two- and four-passenger bodies were available.

WHITE (iii) 1914
White Mfg Co, Waterloo, Iowa
The White cyclecar used a 9hp ohv V-twin engine, and chain final drive.

WHITE STAR 1908–1910
White Star Co, Atlanta, Ga.
This vehicle was a two-passenger buggy with large diameter wheels and solid rubber tires. The 2-cylinder opposed engine developed 20hp. This was mounted beneath the seat and drove through a planetary transmission and double chains. A larger car with its engine under the hood was also made.

WHITING 1910–1912
1 Flint Motor Wagon Works, Flint, Mich. 1910
2 Whiting Motor Car Co, Flint, Mich. 1911–1912
The Whiting was offered as a 20hp two-passenger car with a 2-speed transmission, and as a 40hp five-passenger car with a 3-speed transmission. Both used 4-cylinder engines. Prices were $775 and $1,600 respectively.

WHITING-GRANT *see* GRANT

WHITNEY (i) 1895–1898
1 G. E. Whitney Motor Wagon Co, Boston, Mass. 1895–1897
2 Whitney Motor Wagon Co, Kittery, Me. 1897–1898
George Whitney spent several years experimenting before a company was formed to make his steam cars, and few were in fact made under the Whitney name. After the Stanley brothers had sold their patents to Locomobile and Mobile, they began to make cars of Whitney pattern under the name Stanley-Whitney or McKay (from McKay sewing machines, a company owned by Frank E. Stanley). The original Whitney was a very high, tiller-steered buggy powered by a 2-cylinder vertical engine, and using a fully automatic boiler.

WHITNEY (ii) 1899–1905
Whitney Machine Co, Brunswick, Me.
R. S. Whitney made only three cars during his six-year manufacturing period. The first two were conventional 2-cylinder steamers, a two-passenger runabout and a four-passenger surrey, but the last model, in 1905, showed some originality in having a front-mounted boiler and integral construction of body and chassis.

WICHITA 1914
Wichita Falls Motor Co, Wichita Falls, Tex.
This 2-cylinder cyclecar used belt drive, and the front axle pivoted for steering. It was a tandem two-passenger car with a track of 36in. Unusual features were bicycle fenders for the front wheels, and a half steering wheel to allow clearance for the driver.

WICK 1902–1903
The Wick Co, Youngstown, Ohio
The Wick was a large, expensive car with a 30hp 4-cylinder engine of 340ci displacement. It carried coachwork by Quimby, one of America's finest coach-builders, and was priced at $8,000.

WILCOX *see* WOLFE

WILLIAMS (i) 1905
W. L. Casaday Mfg Co, South Bend, Ind.
The Williams was a cleanly designed five-passenger car with an air-cooled flat 4-cylinder engine of 25hp. The hood was circular in cross-

section and the same diameter (36in) as the tires, a spare being mounted on the front. This car had an early example of a permanent windshield.

WILLIAMS (ii) *see* DE MARS

WILLIAMS (iii) 1957–1968
Williams Engine Co, Inc, Ambler, Pa.

Calvin C. Williams and his twin sons began experimenting with steam cars in 1940, and by 1957 were advertising that they would build complete cars, or convert gasoline autos to steam power. At least one original car was built, using a flash boiler, 4-cylinder single-acting engine and fiberglass body. In 1966 they were offering a steam converted Chevrolet Chevelle for $10,250, and received orders for nine of these, together with one for a Ford Fairlane from the Ford Motor Company. However difficulties in obtaining small quantities of components at reasonable prices delayed the project, and rather than raise extra capital the Williams closed their business in late 1968.

WILLS SAINTE CLAIRE 1921–1927
Wills Sainte Claire Co, Marysville, Mich.

The Wills Sainte Claire, named after its devisor, Childe Harold Wills, who had helped to develop the Ford Model T, and Lake Sainte Claire near his factory, was a beautifully made luxury car. From 1921 to 1924, it had a V-8 engine of 265ci, with the advanced feature of two overhead camshafts (one to each bank of cylinders). In spite of this, it produced a modest 67bhp at 2,800rpm. However, considering the car's quality and specification, $2,475 in 1923 was not a high price. Such a figure was only possible with production of the order of 1,500 a year, which Wills Sainte Claire attained in 1923. In 1925, a long-stroke ohc engine, with 6 cylinders in line, replaced the V-8, and this model remained in production, with slight changes, until 1927.

WILLYS 1909; 1916–1918; 1930–1963
including **OVERLAND** 1903–1929; 1939 and **WILLYS-KNIGHT** 1914–1932
1 Standard Wheel Co, Terre Haute, Ind. 1903–1905
2 Overland Co, Indianapolis, Ind. 1905–1907
3 Willys-Overland Co, Toledo, Ohio 1908–1963

These makes are inseparable, if only because of their confusing nomenclature. The original product of the Standard Wheel Co was a tiller-steered single-cylinder runabout with solid tires which differed from most of its contemporaries in having its engine mounted in front under a real hood. It sold for $595. This had grown up by 1905 into a wheel-steered 77ci twin, still with planetary transmission, and the company changed its style and moved to Indianapolis. Financial difficulties in 1907 brought John North Willys, an Elmira, N.Y., automobile dealer into the picture, and under his ownership a $1,250 4-cylinder model was produced, this having a pedal-controlled planetary transmission in the Ford manner, separately-cast cylinders, and a transaxle. There were two sixes in 1909, an Overland at $2,000, and the 45hp Willys costing $250 more. Both the Willys name and multi-cylinder engines disappeared in 1910, and production of 4-cylinder cars was concentrated in the old Pope factory at Toledo. During these years Willys continued to distribute the Marion, for which he had held an agency in the Elmira days. High-tension magneto ignition was used on the 1912 Overlands, which included a 199ci 2-speed Model 58 at $850, a 3-speed version (Model 59) with conventional transmission at $900, and two bigger fours at $1,200 and $1,500 respectively. By 1914 Overland had moved into the ranks of the best-sellers with the 79 series at $950, a 241ci car which helped to sell 80,000 that year. New also was the Willys-Knight with Knight double sleeve-valve 4-cylinder engine: this was in fact the former Edwards-Knight, which concern Willys had acquired, and early production was undertaken for Willys-Overland by Garford of Elyria, hitherto associated with the manufacture of cars for sale by Studebaker. In 1915 there was an Overland 6 at $1,145, with the group moving up into second place behind Ford in the sales race. Willys-Knight, still a young make, was

1925 WILLS SAINTE CLAIRE Six sedan. *Automobile Manufacturers' Association*
1906 OVERLAND Model 22 8hp roadster. *Kaiser-Jeep Corporation*

1926 OVERLAND Whippet touring car. *G. N. Georgano Collection*

1933 WILLYS 77 coupé. *Kaiser-Jeep Corporation*
1942 WILLYS Americar coupé. *Kaiser-Jeep Corporation*

placed eighteenth: and in 1916 a second Willys 6, with 303ci engine, joined the range, to remain there for three seasons. Willys-Knight had a V-8 on a 125in wheelbase for $1,950 in 1917, but in 1919 fours only were being made, the classic L-head Overland having made its appearance at the low price of $495. The 4-cylinder Willys-Knights had 240ci engines and sold around the $1,400 mark.

In 1920 Willys Overland Crossley Ltd was formed in England with

1949 WILLYS Jeepster touring car. *Kaiser-Jeep Corporation*

works at Stockport: this was a subsidiary of Crossley Motors Ltd, and assembled cars for the British market. It originated nothing save a 1924 version of the Overland powered by a 110ci Morris-Oxford engine. Overlands continued to sell well in America, the Model-92 'Redbird' appearing in 1923 and helping to push the year's sales up to 196,000. Sixes were back in the program for 1925, the Overland being a straight-forward 170ci L-head machine selling for $895, while Willys-Knight's Model-66 had a 66bhp 237ci unit and fwb, and cost $1,845. It supplanted the sleeve-valve fours the following year, and 1926 also saw the first of Overland's 154ci 4-cylinder 'Whippet' series, priced at $625: these repeated the success of the 1919 type. 'Whippets' had fwb in 1927, in which year a companion 170ci six was listed, as well as a smaller and cheaper Model-70 Willys-Knight. This could be bought for only $1,145 in 1928 — a record year both for the group and for the Knight-engined machines, which found 55,000 customers. Other Willys-Overland products during this period were the Stearns-Knight and Falcon-Knight. The 'Whippet' was restyled for 1929, and the Willys range was now headed by a handsome Willys-Knight Great Six; this competed with the bigger Chryslers at $1,850. In 1930 the Willys name was once again seen on a 193ci six and 245ci straight-8, both with L-heads: the former was made in small-bore 146ci 'Palatine' form for the British market. The 'Whippet' was now a Willys rather than an Overland, and in 1931 the 4-cylinder cars were dropped. Sales also slumped, and the sleeve-valve Willys-Knights were allowed to die out with the 87bhp Model-66E of 1932. From 1933 to 1936 the company struggled through a receivership, making only a 134ci L-head four, the Model 77, with some pretensions to aerodynamic shape and a low price of $445, but this was brought up to date in 1937 with new styling and synchromesh. It acquired hydraulic brakes in 1939, reverting briefly to the name of Overland: both name and styling were different again by 1941, when it went under the designation 'Willys-Americar', with roomier bodywork, hypoid final drive, and a list price of $705.

During World War 2, Willys-Overland, along with Ford, were responsible for series production of the famous 4 × 4 Bantam inspired 'Jeep', and Willys continued its manufacture to civilian account after the war, licenses being sold to Hotchkiss in France and Mitsubishi in Japan among others. Station wagon and sports four-passenger versions with 2-wheel drive and 6-cylinder engines were added to the range. It was not until 1952, however, that the company again offered orthodox passenger cars, these being fairly small vehicles with either the well-established four- or a 161ci F-head six, unitary construction, and coil-and-wishbone ifs, selling in the region of $1,750. An L-head six was available in 1953, when 4-door sedans were offered alongside the 2-door type. That year also brought the purchase of the company by Kaiser, and the 'Aero' line was dropped for 1956, though development and production have continued in the Willys-Overland do Brasil factory at São Paulo. Activities at Toledo have centered round the 'Jeep' family. The firm's name was changed to Kaiser-Jeep Corporation in 1963. For subsequent products, see Jeep.

WINDSOR 1906
Windsor Automobile Co, Evansville, Ind.

The only model of this make was a five-passenger touring car priced at $2,500. This car used a 6-cylinder, 30hp engine driving through a friction transmission with shaft drive to the rear axle. This later became the Simplicity made by Evansville Automobile Co.

WINDSOR STEAM CAR *see* DETROIT STEAM CAR

WING MIDGET 1922
H. C. Wing & Sons, Greenfield, Mass.

The Wing Midget was a miniature one-passenger car with the appearance of a scaled-down racing car of an earlier era. It had outside exhausts and double chain drive, and was advertised as being capable of 80mph, and 40 to 50mpg, though not, presumably at the same time.

WINNER 1907
Winner Motor Buggy Co, St Louis, Mo.

The Winner was a typical high-wheel buggy with tiller steering. At $300 it was one of the cheapest ever made.

WINNIPEG (CDN) 1921
Winnipeg Motor Cars Ltd, Winnipeg, Man.

'As Good as the Wheat' was the slogan of this car, which had a 4-cylinder Herschell-Spillman engine and a radiator guaranteed not to burst even if it froze in the bitter Prairie winter.

WINTHER 1920–1923
Winther Motor, Inc, Division of Winther Motor Truck Co, Kenosha, Wis.

A short-lived car produced by a truck concern, the Winther used a 6-cylinder Herschell-Spillman engine and did not differ much from other assembled cars, either in appearance or design. Probably less than 500 passenger cars were built in the four years of manufacture.

1923 WINTON Model 40 34hp touring car. *Keith Marvin Collection*

1922 WING MIDGET roadster. *Keith Marvin Collection*
1904 WINTON 30hp touring car. *G. N. Georgano Collection*

WINTON 1897–1924
Winton Motor Carriage Co, Cleveland, Ohio

Alexander Winton, a Cleveland bicycle maker, built a 12hp twin-cylinder experimental car in 1897, which recorded 33.7mph over a mile. He produced his first vehicle for commercial sale the following year; this was a two-passenger phaeton with a horizontal single-cylinder engine, 2-speed transmission, and laminated wood frame, listed at $1,000; 25 cars were sold in the first season, early customers including the Packard brothers.

The first of the Gordon Bennett Cup races in 1900 stemmed from a challenge issued by Winton to Fernand Charron, and the designer himself took part on a Benz-like vehicle with an enormous single cylinder of 233ci displacement, said to produce 14bhp. It failed to make any impression, but by 1901 Winton was producing a large horizontal-twin with its 2-speed transmission mounted under the floor and alongside the engine. The hood was devoted to tankage, wheel steering was provided, and 40bhp was claimed. A Winton characteristic, which persisted for several years, was a variable-lift inlet valve actuated by compressed air, a medium to which Alexander Winton was addicted. A 15hp touring car on similar lines, with central chain drive, sold for $2,000 in 1902, increased to $2,500 in 1903, when nominal output went up to 20hp. One of these cars was used for Jackson's successful trans-Continental run; also in 1903 Winton made another bid for international racing laurels with his two Bullets. Both of these had in-line engines lying on their sides in the frame, and the inevitable pneumatic governor. Percy Owen's Gordon Bennett car was a 472ci four, but Winton himself drove an 80bhp eight of 943ci displacement, and with only a single forward speed. Both cars retired, though the Bullets later did fairly well in American sprint events.

Vertical 4-cylinder engines and conventionally-located transmissions were the order of the day in 1905, and ht magneto ignition was also used, but two forward speeds were still deemed sufficient. Three types were marketed, ratings being 16, 24, and 40hp. The 354ci Model K of 1906 retained the 2-speed transmission. Sliding-type transmissions were found in Winton's 1907 offering, the 35hp 4-cylinder Model M, which had four speeds with direct drive in third, and the 477ci Model Six-Teen-Six of 1908, which was a 3-speed model. Two sixes were sold in 1909, the larger of the two having a displacement of over 580ci and a wheelbase of 130in. It cost $4,500, and Winton offered a compressed-air starter; by 1911 this was being used to pump up the tires as well. Thereafter pair-cast sixes were standard and electric starting was adopted finally in 1915. No major changes occurred after 1920, when the earlier types gave way to the 348ci Series 25 with a 4-speed transmission.

Winton elected to abandon car manufacture in 1924 in favor of marine diesel engines, and the company is still active in this field as a division of General Motors.

WISCO 1910
Wisconsin Motor Car Co, Janesville, Wis.

The Wisco chassis had a 285ci 4-cylinder engine, with 3-speed selective transmission, on a wheelbase of 118in. Body styles were a four-passenger tonneau and a five-passenger touring car.

WIZARD 1921–1922
Wizard Automobile Co, Charlotte, N.C.

The Wizard was more of a plan than a reality, although probably a few cars were actually produced. The Wizard Jr was a small roadster selling at $395, equipped with artillery wheels and planetary transmission, and powered by a 2-cylinder air-cooled V-type ohv engine. A planned 4-cylinder series failed to materialize.

WOLFE 1907–1909
H. E. Wilcox Motor Car Co, Minneapolis, Minn.

The Wolfe was a five-passenger car on a 108in wheelbase. Continental water-cooled or Carrico 4-cylinder air-cooled engines were used. These were of 201ci displacement and had overhead valves. The drive was by 3-speed selective transmission and double chains to the rear wheels. The car weighed 1,950lb and sold for $1,800. The company continued to build water-cooled cars under the name Wilcox until 1912, and trucks until 1928.

WOLVERINE (i) 1904–1906
1 Reid Mfg Co, Detroit, Mich. 1904–1905
2 Wolverine Automobile & Commercial Vehicle Co, Dundee, Mich. 1905–1906

The Wolverine used 2-cycle, 2-cylinder engines of 10hp and 15hp. It was produced as a four-passenger tonneau and a two-passenger runabout. This make was superseded by the Craig-Toledo.

1907 WOLFE Model D 30hp touring car. *Clarion Larson*
1927 WOLVERINE (iii) 25hp sedan. *Autocar*

WOLVERINE (ii) (WOLVERINE SPECIAL) 1917–1920
Wolverine Motors, Inc, Kalamazoo, Mich.

Announced in September 1917, the Wolverine was built in a single speedster model. A large amount of aluminum was used in its construction. It had a Rochester-Duesenberg 4-cylinder engine and a speed of 75mph was guaranteed. The Wolverine was equipped with wire wheels, a pointed radiator, bicycle fenders, step plates and a large 30 gallon gasoline tank to the rear of the seat, as on the Stutz Bearcat. Its price was $3,000.

WOLVERINE (iii) 1927–1928
Reo Motor Car Co, Lansing, Mich.

This Wolverine was in fact a smaller companion car to Reo's Flying Cloud models of 1927 and 1928, but was marketed as a make of its own and carried its individual radiator and hub-cap insignia. Introduced in April 1927, the car had a Continental 6-cylinder engine and artillery spoke wheels, and differed from the Flying Cloud in the grouping of its horizontal hood louvres. A 2-door and 4-door sedan and a two/four-passenger cabriolet constituted the line, with prices ranging from $1,195, to $1,295.

WONDER 1917
Wonder Motor Truck Co, Chicago, Ill.

This truck company made a touring car with a 22hp 4-cylinder engine, for one season only. It was of conventional design and cost $800.

1956 WOODILL WILDFIRE coupé. *Woodill Fibreglass Body Corporation*

WOOD 1902–1903
Wood Vapor Vehicle Co, Brooklyn, N.Y.

The Wood was a light two-passenger steam car powered by an 8hp 3-cylinder engine. A horizontal water-tube boiler was slung beneath the frame, and the price was $450, making it one of the cheapest steamers ever produced.

WOODILL WILDFIRE c.1952–1958
Woodill Fiberglass Body Corp, Tustin, Calif.

The Wildfire was a sports car with a two-passenger fiberglass body mounted on Willys running gear. The choice of power unit included Willys 90hp, Cadillac 300hp, and Ford V-8 engines. A Brushfire model was built for children (ages 6–12) and was equipped with a single-cylinder 3hp engine with one forward speed. The body design was the same as the Wildfire but scaled down to a 63in wheelbase.

WOOD-LOCO 1901–1902
Wood-Loco Vehicle Co, Cohoes, N.Y.

Powered by a 2-cylinder horizontal 8hp steam engine, the Wood-Loco was available as a passenger car of buggy type, as a delivery van and as a ten-passenger commercial vehicle. Very few Wood-Locos were built.

WOODRUFF 1904
Woodruff Automobile Co, Akron, Ohio

The Woodruff was not an attractive car, as it had a peculiar sloping hood. It had a 3-cylinder engine, and a 3-speed transmission with shaft-drive.

WOODS 1899–1919
Woods Motor Vehicle Co, Chicago, Ill.

The Woods Electric was one of the longest-lived American electric makes, although its sales never reached those of the Detroit, Baker or Milburn. The usual range of town cars was made, including a hansom cab, powered by a single 3hp motor mounted on the rear axle. In 1903 a four-passenger tonneau was made complete with hood which made it look exactly like a gasoline car. Woods Electrics were expensive, with prices up to $4,500. The most interesting Woods was the Dual Power of

1914 WOODS Model 1334 electric brougham. *The Veteran Car Club of Great Britain*

1917 WOODS Dual Power 12hp coupé. *Henry Ford Museum, Dearborn, Mich.*

1915 WOODS MOBILETTE 12/14hp cyclecar. *Kenneth Stauffer*

1917 onwards. This had a 12hp 4-cylinder Continental gasoline engine as an auxiliary to the electric motor. Maximum speed was 20mph with the electric motor alone, or 35mph with both engines.

WOODS MOBILETTE 1914–1916
Woods Mobilette Co, Harvey, Ill.

The first prototype of the Woods Mobilette appeared in 1910, but production did not start until early 1914. It was a two-passenger cyclecar with 12/14hp 4-cylinder engine and tandem seating. Although the prototypes were air-cooled, all production Mobilettes used water-cooled engines. Staggered side-by-side seating appeared on 1916 models, with electric lighting and starting as optional extras. These were standardized on the models announced for 1917, but production did not continue beyond the end of 1916.

WORLDMOBILE 1928
Service-Relay Motors Corp, Lima, Ohio

The Worldmobile was a large six-passenger sedan powered by a 276ci L-head Lycoming straight-8 engine. Service-Relay were truck builders and intended to put the Worldmobile into production, but only seven were made. One survives in Harrah's Automobile Collection.

WORTH 1909–1910
Worth Motor Car Mfg Co, Kankakee, Ill.

This was a high-wheeler with a false hood and the engine beneath the body. The only model, a two- or four-passenger car, had an air-cooled, 2-cylinder engine. The drive was through a friction transmission and double chains to the rear wheels. The gross weight was 1,400lb.

WORTHINGTON BOLLÉE 1904
Worthington Automobile Co, New York, N.Y.

This was a slightly modified 24/32hp 4-cylinder Léon Bollée from France sold by the Worthington Company. In 1905 the company merged with the Berg Automobile Company, of Cleveland.

WRIGHT (CDN) 1929
Montreal, Que.

The rakish Wright Flexible Axle car was a final attempt to base a car on the excellent Wright-Fisher independent suspension system. It was built by Benjamin Wright, formerly of Wright-Fisher, whose suspension was used in the U.S. Birmingham, which was related to the Montreal-built Parker. Production believed limited to one touring car, which performed well but never had a chance.

X & Y

1914 XENIA 13hp cyclecar. *The Veteran Car Club of Great Britain*

1905 YALE (i) 24/28hp touring car. *Keith Marvin Collection*
1905 YORK 18/20hp touring car. *Floyd Clymer Publications*

XENIA 1914–1915
Hawkins Cyclecar Co, Xenia, Ohio
This two-passenger cyclecar was for a short time called the Acme or Hawkins. It had a V-twin air-cooled engine of 9/13hp. A 2-speed transmission with belt drive was used.

YALE (i) 1903–1907
1 Kirk Mfg Co, Toledo, Ohio 1903
2 Consolidated Mfg Co, Ohio 1903–1907
One model of the Yale, with a single-cylinder engine, remained virtually unchanged through the life of the make. There was also a 2-cylinder car, while a larger model, a five-passenger touring car, used a 4-cylinder engine of 24/28hp. The advertising slogan of the Yale was 'The Beau Brummell of the Road'.

YALE (ii) 1916–1918
Saginaw Motor Car Co, Saginaw, Mich.
The Yale appeared as an ivory and black seven-passenger touring model and roadster. It had a V-8 engine of 276ci, with a 3-speed transmission.

YANK 1950
Custom Auto Works, San Diego, Calif.
The Yank was an assembled sports car using a 4-cylinder Willys engine and an aluminum two-passenger body. A maximum speed of 78mph was claimed.

YANKEE 1910
Yankee Motor Car Co, Chicago, Ill.
The Yankee was built as a high-wheeler with solid-rubber tires, and as a two-passenger Racy Roadster model with pneumatic tires. Both were powered by a 2-cylinder air-cooled engine, and both used a planetary transmission.

YENKO 1965–1969
Yenko Sportscars, Cannonsburg, Pa.
The Yenko Stinger was a Chevrolet Corvair Corsa 2-door coupé modified by Don Yenko for club racing. The normal 164ci engine was bored out to 168 or 176ci and various stages of tune were available. Jerry Thompson won the 1967 SCCA 'D' class production national championship in a Stinger. A total of 185 were made.

YORK 1905–1907
York Automobile Co, York, Pa.
The initial York model was a five-passenger surrey, with very curving lines. It was powered by a 4-cylinder engine of 18/20hp, and had shaft drive. It is possible that this make may have been made as late as 1909.

Z

ZENT 1902–1907
1 Zent Automobile Mfg Co, Bellefontaine, Ohio 1902–1907
2 Bellefontaine Automobile Co, Bellefontaine, Ohio 1907

The Zent was built in two- and five-passenger models, with 2-, 3-, and 4-cylinder engines. The transmissions were of the planetary type, and the later models at least used shaft drive. The Zent was succeeded by the Bellefontaine.

ZIEBEL 1914–1915
A. C. Ziebel, Oshkosh, Wis.

The Ziebel cyclecar had two-passenger side-by-side seating. It was driven by a 4-cylinder, water-cooled Badger engine. Wheelbase was 96in with tread of 42in.

ZIMMERMAN 1908–1914
Zimmerman Mfg Co, Auburn, Ind.

The original model of this make was a high-wheeler with solid rubber tires and a 12hp engine. In 1910, standard cars replaced the high-wheelers. The 1910 cars used 4-cylinder engines of 270ci. The first 6-cylinder model was the Z-6 of 1912 with a 331ci engine. During the last four years of manufacture, 4-cylinder engines were also used. In 1911 the company had been bought by Auburn.

ZIP 1913–1914
Zip Cyclecar Co, Davenport, Iowa

1909 ZIMMERMAN 12hp motor buggy. *Eugene Zimmerman*

The Zip cyclecar carried two passengers, side by side. Its V-twin air-cooled engine delivered 10/14hp. A 6-bladed fan provided cooling. Friction transmission and belt drive were used. With sporting wire wheels, this cyclecar cost $395.

GLOSSARY

A guide to the more frequently used technical and general terms which may not be familiar to the present day reader. No attempt has been made to give a complete glossary of the automobile.

The definitions of body styles are very general, as there have been few standard definitions laid down, and these few have been frequently ignored by automobile makers and coachbuilders.

ALAM formula rating – *see* horsepower.

Automatic inlet valves (aiv). Inlet valves opened atmospherically, without any mechanical control. A primitive system, soon replaced by mechanical actuation (moiv).

Avant-train. A two-wheeled power unit consisting of engine, transmission, final drive, steering wheel and other controls, which could be attached to a horsedrawn vehicle, or to enable various bodies to be used with the same engine. *Avant-train* units were the earliest examples of front wheel drive, but were outmoded soon after 1900. Electric as well as gasoline engines were used.

Belt drive. A system whereby the final drive is conveyed from countershaft to rear axle by leather belts

bhp – *see* horsepower.

Cardan (shaft). The drive shaft which conveys power from transmission to rear axle. More usually known as the propeller shaft, the word was widely used in France (*transmission à cardan*) in early days to distinguish shaft drive from chain drive. The principle is said to have been invented by the Italian philosopher, Girolamo Cardano (1501–1576).

Chain drive. A system whereby the final drive is conveyed from countershaft to the wheels by chains. Double chain drive was widely used on powerful cars until about 1908, but could still be found on some old fashioned machines as late as 1914. A number of light cars used centrally-mounted single chain drive to a live axle.

Convertible (orig. convertible sedan or convertible coupé). Any car with folding roof and wind up windows, the term dates only from the early 1930s. In the 1950s the term 'hard top convertible' came into use, meaning a style resembling a convertible, but whose roof could not, in fact, be folded.

Coupé de ville – *see* Town Car.

Cyclecar. A simple light car whose design owed much to motorcycle practice, of which a large variety were made from 1912 until about 1922. The typical cyclecar had an engine of less than four cylinders, often air-cooled, with final drive by belts or chains.

De Dion axle. A system of final drive in which the rear axle is 'dead', or separate from the drive shafts. The drive is transmitted by independent, universally-jointed half shafts. The system was first used on the French De Dion-Bouton steamers of the 1890s, but was abandoned by the firm after 1914. It is, however, used on a number of modern sports cars.

Dos-à-dos. A four-passenger car in which the passengers sat back to back.

Fast and loose pulleys. A system of transmission in which the countershaft carried a loose pulley for neutral, and two fixed pulleys meshing with spur gears of different ratios on the axle. Moving a belt from loose to fixed pulley provided a clutch action.

F-head. Cylinder head design incorporating overhead inlet and side exhaust valves. Also known as inlet over exhaust, or ioe. *See also* L-head, T-head.

Friction transmission. A system of transmission using two discs in contact at right angles. Variation in gear ratio was obtained by sliding the edge of one disc across the face of the other. This theoretically provided an infinitely variable ratio, although in some systems there were a limited number of positions for the sliding disc.

High-wheeler. A simple automobile with the appearance of a motorized buggy which enjoyed a brief period of popularity in the United States and Canada, between 1907 and 1912. Over 70 firms built high-wheelers, the best-known being Holsman, International and Sears.

Horsepower (hp, bhp). The unit for measuring the power of the engine, defined mechanically as 33,000 foot-pounds per minute. Up to about 1910 the horsepower quoted by makers was meant to correspond to the actual output, though often used with more optimism than accuracy. Sometimes a double figure would be quoted such as 10/12 or 24/30; here the first figure represented the power developed at 1,000rpm, while the second was the power developed at the engine's maximum speed. In 1904 the Automobile Club of Great Britain & Ireland's rating (the RAC rating from 1907 onwards) of horsepower was introduced, calculated on the bore of the engine only, and as engine efficiency improved, the discrepancy between rated and actual horsepower grew. The American ALAM (later NACC) horsepower rating followed the

English system of calculation on the cylinder bore alone. Today horsepower rating has largely been abandoned; engine capacity is indicated in cubic inches (ci), and power in developed or brake horsepower (bhp).

Hot-tube ignition. An early system in which the mixture was ignited by a small platinum tube, open at its inner end, which was screwed into the cylinder head. The outer, closed end was heated to red heat by a small, gasoline-fed burner, and when the mixture passed into the tube, it ignited. The system was outdated by 1900, though some firms continued to fit tubes as an auxiliary to electric ignition.

Inlet over exhaust valves – *see* F-head.

Landau. A body style with a folding roof in two parts, so that it could be half open at front or back, or entirely open. The term was used for horsedrawn carriages, but seldom applied to automobiles.

Landaulet (or landaulette). A closed car, the rear portion of which could be opened in fine weather.

L-head. Cylinder head design in which inlet and exhaust valves are mounted on one side of the engine. It was the most commonly used design for all but high performance engines, from about 1910 until after World War 2. Also known as side valves (sv). *See* T-head.

Limousine. A closed car with glass division between driver and the passenger compartment.

Live axle. An axle which transmits power, as opposed to a dead axle, where the power is either carried by separate half shafts (*see* De Dion axle) or by side chains.

Mechanically operated inlet valves (moiv) – *see* automatic inlet valves.

Monocar. One-passenger car. The expression is never used for race cars, most of which have been one-passenger since the late 1920s, but refers to the ultra-light one-passenger cyclecars of the 1912 to 1915 period.

Motor buggy – *see* high-wheeler.

Overhead valve. Cylinder head design in which the valves are mounted above the combustion chamber, either horizontally, or inclined at an angle. Generally abbreviated to ohv.

Over-square. An engine in which the cylinder bore is greater than the stroke (e.g. $5\frac{1}{4}$in × 5in). A 'square' engine is one in which bore and stroke are identical (e.g. 5in × 5in).

Phaeton. An early word for an open car, especially used in the term 'double phaeton', meaning a four- or five-passenger car. One with three rows of seats was a triple phaeton. The term was also applied to some American four-door convertible sedans of the 1920s and 1930s. *See also* Roi des Belges.

Planetary transmission. A form of gear in which small pinions (planetary pinions) revolve around a central, or sun gear, and mesh with an outer ring gear, or annulus. Best known for their use in the Ford Model T, planetary transmissions were found in a wide variety of early American cars.

Roadster. A two-passenger open car of sporting appearance.

Roi des Belges. A luxurious style of open touring car, named after King Leopold II of Belgium. The style is said to have been suggested to the King by his mistress Cléo de Mérode. The style was sometimes known as the Tulip Phaeton.

Rotary valves. Valves contained in the cylinder head whose rotary motion allows the passage of mixture and exhaust gases at the appropriate times.

Rumble seat. A folding seat for two passengers, used to increase the carrying capacity of a standard two-passenger car.

Runabout. A general term for a light two-passenger car of the early 1900s.

Sedan. A closed car for four or more passengers, with either two or four doors. Sports sedan is a loose term for a high performance version, generally with only two doors.

Sedanca de ville – *see* Town Car.

Selective transmission. The conventional transmission in which any gear may be selected at will, in distinction to the earlier progressive transmission in which the gears had to be selected in order.

Side valves. Cylinder head design in which the valves are mounted at the side of the combustion chamber. They may be side-by-side (L-head), or on opposite sides of the engine (T-head). The usual abbreviation, sv, applies to the L-head design, the rarer T-head design being specifically mentioned.

Sleeve valves. Metal sleeves placed between the piston and the cylinder wall. When moved up and down, holes in them coincide to provide passage for gases at the correct times.

'Square' engine – *see* over-square.

Supercharger (colloquially, 'blower'). A compressor fitted to an engine to force the mixture into the cylinders at a pressure greater than that of the atmosphere. First seen on the 1908 Chadwick, the supercharger was widely used on sports and racing cars between the wars, and on Formula 1 racing cars up to 1954.

Surrey. An open four-passenger car, often with a fringed top.

T-head. Cylinder head design in which inlet valves are mounted on one side of the engine, and exhaust valves on the other. Two camshafts were needed, and in order to make do with only one, the side by side or L-head design was developed, and the T-head was outmoded after about 1910.

Tonneau. Strictly speaking, a four-passenger car in which access to the rear seats was by a door at the rear of the body. This layout was used up to about 1904, after which longer wheelbases enabled doors to be mounted at the sides. This design was sometimes called the side entrance tonneau, but in this book we are calling all side entrance open cars, touring cars.

Torpedo (or **torpedo tourer**). An open touring car with an unbroken line from hood to windshield, and from windshield right through to the back of the car, the seats being flush with the body sides. Bodies of this design began to appear in about 1910, and by 1920 were taken for granted, so the name torpedo was usually dropped in favor of touring car.

Touring car. An open car with seats for four or more passengers. Early touring cars had no weather protection at the sides, later ones being provided with detachable side-screens and curtains. Those with wind-up or fixed windows were more often called all-weather touring cars. After about 1930 the mass produced closed car replaced the open car as the most popular type, and the average manufacturer soon abandoned the production of such cars.

Town Car. A body style in which the passenger compartment was closed, but the driver was exposed to the weather, although from the 1920s onward a sliding roof was often provided. The sedanca de ville was a similar style, although often with four windows in the passenger compartment, whereas the coupé de ville had two windows and closed panels with imitation hood irons. Some town car bodies had folding rear quarters, as in the landaulette.

Trembler coil ignition. Ignition by induction coil and electro-magnetic vibrator which broke the primary circuit and induced the high tension current in the secondary windings. Used by Benz and many other pioneers, but superseded by the De Dion-Bouton patent contact breaker, invented by Georges Bouton in 1895.

Victoria. A two-seater open car, often with a large, folding top.

Vis-à-vis. A four-passenger car in which two passengers sat facing the driver.

Waggonette. A large car usually for six or more passengers, in which the rear seats faced each other. Entrance was at the rear, and the vehicles were usually open.

INDEX

Italic figures refer to captions

A.C. Cars Ltd, 80
Adams, 98
Advanced Motors, 170
Aerojet (engines), 152
Air-Cooled Motors Corp, 83
Alfa Romeo (engines), 29, 74
Alfonso XIII, King of Spain, 66, 170
Allard (cars), 35, 44, 118
Amco (engines), 17
American & British Mfg Co (engines), 45
  104, 143, 200
American Hardware Corp, 50
American Wire Wheel Co, 173
Andrews, Archie M., 175
Anglada, Joseph A., 117
Anglo-American Rapid Vehicle Co, 155
Ansted (engines), 67, 117, 163
Apperson, Edgar, 20, 95, 96
Apperson, Elmer, 20, 95, 96
Apple (ignition), 49
Arden, Elizabeth, 66
Arrol-Johnston, 60
Association of Licenced Automobile
  Manufacturers (A.L.A.M.), 79
Astor (taxicabs), 56
Atalanta (cars), 118
Atlas Engine Co, 122
Audi (cars), 171
Austin (cars), 77, 101, 132, 141
Automotive Corp of America, 57, 143
Auto Union (cars), 134

Babcock, F. A., 24
Badger (engine), 213
Bailey, S. E., 112
Bailey (transmission), 20
Baker, H. O., 24
Ball, C. A., 25
Banner Buggy, 87
Barber, A. L., 119, 135, 185
Barley, Albert C., 172
Bastien, Paul, 192
Bauer, Jack, 104
Beach, Eugene, 26
Beaver (engines), 37, 47, 85, 105, 122, 143
Bela Body Co, 194
Belcher Engineering Co., 27
Bendix (brakes), 57
Bennett, F. S., 35
Bergere, Cliff, 191
Bertone (bodies), 21, 190
Biddle & Smart (coachbuilders), 45
Birdsall, W. H., 32

Bijou (cars), 155
Bissell, Dr., 105
Bizzarrini (cars), 42
Bizzarrini, Giotto, 18
Bohman & Schwartz (coachbuilders), 65
Bosch (ignition), 24
Bourassa, H. E., 29
Bournonville, Eugene, 174
Bramwell, W. C., 30
Breese, S. S., 29
Brewster (coachbuilders), 30–31, 162, 173,
  173, 182
Briggs-Stratton (engines), 25, 57, 61, 181
Brighton Beach races, 151, 182
Brightwood Mfg Co, 147
Brill Company, 88
Briscoe, Benjamin, 21, 31, 127
Briscoe, Frank, 21, 32
Bristol (cars), 44
Bristol (chassis), 21
Bristol (engines), 21
British Ensign (cars), 148
British Motor Syndicate, 155
Broesel, Herman, 182
Brooklands Motor Course, 89
Brough Superior (cars), 101, 118
Brown & Lipe (transmissions), 82
Brownell (engines), 27, 171
Brush, Alanson P., 32, 144
Buda (engines), 21, 27, 28, 94, 114, 116, 128,
  159, 196
Budd (bodies), 62, 175
Buehrig, Gordon, 50, 194
Buffalo (engines), 55
Bugatti, Ettore, 134
Buick (brakes), 29
Buick (engines), 19, 106
Burman, Bob, 33, 133
Burnell (kerosene burner), 26
Burns, W. R., 39
Burr, Richard, 190

Cadillac (engines), 22, 55, 57, 78, 131, 139,
  210
Caldwell, Ray, 22
Cameron, E. S., 51
Canadian Top & Body Co, 85
Cantlon, Shorty, 134
Carling's Brewery, 154
Carlton (coachbuilders), *159*
Carnes, Bob, 29
Carpenter, Miles H., 126
Carrell, Joseph C., 112

Carrera Panamericana, 118
Carrico (engines), 120, 210
Caufflel (engines), 163
Chadwick, L. S., 179
Chalmers, Hugh, 39
Champion (transmission), 186
Chandler, Frederick C., 121
Chapin, Roy D., 39, 101
Chapman, W. H., 40
Charron, Fernand, 209
Chapudy Auto Coach (bodies), 25
Chevrolet (engines), 23, 29, 41, 50, 75, 78
Chevrolet, Louis, 41, 50, 84
Chicago–Evanston Race, 67, 138, 139, 154–5
Chicago World's Fair, 158
Christie, J. Walter, 43
Chrysler (engines), 22, 50, 55, 65, 66, 92
Chrysler, Walter P., 39, 43, 62, 127
Clark, Edward, 44
Clement-Bayard (cars), 48
Cleveland (engines), 126
Cleveland Machine Screw Co, 27
Clinton (engines), 107, 131, 193
Cobra, 80, 181
Coffin, Howard Earl, 39
Cole, A. B., 13
Columbia (axles), 21, 104
Commander Motors Corp, 144
Continental (engines), 13, 16, 19, 21, 25, 26,
  27, 28, 30, 31, 34, 37, 38, 41, 47, 48, 52,
  54, 55, 56, 57, 58, 60, 61, 66, 67, 70, 73,
  74, 78, 83, 85, 91, 96, 98, 100, 101, 102,
  104, 105, 107, 108, 109, 110, 112, 114, 116,
  117, 124, 129, 130, 131, 132, 136, 137, 138,
  142, 143, 151, 152, 154, 156, 158, 163, 169,
  170, 171, 172, 173, 174, 175, 177, 178, 179,
  180, 181, 185, 186, 187, 188, 189, 192, 200,
  201, 203, 205, 210, 211
Continental (spark plug), 155
Cook Electric Research Labs, 113
Coolidge, President Calvin, 117
Cooper, Gary, 66
Cord, E. L., 21, 50, 65, 128
Covert, M. B., 129
Covert (transmission), 66
Crane, Henry M., 52, 182
Crawford, J. M., 21
Crawford, R., 193
Cristea, 80
Crocker-Wheeler (electric motors), 145
Crosley (engines), 49
Crosley, Powel, 53
Crossley Motors Ltd, 208

Crosthwaite, John, 63
Crown Magnetic (cars), 148
Croxton, H. A., 54
Cunningham, Briggs, 35, 55
Curtiss (engines), 91, 162, 205
Cushman (engines), 193
Cutler-Hammer (transmission), 71, 163

Daimler (cars), 160
Dalton, Hubert K., 56
Daniels, G. E., 56
Darrin (coachbuilders), 150
Darrin, Howard A., 56, 83, 108
Davidson, Anna F., 109
Davis (engines), 70
Davis, George W., 57
Dawson, Joe, 39, 142
De Causse, 82
De Dion (axle), 125, 134
De Dion-Bouton, 35, 52, 107, 131, 153, 156, 164, 203, 205
Delaunay-Belleville, 82
Delco (electric lighting), 33, 35, 145
Delling, Eric H., 58, 129
De Luxe (engines), 36, 54, 55, 73, 77, 113, 123, 131, 164, 182, 201
Demarest (coachbuilders), 162, 182
de Palma, Ralph, 149
de Paolo, Peter, 134
Derby-Miller (car), 134
Derham (coachbuilders), 65, 82, 121, 194
Derr, Thomas S., 18
De Tamble (engines), 110
De Vaux, Norman, 61
Dewar Trophy, 35
Dey, Harry E., 61
Dietrich (coachbuilders), 82
Disbrow, Louis, 61
D.K.W. (chassis), 57
Doble, Abner, 62
Dodge (engines), 65, 190
Dodge, John, 62, 63
Dodge, John Duval, 63
Doman, 117
Dorris (engines), 58
Dorris, George P., 63, 176
Dort, Joshua Dallas, 64
Dubonnet (suspension), 33, 41, 160
Duco (cellulose finish), 35, 41, 144
Duesenberg (engines), 21, 28, 37, 78, 130, 131, 151, 163, 170, 172, 180, 181, 210
Duesenberg, August, 65
Duesenberg, Fred, 65, 126, 127
Dumont (cyclecar), 66
du Pont, E. Paul, 66, 67
Durant, W. C., 33, 35, 41, 67, 69, 79, 105, 119, 120, 129, 163, 181, 187
Duray, Leon, 134
Duryea, Charles E., 67, 68
Duryea, Frank, 67, 188
Dyke, A. L., 178
Dynaflow (transmission), 33

Earl, Harley, 33, 115
Eck, James L., 29
Eckhart, Frank, 21

Eckhart, Morris, 21
Edge, S. F., 155
Edward, Prince of Wales (afterwards King Edward VIII), 129, 137
Edwards, H. S., 189
Egerton, Hubert, 155
Electric Vehicle Co, 171
Elektron Mfg Co, 193
Elgin Races, 121, 142
Elysée (trucks), 185
English, William, 193
Entz (transmission), 58, 112, 129, 148
Erskine, Albert R., 73
European Grand Prix, 134
Exner, Virgil, 192

Facel Vega (cars), 44
Falls (engines), 20, 40, 51, 64, 71, 77, 84, 94, 99, 110, 123, 152, 163, 203
Fangio, Juan Manuel, 41
Farmer (engines), 65, 76, 135, 163, 195
Farnsley, Charles Peaslee, 121
Fawick, T. L., 182
Fawkes (tires), 38
Ferguson, J. B., 77
Ferro (engines), 105, 178
Fetch, Tom, 149
Fiat (cars), 99, 113
FIAT—Portola (cars), 161
Field, Marshall, 55
Filer Stowell Co, 156
Fischer (engines), 136
Fishback, R. W., 97
Five Boro (taxicabs), 56
FN (engines), 93
Ford (engines), 21, 29, 33, 50, 63, 68, 70, 107, 140, 172, 174, 178, 181, 210
Ford, Edsel, 118
Ford, Henry, 59, 79, 121, 180
Fore River Ship & Engine Co, 122
Fournier, Charles, 179
Franquist, Edward, 182
Frantz, Revd H. A., 83
Frazer, Joseph A., 90, 108
Freestone & Webb (coachbuilders), 50, 149
French Grand Prix, 43, 65
Fuller (transmission), 93
Fuller, Buckminster, 68
F.W.D. (engines), 136

Gable, Clark, 66
Gaeth, Paul, 86, 155
Gardner, Russell E., 87
Gas Engine & Power Co, 100
Gates-Kelly Automotive Co, 36
G.B.S. (engines), 16, 27, 73, 88, 93, 94, 95, 115, 137, 138, 155, 163, 187
General Electric (electric motors), 29, 47
General Motors Corp, 33, 35, 41, 43, 72, 105, 115, 125, 144, 145, 160, 177, 179, 181, 201, 209
George, Prince of Wales (afterwards King George V), 48
George VI, King of England, 129
Ghia (coachbuilders), 65, 66

Gilmore-Yosemite Economy Run, 90
Girling (brakes), 29
Gladden (engines), 103
Glidden Tour, 113, 120, 127, 157, 205
Goodrich (suspension), 197
Goossen, Leo, 134
Gordon Bennett Cup Race, 120, 177, 209
Gordon-Keeble (cars), 42
Gormully & Jeffery, 165
Graber (coachbuilders), 149
Graham Brothers, 89
Grand Central Palace, New York City, 116
Grant-Lees (transmission), 104
Grantura Engineering, 92
Graves, Dr Charles H., 40
Gray (engines), 110
Gray, William & Sons Ltd., 40, 90
Gray-Bell (engines), 13
Great Horseless Carriage Co, 155
Green Dragon (racing car), 153, 154
Gregory, Ben F., 91
Greuter, Charles R., 99, 127
Grossman, G. J., 89
Gunn, E. G., 36

Hall-Scott (engines), 47, 76
Hammond, E., 145
Hampden Automobile & Launch Co, 188
Hardy, A. B. C., 79, 205
Hare's Motors, 52, 120, 182
Harley-Davidson (engines), 90
Harrahs' Automobile Collection, 195, 211
Harroun, Ray, 94, 124
Haskelite (bodies), 152
Hassler (transmission), 120
Hawkes, Douglas, 134
Hayes (coachbuilders), 50
Haynes, Elwood, 95, 96
Hazard (engines), 87
Healey (cars), 141
Healey (coachbuilders), 42, 76
Hearst, William Randolph, 55, 66
Hele-Shaw (clutch), 48
Henry J. (engines), 74
Hercules (engines), 57, 109, 126, 140, 158
Herschell-Spillman (engines), 13, 14, 16, 17; 27, 28, 38, 40, 45, 50, 53, 55, 56, 62, 64, 65, 66, 81, 88, 95, 98, 113, 120, 121, 123, 148, 158, 165, 174, 182, 183, 188, 189, 198, 201, 209
Hertel, Max, 98
Hertz, John, 98
Hewland (transmissions), 29
Hines, William R., 98
Hispano-Suiza, 114
Hoff, R. C., 193
Holbrook (coachbuilders), 82, 162, 182
Hollister (transmission), 169
Houk (wheels), 94, 177
Howard, W. S., 20, 100
Hudson (engines), 113
Hudson, J. L., 101
Huffaker, J., 88
Hupp, Louis, 101, 196
Hupp, Robert, 101, 166
Hydramatic transmission, 35, 145, 161

Ilin of Haifa, 97
Indian (engines), 21
Indianapolis Speedway, 33, 51, 55, 65, 93, 94, 101, 113, 121, 124, 134, 142, 189, 191, 192
Intermeccanica (bodies), 140, 146
Irish Motor & Cycle Co, 155
Iso (cars), 42

Jaguar (cars), 29, 80
J.A.P. (engines), 36
Jay, Webb, 205
Jenkins, Ab, 158
Jensen (cars), 44, 141
Jericho Motor Parking Sweepstakes, 39
Jewett, H. M., 106
Jordan, Edward S., 107
Judkins (coachbuilders), 65
Juliano, Father Alfred, 22

Kaiser, Henry J., 90, 97, 108
Keech, Ray, 134
Keeton, F. M., 54
Kelecom (engines), 110
Kelsey, C. W., 109, 139
Kennedy, President John F., 118
Keystone Motor Co, 179
Kilbourn, Orson, 147
King, Charles B., 110, 143
Kinmont (brakes), 57
Kirkham Machine Co., 112
Kline, James A., 112
Klingensmith, F. L., 90
Knight (engines), 31, 47, 70, 76, 136, 166, 182, 187, 188, 189, 207, 208
Knight, Charles Y., 182
Knight, Margaret E., 109
Knox, Harry A., 21, 113, 147
Kodak (camera), 194
Koeb, Emil, 113
Kohler (engines), 111, 152, 178
Krarup, Marius, 149
Kurtis, Frank, 113, 139

Lake St Clair, 79, 207
Lambert, John W., 114
Lammas-Graham, 90
Land Speed Record, 89, 134, 192
La Vigne, J. P., 92, 107, 115
Lawrence, Charles L., 29
Lawson, H. J., 155
Lawson Motor Wheel, 197
Lawwell, 83
Lea-Francis (cars), 134
Le Baron (coachbuilders), 65, 104, 118, 150, 157
Le Blond-Schacht (trucks), 178
Leland & Faulconer, 59
Leland, Henry M., 35, 59, 79, 117
Leland, Wilfred, 117
Le Mans, 35, 43, 55, 66, 192
Léon Bollée (cars), 211
Le Roi (engines), 25, 28, 180, 188
Lewis (engines), 48
Lewis, William, 117
Lincoln (engines), 22, 70, 139

Lindbergh, Col Charles, 82, 82
Little, William H., 119
Lloyd, Harold, 55
Lockhart, Frank, 134, 192
Lockheed (brakes), 39, 66, 79, 82, 100, 101, 112, 137
Loewy, Raymond, 191
London-Brighton Emancipation Run, 67, 155
London-Pullman (cars), 163
Longuemare (carburetors), 51
Loomis, Gilbert, 120
Lowell Motor Co, 131
Lozier, E. R., 121
Lozier, H. A., 93, 121
Lundell (electric motors), 138
Luxor (taxicabs), 56
Lycoming (engines), 15, 16, 20, 27, 28, 30, 34, 40, 50, 62, 64, 65, 70, 87, 89, 91, 93, 96, 98, 110, 120, 125, 128, 152, 156, 168, 180, 182, 184, 195, 197, 200, 211
Lynite (pistons), 64

Madison Square Gardens (auto show), 104, 121
Magic (engines), 151
Manville, Tommy, 66
Marble-Swift (transmission), 168
Marks, 117
Marmon, Howard, 124
Marriott, Frank, 185
Martin, James V., 126
Martin, Karl H., 58, 203
Marvel (delivery car), 48
Maserati (cars), 55
Mason (engines), 26, 41, 137, 152, 163, 179, 181
Massachusetts Institute of Technology, 18
Massnick-Phipps (engines), 176
Maxim, Hiram, 47, 105
Maxwell, Jonathan, 127, 143
Mazzci, William, 102
McCarthy, John J., 140
McCue (wheels), 96
McCulloch (supercharger), 108
McKee, J. A., 77
Mead (engines), 184
Merchant & Evans, 45
Mercury (engines), 131, 142
Merrill, Frank, 200
Métallurgique (cars), 192
Metz, C. H., 125, 132, 203
Meyer, Lou, 134
M.G. (chassis), 21
Michellotti, 55
Midwest (engines), 94, 96
Miller, Harry A., 91, 133, 134
Milton, Tommy, 134
Milwaukee (engines), 55, 133
Minerva (cars), 137
Mitchell, General Billy, 126
Model (engines), 55, 94, 131
Mohs, Bruce Baldwin, 136
Moline-Knight (engines), 112
Möller, M. P., 52, 56, 61, 185
Möller (taxicabs), 56

Monte Carlo Rally, 80
Montgomery-Ward (mail-order firm), 135
Mooers, Louis P., 137, 153
Morgan (coachbuilders), 138
Morriss, F. E., 138
Morris-Oxford (engines), 208
Moskovics, Frederick E., 192
Mueller, Hieronymus A., 139
Mueller, Oscar B., 139
Muntz, Earl, 139
Murphy (coachbuilders), 50, 65, 154
Murphy, Jimmy, 134

Nash, Charles W., 14, 106, 141
National Cash Register Co, 39
Nelson, Emil A., 142
New Era Motors, 112, 137
New Mexico (battleship), 148
New York Motor Co, 82
New York—Paris Race, 195
Nissan (cars), 90
Norden (cars), 143
Northway (engines), 46, 77, 105, 143, 145, 179, 181
Notre Dame University, 173
Nyberg, Henry, 168

Offenhauser (engines), 55
Offenhauser, Fred, 134
Ogren, Hugo W., 144
O'Halloran Brothers, 53
Oldfield, Barney, 134, 154
Olds, Ransom Eli, 145, 169
Onan (engines), 195
Opel (cars), 42
Osca (engines), 29
Owen, J. L., 148
Owen, Percy, 209
Owen, Ray M., 148

Packard (engines), 141
Packard, J. W., 149
Packard, W. D., 149
Padana (coachbuilders), 193
Pagé, Victor W., 151, 200
Pak-Age-Car (trucks), 192
Pandolfo, Samuel Conner, 151
Paramount (taxicabs), 56
Parkmobile (parking attachment), 57, 143
Pennant (taxicabs), 25
Pennington, Edward Joel, 154, 155, 196
Pennsylvania Supply Co, 170
Perkins (engines), 78, 160, 172
Perkins Diesel (engines), 106, 141
Pershing, General, 62
Petard, René, 117, 135
Peugeot (cars), 133, 134
Pickford, Mary, 55
Pierce, George N., 156
Pininfarina (coachbuilders), 166
Piper, John, 202
P. J. Dasey Co, 136
P.L.M. (station wagons), 109
Polymobil (cars), 145
Pomeroy, L. H., 160
Ponder, J. M., 160

Pontiac (engines), 29, 192
Poole, Al, 182
Pope, Colonel, 197
Porsche (engines), 29, 91
Porter, Finlay Robertson, 85, 129, 162
Powell Lever (engines), 70
Power, W. M., 151
Powerglide (transmission), 42
Pray, Glenn, 21, 50
Prugh (engines), 26

Quimby (coachbuilders), *177*, 182, 206

Radford, William H., 110
Railton (cars), 101, 195
Rambler (engines), 106
R. & L. (taxicabs), 166
Rasmussen, J. S., 171
Reeves (engines), 124
Reeves (transmission), 99
Reeves, Milton O., 168
Reinertsen, Rex, 170
Remington, Philo E., 169
Renault (engines), 18, 123
Renault Dauphine, 96
Rice Tuckermatic (transmission), 197
Rickenbacker (chassis), 29
Rickenbacker, Capt Eddie, 170
Riker, A. L., 120, 147, 171
Robertson, George, 120, 182
Rochester-Duesenberg, *see* Duesenberg
Rochet-Schneider (cars), 139
Rockne, Knute, 173
Rollston (coachbuilders), *66*, 150, *192*
Romanelli, Francesco, 173
Romney, George, 166
Roosevelt, President Franklin D., 118
Roosevelt, President Theodore, 174, 205
Rootes Group, 44
Rothwell (cars), 155
Rudge-Whitworth (wheels), 15
Rumpler (cars), 102
Rutenber (engines), 17, 21, 45, 54, 89, 93,
    103, 110, 114, 122, 123, 137, 142, 152, 172,
    184, 189, 195, 201
Ruxton, William V. C., 175

SAAB (engines), 29
Sager, Frederick, 176
Saknoffsky, Count Alexis de, 154, 169
Salmons (coachbuilders), 111
Sanders (coachbuilders), 80
Savannah Grand Prize, 39
Schebler (carburetor), 163
Schebler, George, 124
Schmidt, Charles, 149
Schulz, A. C., 129, 142
Schut, Bakker, 80
Scott-Newcomb (engines), 185
Seabrook—R.M.C. (cars), 168
Seagrave (fire apparatus), 136
Sears Roebuck, 16

Selden, George B., 180
Service-Relay (trucks), 211
Sheepshead Bay, 39
Shelby, Carroll, 181
Selby, Eugene, 181
Silver, C. T., 20, 112
Simca (cars), 44
Simpson, Mrs Ernest, 33
Sinatra, Frank, 65
Sintz (engines), 168
Sloan, A. P., 129
Smith, H. Anton, 183
Smithsonian Institution, 25
Sofield, Hilton W., 98
Spacke (engines), 31, 32, 55, 57, 69, 103,
    120, 178, 185
Speedwell (engines), 74, 98, 109
Spohn (coachbuilders), 88
Springfield Metal Body Co, 139, 147
S.S. (tires), 64
Stanley, F. E., 128, 185, 206
Stanley, F. O., 128, 185, 206
Stansell Motors Ltd, 31
Star (engines), 119
Startix (starter), 74
Stearns, E. C., 188
Sterling (engines), 50, 94, 123, 137, 178
Stevens, Brooks, 74, 75, *87*, 88, 97
Stirling of Granton (bodies), 155
Stout, William B., 178
Stratton, Frank S., 190
Streite (engines), 84
Studebaker (engines), 75
Studebaker, Clem, 190
Studebaker, Henry, 190
Sturgis, Harold, 138
Stutz (transmission), 96
Stutz, Harry C., 96, 191, 192
Supreme (engines), 15, 21, 89, 104

Taylor, Molt B., 15
Teetor-Hartley (engines), 18, 21, 73, 127, 158
Thomas (engines), 57
Thompson, Jerry, 212
Thompson, R. P., 113
Tiley, Dr C. Baxter, 27
Tinker, George, 202
Titan (taxicabs), 32
Tjaarda, John, 178
Tootsie Toys, 89
Tourist Trophy, 101
Tracy, Joe, 120, 182
Tremulis, Alex, 197
Truman, President Harry S., 118
Tucker, Preston T., 197
T.V.R., 92, 107
Twentieth Century (taxicabs), 56

Ultramobil (cars), 145
United States Motor Co, 51, 127

Vail, Ira, 101
Valley Despatch (trucks), 176

Vanderbilt Cup, 15, 21, 39, 82, 83, 120, 121
van Ranst, C. W., 84
Van Wagoner, William, 193
Van Zandt, Newton, 170
Vauxhall (cars), 160
Vehicle Equipment Co, 201
Veracity (cars), 183
Victor (bicycles), 147
Vignale (coachbuilders), 55, 78
Vim Motor Truck Co, 196
Volkswagen (cars), 40, 78, 200
Vulcan (electric gearshift), 180

Waco (airplane), 82
Wagner (electric motor), 195
Wahl, George, 63
Waldorf-Astoria Hotel, 61
Walker, Jimmy, 66
Walker, J. B., 119, 135, 185
Warner (transmission), 58
Warren (transmission), 89
Watkins Glen, 55
Waukesha (engines), 77, 139
Weidely (engines), 21, 93, 96, 111, 130, 131,
    152, 181, 182
Weidely, G. A., 162
West, Mae, 66
Westinghouse (airsprings), 46
Westinghouse (electric motors), 20, 39, 102,
    105
Westinghouse-Schneider (torque converter),
    197
White, D. McCall, 114
White, Rollin, 173, 205, 206
Whiting Ltd, 90
Whitman, L. L., 145
Whitney, George, 206
Whitney, R. S., 206
Wilder, Steve, 146
Wilkinson, John, 82
Willans & Robinson (engines), 67
Williams, Captain Al, 68
Williams, Calvin C., 207
Willoughby (coachbuilders), 82
Wills, Childe Harold, 207
Willys (engines), 42, 97, 139, 210, 212
Willys, John North, 76, 124, 207
Wilson, President Woodrow, 133
Winton, Alexander, 209
Wisconsin (engines), 46, 50, 55, 61, 66, 111,
    127, 148, 182, 191, 203
Wizard (engines), 36, 167
Wonder Motor Truck Co, 45, 210
Woodlite (headlights), 66, 107
Wright, Benjamin, 211
Wright-Fisher (suspension), 152, 211

Yellow Cab Company, 181
Yenko, Don, 212
Ypsilanti (transmission), 197

Zamfirescu, 80
Zimmermann (coachbuilders), *102*
Z.I.S. (cars), 150